THE PHIL

of the Holy Neptic Fathers

Volume 5

Compiled by
St. Nikodemos of the Holy Mountain and St. Makarios of Corinth

St. George Monastery

Published by: Virgin Mary of Australia and Oceania 2020 ©
www.oceanitissa.com.au

ISBN 978-0-6450009-0-0

The Greek version of the Virgin Mary of Stillness as depicted on the front cover in English. This icon and all graphics in this book were created by Anna Skoubourdis.

CONTENTS

]THE HOLY METROPOLIS OF LIMASSOL

PROLOGUE

It is with great joy that I write the prologue of this English-language publication of the fifth volume of the *Philokalia*, which has been undertaken with great care and diligence by the novice nun Anna Skoubourdis for the benefit of our English-speaking brothers and sisters in Christ who are unable to immerse themselves in the Philokalic texts of the Holy Neptic Fathers of our Orthodox Church owing to the difficulty of the language.

The interior, spiritual work of unceasing prayer is the most precious treasure of the experience of our Holy Fathers, who "by practice and by contemplation," and after struggles and giving their own blood, experienced the sweetness of the work of *nepsis* and unceasing prayer, which draws the grace of the Holy Spirit to the heart of man and brings about his purification from the passions, the illumination of his intellect, and the purity of his heart, in confirmation of the infallible word of our Lord Jesus Christ: *Blessed are the pure in heart, for they shall see God* (Mt. 5:5).

In the Orthodox patristic teaching concerning the purification, illumination, and deification of man, it is necessary for the person engaged in spiritual struggle to recognize that none of the things described by the *Philokalia* are the result of human effort alone, as great and rigorous as this effort may be, but of the cooperation between the divine uncreated grace of the Holy Spirit and human freedom. God never violates or overlooks the person's free will, and neither can the human person make spiritual progress without the synergy of the All-Holy Spirit. The salvation of man is not a product of human self-deification, or of techniques and methods of concentration, or of any other psychosomatic practice, but is rather the fruit and result of the person's journey in the Church and through the Church, through humility, repentance, and by calling out and seeking for the mercy and grace of our Lord Jesus Christ from the depths of the heart.

The tradition of the *Philokalia* bears absolutely no real similarity to the various systems and methods of self-realization, self-liberation, and self-divinization originating from Hinduism which are in such wide circulation today; for through their experience our Holy Fathers handed down the tradition that without the uncreated Grace of the All-Holy Spirit, and also, apart from or outside of the Church, we cannot attain any of the realities which the *Philokalia* describes with such clarity and total precision.

The Church speaks about how prayer is done with the deepest humility, complete repentance, and with absolute reference to the "only One who can save," our Lord Jesus Christ. Prayer is not an activity that is transferred from person to person, but a heart-wrenching existential cry of agony in pursuit of divine mercy; this prayer proceeds from the person to the Lord Jesus Christ, and in turn, through Him, mercy and uncreated Divine Grace are granted to the praying person, as and when the Lord wills it.

I humbly pray that our brothers and sisters who will study the *Philokalia* will find this way of Life through the teaching of the Holy Fathers of our Orthodox Church, and for the novice nun Anna Skoubourdis to find rich reward from God for her efforts and care for this publication.

With many paternal blessings

in Christ,

† ὁ Λεμεσοῦ Ἀθανάσιος

+Metropolitan Athanasios of Limassol

TRANSLATORS' INTRODUCTION

The *Philokalia*, compiled by St. Nikodemos of the Holy Mountain and St. Makarios of Corinth, first published in Greek in 1782, and shortly thereafter translated into Old Slavonic and Russian, has influenced Orthodox Christianity for centuries. It is the distillation of a spiritual tradition that can be traced back to the beginnings of Christian monasticism in the 4th century and ultimately to Holy Scripture and the teaching of Jesus Christ and His Apostles. Its rich assortment of spiritual texts provide boundless wisdom and guidance concerning prayer, the knowledge of God, and the struggle to overcome our passions and internal fragmentation.

The fifth and final volume of the *Philokalia* is made up of two parts. The first part is composed of mystical theological writings from around the 14th century AD, which explore aspects of both *practice* (πρᾶξις) and *contemplation* (θεωρία) in Hesychasm, and was originally intended primarily for monastics engaged in the life of stillness (*hesychia*). Thus the *Exact Rule and Method* provides detailed practical instruction for hesychasts, while St. Kallistos Angelikoudes' *Chapters* and the treatise *On Union with God and the Contemplative Life* delve deeper into the contemplative aspect of Hesychasm, with devotional prayers, spiritual interpretations of Scripture, and profound meditations on the ineffable experience of God. This period of theology is only beginning to be rediscovered and appreciated in all its depth, and the fact that it flourished in the last century before the Fall of Constantinople in 1453 lends a certain poignancy to this final spiritual testimony of the Eastern Roman Empire. But it should also be stressed how the tradition of Hesychasm and Orthodox spirituality has persisted to this day, and continues to be an abiding source of inspiration for Christians throughout the world.

The second part, beginning with section 6 (Symeon of Thessaloniki) was compiled for the benefit of all Christians, especially laypeople and Christians "living in the world". Not only do the titles, subtitles, and content of these texts indicate this, but also the fact that in the original publication the texts themselves were Modern Greek (18th century) translations and paraphrases of the primary Byzantine Greek sources. This may be compared to the *Synaxaria* (Lives of the Saints) of the Orthodox Church, which are often edited and compiled from older sources for the specific purpose of accessibility and readability. Thus it includes vivid narrations of Saints' experiences of the Jesus Prayer, as in the story of how St. Maximos the Hut-Burner received the gift of prayer from the Mother of God and St. Symeon the New Theologian's account of how the young man George acquired noetic prayer while living and working in the world. It further contains exhortations for all Christians to pray unceasingly, in accordance with St. Paul's injunction to *pray without ceasing* (1 Thess. 5:17).

So then, let the following be noted about our translations of the second part. All these translations are from the Modern Greek editions prepared by the original compilers of the Greek *Philokalia.* Translations from the original Byzantine Greek *Discourse on Faith* by St. Symeon the New Theologian and *On the Three Forms of Prayer* ascribed to the same Saint can be found in Volume 4 of the *Philokalia*, translated by Palmer, Sherrard, and Ware, which they moved from Volume 5 to be next to the *Practical and Theological Chapters* of St. Symeon the New Theologian (on a more chronological basis). While we could have decided not to include these texts because they have already been translated in Palmer, Sherrard, and Ware's translation of Volume 4, we judged it most spiritually beneficial and faithful to the intentions of the original compilers to include them, since they offer elegant testimonies to the second part's thesis that all Christians can and should pray unceasingly, as well as providing helpful information about the danger of delusion (πλάνη) and the need for spiritual guidance. The one section that is not included is that of St. Gregory of Sinai, both because it is already translated in Volume 4 and it is the only text that is repeated twice (in both Byzantine and Modern Greek) in the *Philokalia*, a repetition meant for Modern Greek readers who had difficulty reading Ancient and Byzantine Greek. We have translated from the Greek edition *Φιλοκαλία τῶν ἱερῶν Νηπτικῶν* published by Aster-Papademetriou, and have consulted the Modern (Demotic) Greek translation by Antonios G. Galitis and edited by Ignatios Sakalis, published by *To Perivoli tis Theotokou* Publications.

The Language of the *Philokalia*

The luminosity and spiritually rich quality of the Greek language are well described in the words of the Irish author James Joyce:

> 'I speak the tongue of a race the acme of whose mentality is the maxim: time is money. Material domination. *Dominus!* Lord! Where is the spirituality? Lord Jesus? [...] 'The Greek!' he said again. 'Kyrios! Shining word! The vowels the Semite and the Saxon know not. Kyrie! The radiance of the intellect. I ought to profess Greek, the language of the mind. Kyrie eleison!'[1]

[1] *Ulysses*, 7.563-4.

The reader and student of the *Philokalia* encounters such qualities of "spirituality," "radiance", and "intellect" in abundance, streaming from a tradition that sought for both the transcendence of eternity and the illumination of the intellect in the present age, through the grace of Jesus Christ. It cannot be sufficiently emphasized just how important the Greek language and terminology are to this spiritual vision and to the overall structure of the fifth volume of the *Philokalia.* A good indication of this is that the title itself has two Greek words transliterated into English: *Philokalia*, meaning "love of the beautiful" and "love of the good", and *neptic*, an adjective describing *nepsis,* that is, "watchfulness, sobriety, and attention in prayer". This is one of the many reasons we have decided to provide notes about the key Greek terms. While these explanations are incorporated into the main body and footnotes of the text, we should like to comment briefly on the following essential concepts.

Let it first be noted that we have consistently translated *nous* (νοῦς) as "intellect" with a few considerations in mind. In Latin translations of Greek texts, *intellectus* was regularly used to render *nous*, and the translators of the first four volumes of the *Philokalia* have likewise upheld this time-honored tradition. *Intellectus* there originally referred to "the part of the soul responsible for contemplation and perception", and had not yet acquired the later nuances of "intellectual" or "intellectualism"; we must try to go beyond these secondary connotations, and it is hoped that the frequent use of the relatively uncommon term "intellect" in the spiritual context of the *Philokalia* will serve as a constant reminder that the inner faculty being signified is not simply the "thinking mind" and the sum total of mental processes, but something much more profound and holistic. Another reason to translate it this way is the frequent translation of the *noetic* realities perceived by the *nous* as "intelligible" (νοητός, νοούμενος), and the proper activity of the *nous* as "intellection" (νόησις). Now, in the *Philokalia*, the intellect naturally *knows* and *understands*, not with the fragmented, rationalistic, or logical thinking and reflection we often think of today, but in a mode of contemplation, prayer, and insight. Moreover, the *nous* is eminently understood as the faculty by which we commune with God and apprehend His love. At the same time, this does not altogether exclude the role of reason (*logos*), since rational reflection on creation and Scripture by the guidance of the Holy Spirit are meant to help raise the intellect to the reality of God beyond reason, and ultimately even beyond intellect (*nous*) through apophatic theology and mystical experience. Perhaps the most apt characterization of the intellect (*nous*) can be found in this volume of the *Philokalia*: St. Kallistos Kataphygiotes says the intellect is by nature *philokalic* (φιλόκαλος), that is, it was created to be a natural "lover of goodness and beauty" (*On Union with God* 35, 91) Thus, we can even see how the *nous* is what gives coherence to the whole *Philokalia*, since all these spiritual texts are meant to cultivate the intellect's natural "love for the beautiful" and to direct it to the Triune God, the Highest Good and Supreme Beauty.

While it can certainly be said that Greek is "the language of the mind", it is no less a "language of the heart." All of the texts of this volume speak at length about the Prayer of the Heart, the heart's experience of the grace of the Holy Spirit, acquired through unceasing prayer to Jesus, Κύριε Ιησοῦ Χριστέ, Υἱὲ τοῦ Θεοῦ, ἐλέησόν με: "Lord Jesus Christ, Son of God, have mercy on me." The natural response to the experience of God's love and beauty is yearning, delight, and *divine eros*, the term used to describe the purified soul's love for God. As St. Kallistos Angelikoudes writes, "Rationality clearly does not possess the natural power to animate the throne of the soul's faculties – that is, the heart – from within, but only from without. [...] But the power and energy of the Holy and Life-Giving Spirit wholly takes possession of this abode of the soul from within" (*Chapters* 46), that is, through the beauty of the Lord. It is perhaps this beauty that Dostoevsky was hinting at with his enigmatic words, "Beauty will save the world."[2]

The whole liturgical, ascetical, and spiritual life of the Orthodox Church is dedicated to the supreme Beauty, God the Trinity. It also has its own unique language and terminology, from *neptic* and *hesychia* to *noetic* and *theosis*. Many of the writings in this volume provide detailed explanations of these terms, and while much can also be learned from context, we have found it necessary to provide some commentary as well, especially when the teachings and arguments are based on the subtle and precise meanings of the original Greek terms. For example, the meaning of the cognate adjectives of *nous*, *noetic/intelligible* (νοερός, νοητός), which is often confused with the word *spiritual*, should be understood in the context of the *Philokalia* as relating to the intellect (e.g. as an object of the intellect's contemplation, or supernaturally manifested to the intellect). On the other hand, *spiritual* (πνευματικός) usually specifically denotes the grace and uncreated energy of the *Holy Spirit*. As unfamiliar a term as *noetic* may be to some readers, the distinction between terms such as *rational, noetic,* and *spiritual* must be strongly maintained, especially since according to the Orthodox theology of Hesychasm, the *nous* and all noetic beings (humans and angels) are created, while the essence, hypostases, and energies of the Holy Trinity are uncreated.

In addition to drawing extensively from Holy Scripture, the *Philokalia* is replete with references to the writings of the Church Fathers and the liturgical life of the Orthodox Church. Aside from being enriched with succinct and illuminating patristic instructions, much attention is also given to sublime but difficult

---

[2] Fyodor Dostoevsky, *The Idiot*, trans. Constance Garnett (New York: Bantam, 1981), 370.

doctrines, such as the teaching of *theosis* and "seeing and 'suffering' the splendor of God" according to St. Gregory the Theologian[3] and the "enhypostatic illumination" and "unoriginate deification" according to St. Maximos the Confessor (cf. *Xanthopoulos* 68).[4] Furthermore, a special liturgical idiom, formulated by figures such as St. Dionysios the Areopagite, inform a significant portion of the mystical language of the *Philokalia*. The language of Late Antiquity primarily associated with mystery religions and rites had been thoroughly Christianized by this point of Byzantine history,[5] and Late Byzantine theologians took many of these terms for granted and understood them in a thoroughly Christian sense. It would be a mistake to interpret the meaning of Hesychasm apart from the liturgical life of the Church, and the most mystical and indescribable experiences are described with the liturgical language of illumination, spiritual rebirth (i.e. Baptism), *mystery* (i.e. sacrament), and the Eucharistic imagery of food and drink, with further references to the rites and vows of Eastern Orthodox monasticism. It is characteristic that the *Exact Rule and Method*, a rule for Hesychasts written by Kallistos and Ignatios Xanthopoulos, begins with a detailed explanation of Baptism and includes a lengthy passage about the Holy Eucharist towards the end. Even the deeply philosophical and syllogistic work *On Union with God and the Contemplative Life* revolves around the thesis that the gift of grace and divine adoption constitutes the foundation of the contemplative life.

The sheer variety of biblical and patristic citations, phrases, paraphrases, and commentary contained in the *Philokalia* has necessitated a somewhat complex system of citation. Biblical citations and phrases are written in *italics* (in addition to some transliterations from the original Greek, e.g. *philokalic, hesychia, logoi*); patristic quotations, certain quoted phrases, and dialogue are put in "double quotation marks"; lastly, Scriptural and patristic phrases being explained and exegeted are put in 'single quotation marks'. All biblical references from the Old Testament are taken from the Greek Septuagint (LXX), the canonical Old Testament of the Eastern Orthodox Church, and are very loosely based on the classic translation by Sir Lancelot Brenton. Biblical references from the New Testament are based on the New King James Version translation, which underlies the Orthodox Study Bible. Nevertheless, the extremely detailed exegesis of the *Philokalia* has usually required us to modify and adapt these translations to the context of patristic texts. Lastly, we have used the translation of St. John Climacus'

---

[3] *Oration* 45.7, On Holy Pascha. This quote from St. Gregory Nazianzen served as one of the most foundational texts for describing union with God in Byzantine mystical theology, and is one of the reasons we have often translated it 'to suffer', to more easily identify its source.

[4] St. Maximos the Confessor, *On Difficulties in Sacred Scripture: The Responses to Thalassios* (trans. Fr. Maximos Constas), 57

[5] This process began as early as St. Ignatios of Antioch in the first century AD.

Ladder of Divine Ascent by Fr. Lazarus Moore in certain passages, occasionally with slight modifications. These quotations are cited in the footnotes.

We have made the editorial decision to provide parenthetical glosses of Greek words in the main body of the text. These glosses highlight key terms and theological concepts (especially when we needed to deviate from the traditional pairings given in the Glossary of Theological Terms), idiomatic renderings, wordplay, metaphors, proverbs, and in short, all the intricacies of Patristic Greek that would otherwise be forfeited for the sake of readability. These texts are brimming with neologisms and flourishes that defy translation, be it the mystical raptures of St. Kallistos Angelikoudes or the pith and power of St. John Climacus. The Fathers were pushing the limits of their language's expressive power, warping and twisting it to convey what could hardly be put into words. An overly literal translation of this would be almost incomprehensible. That is why we settled on a hybrid text. This way, we could reproduce a bit of the flavor of the original and hold onto its most salient features, while still yielding a dynamic translation with an eye for English style and rhythm. We hope and pray that it will benefit monastics, clergy, and laypeople, and student and teacher alike.

We wish to thank Sister Anna Skoubourdis, the Holy Monastery of St. George, and J. D. Candelario for their guidance and support during the whole duration of the research and writing of this translation, as well as His Eminence Metropolitan Athanasios of Limassol for his blessing and prayers, and the monks of Mt. Athos for their prayers and counsel. We also owe tremendous thanks to Euphrosini Candelario, Eleftheria Deligianni, and Jonathan Vladimir Howry for their assistance.

We would also like to express our gratitude for all the contributions of His Eminence Metropolitan Kallistos Ware, G. E. H. Palmer, and Philip Sherrard toward research on the *Philokalia*, for their translations of the first four volumes of this anthology, and for introducing the study of the *Philokalia* to so many generations of students. We humbly offer this edition as just one of several contributions to the study of the *Philokalia* made in recent decades.

Feast of St. Demetrios 2020

Jonathan Gardner
Timothy Fisher

Saints Kallistos and Ignatios Xanthopoulos

AN EXACT RULE AND METHOD FOR HESYCHASTS

Biographical Note on Sts. Kallistos and Ignatios

St. Kallistos Xanthopoulos, the Most-Holy Patriarch of Constantinople, flourished around 1360 AD under Andronikos II Palaiologos; he was a disciple of St. Gregory of Sinai (whose lengthy biography he would go on to write), and lived the ascetic life on the Holy Mountain at the Skete of Magoulas, across from Philotheou Monastery. He lived together with his fellow ascetic Mark for twenty-eight whole years, and during this time he also formed such a great friendship with Ignatios, also surnamed Xanthopoulos, that it was as if they were "one soul in two bodies."[6] He later became Patriarch of Constantinople and set out for Serbia together with his clergy because of the Church's peaceful unity there, and on his way he passed through the Holy Mountain. There St. Maximos the Hut-Burner met him with the comical yet prophetic greeting, "This old man will never see his old lady again!"[7] St. Maximos then bid him farewell by chanting the funeral psalm after him, "*Blessed are the blameless in the way*" (cf. Ps. 118). And as foretold, when he arrived in Serbia, he exchanged this corruptible life for the incorruptible.

St. Symeon of Thessaloniki also writes the following about these two saints in a passage on the deifying prayer, "Lord Jesus Christ, Son of God, have mercy on me" (Ch. 295):

> Now in our days, the subject [of the Jesus prayer] has been treated most exceptionally by two men who are themselves of God and wrote in the Spirit. These two men spoke from God, as true God-bearers and Christ-bearers, indwelt by God Himself: our Holy Father Kallistos, appointed by God as Patriarch of our Capital, the New Rome, and his brother in spirit and fellow ascetic St. Ignatios. They co-authored a book on this subject and wrote lofty spiritual

---

[6] The phrase St. Gregory the Theologian used to describe his friendship with St. Basil the Great, *Oration 43*, Funeral Oration on St. Basil the Great, 20.2.

[7] St. Maximos Kavsokalyvis (Καυσοκαλύβης) was a holy fool for Christ and hesychast whose feast is celebrated in the Orthodox Church on January 13. He feigned foolishness for Christ's sake (for instance, by burning down his own huts) and possessed the gift of foresight. Here his humorous greeting and his chanting of the funeral service prophesy St. Kallistos' imminent repose and his permanent separation from Constantinople, the city ("old lady") of his episcopacy.

philosophy with divine wisdom; in their chapters, which add up to the perfect number one hundred, they have expressed their perfect knowledge of this prayer. Though both were heirs of the Imperial City, they left this all behind, and while they had lived until then in purity and monastic submission, from then on they spent their lives bound together in heavenly asceticism, preserving their unity in Christ, the unity which Christ Himself had prayed to the Father for all of us to preserve (Jn. 17:11), and they *shone as lights in the world, holding fast the word of life,* as St. Paul says (Phil. 2:15-16). For they surpassed nearly all other saints in unity with Christ and in love, so that there was never even a hint of a quarrel between them, either in thought or in deed, nor even the slightest grievance, which is something almost unheard of among mankind.

And thus they became angelic and, just as they had prayed, they held fast to God's peace and acquired it in themselves; for Jesus Christ *is our peace*, as St. Paul says, *who has made the Jews and Gentiles one* (Eph. 2:14), and His *peace surpasses all understanding* (Phil. 4:7). They departed this life in peace and now enjoy divine serenity, seeing more clearly than ever Jesus, whom they earnestly sought and loved with all their souls. At last they are with Him and share unceasingly in His sweetest and divine light, the pledge of which they received here on earth after having been purified through contemplation and the practice of the virtues, and attaining that divine illumination which the Apostles beheld on Mt. Tabor (Mt. 17:1-2). Moreover, this fact has been clearly attested to by many people who have testified that they saw their faces shining like Stephen's (Acts 6:15), since the grace was not poured into their hearts alone, but also filled their countenances. So did they shine for all to see, like the sun in its brilliance (as those who saw them have given testimony), just as the great Moses of old (Ex. 34:29-30). Having truly 'suffered' this blessed passion and come to know it by experience, these men provide a clear account concerning the divine light, the natural energy and grace of God, and holy prayer, and they bring forth the Saints as witnesses also.

AN EXACT RULE AND METHOD

WITH GOD'S HELP

FOR THOSE WHO CHOOSE TO LIVE

AS HESYCHASTS AND MONASTICS

BY THE MONKS

KALLISTOS AND IGNATIOS XANTHOPOULOS

INCLUDING TESTIMONIES FROM THE SAINTS

About their own conduct, practice, and way of life, and the manifold and great benefits of *hesychia*[8] for those who practice it correctly. The present treatise and discourse is divided into one hundred chapters. The preface and first chapter of the discourse is about the divine and supernatural gift and grace that indwells the faithful through the Holy Spirit.

1. According to divine Scripture we are *taught by God* (1 Thess. 4:9) and bear the new law wordlessly written on our hearts (cf. 2 Cor. 3:2-3); we shine brighter than beacons, have the good and infallible Spirit as our helmsman, and are *children and heirs of God, co-heirs with Christ* (Rom. 8:17). Thus, we should be living as angels and not even require anyone to teach us to know the Lord. But given the way we turn away what is greater from our earliest years (ἐκ πρώτης ἡμῶν τριχός) and going wandering (ἀποβουκόλησις) after the lesser, and the dread Belial's deception and his fierce tyranny (τυραννὶς ἄσπονδος) over us, we tend to run in our wretchedness even further away from the saving and deifying commandments, over cliffs that lead down to the soul's desolation; and most pitiful of all, we have been led (ἠρέθισεν) to think and act against our own nature, just as the divine Scriptures say: *There is no one who understands, there is no one who seeks God, they have all turned aside from the straight path and have together become worthless* (Ps. 13:2-3.); hence we are but *flesh* (Gen. 6:3) and fall short of God's light-giving (σελασφόρου) grace (cf. 3:23). Therefore, we stand in need of each other to be mutually encouraged and assisted in our pursuit of virtue.

The present treatise was written with the purpose of answering a brother's question, and in obedience to an ordinance of the Fathers.

2. Since you have often asked us, worthless though we are, for a discourse and written rule for your own spiritual benefit (and perhaps for others too, as you suggest) – for you yearn to *search* the divine and live-giving *Scriptures*, as the Lord says (Jn. 5:39), and desire to be securely initiated (μυεῖσθαι) – we have decided that it is high time for us, by God's help, to satisfy your laudable desire. Hence, out of love for you and for the sake of your benefit, we have shrugged off our habitual laziness; for we are deeply impressed by the earnest desire for good things and ceaseless diligence expressed by you, our dearly beloved spiritual child. But even more so, we dread that fearful condemnation that God threatens against those who hide their talent (Mt. 25:25); moreover, we seek to fulfill a paternal command that our Fathers and spiritual teachers left us, namely, that we entrust what they have taught us to others who love God. Now may God, the Father of

[8] *Hesychia* ("stillness," "silence") is a theological term referring to the hesychastic life of solitude and pure prayer practiced since the beginning of Eastern Orthodox monasticism.

love, the Lord who gives every good thing in abundance, grant us a suitable word (καίριος λόγος) *as we open our mouths* (Eph. 6:19), though we are *weak in speech* and *slow of tongue* (Ex. 4:10); for He has often breathed His word (λόγος) even into irrational and mute beasts (ζῷα ἄλογα) for the benefit of those who heard (Num. 22:28). Thus, may He grant to you (and to any others who read this, as you have suggested) an ear to hear with wisdom and discernment, and to proceed without error, in a way pleasing to Him. For as it is written, *without Him we can do nothing* that is beneficial and leads to salvation (Jn. 15:5); and *unless the Lord builds the house, the builders labor in vain* (Ps. 126:1).

Prior to every work is a plan, and the plan of our present endeavor is to learn what the foundation of the spiritual life is.

3. Prior to every work (πρᾶγμα) is a plan (σκοπός); our plan is to give you counsel pertaining to your spiritual growth, as far as we can, and you must plan to live genuinely in accordance with what we write. Thus, we must first of all reflect on (ἐνοπτριζόμενοι) how we should plan to complete this building in Christ and how to lay its solid foundation. Then when the proper time comes (καιροῦ καλοῦντος), and even more so, with abundant help from above, we will be able to build a roof worthy of such a temple with the Holy Spirit as our architect.

The beginning of every God-pleasing undertaking is to live according to the Savior's commandments. Its end is to return to the perfect grace of the All-Holy and Life-Giving Spirit, which was given to us through divine Baptism.

4. Now the beginning of every God-pleasing undertaking (πραγματεία) is, in a word, to seek (σπεύδειν) to live in every way and with all our might according to all the deifying commandments that the Savior has given us, with the goal of keeping them and recovering thereby the free gift (προῖκα) that was originally given to us from on high at the sacred baptismal font – namely, our perfect spiritual reformation (ἀναμόρφωσις) and renewal (ἀνάπλασις) accomplished through grace, or however you wish to call so great a gift. This is done by *putting off the old Adam with his deeds* and desires and *putting on the new* spiritual *Adam* (Col. 3:9-10), the Lord Jesus Christ. As the divine Paul says: *My little children, I travail in birth again for you until Christ be formed in you* (Gal. 4:19) and, *As many of you as have been baptized into Christ have put on Christ* (Gal. 3:27).

What this grace is and how we may obtain it; what are the things that obscure this grace, and those that make it shine again.

5. St. John Chrystostom, whose soul and tongue outshine the brightest gold,[9] will tell you what this grace is, and how we may obtain it, and also what are the things that obscure (θολοῦντα) it and those that make it shine again (ἀνακαθαίροντα): "What does it mean that by *reflecting the glory of the Lord we are changed into the same image [from glory to glory* (εἰς δόξαν) *just as by the Spirit of the Lord]* (2 Cor. 3:18)? This was more apparent when miraculous gifts were active (τῶν σημείων τὰ χαρίσματα ἐνήργει), but even now it is not difficult for the eyes of faith to see. For when we are baptized, our soul shines brighter than the sun, being washed clean by the Spirit, and not only do we gaze on the glory of God, but we even take on some of its radiance. For just as polished silver, when set in the sunlight, gives off rays of its own, not only by its own virtue but through the brilliance of the sun, in the same way when the soul is purified and outshines the brightest silver, it receives radiance *from* the Spirit's *glory* and participating *in the glory* itself (εἰς δόξαν); and this, of course, is the work of the Spirit of the Lord."

And further, "Shall I give you a more tangible example from the Apostles? Consider Paul, whose clothes worked miracles (ἐνήργει) (Acts 19:12), or Peter, whose mere shadow had this power (ἴσχυον) (Acts 5:15). Their clothes and shadows would have been powerless had they not borne the image of the King and His unapproachable radiance; for the mere sight of the king's garments frightens thieves. Do you wish to see how this light also shone through their bodies? It is said that *as they gazed* on Stephen's face, *they saw that it was like the face of an angel* (Acts 6:15); but even this paled in comparison to the beams of glory within. The same light that once shone from Moses' face these men bore in their souls, and how much more (Ex. 34:30)! For Moses' light was sensible while theirs was immaterial. And just as material bodies all lit up with fire shed light on other bodies surrounding them, much the same happens with believers; and thus those who experience (πάσχοντες) this are taken up from the earth and dream of heaven with their waking eyes (ὀνειροπολοῦσιν). But alas! we should pause here and heave a deep sigh... For although we enjoy something so noble, we do not even understand it, since we are quickly distracted from these things and inclined toward sensible realities. For this unspeakable and awesome glory dwells within us for just a day

---

[9] St. John Chrysostom was given the epithet Χρυσόστομος ("golden-mouthed") for his rhetorical eloquence, and as Angelikoudes indicates, the radiance of his soul. The way Angelikoudes introduces Chrysostom (παντός χρυσίου λαμπρότερος) also amplifies Chrysostom's own words to describe the baptized soul (ἀργύρου παντός λαμπροτέρα)

or two before we then douse it with the river of daily affairs and keep off its rays with dense clouds."

And elsewhere he says: "The bodies of those who are pleasing to God are clothed in such glory as cannot be seen with these eyes; yet God has procured us some faint, dim signs of this in both the Old and New Testaments. In the Old Testament Moses' visage radiated such glory that the Israelites could not even look upon him (Ex. 34:30), and in the New Testament, Christ's countenance shone even brighter (Mt. 17:2). Have you heard the utterances of the Spirit? Have you understood the power of this mystery? Do you realize how great are the birthing pangs of our perfect spiritual reformation out of that holy baptismal font? How great are the fruits of its yield, its fullness, and its rewards? And how it lies within our power either to increase or diminish this supernatural grace, either by obscuring it or manifesting it such as we can. This is due to the storm of earthly affairs and the moonless night of the passions that comes from them, and like a squall or a raging torrent they surge over us and deluge our souls till we can no longer breathe or attend to what is truly beautiful and blessed, the very thing for which we were made. But as it is, our souls are quite tossed about by the tumult and choked by the smoke of pleasures, blackened and dragged under water. But those who walk by the Spirit and not the flesh possess the exact opposite, that is, all that is born of the deifying commands; for as it is written, *walk by the Spirit, and you shall not fulfill the lust of the flesh* (Gal. 5:16); these are profitable for salvation and will bear you up to the top of the ladder, to the highest rung: love, *and God is love* (1 Jn. 4:8)."

Although we receive divine grace purely as a gift through Holy Baptism, we obscure it with the passions, and make it shine again by fulfilling the commandments.

6. At that moment in the divine womb (θεία μήτρα), the holy font, we receive the perfectly free gift (δωρεὰν τὸ ὅλον) of divine grace. And when we later cover over it – though we ought not to – by misusing these earthly things and worrying over mundane cares and the beguiling mist (ἀχλύς) of the passions, we can still repent and fulfill the divine commandments, and thus return to that supernatural radiance and be restored to gaze on it in all its brilliance; this vision is revealed to each person according to the measure of his diligence in the faith, and even prior to that, by the Lord Jesus Christ's help and good pleasure. As St. Mark says, "Christ, being perfect God, has given perfect grace to those baptized in the Holy Spirit. In no way can we add (προσθήκην) to this grace; it is revealed to us and manifests itself in proportion to our labor in the commandments. Rather, it adds to our faith *till we all come to the unity of the faith, to the measure of the stature of the fullness of Christ* (Eph. 4:13)." Therefore anything that we have to offer after we have been

regenerated in Him has already been given to us by Him, and it was already lying hidden within us.

Anyone who wishes to live in a God-pleasing manner must strive to keep all the commandments. One's chief concern, however, should be for the chiefest and most universal commandments.

7. As we have mentioned, the beginning and root of this whole undertaking is to walk according to the commandments that lead to salvation. Its fulfillment and fruit is our recovery of the perfect grace of the Spirit that was first given to us through baptism; and this grace is assuredly within us, *for the gifts of God are irrevocable* (Rom. 11:2). But since we have buried it under the passions, it is to be uncovered again by practicing the deifying commandments. We must therefore strive to purify ourselves in every way for *the manifestation of the Spirit* (1 Cor. 12:7), that it might be seen manifestly. For as the blessed David says to God, *Your law is a lamp unto my feet and a light unto my paths* (Ps. 118:105), and, *The commandment of the Lord is resplendent, giving light to the eyes* (Ps. 18:9), and, *I have kept all your commandments well* (Ps. 118:128). And the beloved disciple, *He who keeps His commandments abides in Him, and He in him* (1 Jn. 3: 24), and, *His commandments are not burdensome* (1 Jn. 5:3). And in the words of the Savior Himself, *He who has My commandments and keeps them, it is he who loves Me. And he who loves Me will be loved by My Father, and I will love him and manifest Myself to him; if anyone loves Me, he will keep My word; and My Father will love him, and We will come to him and make Our home with him. He who does not love Me does not keep My words; and the word which you hear is not Mine but the Father's who sent Me.* (Jn. 14:21-24). So let us devote our fullest effort above all to the chiefest and most universal commandments, and they will give birth to the rest. In this way, with God's help, we may proceed without stumbling toward the goal laid before us, so that by starting off with a good beginning (καλὴ ἔναρξις) we may attain to the end that we so desire: *the manifestation of the Spirit* (cf. 1 Cor. 12:7).

The beginning of any work of love toward God is the invocation of the name of our Lord Jesus Christ in faith, along with the peace and love that arise from it.

8. Now the beginning of any God-pleasing work is the invocation of the saving name of our Lord Jesus Christ with faith, for He Himself declared, *Without Me, you can do nothing* (Jn. 15:5). And along with faith, we need peace, for Scripture says that we must *pray without wrath and doubting* (1 Tim. 2:8). And lastly, we are in need of love, for *God is love, and he who abides in love abides in God, and*

God in him (1 Jn. 4:16). This peace and love do not only render our prayers acceptable to God, but they are also born from this prayer, and dawn forth from it like twin rays of divinity that increase to perfection.

An abundance of spiritual goods is lavished on us through each of these principles in particular, and through all three in unison.

9. So then, from prayer in faith, peace, and love – through each one in particular, and all three together – a wealth of spiritual goods washes over us in abundance. By calling on the name of our Lord Jesus Christ with faith we firmly hope to receive the mercy and the true *life that is hidden* in Him (Col. 3:3). For the name of the Lord Jesus Christ bubbles over with these virtues like a divine perennial spring, inasmuch we call on it with a pure heart. Through the *peace that surpasses all understanding* and *has no end* (Phil. 4:7; Is. 9:7), we are made worthy of reconciliation (καταλλαγή) with God and with each other. Lastly, through love – whose glory is beyond compare – we become wholly joined to God, since it is the end and summation of the law and the prophets (Mt. 22:40), and indeed God Himself is called love (1 Jn. 4:8). Our sin is abolished through God's righteousness and through the gracious, loving adoption that works so wondrously in us. For *love covers over a multitude of sins* (1 Pet. 4:8), and *love bears all things, believes all things, hopes all things, endures all things patiently; love never fails* (1 Cor. 13:7-8).

The Lord Jesus Christ left His disciples final parting commandments and a divine inheritance at the time of His saving passion, and did likewise after His resurrection.

10. Hence, when the time came for our all-good and dearest Lord Jesus Christ to endure His passion willingly for our sake, and when He later appeared to the Apostles after the resurrection (that is before returning to the Father, who is His Father by nature and ours by grace), He left final parting commandments (ἐξιτηρίους ἐντολάς) and consolations to those who are in His care in a most kindly, reassuring, and gentle manner, just as a true and affectionate father would do. Moreover, they are an inalienable, divinely-bestowed inheritance. And this is what He said to His disciples when His saving Passion was upon him: *Whatever you ask in My name, I will do* (Jn. 14:13); *Truly, I say to you, whatever you ask the Father in My name He will give you. Until now you have asked nothing in My name. Ask, and you will receive, that your joy may be full* (Jn. 16:23-24); *In that day you will ask in My name* (Jn. 16:26). And again after the resurrection: *And these signs will follow those who believe: In My name they will cast out demons; they will speak with new tongues* (Mk. 16:17), and so on. Likewise, St. John the

Beloved said, *And truly Jesus did many other signs in the presence of His disciples, which are not written in this book; but these are written that you may believe that Jesus is the Christ, the Son of God, and that believing you may have life in His name* (Jn. 20:30-31). And the divine Paul: *In the name of Jesus every knee shall bow* (Phil. 2:10), and so on. Moreover, the following is recorded in the Acts of the Apostles: *Then Peter, filled with the Holy Spirit, said to them [...], "Let it be known to you all, and to all the people of Israel, that by the name of Jesus Christ of Nazareth, whom you crucified, whom God raised from the dead, by Him this man stands here before you whole* (Acts 4:9-11). And a little further: *Nor is there salvation in any other, for there is no other name under heaven given among men by which we must be saved* (Acts 4:12). Again, the Savior said, *All authority has been given to Me in heaven and on earth* (Mt. 28:18).

Furthermore, the Lord, the God-man, said to the Apostles before the cross, *Peace I leave with you, My peace I give to you* (Jn. 14:27), and, *These things I have spoken to you, that in Me you may have peace* (16:33). And, *This is My commandment, that you love one another* (15:12), and, *By this all will know that you are My disciples, if you have love for one another* (13:35), and, *As the Father loved Me, I also have loved you; abide in My love. If you keep My commandments, you will abide in My love, just as I have kept My Father's commandments and abide in His love* (15:9-11). Once again after His resurrection He appears to have revealed Himself to His disciples at different times and to have frequently granted them peace, saying, *Peace be with you* (Jn. 20:19). And to Peter, to whom He entrusted the leadership of His disciples, He said this in his third reply: *If you love Me more than the others, Peter, feed my sheep* (Jn. 21:15). In this way He indicated that care for the flock is a kind of reward (ἀντέκτισιν) for a flaming love towards the Lord Jesus Christ Himself. And one would not be missing the mark (ἀπὸ σκοποῦ) by saying that these three principles that we have mentioned engender three other extraordinary spiritual states: the purification of the soul, illumination, and perfection.

All the virtues are bound together by these three principles.

11. If someone wished to examine the matter carefully, he would find that this threefold and unbreakable cord (cf. Eccl. 4:12) sustains and binds together the whole pure purple robe of virtues woven by God (ἄφθορον καὶ θεότευκτον ἁλουργίδα). For a life pleasing to God is like a precious chain and gilded necklace, with one gleaming virtue interlocking with the next, and all fastened together to form a unified whole. Moreover, the many different virtues constitute a single work: the deification of the person who sincerely lives by them. The bonds and links by which they are fastened together are, as it were, the most precious and

saving invocation of the name of the Lord Jesus Christ in faith (together with hope and humility), and peace, and love; this is truly the three-trunked life-giving tree planted by God Himself (τὸ θεοφύτευτον ὄντως καὶ τριστέλεχον δένδρον καὶ ζωοπάροχον). He who lays ahold of it in due season and partakes of its fruit as he should, will not reap death like the first-formed man, but indestructible and eternal life.

The gift and visitation of the Holy Spirit from God the Father to the faithful is granted through Christ Jesus and in His holy name.

12. Furthermore, the gift and visitation of the Holy Spirit from God the Father is conferred on the faithful through Christ Jesus and in His holy name. As the exceedingly divine and tender-hearted Lord Jesus Christ Himself said to the Apostles, *It is to your advantage that I go away; for if I do not go away, the Helper will not come to you; but if I depart, I will send Him to you* (Jn. 16:7), *the Helper [...] whom I shall send to you from the Father, the Spirit of truth who proceeds from the Father* (Jn. 15:26). And again, *The Helper, the Holy Spirit, the Father will send Him in My name* (Jn. 14:26).

Our Holy Fathers have wisely enjoined us through the inspiration of the Holy Spirit who dwelt within them to pray to our Lord Jesus Christ and seek mercy from Him.

13. Therefore, our illustrious guides and teachers very wisely taught us through the inspiration of All-Holy Spirit who dwelt within them that before every good work or spiritual study, we should all pray in the Lord and seek mercy from Him with confidence; especially those who have struck out into the arena of deifying stillness (τὸ στάδιον τῆς θεοποιοῦ ἡσυχίας), who wish to consecrate themselves to God and break with the world, living a truly still life as hesychasts. We should make His most hallowed and sweet name our ceaseless work and study, bearing it continually in our hearts and minds and on our lips. In it and through it we should breathe and live and sleep and rise and move about and eat and drink; in short, it is crucial that we do everything in this way. For if this is missing, all sorts of evils overwhelm us, or at any rate we are left with nothing of value. But as long as this is present in us, all obstacles are removed. Indeed, then we lack no good thing and nothing remains out of reach, just as the Lord Himself declares: *He who abides in me, and I in him, bears much fruit; for without Me you can do nothing* (Jn. 15:5). For His name is feared and worshiped by all creation, and is the Truth and Name above all truths and names (Phil. 2:9). So then, after we have first called upon His name in faith and done all we can to spread the sails of the present treatise by it, unworthy as we are, let us begin our discourse and set out for what lies ahead.

He who desires to walk without stumbling in the godly way of stillness must first of all renounce the world and choose complete obedience.

14. In the name of our great God and Savior Jesus Christ, who said, *I am the light, the life, and the truth, the way and the door that leads to God the Father, and whoever passes through Me will be saved, and will go in and out and find the pasture* of salvation (Jn. 8:12; 14:6; 10:9), we ask that you hearken to the words we say and the sincere counsels we give to you. First and foremost, together with the universal rejection (ἀποταγή) of the world in accordance with the sacred monastic rite, you should choose for yourself genuine and complete subjection (ὑποταγή). That is, take great care to find an unerring guide and teacher. You will recognize him by how he testifies to what he says on the basis of the Holy Scriptures, and how he is Spirit-bearing, with a life that harmonizes with his words. Moreover, he should be lofty in thoughts but humble in mind, gracious (χρηστόν) in his manners and resembling the Christian (κατὰ Χριστόν) teacher as described in the divine teachings. Once you have found him and dedicated yourself to him physically and spiritually, as an affectionate son to a genuine father, you must wholly abide by his instructions and follow them faithfully, looking to him as to Christ Himself and not to man. After casting any unbelief and hesitation from yourself, even every thought and will of your own (μετὰ θελήσεως θέλημα), follow in the footsteps of your teacher with simplicity and without curiosity (ἀπεριέργως), having your conscience as a kind of mirror reflecting the clear and pure testimony of your unconditional and total obedience to your spiritual guide. But whenever the devil, who opposes all that is good, secretly sows a disobedient thought in your mind, draw back from it as from fornication and fire, and come to yourself. Further, wisely rebuke the deceiver (ἀπατεών) who insinuates these thoughts, saying, "It is not the traveler who leads the guide, but the guide who leads the traveler," and, "I have no responsibility for judging my elder, but rather he has responsibility for me; I was not appointed to be his judge, but he to be my judge," as St. John Climacus and others have written. For there is nothing more authentic than this way of life – the life of subjection – for a man who has decided with full consent to tear apart the record of his iniquities (τὰ χειρόγραφα τῶν οἰκείων ἀμπλακημάτων) and to be enrolled in the divine book of the saved. For if, according to the blessed Paul, the Son of God, our God and Lord Jesus, by becoming human for our sake and fulfilling in all wisdom the Father's will for our salvation, laid down the path of obedience, through which He, as a human being, was pleasing to the Father and honored by the paternal decree (for Paul says: *He humbled Himself and became obedient to the point of death, even the death of the cross. Therefore God also has highly exalted Him and given Him the name which is above every name* [Phil. 2:8-9]), then what shall we make of him who so audaciously, not to say ignorantly, expects to achieve the glory of our Lord and God and Savior Jesus Christ and rewards of the Father (τῶν πατρικῶν ἐπάθλων) without having chosen to walk the

same path as our instructor and teacher Jesus Christ? For if the pupil wishes to become like his teacher, he must with all his soul look steadfastly to the life and works of his instructor as his best example and archetype, and be earnest in imitating him every day. Hence it is also written about our Lord Jesus Christ Himself that *He was subject to His father and mother* (Lk. 2:51; cf. Ex. 20:12), and the Savior Himself says that He came *not to be served but to serve* (Mt. 20:28). But as for someone who wishes to live otherwise, that is, in a manner pleasing to himself, independently, and without any guide, is he justified in thinking that he is genuinely pursuing a God-pleasing life? Of course not! On the contrary, he has broken all the rules (ὡς ὑπὲρ τὰ ἐσκαμμένα πηδῶν). John Climacus says, "Just as the one who has no guide easily loses his way, so does the one who pursues the monastic life independently easily get lost, even if he possesses all the wisdom of the world." That is why most people, not to say all, who are not submissive and who walk without counsel, even when they seem to sow much in sweat and labour in reality reap very little, as if they were daydreaming (ὀνειροπολοῦντες). Some even gather tares instead of wheat, because they follow, as it is said, an idiorrhythmic way of life in self-pleasing conceit, and there is nothing worse than this. Again, John Climacus testifies to this when he writes: "You who have decided to strip away all hindrances (ἀποδύσασθαι) for the arena of this spiritual confession, you who wish to take on your neck the yoke of Christ, you who are therefore trying to lay your own burden on another's shoulders, you who hasten to sell yourselves into voluntary slavery (τὰς ἑαυτῶν ὠνάς) in return for your freedom, you who are being supported by the hands of others as you swim across this great sea – you should know that you have decided to travel by a short but rough way, from which there is only one deflection, and it is called self-reliance.[10] But he who has renounced this entirely, even in matters that seem to be good and spiritual and pleasing to God, has reached the end even before setting out on his journey. For obedience is distrust of oneself in everything, however good it may be, right up to the end of one's life."[11] Therefore, wisely take these things to heart, and as you strive to practice the *good portion* of celestial stillness (αἰθεροδρόμου ἡσυχίας) which *shall not be taken from you*, follow these well established laws which have been made known to you (cf. Lk. 10:42). First, embrace obedience with joy (ἀσπασίως ἄσπασαι). And only then embrace stillness. For just as practice is the foundation of theory, so is obedience the foundation of stillness. And, as it is written, Do not desire to *remove the boundaries laid down by the Fathers* (Prov. 22:28), and, *Woe to him who is alone* (Eccl. 4:10). In this way, by making a good beginning by laying the foundation, in the course of time you will raise a most-

---

[10] *Idiorrythmia*: an ascetic term which means that the monk gives himself his own rule and establishes his own individual rhythm of life by following his own opinion and will, without obeying or consulting an elder.

[11] *Ladder of Divine Ascent* 4.5 (trans. Lazarus Moore, with slight modifications), 11.

glorious roof by the architecture of the Spirit. For, as the saying goes, a bad beginning (ἀρχὴ ἀδόκιμος) will spoil the whole, but where the beginning is proper, the whole will be well-ordered and harmonious. And even if occasionally the opposite turns out to be the case, this failure too will be owing to our own intention and free will (προθέσει καὶ προαιρέσει).

What are the signs of true subjection, such that the truly obedient person who possesses them will be practicing subjection without error.

15. However, considering that the word of obedience (ταύτης ἀγωγῆς) is so great and difficult to carry out (hence those who practice obedience do so in various ways), it is necessary that we make some notes for you to serve as reminders; if you keep them as a rule and unfailing standard, you will conduct your life in a lawful and holy manner. This is what we have to say: one who practises true obedience must, we think, preserve the following five virtues in every case. The first virtue is faith, that is to have a pure and sincere faith in one's spiritual director (ἐπιστάτης), so much so that it seems to him that he is looking upon Christ and submitting to Him, for as the Lord Jesus says, *He who listens to you, listens to Me, and he who rejects you, rejects Me; and whoever rejects Me, rejects Him who sent Me* (Lk. 10:16), and also, *Everything that is not of faith is sin* (Rom. 14:23). The second virtue is truth, that is, to be truthful in word and deed, as well as in the exact confession of one's thoughts and passions. For as it is written, *The beginning of your words is truth* (Ps. 118:160), and, *The Lord loves the truth* (Ps. 30:24). Moreover, Christ says, *I am the truth* (Jn. 14:6), and is called the Truth-Itself. The third virtue is not to do one's own will. For it is said that it is harmful for someone in obedience to do his own will, but he must continually cut it off willingly, which means without being forced by his spiritual father. The fourth virtue is to completely refrain from contradicting or quarrelling, since talking back and quarrelsomeness are unbecoming to the pious. As the holy Paul writes, *If anyone is inclined to be quarrelsome, we have no such custom, nor do the churches of God.* (1 Cor. 11:16). If these things are completely forbidden to all Christians in general, how much more so to monastics. For in these matters they have promised to be strictly obedient in accordance with the Lord's will. In any case, contradicting and quarreling come about from a mind fettered with disbelief and conceit, as it is said, "The conceited monk stubbornly contradicts." The converse is also true, that is, the habit of not contradicting or quarreling proceeds from faith and a humble disposition. The fifth virtue that a monastic in obedience must preserve is exact and honest confession to one's elder (προεστῶτα), just as we have promised at the rite of the monastic tonsure, as before Christ's dreadful tribune, before God and the holy angels: to keep from beginning to end the practice of disclosing the hidden things of the heart, among our other promises and covenants with the Lord. It is

also said by the divine David, *I said, I will confess my iniquity to the Lord against myself, and You forgave* (Ps. 31:5), and so on. And John Climacus says, "The bruises that are exposed (μώλωπες θριαμβευόμενοι) will not grow worse, but will be healed." May the one who keeps these five virtues with wisdom and diligence be wholly assured that he will obtain even at the present time the blessedness of the righteous as a pledge of what is to come.

These are the characteristics of honorable obedience, and they constitute a kind of root and foundation. Hear, then, what the branches and the fruits are, and what the canopy is. We are told again by John Climacus, "From obedience is born humility, from humility discernment, from discernment insight, and from insight foresight," which is the work of God alone and is granted as a wondrous and supernatural gift to those who are deified and blessed. In addition to this, let the following be clear to you: humility springs up within you according to the measure of your obedience, and again, discernment according to the measure of your humility, and so on for the other virtues. Strive then with all your might to run in the way of obedience without stumbling, and in this manner you will securely attain to the most advanced virtues. But if you stumble and limp at the turning-post in this course of obedience, know that you will not finish well the remainder of the race – the life dedicated to Christ – nor will you be crowned with the wreath awarded to the victors. But let obedience and its attributes as we have described them be a guide to you, just as sailors keep watch to preserve a straight course, so that by keeping an unshaken orientation you will be able to sail over the great sea of virtues and finally anchor in the tranquil haven of dispassion. If you experience any storm or tempest, it will be due to your disobedience (cf. Acts 27:10-44). For, as the Fathers say, the person who is truly obedient cannot even be harmed by the devil himself.

In order to show you briefly how great the sublime height of obedience is, we will call to mind one more phrase from a holy Father. John, that most-luminous beacon of the life dedicated to Christ and new Bezalel of the Heavenly Ladder (Ex. 31:2), says, "The Fathers call chant a weapon, prayer a fortification, blameless tears a bath; but they considered blessed obedience martyrdom (ὁμολογία), *without which none* of those subject to the passions *will ever see the Lord* (Heb. 12:14)."[12] We think that these words suffice as the clearest statement and praise of a virtue as inimitable and ineffable as thrice-blessed obedience. We might learn and acquire even more knowledge by experience if we look back and consider what caused our destruction and mortality, although we were not so created from the beginning, and again what causes our renewal and immortality.

---

[12] *Ladder* 4.8.

We see, then, that the cause of that former corruption was the first Adam's belief and trust in himself, his self-reliance, and his disobedience (ἰδιοπιστίαν τε καὶ ἰδιορρυθμίαν καὶ τὸ ἀνυπότακτον), which resulted in the transgression and violation of the divine commandment. The latter, the cause of incorruption, was achieved for us by the second Adam, our God and Savior Jesus Christ's consent and submission to His Father, whose commandment He kept. For, as the Savior says, *I have not spoken from Myself; but the Father who sent Me gave Me a command, what I should say and what I should speak. And I know that His commandment is everlasting life. Therefore, whatever I speak, I speak just as the Father has told Me* (Jn. 12:49-50). For as in the forefather Adam, and those like him (τοῖς κατ' αὐτόν), the root and mother of all sorrows is self-conceit, so in the new Adam, the God-man Jesus Christ, and in those who desire to live in Him (κατ' αὐτόν), the beginning and source and foundation of all blessings is humility. We see this order and attitude being preserved even among the chorus of those supreme deiform angels who hold their station far above us, as well as in our Church here on earth. Moreover, we have been taught and believe that those who stray from this ordinance and wish to live singularly and irregularly, not to say arrogantly, are cut off from God and the radiant and heavenly inheritance and the universal Church, and are excommunicated and sent off to the darkness and fire of Gehenna. And this is what has befallen the wicked evildoers accompanying Lucifer, and the prattling malicious heretics who have appeared at times, as we are told by the God-inspired words: it is said that they were piteously rejected from the glory and tenderness of God, and the heretics were excommunicated from the sacred association of Christians, all because of their complacency and pride.

A wise man once said that contraries are cures for their contraries.[13] Since then the cause of all sorrows (σκυθρωπῶν) is insubordination and arrogance, while being subjected and humbled gives rise to bright joys (φαιδρωπῶν), he who wishes to live without condemnation must therefore live in subjection to a tested and unerring father who derives his authority from the experience of many years, knowledge of divine things, and whose life is adorned with the crown of virtues. Moreover, one should consider this father's instruction and counsel as if it were the voice and will of God. For, as Scripture says, *Salvation is found in abundant counsel* (Prov. 11:14), and, *A man without counsel is his own enemy.* But if some of the venerable Fathers have happened to attain deifying stillness and perfection in God without this kind of discipline in obedience, this was accomplished by divine revelation and rarely does it occur. Furthermore, it has been written that the

[13] Galen of Pergamon (2-3rd cen. AD), renowned physician and philosopher. See *On The Therapeutic Method* 11.12.

exception does not become the law of the Church, just as one swallow does not make a spring.

So then, believe genuine submission to be a preliminary lesson for the stillness of surpassing beauty and do not regard the singular instances of God's economy, but rather follow what the venerable Fathers have universally prescribed (τὰ κοινῇ ψηφισθέντα). In this way you will be made worthy of the rewards for those who live lawfully. Besides, is it not the case that no one would choose to set out on an unknown road without a guide pointing out the right way? Nor would anyone brave the open sea without an experienced captain. Such is the case for any art and science given the absence of a proper teacher. But as for the art of arts, and the science of sciences, and the path that leads to God, and the infinite noetic sea, that is to say the solitary life which is akin to the life of the angels, who would dare to take it up and trust himself to reach his goal without a guide or captain or a true and experienced teacher? Whoever does this is truly *deceiving himself* (φρεναπατᾷ ἑαυτόν) (cf. Gal. 6:3), and has already strayed even before he has begun, since he is not training according to the rules (cf. 2 Tim. 2:5). On the other hand, he who obeys the institutions of the Fathers has achieved his goal before even setting out. For how else can we properly learn to fight against the flesh or to take up arms against passions and demons? Indeed, as it is written, "Next to the virtues there are neighboring (ἀγχίθυροι) evils set up as traps." Or how else will we learn to train our body's senses and attune the faculties of the soul as the strings of a lyre? Even more so, how will we be able to distinguish between divine prophecies (ὀμφάς), revelations, consolations, and contemplations on the one hand, and demonic delusions, deceptions, and fantasies on the other? In short, how will we be made worthy of being united with God and the divine rites and mysteries without being initiated by a true and illumined guide? It is impossible – truly impossible. Let us consider the chosen vessel, blessed Paul – the initiate into ineffable realities, the mouth of Christ, the light of the world, the universal sun, the teacher of the whole world – and how he says that he discussed and convened with his fellow apostles about the Gospel *in order to make sure that he was neither running nor had run all in vain* (Gal. 2:2). Let us also attend to Wisdom-Itself, our Lord Jesus Christ, who says of Himself, *I have come down from heaven, not to do My own will, but the will of Him who sent Me* (Jn. 6:38) and about the All-Holy and Life-Giving Spirit that *He shall not speak of Himself, but whatever He hears He will speak* (Jn. 16:13).[14] May this proper order (τάξις), which holds together (συνέχει) both heavenly things and earthly things, fill us (συνεχόμεθα) with dread and astonishment and anguish both on account of our own nothingness and indifference and for the sake of those who, through madness and self-will, prefer to live

[14] Kallistos and Ignatios are of course not implying any subordination or hierarchy between the divine persons of the Holy Trinity, but rather an "order", or *taxis*, of perfect equality and mutual love.

shamelessly and dangerously in self-reliance and unruliness. For this struggle we face is truly terrible, and there are packs of thieves (λωποδύται), countless pirates waiting in ambush, and a host of wrecked ships. This is why among the many, only a very few are saved (Lk. 13:23-4).

However, let them live as they wish, for *each one's work will be tested by fire*, as the Scripture says (1 Cor. 3:13); and the Psalmist says, *You will give to each according to his works* (Ps. 61:13). Or rather, let them not simply live as they want, but may they desire to live as they ought to live, and may the Lord grant understanding to all. Since you have learned the nature of the whole golden and spiritual robe of blessed obedience by merely touching its fringe through these words of ours (cf. Lk. 8:44), you and anyone else who wishes to live the God-pleasing life should strive to find a teacher unerring and perfect, as we have indicated. According to the Christ-bearing Paul, *Solid food is for the perfect who have trained the senses to distinguish between good and evil* (Heb. 5:14), and in this way, by seeking with diligence and faith, you will not fail in your purpose. For as the Scripture says, *Everyone who asks receives, and whoever seeks finds, and to whomever knocks it will be opened* (Mt. 7:8). Then the teacher you find will mystically teach (μυσταγωγήσει) you in due time and in good order all that is right and dear to God. Further, he will guide you into those mysteries that are God-pleasing, spiritual, and inaccessible to most people as soon as he sees that you rejoice with all your soul in moderation, austerity, and simplicity in food, drink, shelter, and clothing, and that you are content with what is really profitable, appropriate, and necessary for each occasion, without seeking frivolous and silly things, which those who live in folly and arrogance pompously boast about, and so turn their swords against themselves and against their own salvation. As the great Apostle Paul says, *Having food and clothing, with these we shall be content* (1 Tim. 6:8).

But do you indeed seek and desire for us to instruct you in writing about what is appropriate to the beginning, middle, and end of the life dedicated to Christ? While your request is commendable, it is difficult to give a response offhand (ἐκ τοῦ προχείρου). Nevertheless, with Christ's help (Χριστοῦ δεξιὰν ὀρέγοντος) and at your behest, we will do our best to fulfill this request. We will set out to build upon the solid and unshakeable foundation of glorious and perfect obedience that house which is most celebrated in the whole domain of spiritual edification: deifying *hesychia*. Hence we shall speak hereafter by resting on the Spirit-inspired (πνευματοφθόγγοις) testimonies of the Fathers as upon steadfast pillars.

Anyone who desires genuine and godly *hesychia*[15] must, along with Orthodox faith,[16] be full of good works. Faith is twofold. The hesychast must have faith, but also be peaceful, undistracted, free from anxiety – that is, without concerns – silent, still, thankful to God in all things; he should acknowledge his weakness, endure temptations bravely, hope in God, and expect what is beneficial from Him.

1. The Lord says, *Not everyone who says to Me, 'Lord, Lord,' shall enter the kingdom of heaven, but he who does the will of My Father in heaven* (Mt. 7:21). So then, dear one, if it is not only in words that you yearn for (ἐρᾷς) holy *hesychia* – which makes those who genuinely practice it purely receptive of manifestations of God and the Kingdom of Heaven even in this present life, and then in the age to come more completely and perfectly – if you yearn for it in truth and in deed, make sure that in addition to your Orthodox faith you are also full of good works.

So then, be at peace with everyone (such as it depends on you), undistracted, free from anxiety, that is, without any concerns, silent, quiet, thankful to God in everything, aware of your own weakness, with your eyes ever watchful and alert to the manifold temptations that assault you every day, and struggle against any turmoil and affliction that comes upon you with patience and forbearance. For the first and the second points, that is, to be adorned with the Orthodox faith and good works, let the glorious brother of God James teach you plainly, saying, *Faith without works is dead,* as are works without faith. Show me your faith by your works (cf. Jas 2:26,18). And even more importantly, the Master and Teacher of all, our Lord Jesus Christ, said to His disciples, *Go therefore and make disciples of all the nations, baptizing them in the name of the Father and of the Son and of the Holy Spirit, teaching them to observe all things that I have commanded you* (Mt. 28:19-20). Moreover, Gregory the Theologian says that God requires three things of everyone who is baptized: right faith in the soul, prudence in the body, and truth on the tongue.

---

[15] We note once again that *hesychia* ("stillness") is sometimes untranslated because it is being used in a more specific sense, as a description of the life of the *hesychast*. For example, the list that follows includes "stillness" (ἡσυχία) as one of many aspects of "*Hesychia*" (along with peace, silence, gratitude, etc.).

[16] "Orthodox faith" (ὀρθόδοξος πίστις) refers to both "the faith of the Orthodox Church" as well as "right doctrine," "right worship".

Faith is twofold.

2. Note that, according to the words of divine tradition, faith is twofold. One is the universal (καθόλου) faith of all Orthodox Christians, in which we were first baptized and in which we hope to depart from this life (συναπέλθοιμεν). But those who have the other kind of faith are rare: they are those who through fulfillment of all the deifying commandments have been restored to being *in the image and likeness of God*, and have thus been enriched by the light of divine grace, placing all their hope in the Lord (cf. Ps. 72:28), so that – what wonder! – they have no doubts in their petitions to God during prayer, but by pleading with faith they immediately receive what is profitable, as the Lord promises (Mt. 21:21). Thus did these blessed ones gain sure faith from sincere works, since they cast off all knowledge, uncertainty, doubt, and hesitation, became completely immersed in the divine intoxication (μέθη) of faith and hope and love in God, and experienced (πάσχειν) that good and blessed *transformation* which, according to David, is the work of *the right hand of the Most High* (Ps. 76:11). Now, while it is not the proper time for us to speak extensively about the first kind of faith, it is an excellent opportunity to talk about the second kind, which blooms and bursts forth from the first as a divine fruit. For faith is as it were the root and crown of deifying *hesychia*, as John Climacus says: "If you do not believe, how will you find *hesychia*?"[17] And as the divine David says, *I believed, wherefore I spoke* (Ps. 115:1). Again, the great Apostle Paul says, *Faith is the substance of things hoped for, the evidence of things not seen* (Heb. 11:1), and, '*The righteous shall live by faith'* (Rom. 1:17; Hab. 2:4). Furthermore, when the Lord's disciples asked Him to increase their faith, He told them, *"If you have faith as a mustard seed, you can say to this mulberry tree, 'Be pulled up by the roots and be planted in the sea,' and it would obey you* (Lk. 17:5-6). Again, He said: *If you have faith and you do not doubt, you will not only do the miracle of the fig tree, but if you say to this mountain, 'Rise up and fall into the sea,' it will be done; and all that you ask in prayer by faith, you will receive* (Mt. 21:21-22), and, *Your faith has saved you* (Mt. 9:22).

Furthermore, St. Isaac writes: "Faith is subtler (λεπτοτέρα) than knowledge, and knowledge subtler than sensible things. Hence, all the Saints who were made worthy of reaching the state of ecstasy in God live by the power of faith in the bliss of that supernatural state. When we say faith we do not mean faith in the sense of belief in the three worshipful and divine Hypostases and in the supreme unique nature of the Divinity itself, nor in the miraculous economy of the Incarnation of the Word whereby He assumed our own nature, even though this faith too is very exalted. Rather we mean that faith which arises in the soul from the light of grace

---

[17] *Ladder*, 27.68.

through the experience of the mind, and which preserves the heart without any doubts, in the full assurance of hope and far from any conceit. This faith reveals itself not through the hearing of the ears, but to spiritual eyes it uncovers mysteries hidden in the soul and that secret divine treasure which is hidden from the sight of the sons of the flesh, but revealed in the Spirit to those who dine at Christ's table by relishing His laws. For as He said, *If you keep my commandments, I will send to you the Comforter, the Spirit of Truth, whom the world cannot receive, and He will teach you the whole truth* (Jn. 14:17, 16:13), and so on. St. Isaac further says, "Until He comes, who is the consummation of the mysteries, and until we are counted worthy of receiving the manifest revelation of those mysteries, faith is what enables us to participate in the ineffable mysteries of God and the Saints. May it be granted that we might partake of them by the grace of Christ, both here as a pledge and there in the Kingdom of Heaven in tangible truth, together with all who love Him."

You should be peaceful.

3. Now we come to the third point, to be peaceful with everyone. Let the words of the blessed David, as well as those of the Christ-bearing Paul, louder than the blast of a trumpet, provide clear counsel to you: the first says, *Those who love Your law have much peace, and there is no offense in them* (Ps. 118:165), and *With those who hate peace, I was peaceful* (Ps. 119:7), and, *Seek peace and pursue it* (Ps. 33:15). Then the Apostle Paul says, *Pursue peace with all and holiness, without which no man shall see the Lord* (Heb. 12:14), and, *If it is possible, as much as depends on you, live peaceably with all* (Rom. 12:18).

You should be undistracted.

4. As to the fourth point, that is being undistracted, St. Isaac will instruct you, "If it is indeed true that desire is born of the senses, then let all those be silenced who claim that they preserve peace of mind while living amidst distractions," and, "Do not have dealings with distracted men."

You should be free from anxiety and care.

5. For the fifth, that is, being free from anxiety and care (ἀμέριμνον καὶ ἀφρόντιστον) about either reasonable (εὐλόγων) or unreasonable (ἀλόγων) matters,[18] let the Lord's words in the Gospels instruct you: *Therefore I say to you, do not worry about your life, what you will eat or what you will drink; nor about*

[18] That is, rational concerns or irrational anxieties.

your body, what you will put on. Is not life more than food and the body more than clothing? Look at the birds of the air, for they neither sow nor reap nor gather into barns; yet your heavenly Father feeds them. Are you not of more value than they? Which of you by worrying can add one cubit to his stature? So why do you worry about clothing? (Mt. 6:25-28) And further, *Therefore do not worry, saying, 'What shall we eat?' or 'What shall we drink?' or 'What shall we wear?' For after all these things the Gentiles seek. For your heavenly Father knows that you need all these things. But seek first the kingdom of God and His righteousness, and all these things shall be added to you. Therefore do not worry about tomorrow, for tomorrow will worry about its own affairs. Sufficient for the day is its own trouble* (Mt. 6:31-34). Also, St. Isaac says, "Without freedom from anxiety do not seek light in your soul, nor seek for tranquility and *hesychia* as long as you have indolence in your senses." And as John Climacus says: "A small hair disturbs the eye, and a small care ruins *hesychia*; for *hesychia* is the banishment of thoughts and ideas, and the rejection of even reasonable cares. He who has really attained to *hesychia* does not give a thought to his flesh; for He who has promised will not prove false."[19]

You should be silent.

6. The order of our discourse now compels us to discuss the sixth point: silence. On this, St. Isaac says the following: "Whoever keeps his mouth from backbiting (καταλαλιά) guards his heart from the passions. And whoever cleanses his heart from the passions sees the Lord at all times. If you place all the works of solitude on one side of the scale and place silence on the other, you will find that silence outweighs all the others. Above all, love silence, since it brings you near to that divine fruit which the tongue cannot describe. Therefore, let us begin by forcing ourselves to keep silent, and then the habit of keeping silent will engender within us that which leads us to silence itself. May God grant you to experience that which is born of silence. And if you begin this way of life, I cannot say how great a light will arise from within you." Again, "Silence is a mystery of the coming age, while words and speech are an instrument of this world." And to St. Arsenios this was commanded a second time by the voice of God, "Arsenios, depart, be silent, be still, and you shall be saved."

You should be still.

7. Furthermore, for the seventh point, that is, to live in stillness, Basil the Great and St. Isaac once again are reliable witnesses. The first said, "Stillness is the

---

[19] *Ladder* 27.51-52 (Trans. Moore, with slight modifications), p. 116.

beginning of the soul's purification," and the second: "The end (ὅρος) of stillness is to be silent about all things." Here Basil succinctly states its beginning, and Isaac its end. Furthermore, in the Old Testament it is said, *Have you sinned? Be still* (Gen. 4:7), and, *Be still* (σχολάσατε) *and know that I am God* (Ps. 45:11). And John Climacus says: "The preliminary task of *hesychia* is the disengagement from all affairs, whether reasonable or not; for he who allows even reasonable ones will certainly fall into those which are not. The second task of *hesychia* is earnest prayer (προσευχὴ ἄοκνος). And the third is inviolable (ἄσυλος) activity of the heart. It is of course impossible for one who does not know the alphabet to study books. It is still more impossible for one who has not attained to the first to progress properly (λόγῳ) to the last two tasks."[20] Moreover, St. Isaac says, "Yearning for stillness means the continual expectation of death. He who enters into the work of stillness without this meditation will be unable to bear those things we ought to endure with fortitude in the future."

You should thank God in all things.

8. Likewise, for the eighth point, to give thanks in all things, let the divine Apostle Paul be your teacher, as he commands: *In everything give thanks* (1 Thess. 5:18). Furthermore, St. Isaac writes, "The thanksgiving of the recipient prompts the benefactor to give more gifts, even greater than the first. But he who does not give thanks for the smaller gifts will be unfaithful (ψεύστης) and unjust in regard to the greater ones. What brings the gifts of God to man is the heart that moves with ceaseless thanksgiving. But what brings temptation to the soul is the thought of murmuring that constantly stirs in the heart. A mouth that always gives thanks receives a blessing from God, and grace comes into the heart that perseveres in gratitude."

You should recognize your own weakness.

9. You will learn how great a profit accrues to him who has come to know his own weakness – the ninth point – by considering the example of the divine David, who says in the sixth psalm, *Have mercy on me, Lord, for I am weak* (Ps. 6:3). And in another psalm he says, *But I am a worm, and no man; a reproach of men, and a scorn of the people* (Ps. 21:7). Again, St. Isaac writes, "Blessed is he who knows his own weakness, for this knowledge becomes the foundation and root and beginning of all goodness. When one realizes and truly perceives his own weakness, then he tightens the looseness of his soul (περισφίγγει τὴν ἑαυτοῦ ψυχὴν ἀπὸ τῆς χαυνότητος) that obscures knowledge, and stores up watchfulness

[20] *Ladder* 27.46 (Trans. Lazarus Moore, with slight modifications), 115.

(παραφυλακή) for himself. The person who has come to know the true measure of his own weakness has attained to the perfect degree of humility. "

You should bravely endure temptations.

10. The last point that remains in our discourse, and completes the number ten, is that you should endure bravely and resist with patience and forbearance the manifold temptations that assault you. Hear then what is written in the Holy Scripture about this, for the Christ-bearing Paul says, *Brethren, we do not wrestle against flesh and blood, but against principalities, against powers, against the rulers of the darkness of this age, against spiritual hosts of wickedness in the heavenly places* (Eph. 6:12), and, *If you are without chastening, of which all have become partakers, then you are illegitimate and not sons* (Heb. 12:8), and, *For whom the Lord loves He chastens, and scourges every son whom He receives* (Heb. 12:6). Moreover, James, the Brother of God, says that a man who does not endure temptation is not approved (Jam. 1:12). Further, St. Elias the Presbyter says, "Every Christian who truly believes in God must not be carefree (μὴ ἀμεριμνεῖν), but should always anticipate and be prepared for temptation, so that he is never surprised or perplexed when it comes. Even more so, he should gratefully endure the toil of affliction and really mean what he says when chanting with the prophet, *Lord, put me to tests and temptations* (Ps. 25:2). Now the prophet did not say, *Your chastening* 'has destroyed me', but that it *has upheld me to the end* (Ps. 17:36)." But again, neither should you seek to know the causes of the temptations by asking where they come from, but only pray to God and endure them with thanksgiving, as St. Mark says: "When a temptation comes, do not seek to know why and where it came from, but how to endure it with thanksgiving and forgiveness (ἀμνησικάκως)." And again, "Considering how difficult it is to find a man who has been pleasing to God without suffering temptations (ἐκτὸς πειρασμῶν), we should thank God amidst all that happens to us." Again, "Every affliction reveals the inclination of the will, whether it is turned to the right or to the left. For this reason every affliction that occurs is called a 'temptation' (πειρασμός), because it provides to the one who experiences it a test of his hidden desires." Moreover, St. Isaac, along with many others, writes: "Temptation can benefit (ὠφελεῖ) everyone. For if it even benefits St. Paul (2 Cor. 12:9-10), let *every mouth be stopped, and all the world become guilty before God* (Rom. 3:19). Contestants are tested (πειράζονται) that they might increase in their wealth; the sluggish, so that they might guard themselves from what harms them; those who slumber, that they might be urged to wakefulness; those who are far from God, that they might draw near to Him; and those who are His own, that they might enter into the house of the Father with boldness. No son who remains undisciplined (ἀγύμναστος) is given the wealth of his father's house for his own use. And it is for this reason that God tries and tests first, and afterwards presents the gift. Glory be to the Lord, who by means of bitter medicine (φαρμάκοις στρυφνοῖς) grants us the enjoyment of our health. There is no one exempt from the pain of discipline, and there is no one exempt from the bitter draught of the poison of temptations. But without them no one can indulge in a strong mixture that would otherwise be lethal. Again, to endure patiently is not something in our own power. For how does the earthen jug get the power to hold water, except by the divine fire that makes it solid? If we submit and humbly entreat God with unceasing desire, we will be able to endure everything with perseverance, in Christ Jesus our Lord." It is also said in the Wisdom of Sirach, *My son, if you come to serve the Lord, prepare your soul for temptation. Set your heart aright, and persevere, and make not haste in time of trouble* (Sir. 2:1-2).

You should hope in God and expect from Him what is beneficial.

16. Put the anchor of your hope in God who has the power to save, and await from Him the best way out of temptations. For the Scripture says, *God is faithful, who will not allow you to be tempted beyond what you are able, but with the temptation will also make the way of escape* (1 Cor. 10:13); *Affliction produces perseverance; perseverance produces character; character produces hope, and hope does not disappoint* (Rom. 5:3-5); *He who endures to the end will be saved* (Mt. 10:22); and, *By your patience, gain your souls* (Lk 21:19). Moreover, James, the Brother of God, says, *My brethren, count it all joy when you fall into various trials, knowing that the testing of your faith produces patience. But let patience have its perfect work, that you may be perfect and complete, lacking nothing* (Jas. 1:2-4); and, *Blessed is the man who endures temptation; for when he has been approved, he will receive the crown of life which the Lord has promised to those who love Him* (Jas. 1:12). And as St. Paul says: *I consider that the sufferings of this present time are not worthy to be compared with the glory which shall be revealed in us* (Rom. 8:18). And the Psalmist: *I waited patiently for the Lord; and he attended to me, and hearkened to my supplication. And he brought me up out of a pit of misery, and from miry clay: and he set my feet on a rock, and ordered my ways aright. And he put a new song into my mouth, a hymn to our God* (Ps. 39:2-4). Blessed Symeon Metaphrastes also writes, "The soul caught in the bonds of God's love thinks nothing of her sufferings, but revels in her sorrows and flourishes amidst distress. And when she does not experience any grief for the sake of her Beloved, she considers this to be a greater affliction, and flees comfort as though it were torment."

The fear of God is twofold: the fear proper to beginners and the fear proper to the perfect.

17. At this point we should not neglect to discuss the twofold fear of God. We slightly changed the order of the first fear (for the Fathers list fear after faith) because we decided to mention the perfect fear after the conclusion of the above ten chapters.

On the first fear, which is proper to beginners.

So then, dear one, understand that there are two kinds of fear of God: the fear proper to beginners and the fear proper to the perfect. About the first kind it is written, *The fear of the Lord is the beginning of wisdom* (Prov. 1:7), and, *Come, children, listen to me; I will teach you the fear of the Lord* (Ps. 33:12), and that *by the fear of the Lord everyone departs from evil* (Prov. 15:27), and, *Where there is fear, there is keeping of the commandments*. St. Isaac says, "The fear of God is the beginning of virtue; they say that it is born of faith and sown in the heart when the mind departs from the distraction of the world to gather its intellections, which were wandering through vain imagining (μετεωρισμός), and directs them instead to meditation on our future restoration." Further, "The beginning of the true life of man is the fear of God. However, it does not consent to reside in the soul together with any vain imagination. Be wise and set the fear of God as a foundation for your journey, and in a few days you will be restored to the gate of the kingdom by the straightest possible path."

On the second and perfect divine fear.

About the second kind, that is, the perfect fear of God, it is written: *Blessed is the man that fears the Lord; he will delight in His commandments with all his will* (Ps. 111:1), and, *Blessed are all those who fear the Lord, who walk in His ways* (Ps. 127:1), and, *Fear the Lord, all you His saints, for those who fear Him lack nothing* (Ps. 33:10), and, *Behold, thus shall the man who fears the Lord be blessed* (Ps. 127:4), and, *The fear of the Lord is pure, enduring forever and ever* (Ps. 18:10). St. Peter of Damascus also writes, "The sign of the first kind of fear is to hate sin and to feel anger against it, as if wounded by a beast. The sign of perfect fear is to love virtue and to fear turning away (τροπή), for no one is immune to change. Regarding everything in this life, we should always fear lest we fall." So then, in heeding these things with understanding, strive to preserve the first kind of fear within you unceasingly, together with all that we have mentioned, for it is a treasure trove of every good deed. By keeping these, your steps shall be guided (cf. Ps. 39:3) toward the fulfillment of all the commandments of our Lord Jesus

Christ, and as you make progress on this path, you will also eventually acquire the fear that is perfect and pure (cf. Ps. 18:10), through your desire for the virtues and the mercy of our good God.

We ought to sacrifice our very lives for the sake of the commandments and faithfulness to the Lord Jesus Christ if it is required of us.

18. In addition to the above, you should also know that, for the sake of the life-giving commandments and faithfulness to Jesus Christ in accordance with the commandments, we ought to sacrifice our lives willingly and without regret if this is ever required of us (καιροῦ καλοῦντος). As the Lord Jesus Christ Himself says, *Whoever loses his life for My sake and the gospel's will save it* (Mk. 8:35). And you should believe without any doubt or hesitation that the God-man Jesus, our Savior, is Himself the Resurrection and the Life and all that pertains to our salvation, as He Himself has said: *I am the resurrection and the life. He who believes in Me, though he may die, he shall live. And whoever lives and believes in Me shall never die* (Jn. 11:25-26), and, *God so loved the world that He gave His only begotten Son, that whoever believes in Him should not perish but have everlasting life*. (Jn. 3:16), and, *I have come that they may have life, and that they may have it more abundantly* (Jn. 10:10). Therefore, no matter what state you find yourself in, run along the path together with Christ Jesus our Lord without turning back, *forgetting the things which are behind and reaching forward to the things which are ahead*, as it is written (Phil. 3:13).

Now seems a good and quite suitable time to give a preliminary explanation of a natural method suggested by the great and blessed Nikephoros on how to enter the heart by breathing in through the nose (δι' εἰσπνοῆς ῥινός), which contributes in a certain manner to the concentration of the intellect. In this way the present discourse will proceed in good order with God's help. This holy man, along with many others who have their authority from the written testimonies of the Saints, says the following:

Natural method of entering the heart by breathing through the nose and the accompanying prayer that is performed: "Lord Jesus Christ, Son of God,

have mercy on me". How this method contributes to the mind's concentration.[21]

19. "Brother, as you know, the breath we breathe is air, and we breathe it specifically for the heart, which supplies life and warmth to the body. Thus the heart carries the breath of air into itself as a means of carrying out, upon exhalation, some of its heat in order to maintain the body's proper temperature. The cause, or rather, the servant of this function is the lungs, which were made by the Creator with a thin structure, so as to inflate and inhale the air without difficulty like a pair of bellows. Thus, the heart cools with breathing, releases heat, and impeccably performs the function for which it has been designed unto the preservation of life. So then, after having sat down in a quiet (ἡσύχῳ) cell and concentrated your intellect, let the intellect pass through the nose into the airway, where the breath enters into the heart; and push your intellect and force it to descend along with the inhaled air into the heart. And when it has entered there, what follows will not fail to cheer and delight you: for just as a man who was absent from his home cannot help but feel joy in greeting his children and his wife when he returns, so the intellect too, when it is united with the soul, is filled with unspeakable delight and gladness.

"So then, brother, accustom your intellect to stay there and to avoid quickly departing from there. At first it is quite distressed (καταρρᾳθυμεῖ) by the closure and restraint; however, once it gets used to it, it is no longer fond (οὐκ ἔτι στέργει) of wandering about, *for the Kingdom of God is within you* (Lk. 17:21), and as the intellect perceives it there and pursues it in pure prayer, everything outside seems wretched and unpleasant." And further he says, "You should know this too, that while your intellect is there, do not let it stay quiet and idle, but give it the prayer: 'Lord Jesus Christ, Son of God, have mercy on me', as its task and ceaseless study, and let it never cease from it. For it keeps the intellect undistracted (ἀμετεώριστον), makes it invincible and inviolable against the enemy's attacks, and daily increases love and divine longing."

The blessed Nikephoros writes this with the above-mentioned goal in mind, in order that by practicing this natural method the intellect might come back from its habitual roaming, wandering, and captivity, and return to attentiveness, so that through attentiveness it becomes reconnected with itself and united to prayer, and from then on the intellect may enter into the heart with this prayer and perpetually

[21] If this psychosomatic method is used to aid concentration in prayer it should be done with spiritual guidance, as Kallistos and Ignatios explain more generally at the beginning of the *Exact Rule and Method.*

abide in it. Another teacher wise in divine matters, while explaining the above passage as someone who has experience in this sacred work, says the following:

The natural method of breathing through the nose while invoking the Lord Jesus Christ.

20. "We should also make this clear to the person who is eager to learn: When we train our intellect to go down into the heart while breathing in, then we will surely learn that as it descends the intellect does not enter there until it has renounced every thought and become single and bare, occupied only with the invocation of our Lord Jesus Christ and nothing else. But again, when it departs from there and returns to external things, it reemerges into fragmented thinking and is even divided against its will."

The divine Chrysostom, like other holy Fathers of old, enjoins us to pray in Christ Jesus our Lord within the heart, and to say the prayer, "Lord Jesus Christ, Son of God, have mercy on me".

21. The great Chrysostom also says, "Brethren, I entreat you never to break or neglect the rule of prayer." And further, "Whether he is eating or drinking or sitting or serving or traveling or doing anything else, the monk ought to cry unceasingly, 'Lord Jesus Christ, Son of God, have mercy on me', [...] in order that the name of the Lord Jesus, by descending into the bottom of the heart, might humiliate the dragon that has taken possession of the pastures of the heart, and save and give life to the soul. Therefore, abide unceasingly in the name of the Lord Jesus, so that the heart might envelop the Lord, and the Lord the heart, and the two become one."[22] And again, "Do not separate your hearts from God, but always persist and guard them with the remembrance of our Lord Jesus Christ; until the name of the Lord is planted in the heart, and it thinks of nothing else, that Christ may be magnified in you."

More about the remembrance of Jesus within the heart by breathing with attention.

22. John Climacus also writes, "Let the remembrance of Jesus cling to your every breath, and then you will know the value of stillness."[23] And as St. Hesychios says, "If you really wish to put distracting thoughts to shame, to find stillness easily and

---

[22] See ch. 49.

[23] *Ladder* 27.61 (Trans. Moore) 116.

watchfulness of heart without difficulty, let the prayer of Jesus cling to your every breath, and in a few days you will see this happen."

Anyone who wishes to be watchful in intellect, especially the beginner, should sit in a quiet and dark room during the time of prayer, so that the mind and the intellect can be recollected from division in a natural manner.

23. These things have been established from above and by great and holy Fathers, that is, all that we have explained with testimonies about breathing through the nose, descending into the heart, praying to our Lord Jesus Christ, the Son of God, meditating, being watchful, and seeking mercy from Him in His holy and saving name. But we should also add that the one who is intent on being noetically watchful in his heart, especially the beginner, should always be in a quiet place (ἐν ἡσύχῳ), and that especially during the appointed time of prayer he should sit in a quiet and dark corner, as we have been mystically taught and instructed by the divine Fathers and teachers experienced in this most-blessed work.

For since the gaze of the eyes and looking at visible phenomena naturally become a cause for scattering and diverting the mind toward what is seen, and consequently it becomes troubled (σκύλλεσθαι) and altered (ποικίλλεσθαι), so by contrast when the mind is enclosed in a quiet and dark room, it ceases to be divided and distracted by the sense of sight and the habit of glancing at things. In this way the intellect, willingly or unwillingly, tends to become calm and free from division, and grows accustomed to being recollected to itself, as Basil the Great says, "The intellect that is neither scattered towards external things nor diffused in the world by the sense faculties returns to itself."

It is first and foremost through Jesus Christ and the invocation of His holy name with faith in the heart that cessation from anxiety and mental wandering is granted to the intellect. But the natural methods of entering the heart by breathing through the nose, sitting in a quiet and dark space, and the like, also contribute in a certain manner.

24. More importantly, and indeed what is most important of all, is that this accomplishment of the intellect is achieved by the assistance of divine grace, through the heartfelt, pure, and unwandering invocation of our Lord Jesus Christ, which is done with faith, and not simply by the simple natural method of breathing through the nose or by sitting in a quiet, dark place – why of course not! For the Divine Fathers did not devise these methods for any other purpose than to assist (ὡς συνεργά) in some way in the concentration of the mind, returning it back to itself, and recalling it from its habitual wandering back to a state of attentiveness,

as we have explained, and by these means constant, pure, and unwandering prayer is engendered in the intellect, as St. Neilos says: "The attentive intellect that seeks prayer shall find it (cf. Mt. 7:8). For praying attentively follows from paying attention more than anything else, so we should strive to acquire attentiveness."[24] So then, dear child, since you *desire life and love to see good days* (Ps. 33:13), and wish to live in the body as though bodiless (ἐν σώματι ὡς ἀσώματος), live by the following rule and canon.

How the hesychast should spend the time between vespers and orthros; the beginning of detailed instruction.

25. When the sun goes down, after calling upon the most-good and almighty Lord Jesus Christ to help you, sit on a stool in a quiet, dark cell. And as you gather your intellect from its usual external wandering and rambling, and push it gently into your heart by breathing through your nose, persist in the prayer, "Lord Jesus Christ, Son of God, have mercy on me."

That is to say, concentrate on the words of the prayer, uniting them in a certain manner to your breath, as St. Hesychios says: "While breathing in, unite watchfulness with the name of Jesus, together with humility and the unwavering remembrance of death, for these too bring benefit," and together with the Jesus prayer keep in mind the other thoughts that we have said to you, along with the remembrance of the Judgment and retribution for good and evil deeds; moreover, wholeheartedly consider yourself to be more sinful than all men and more impure than the demons themselves, and hence deserving of eternal torment (ὅπως μέλλῃς αἰωνίως κολάζεσθαι). As you ponder these things compunction and mourning and tears will come to you, and you should persist in this meditation until they come of themselves.

But if you have not yet been counted worthy to receive the gift of tears, then struggle and pray humbly to obtain it. For through tears we are purified of our passions and defilements and become partakers of all that is good and saving, as John Climacus says: "Just as fire consumes (ἀναιρετικόν) stubble, so do pure tears consume every bodily and spiritual impurity."[25]

And another holy Father says: "He who wishes to destroy evils, by weeping will he destroy them; and he who wishes to obtain virtues, by weeping will he obtain

---

[24] In Greek, there is an alliterative wordplay on the words "attentiveness" (προσοχή) and "prayer" (προσευχή).

[25] *Ladder* 7.31.

them." If you do not have compunction, you should know that this is a sign of vainglory, which prevents the soul from feeling compunction. If tears still do not come to you, sit down and ruminate (προσέχων) on these thoughts while saying the Jesus Prayer for an hour. Then arise and chant the Small Compline service (τὸ μικρὸν ἀπόδειπνον) attentively (σὺν προσοχῇ). Afterwards sit down again and continue the prayer[26] according to your strength, purely and without reverie, that is, without any anxiety or thought or any kind of imagining, in great sobriety, for half an hour, according to the saying, "If you desire to commune with the intellect alone (μετὰ μόνου γενέσθαι τοῦ νοῦ), isolate yourself from everything but eating and breathing, and pray."

Then, after sealing yourself with the sign of the precious and life-giving Cross, do likewise while sitting on your cot: bring to mind the joys and punishments of the coming age, the flux (ῥευστός) and deceptiveness of temporal things, and that debt which comes upon us swiftly and suddenly and which all are obliged to pay – death – and the dreadful reckoning that will take place at the end, and even before the end (cf. Mt. 12:36). After remembering all your sins briefly, fervently asking for forgiveness, and examining (λογοπραγήσας) exactly how you spent the day, go lie down as you continue the Jesus prayer, as it is said: "Let the remembrance of Jesus sleep with you." Then sleep for five or six hours; or rather, sleep for as long as the nighttime lasts.

How to spend the time between orthros and morning.

26. When you have woken up, glorified God and again called upon Him for help, begin that task of yours which comes first and foremost: praying in the heart purely and without reverie for up to an hour. For at that time the intellect tends to be serene and undisturbed; moreover, we have also been commanded to offer to God our first-fruits and first-born (Ex. 22:29), which means to lift up as far as possible our first thoughts (πρωτόνοια) unwaveringly unto our Lord Jesus Christ through pure prayer of the heart. Further, as St. Neilos says: "He who always offers the first-fruits of his thought to God is one who really prays."

After this, chant the Midnight Office (τὸ μεσονυκτικόν). If, however, you do not have strength for more perfect *hesychia*, and therefore cannot make a beginning as we have said, or perhaps for some other reason, as is often the case for beginners, though rarely for those who have made progress but have yet to reach perfection (since the perfect *can do all things through Christ who strengthens* them [Phil.

---

26 This phrase, "continue the prayer" or "hold onto the prayer" (κράτησον τὴν εὐχήν), is repeated throughout the following chapters during all the various daily tasks of monastic life.

4:13]), in this case do the following: after arising from sleep, first chant the Midnight Office with as much wakefulness as possible, with all your attention and understanding. Then sit down and pray in your heart purely and without reverie for an hour, as we have said; or rather, as much as the Giver of all good things provides to you. For John Climacus says, "Devote the greater part of the night to prayer and only what is left to recital of the psalter. And during the day again prepare yourself according to your strength."[27] If however, despite your struggle you are still overwhelmed by negligence and despondency or your mind is blurred by something that has happened, arise and stir yourself awake, and continue the Jesus prayer. Then, after sitting down, endeavor to pray as we have said, always taking care to commune with God, who is pure, through pure prayer. Then stand up and chant the Six Psalms (ἑξάψαλμος) with understanding, Psalm 50, and any canon you like.

Next, sit down again and pray earnestly (εἰλικρινῶς) for half an hour, struggling to keep yourself awake. Then arise again and chant the Lauds (οἱ αἶνοι),[28] the usual doxology, and the First Hour until the conclusion of the service. Let all that you say with your lips be such that it is only loud enough to reach your ears – for we are commanded to offer the *fruit of our lips* to God (Heb. 13:15) – and give thanks with all your soul and mind to the Protector who loves mankind, our all-wise God, who by His infinite mercy has granted us to pass favorably through the sea of the night and to look upon the bright and joyful expanse of day. Likewise fervently beseech Him to grant that we pass through the moonless and fierce storm of demons and passions without any surges or swells, and that He may have mercy on us.

How to spend the time between morning and mealtime.

27. From morning (ἀπὸ τῆς πρωίας) till mealtime (ἕως τοῦ ἀρίστου), after you have first given all of yourself wholly unto God according to your strength (ὅλος ὅλον ὅλῳ Θεῷ ἀναθείς) and prayed to Him with a *broken heart* to help you who are infirm and indolent and irresolute, begin pure and unwandering prayer of the heart. When you read, stand upright as you read the appointed passages (τὸ τετυπωμένον σοι) from the Psalter, the Apostle, and the Holy Gospel; do the same in your prayers to our Lord Jesus Christ and the Most-Pure Theotokos, but you may sit down for the rest of the readings from the Holy Scriptures. After this, attentively chant the usual Hours which have been prescribed (διετυπώθησαν) by the Fathers of the Church with great wisdom, and with all the strength of your soul

---

[27] *Ladder* 27.77 (Trans. Moore), 118.
[28] Or "Praises".

drive away both sloth, the teacher of all vices, and all the other passions and their causes, even if they seem trivial and appear to be harmless.

On guarding oneself from sloth, and how even the hesychast must adhere to the ecclesiastical order and tradition.

28. St. Isaac says: "Beloved brethren, guard yourselves from sloth (ἀργία), since certain death is hidden within it. When the monk is free of sloth, he does not slip into the hands of the demons that wish to capture him. God will not condemn us in that day concerning psalms or laziness in prayer, but because by neglecting them the way is cleared for the demons to enter. And when they have found an open space (χώρα), entered, and closed the doors of our spiritual eyes, then they will tyrannically and wickedly fill us with all those evils which make those guilty of committing them susceptible to a dreadful punishment by divine judgment, and we will become enslaved because we have forsaken small matters, which are worthy of the utmost care for Christ's sake, as the wisest men say, 'Whoever does not subject his own will to God will be subjected to the enemy.' So let these matters that appear trivial to you be reckoned as walls that guard against our captors. The way we conduct these matters within the cell has been wisely established by those responsible for the order of the Church through the revelation of the Spirit as a guard for our lives; the unwise consider these matters to be of no consequence, but they do not understand the harm that comes of this. For them, the beginning and the means of the hesychastic way of life consist of undisciplined liberty (ἐλευθερία ἀπαίδευτος), which is the mother of the passions. For it is better to strive not to neglect small matters, than to give place to sin in their absence, since the consequence of this untimely freedom is sheer slavery."

Elsewhere St. Isaac writes: "How seductive are the causes of the passions! Occasionally one manages to cut off the passions and upon their removal he becomes tranquil and rejoices that they are abolished, but he cannot abandon the causes of the passions. For this reason we are tempted against our will. We are grieved by the passions, yet we love to indulge their causes within us. We do not desire the sins, but we accept with pleasure the causes that induce them. Hence, the latter actualize (παραίτιοι γίνονται τῇ ἐνεργείᾳ) the former. He who loves the causes of the passions is involuntarily subjected and is enslaved to the passions against his will. But he who hates his own sins ceases from them, and he who confesses them will obtain forgiveness. It is impossible for someone to abandon the habit of sin before first acquiring enmity (ἔχθρα) against it, or to obtain forgiveness before confessing one's faults. For this enmity is the cause of true humility, and confession is the cause of compunction, which springs in the heart from remorse." And elsewhere he says: "The only sin that cannot be forgiven is the one not repented of." But that is enough concerning these things.

After chanting the Hours we have specified, you should then eat, continuing the Jesus prayer while eating, so that by doing so you may acquire the habit, by the power of grace, of *praying unceasingly* according to the commandment (1 Thess. 5:17). As for our discourse on the nourishment that sustains the body by the ineffable wisdom of the Creator, let it wait for now. Let us first speak of the food that forms and animates the soul, according to the Saints, namely, sacred and deifying prayer; and this will be a more reasonable order, since the soul is superior (προτιμοτέρα) to the body.

More about prayer. We should always pray.

29. Just as our body, when it has no soul, is dead and foul, so too the soul, if it does not stir itself to prayer, is dead and wretched and foul; and the great prophet Daniel teaches us well how we ought to consider deprivation of prayer to be more bitter than death, since he preferred to be put to death rather than to be deprived of prayer even for a moment (Dan. 6:10). The divine Chrysostom also teaches us well, saying, "Everyone who prays converses with God. Everyone knows what a great thing it is for man to speak with God, but no one can depict so great an honor in words. For this honor exceeds the majesty of the angels." And again, "Prayer is the common work of angels and men, and nothing separates their respective natures in regard to prayer. It sets you apart from the irrational beasts, and it unites you with the angels. Moreover, one will speedily be raised up to the life, state, conduct, honor, dignity, wisdom, and prudence of angels, if he dedicates all his life to stillness in prayer and the worship of God." Further, "When the devil sees the soul shielded by virtues he dares not approach it, since he fears the strength and power of prayers, which nourish the soul more than food does the body." And again, "Prayers are the sinews of the soul; for just as the body is held and fitted together and stands and lives and is made solid by muscles and sinews (but if one were to cut them, then it would compromise the whole body's integrity (ἁρμονίαν), likewise, through holy prayers, souls are united and held (ἁρμόζονται) together and effortlessly run in the way of piety. But if you deprive yourself of prayer, it is like taking a fish out of water. For just as water is life for the fish, so is prayer for you. By means of prayer one flies through the air like a fish through water, ascends to the heavens, and draws near to God."

Again, "Prayer and supplication make men temples of God. Just as gold, precious gems, and marble make the palaces of kings, so does prayer make people temples of Christ. What then could be a greater praise for prayer than the fact that it raises up temples of God? He whom even the heavens cannot contain enters into the soul that lives in prayer (cf. 3 Kg. 8:27)."

St. John Chrysostom continues, saying, "One may also consider the power of holy prayers from the fact that Paul, as if possessed of wings, raced throughout the whole world, but even as he was imprisoned, endured floggings, wore chains, lived amidst violence and dangers, cast out demons, resurrected the dead, and cured diseases, he did not rely on any of these things for the salvation of men, but it was by prayers that he fortified his soul. Even after performing miracles and resurrecting the dead, he always had recourse to prayer, as a wrestler contends for the victor's laurels (ὥσπερ τις ἀθλητὴς ἐπὶ παλαίστραν στεφάνου). For prayer brings about the resurrection of the dead and all other sorts of miracles. The vitality that water brings to trees, prayers provide to the lives of the Saints." And again, "Prayer is the means of salvation, the cause of immortality (ἀθανασίας πρόξενος), the steadfast fortification of the Church, an impenetrable refuge, terror of the demons, and salvation for all of us who live in piety." Again, "Just as when a queen enters a city she is accompanied by a display of all her wealth, likewise with prayer: when it enters the soul, it brings all the virtues in its train." And further, "What the foundation is to the house, prayer is to the soul. We must lay prayer first as a groundwork and base in the soul, and then zealously build thereon the virtue of temperance, and care for the poor, and all the laws of Christ." And, "Earnest prayer is the light of the mind and the soul, a light constant and inextinguishable. It is for this reason that the evil one suggests so many myriad disparate thoughts to our minds and at the time of prayer pours into our souls notions which he himself devised and which we would never even conceive of." And again, "Prayer is a mighty weapon, a strong protection."

Furthermore, Gregory the Theologian says, "Remembering God is more important than breathing." And, "We should think upon God more often than we breathe." And as St. Isaac says, "Without ceaseless prayer you cannot draw near to God." And, "If after the labor of prayer your mind becomes occupied with some other concern, it causes the mind to scatter. Prayer that involves no labor of body or pangs of heart is reckoned as a miscarriage, for it has no soul."

Further, John Climacus writes, "Prayer by reason of its nature is the converse and union of man with God, and by reason of its action upholds the world and brings about reconciliation with God; it is the mother and also the daughter of tears, the propitiation for sins, a bridge over temptations, a wall against afflictions, a crushing of conflicts, work of angels, food of all the spiritual beings, future gladness, boundless activity, the spring of virtues, the source of graces, invisible progress, food of the soul, the enlightening of the mind, an axe for despair, a demonstration of hope, the annulling of sorrow, the wealth of monks, the treasure of solitaries, the reduction of anger, the mirror of progress, the realization of success, a proof of one's condition, a revelation of the future, a sign of glory. For him who truly prays, prayer is the court, the judgment hall and the tribunal of the Lord before the judgment to come."[29] And elsewhere, "Prayer is nothing other than estrangement from the world, visible and invisible."[30]

And St. Neilos says, "If you have a desire to pray, renounce all things so that you might inherit all things. Prayer is the lifting of the mind to God. Prayer is the fellowship (ὁμιλία) of the mind with God. Just as bread nourishes the body and virtue nourishes the soul, so spiritual prayer is food for the intellect." Now this provides us with a good opportunity to discuss the bodily regimen as concisely as possible: the measure, amount, and kind of food one should eat.

On bodily regimen and how the hesychast should eat.

30. The Scripture says, *Son of man, you shall eat your bread in measure* (σταθμῷ) *and shall drink your water with moderation* (μέτρῳ) (cf. Ezek. 4:10-11), for this amount is sufficient for one who is striving to live the life pleasing to God. As it is said, "If you don't give blood, you won't receive spirit." The great Paul also says, *But I discipline my body and bring it into subjection, lest, when I have preached to others, I myself should become disqualified* (1 Cor. 9:27).

As the divine David says, *My knees have grown weak from fasting, and my flesh has changed for lack of oil* (Ps. 108:24). And again, Gregory the Theologian, "Nothing conciliates God (Θεὸς θεραπεύεται) more than the humbling of the flesh (κακοπαθείᾳ), and His lovingkindness is granted as a reward for tears."[31] Furthermore, St. Isaac writes, "In the same way that a mother cares for her child, Christ cares for a body that is humbled (κακοπαθοῦντος), and is always near to that body." And, "Knowledge of the mysteries of God cannot be found in a full belly. Just as for *those who sow in tears* there follows a *harvest in joy* (Ps. 125:5-6), so does joy follow from the humbling of the flesh for God's sake. Blessed is he who has blunted himself (ὁ ἀποστομίσας ἑαυτόν) to every pleasure that separates him from his Creator." And elsewhere, "After a long time of being tempted from every side (ἐν τοῖς δεξιοῖς καὶ ἀριστεροῖς), and after testing myself often in both these ways and receiving countless wounds from the enemy, and being granted abundant help on many occasions and in secret (κρυπτῶς), I gained many long

---

[29] *Ladder* 28.1 (Trans. Moore), 119.
[30] *Ladder* 28.25 (Trans. Moore, 121.
[31] *Gregory Nazianzen, Oration* 24.11.

years of experience, and through the trial and grace of God I have learned this: that the foundation of all goods, and the restoration (ἀνάκλησις) of the soul from the enemy's captivity, and the path that leads to light and life, are found in these two ways: to settle oneself in one place and to fast always (ἀεί), that is, to follow a wise and prudent regimen (κανονίσαι ἑαυτόν) in self-control (ἐγκράτεια) of the belly, seated in stillness in unceasing rest (σχολῇ) and meditation (μελέτη) on God. This is where subjection of the senses and watchfulness of intellect comes from; this is how the wild passions that stir within the body are tamed; from there comes meekness of thoughts, radiant motions of the mind, diligence in the divine works of virtue, lofty and subtle perceptions, innumerable tears poured forth at every hour, and the remembrance of death; from this source comes pure chastity, which is wholly absent of any imagination that tempts the mind; acuity and a sharp-sighted knowledge of things that are far off (ἡ ὀξυδερκία καὶ ἡ ὀξύτης τῆς γνώσεως τῶν μακρὰν ὄντων); deeper mystical perceptions, which the mind grasps by the power of the divine writings, and inner motions that occur within the soul, and the capacity to discriminate and discern between evil spirits and angelic powers, between true visions and vain fantasies. From this source comes the fear which guards the ways and tracks through the sea of the mind, and which cuts off indolence and negligence; the flame of zeal which tramples over every danger and overcomes every fear; and the fervency which scorns all desire, and by removing desire from the mind, makes one oblivious to any memory of what has transpired between oneself and others. To put it concisely, from this source comes the freedom of the true person, the joy of the soul, the resurrection, and repose with Christ in the Kingdom of Heaven. However, if anyone neglects these two ways, let him understand that he not only deprives himself of all that we have described, but even shakes the foundation of all the virtues by scorning these two. And just as these two virtues within the soul are the foundation and sum (ἀρχὴ καὶ κεφαλή) of divine labor, and the door and the way to Christ, as long as one keeps them and persists in them, so conversely, if he departs from them and abandons them, he will end up falling into their contraries, namely, lack of restraint (μετεωρισθῆναι) in the body and unlawful gluttony and the like." And elsewhere St. Isaac says, "Those who begin the solitary life in indolence and laziness are agitated and dismayed not only by these kinds of struggles, but even by the rustling of the leaves of the trees and the small necessity of having to be hungry; they are overcome by the slightest infirmity, give up the contest, and turn back. But true and tested fighters do not even eat green herbs to satiety (ἐκ τοῦ χόρτου τῶν λαχάνων χορτάζονται), nor do they deign to eat anything before the appointed mealtime, even if they only live off the roots of dry herbs; they even sleep cramped on the ground in great discomfort, and they even lose their eyesight because their bodies are so utterly spent (ἐκ τῆς ἄγαν κενώσεως). Indeed, when they are close to departing from the body from want (ἐκ τῆς ἀνάγκης ἐγγίζουσιν ἐξελθεῖν ἐκ τοῦ σώματος), not even then do they draw back because of their sturdy resolve, lest they be defeated and fall. For they yearn and desire to strain themselves for the love of God, and would rather strive for virtue than enjoy this temporary life or any rest that exists in this life. Moreover, when they are assaulted by temptations, they rejoice all the more since they are brought to perfection and made perfect through them. Nor do they have any doubt in the love of God because of the hardships they experience, but until they depart from this life they are willing to accept temptations courageously and do not shun them, for they are made perfect through them."

Now, on the basis of these and related teachings, which we follow, but also in obedience to Him who says, *Go along the royal way; do not turn aside to the right or to the left* (cf. Num. 20:17), we present to you a rule and canon of moderation with the following standards.

How the ascetic should eat on Mondays, Wednesdays, and Fridays.

31. Three days a week, on Monday, Wednesday, and Friday, always eat once a day in the afternoon. Eat six ounces of bread (ἄρτου οὐγγιῶν ἕξ), dry food in moderation (ἐγκρατῶς τοῦ ἀρκοῦντος), and up to three or four glasses of water, as you wish, following the 69th canon of the Holy Apostles which prescribes: "If a bishop, presbyter, deacon, reader, or chanter does not fast on Great Lent or on Wednesdays or Fridays, let him be defrocked (καθαιρείσθω), unless he is prevented by a physical illness. If he is a layman, let him be unchurched (ἀφοριζέσθω)." At any rate, the fast on Monday was established by the Holy Fathers at a later time.

How one should eat on Tuesdays and Thursdays.

32. Eat twice a day on Tuesdays and Thursdays. At lunch you should eat six ounces of bread and eat cooked food in self-control, in addition to some dry food. Partake of wine mixed with water as needed, up to three or four cups. At dinner, eat three ounces of bread as well as some dry food or fruits, and one glass of wine mixed with water, and if you are quite thirsty drink two cups at most, for thirst contributes to weeping and is a companion to vigilance, as John Climacus says, "Thirst and vigil afflict (ἐξέθλιψαν) the heart, but when the heart is afflicted, waters spring forth."[32]And St. Isaac, "Thirst for God that He might fill you with His love." But if you prefer to eat only once (τὸ μονοφαγεῖν) on these two days, you will do best, since fasting and self-control are the principle, mother, root, source, and foundation of all goods. One pagan author says, "Choose the best life (βίος ἄριστος), and habit will make it pleasant." Basil the Great, too: "Where there is a will, the way is

[32] *Ladder* 6.13 (Trans. Moore), 36.

cleared (ὅπου προαίρεσις, τὸ κωλῦον οὐδέν)." And another divine Father says, "The flower is the beginning of the fruit, and self-control is the beginning of the practical life." Now these things and what comes after them may seem difficult to some, or perhaps even impossible. But whoever takes into account the abundant fruit that is born from them, and reflects on how great is the glory they are wont to bring forth, will consider them easy when he combines his own earnest effort with the help of our Lord Jesus Christ, and then he will declare in word and in deed just how easy they are and attest to their value. Moreover, St. Isaac says, "Humble (εὐτελής) bread from the table of the pure purifies the soul of him who eats of it from every passion." Further, "From the table of those fasting, keeping vigil, and laboring in the Lord, receive for yourself the medicine of life," and, "Be raised up from the deadness (θνῆξις) of your soul, for the Beloved sits among them, and by sanctifying the food He changes the bitterness of their misery into His own indescribable sweetness, and meanwhile His spiritual and heavenly ministers overshadow them and their holy banquet." and, "The fragrance of the faster is delightful, and being in his company gladdens the hearts of the discerning." And again, "The way of the temperate man is dear to God."

How you should eat on Saturdays. About vigils and how one should eat on days and weeks with vigils.

33. Every Saturday (apart from Great Saturday) you should eat twice (διφαγεῖν), as has been appointed for Tuesday and Thursday, on account of the decision of the Sacred Canons and the fact that it is necessary to celebrate vigils on all Sundays of the whole year except during Cheesefare (Τυροφάγον) or whenever there is an approaching vigil for one of the Great Dominical Feasts or for any of the Great Saints, in which case you may omit the Sunday vigil to do the other instead. In any case, eat twice on Saturdays. Nevertheless, it is always profitable to exert yourself (ἐκβιάζεσθαι) in the work of nighttime vigil. Thus, even if there is a vigil later in the week, it is most profitable to do the Sunday vigil as well, and great gain will very quickly follow from it, or as Scripture says, *Thus shall your light break forth as the morning, and your health shall quickly spring forth* (Is. 58:8). Moreover, St. Isaac writes, "In every struggle against sin and desire, the labor of vigil and fasting is the beginning, especially for anyone who is struggling against the *sin that dwells within us* (Rom. 7:17-20); among those engaged in invisible warfare it is also the sign of hatred against both sin and the desire to commit it. For nearly all the assaults of the passions begin to grow weak through fasting. After fasting, nighttime vigil contributes most to ascesis. He who loves the company of this pair (συζυγία) of virtues in all his life becomes a friend of prudence. Just as the contentment (ἀνάπαυσις) of the belly is the beginning of all evils, and sluggishness in sleep enkindles desire for fornication, so by contrast the holy way of God and foundation

of every virtue is fasting and vigil and watchfulness in the service of God." And again, "The Lord provides for the safety of the soul that shines with the remembrance of God and sleepless vigil by day and by night; He sends a cloud to cover it by day and a pillar of fire to illuminate it by night (Ex. 13:21-22), and within its darkness (γνόφος) light will shine." Further, "Treat yourself to a work of delight: continual vigil in the nighttime, by means of which the Fathers stripped off the *old man* (Eph. 4:22) and were made worthy of the *renewal of the intellect* (Rom 12:2). In these hours the soul has a perception of immortal life, and through this perception it strips away the darkness of the passions and receives the Holy Spirit." And again, "Honor the work of vigil to find comfort in your soul." And, "Among all the works done by monastics, consider no activity to be greater than nighttime vigil." Again, "Do not consider the monk who lives in vigil with discernment of intellect as simply a man clothed in flesh (σαρκοφόρος), since this work truly befits the angelic order." Further, "A soul laboring in this angelic activity of vigil shall receive cherubic eyes to constantly gaze and look upon the heavenly vision (θεωρία)."

Spend your vigils in prayer, chanting, and reading, with purity and compunction, without wandering thoughts, either alone or in friendly, like-minded company. And after every vigil, take a little refreshment from the fatigue of the vigil with food and drink at dinner. That is, eat three ounces of bread and some dry food, as needed, and drink three glasses of wine mixed with water. Also, make sure that on a fasting day which has a vigil you do not break the fast up to the Ninth Hour because of the vigil, since you *ought to do the one without leaving the other undone* (cf. Mt. 23:23), and we have already explained how you can take refreshment after the vigil.

How one should eat on Sundays. Concerning other matters, such as labor and humility.

34. Likewise, on all Sundays, as on Saturdays, eat two times a day. Let this rule be kept strictly (σῶα τηρείσθω), unless you are sick. Of course, there are also days which the holy Fathers have appointed to be free of fasting out of long-standing custom, and then there are more recent causes, whether sacred or not (ἐνθέων φαμὲν ἢ καὶ ἐναντίων). On these days we do not eat only once, nor do we eat only dry food, but we partake of all foods that are beneficial (χρήσιμος) and permissible (ἀνεπίληπτος), in addition to vegetables, all with self-control and in limited portions. For it is always best to have self-restraint in all things. But in the case of bodily weakness, as we have said, one should partake without shame of all beneficial and permissible foods that help strengthen the body. For the Holy Fathers have taught us to be killers of the passions (παθοκτόνοι), not killers of the

body (σωματοκτόνοι). Likewise, it is also reasonable to eat a little (μικρὸν ἀπογεύεσθαι) of all that is approved or permissible in the monastic life (τῷ ἐπαγγέλματι), both to glorify and give thanks to God and to avoid pride. But also avoid eating more than enough (τὰ περισσά). For as St. Isaac says, "Lack of things teaches a person self-control even when he does not seek or desire it," since when we have abundance and freedom we are unable to control ourselves. Moreover, we should have no love for bodily contentment and rest (ἀνάπαυσις). For according to St. Isaac, "The soul that loves God finds rest only in God." You should prefer humility, together with labor and toil (κακουχίᾳ). For as one of the Saints writes, by labor and humility we win Jesus Himself.

How one should eat and conduct oneself during the holy forty-day fasts, especially during Great Lent.

35. We consider it unnecessary to explain in any special detail the diet, or even one's basic conduct, during the holy forty day fasts. For we have already instructed you regarding days when you keep the Ninth Hour, and it is right for you to do the same during the holy forty-day fasts, apart from Saturdays and Sundays. Or better yet, do it with even greater strictness and sobriety if possible, especially during Holy and Great Lent, for since it is one tenth of the whole year it is a tithe offering (ἀποδεκάτωσις) to God, and grants prizes to victors in Christ Jesus on the divine and luminous Day of our Lord's Resurrection.

On discernment, and how labor in moderation is of inestimable value. More about submission.

36. Moreover, in addition to practices such as these, it is necessary that you apply them with strict discernment for the sake of the harmonious and peaceful constitution of our twofold nature as body and soul. For as Scripture says, *A house is built by wisdom and is set up by understanding. By good sense the chambers are filled with all precious and fine wealth* (Prov. 24:3-4). And further, the divine Thalassios writes, "Poverty and deprivation with reason (μετὰ λόγου) and discernment constitute the royal way (cf. Num. 20:17; 21:22). By contrast, mortification (ὑπωπιασμός) without discernment and unreasonable self-abasement are not profitable, both being contrary to reason (παρὰ λόγον)." And again, St. Isaac says, "The relaxation of the members is followed by dissipation (ἔκστασις) and confusion of thoughts, while excessive work is followed by despondency (ἀκηδίᾳ), and despondency again gives way to dissipation of thoughts. However, the first kind of dissipation differs from the second. The first gives rise to an assault of fornication, while the second leads to the abandonment of the hermitage and wandering from place to place. On the other hand, labor that is done with diligence

and moderation is of inestimable value. Therefore, deficiency in these matters increases sinful pleasure, while excess in them causes despondency and then distraction." Also, the great Maximos writes, "Do not provide complete rest (σχολή) to the flesh, but appoint to it as much discipline (ἄσκησις) as you can handle, and direct your whole intellect within. *For bodily exercise profits a little, but piety is profitable for all things* (1 Tim. 4:8)," and so on. But if the flesh should dominate (τυραννεῖ) and tip the scales of the soul in its favor, it will drag it into a disorderly downward sweep of soul-corrupting tendencies, as it is written: *For the flesh desires against the spirit, and the spirit against the flesh* (Gal. 5:17); but as for you, mortify the flesh by bridling and curbing it with self-control until it becomes obedient against its impulses (ἄκουσα) and submits to what is superior – the soul. Keep in mind the words of the great Paul, *Even though our outward man is perishing, yet the inward man is being renewed day by day* (2 Cor. 4:16), and St. Isaac, "It is better for you to give yourself over to die in struggles than to live in negligence. Not only those who have accepted death for faith in Christ are martyrs, but also those who die for keeping His commandments." And, "It is better for us to die fighting than to live in transgression."

However, most importantly of all, you should do all things with the counsel and guidance of your spiritual father in the Lord. For in this manner, by the grace of Christ, what seems burdensome to you will become light, and the uphill struggle will seem as easy as sprinting downhill. But let us now return to the point where we had left off.

How the ascetic should spend the time between lunch and sundown. We should believe that divine gifts are granted to us in proportion to our effort and the measure of our labor.

37. After having partaken of a meal befitting an ascetic (ἀγωνιζόμενος), in accordance with the divine Paul when he urges that the *contestant* (ἀγωνιζόμενος) *exercise self-control in all things* (1 Cor. 9:25), go sit and read a while, especially the neptic writings of the Fathers. And if the days are long, sleep for an hour. Then get up and work a little with your handicraft while continuing the Jesus prayer. Afterwards, pray in the manner we have described above; then read, study, and strive to be humble and to consider yourself lower than all people. *For whoever exalts himself will be humbled, and he who humbles himself will be exalted* (Lk. 14:11), as Scripture says, and, *Let him who thinks he stands take heed lest he fall* (1 Cor. 10:12); *The Lord resists the proud, but gives grace to the humble* (Prov. 3:34; Jam. 4:6); *Not knowing the Lord is the beginning of pride* (cf. Wis. 10:12); *The proud have transgressed exceedingly* (Ps. 118:51); and, *Do not set your mind on lofty things, but associate with the humble* (Rom. 12:16). As the divine

Chrysostom says, "He who thinks of himself as nothing knows himself best. For there is nothing so dear to God as reckoning oneself to be among the last." And St. Isaac: "Mysteries are revealed to the humble-minded. Where humility springs up, there the glory of God bursts forth. Humility comes before grace, while self-conceit comes before chastisement (παιδεία)." And St. Barsanuphios says: "If you truly desire to be saved, take heed and do as follows: raise your feet up from the earth, lift your intellect up to heaven, and let your meditation be there night and day. Abase yourself (καταφρονήθητι) as much as you can, striving to see yourself as lower than every man. This is the true way of salvation. There is no other path for him who desires to be saved *through Christ who strengthens* him (Phil. 4:13). Let him who desires it run – let him race forward! – let him run forward to *make it his own* (Phil. 3:12). I bear this testimony before the living God, who desires to grant eternal life to all who desire it." Again, John Climacus says, "Not that I fasted, or kept vigil, or slept on the ground, but that *I was humbled, and the Lord saved me speedily* (Ps. 114:6)." Above all, strive to be of no account, as St. Barsanuphios says: "Being free from anxiety about all things brings you near the city; being disregarded among people makes you an inhabitant of the city; and dying to all men causes you to inherit the city and its treasures." And again, "If you desire to be saved, consider yourself of no account, and run towards what is set before you." Furthermore, according to St. John, a disciple of St. Barsanuphios, this "being of no account" means not equating yourself with anyone, nor boasting in any good work by saying, "I've done that too."

Afterwards, sit down again and pray purely and without reverie until the evening comes. At this time, chant the usual vespers service till the end, believing in all sincerity of heart that God rewards us with consolations and the distribution and bestowal of gifts and prizes in proportion to our labor and suffering for the sake of virtue, and according to the measure of our toil, as the divine Psalmist says, *According to the multitude of my sufferings in my heart, Your consolations have gladdened my soul* (Ps. 93:19). The Savior also says, *Come to Me, all you who labor and are heavy laden, and I will give you rest* (Mt. 11:28). And the great Paul says, *If we suffer with Christ, we will be glorified with Him. For I consider that the sufferings of this present time are not worthy to be compared with the glory which shall be revealed in us* (Rom. 8:17-18). Moreover, the divinely wise St. Maximos says, "The measure of each person's faith is the cause of the distribution of divine goods. For inasmuch as we believe, we will act out our faith with commensurate zeal. Thus, he who does good deeds shows the measure of his faith in proportion to his deeds, and consequently receives a measure of grace to the extent that he has believed. Conversely, he who does not do good deeds shows the measure of his unbelief (ἀπιστίας) in proportion to his non-action (ἀπραξίας), and so receives the deprivation of grace to the extent that he has not believed. Therefore, there is no reason for anyone to envy (βασκαίνων) the accomplishments of another, since it is clearly up to him alone to choose to believe and act in such a manner as to receive the grace that is granted according to the measure of his faith." Let us then pray with all our souls that the rest of our lives, and especially the ends of our lives, be Christian, painless, without shame, peaceful, and that we may be granted a good defense before the awesome judgment seat of our Lord and God and Savior Jesus Christ.[33]

Pure prayer is superior to any work.

38. Brother, in addition to these things you should understand that all methods, rules, and, one might say, every sort of spiritual practice, are so appointed and arranged because we are not yet able to engage in pure and unwandering prayer of the heart. But when we have achieved this through the favor and grace of our Lord Jesus Christ and left behind the many and the varied and the multiplicity that divides, we become united with the One and Single and Unitive in a direct ineffable manner beyond reason, as the renowned Theologian says: "God is united with gods and known by them."[34] This refers to the enhypostatic illumination in the heart through the Holy Spirit, which occurs through pure and unwandering prayer of the heart. However, this is rare, and only one in a thousand is made worthy by the grace of Christ to advance to this state. For "sailing beyond" (ὑπερπλεῦσαι), being made worthy of spiritual prayer, and achieving the revelation of the mysteries of the coming age: these are all attained through divine grace by very few in each generation, as St. Isaac writes: "Just as among myriads of people it is hard to find a single person who has fulfilled the commandments and laws with only slight infractions (μικρὸν ἐνδεῶς) and reached purity of soul, likewise only one in a thousand is granted to attain pure prayer through great watchfulness (παραφυλακῆς), or to surpass even this limit and to achieve the further Mystery. For indeed there are not many who have become worthy of pure prayer, but only very few; and only a few in every generation (μόλις εὑρίσκεται γενεᾷ καὶ γενεᾷ) are able through the grace of Christ to attain to that Mystery which is above and beyond pure prayer." And a bit further, "Now if someone can hardly pray with *purity*, what must we say about *spiritual* prayer? For all truly spiritual prayer is completely free of motion. And any prayer that has motion is inferior to spiritual prayer."

---

[33] One of the petitions read by the priest at every vespers service (and other services of the Orthodox Church).

[34] Gregory the Theologian, *Or. 45*, On Holy Pascha. "gods" here refers to human beings who have been deified, made "gods" by divine grace, a patristic doctrine related to biblical passages, such as Ps. 81, *I have said you are gods and all sons of the Most High.*

So then, if you wish to be made worthy through Jesus Christ of such extraordinary (καινῶν) mysteries in truth and in deed, that is, by experience, then strive at all times, in every hour, and with all your might to acquire pure and unwandering prayer of the heart, so that in this manner you might grow (προκόψῃς) from a nursing babe into *a perfect man, to the measure of the stature of the fullness of Christ* (Eph. 4:13), and that you might achieve the blessing and approval that is given to the *faithful and wise steward* (Luke 12:42), as one who *manages his affairs and words with discretion* (Ps. 111:5) through a life lived according to reason. And then *you will never be shaken* (Ps. 111:6), just as St. Philemon writes about this matter: "Brother, whenever God grants you to pray purely and undistractedly with your intellect, whether it be day or night, do not focus on your rule, but stretch towards God and cling to Him with all your strength, and He will illuminate your heart concerning spiritual activity." And another teacher wise in divine matters (τις τῶν θεοσόφων) says, "If you wish to serve God in the body as though you were a bodiless angel, then acquire unceasing prayer hiddenly in your heart, and your soul will become like an angel before death." Likewise, St. Isaac wrote in reply to someone who asked what the sum (περιεκτικόν) of all the labors of *hesychia* are, so that by reaching it one might know whether or not he has attained perfection in this way of life: "When one has been made worthy of perpetual prayer – that is, when he has acquired this prayer, he has attained the end (ἄκρα) of all virtues and becomes the dwelling place of the Holy Spirit. For unless one has fully received the grace of the Comforter, it is impossible to accomplish this kind of perpetual prayer with comfort. For the Scripture says that when the Spirit makes His dwelling in a human being, the person never leaves off praying (οὐ παύεται ἐκ τῆς προσευχῆς) since the Spirit Himself is always praying in him (cf. Rom 8:26). Then prayer cannot be cut off from his soul either in sleep or in waking, but whether he is eating, drinking, sleeping, or doing anything else, even in deep sleep, sweet scents and fragrances of prayer spring up effortlessly from his heart. From then on prayer is never separated from him, but remains hiddenly at work within him at all times, even if it may seem to fall still on the outside. Moreover, the silence of the pure of heart is called prayer by one of the Christ-bearing Saints, since the thoughts of these people are divine motions, and the movements of the pure heart and mind are meek voices chanting hiddenly unto God." And several other God-bearing Fathers who have been mystically initiated through the experience of divine grace have described many such wonderful things, but we have had to omit them so as not to prolong our discourse.

On the amount of prostrations to be done every day.

39. As for the amount of prostrations (γονυκλισίαι) to be done, the Fathers have prescribed that we do three hundred every twenty-four hours of the five weekdays,

since on Saturdays and Sundays and other established (ἐξ ἔθους σεσημειωμέναις) days, and even some weeks, we are ordered to take a break from prostrations for some mystical and untold reasons (κατά τινας μυστικοὺς καὶ ἀπορρήτους λόγους). But there are some who exceed this number, while others do less, each according to their strength and will (προαιρέσεως). You too should do them according to your strength. But of course truly blessed is he, and indeed many times blessed, who always exerts himself (ἐκβιάζων ἑαυτόν) in all the works of God, *For the kingdom of heaven is taken by force* (βιαστή), *and the forceful* (βιασταί) *seize upon it* (Mt. 11:12).

Divine gifts are not, as we have said, bestowed solely in proportion to our effort and the amount of our labor, but also on the basis of our habit of mind, receptivity, faith, and natural disposition.

40. We should also understand that divine gifts are not distributed only in proportion to our effort and the amount of our labor, as we said before, but also on the basis of our way of life, receptivity, as well as our faith in the things laid before us, and the disposition which naturally suits us (προσφυῶς προσοῦσαν). For St. Maximos says, "The intellect is an organ of divine wisdom, while reason is an organ of divine knowledge. The natural assurance that comes from both is established through the faith that comes from both. Likewise, natural charity is the instrument of the divine gift of healing. For each divine gift corresponds to an organ within us that is suited and capable of receiving it, such as a power or habit or disposition. For example, someone who has purified his intellect of all sensible fantasies receives wisdom. He who has established his reason as master over the innate passions, namely, anger and desire, receives knowledge. He who possesses in his mind and reason an unwavering assurance of the Divine, receives the faith for which *all things are possible* (cf. Mk. 9:23). And he who has achieved natural charity, having completely eradicated self-love, receives gifts of healing." However, make sure that nobody knows about your spiritual work except your spiritual father and guide. Also pray for us who are unworthy and who say what is good, but do not do it, that we may first be granted to do works that are pleasing God, and only then to instruct others and advise them. For as the Lord says, *Whosoever shall do and teach* these commandments, *the same shall be called great in the kingdom of heaven* (Mt. 5:19). Again, may the All-Powerful and All-Merciful Lord strengthen and lead you so that you might learn these things with understanding and earnestly do them. (For as the divine Paul says, *It is not the hearers of the law who are just before God, but the doers of the law shall be justified* [Rom 2:13]). Now may He direct you in every good and saving work, and guide you in the Spirit unto the noetic and sacred labor set before you, by the prayers of the Saints. Amen.

Considering how we have said little about the practical aspect of discernment, now is a good opportunity to speak briefly about the perfect virtue of general discernment, such as we can, since according to our renowned Fathers this is the greatest of all the virtues.

On general and perfect discernment. He who lives against nature and according to the flesh; he who lives according to nature and according to the soul; and he who lives above nature and according to the spirit.

41. He who lives and acts in a carnal manner and against nature (σαρκικῶς καὶ παρὰ φύσιν) has completely lost his ability to discern. However, he who has abstained from evils and begun to do good – as in the verse, *Depart from evil and do good* (Ps. 33:15) – as a novice with his ears inclined to instruction, he approaches a sense of discernment suitable to beginners. Next, he who lives according to nature and according to the soul (κατὰ φύσιν καὶ ψυχικῶς) in the intermediate state – by acting with intelligence and living according to reason – sees and discerns in his own measure realities in himself and in those who resemble him. Lastly, he who lives above nature and according to spirit (ὑπὲρ φύσιν καὶ πνευματικῶς) – having passed beyond the impassioned, beginning, and intermediate stages and advanced by the grace of Christ to a perfect state, that is, to enhypostatic illumination and perfect discernment – sees himself and discerns for himself with perfect clarity; he can also see and discern clearly for others, while he himself, although visible, can be seen and discerned (διακρινόμενος) by no one, nor is he *judged* (ἀνακρινόμενος), since he has become and is rightly called *spiritual*, not as presented in paper and ink (cf. 2 Cor. 3:3), but in truth and in grace, as the divine Apostle says: *He who is spiritual judges all things, yet he himself is judged by no one* (1 Cor. 2:15).

More about discernment by way of example.

42. The first kind of person – the carnal one – resembles one who walks in the deep and moonless night (στυγνῇ σκοτομήνῃ). As he wanders through and is benighted by a darkness that cannot be felt (ἀψηλαφήτῳ) (cf. Ex. 10:21), not only can he not see and discern himself, but he cannot even see where he is going, as the Savior says, *He who walks in darkness does not know where he is going* (Jn. 12:35).

The second one – the beginner – is like one who walks in the night with a clear sky glimmering with the stars. Only faintly guided by the starlight, he walks slowly and stumbles over stones of indiscretion and falls. Thus, he sees himself a little and discerns himself as if in a shadow, and [to this] Scripture says, *Awake, you who sleep, arise from the dead, and Christ will give you light* (Eph. 5:14).

The third one – the intermediate – is like one who walks at night with tranquil weather and a full moon. Guided by the moonlight, he walks a little more steadily and makes progress. Moreover, he sees himself as in a mirror and can also discern those who walk alongside him, as it is said, *You do well, attending to the word as to a light that shines in a dark place, until the day dawns and the morning star rises in your hearts* (2 Pet. 1:19; cf. Ps. 118:105).

The last – the perfect and spiritual – is like one who walks at noon on the clearest day, and is illuminated by the splendid rays of the sun. He sees and discerns himself transparently in the sunlight, and is able to judge most people, or rather, to *judge all*, according to the divine Apostle (1 Cor. 2:15), and indeed he is able to judge everything he comes across; he walks without going astray and unerringly guides those who follow him to the true light, the life, and the truth. About such people it is written: *You are the light of the world* (Mt. 5:14). Also, the most divine Paul says, *It is the God who commanded light to shine out of darkness who has shone in our hearts to give the light of the knowledge of the glory of God in the face of Jesus Christ* (2 Cor. 4:6). And the blessed David says, *The light of Your face has been signed upon us, Lord* (Ps. 4:7), and, *In your light shall we see light* (Ps. 35:10). And again, the Lord says, *I am the light of the world. He who follows Me shall not walk in darkness, but have the light of life* (Jn. 8:12).

On human mutability and change, and the surpassing glory of humility.

43. We want you to know, too, that those who have come to perfection through purification and illumination as much as their strength allows (for there is no perfect perfection in this imperfect age, but rather unconsummated perfection [ἀτέλεστος τελειότης]); thus, these people are not unchanging, on account of natural weakness and the conceit that sometimes sneaks in. That is to say, they too are occasionally susceptible (πάσχουσι) to alterations and [their glory] is stolen away from them that they might be tested. And even then they are able to receive greater help from God. But those who stray from this path are said to be 'a portion for wolves' by the Fathers. Immutability and inalterability are reserved for the coming age. However, in the present age, there are times of purity, peace, and divine consolation, and times when they are caught up by the driving winds, stretched, twisted and dashed against the rocks. This occurs depending on the measure of each person's progress in the spiritual life, for reasons known only to the Lord, but also so that we might always be aware of our weakness. For Scripture says, *Blessed is he that knows his own weakness* (Job 37:7), and as St. Paul writes, *We should not trust in ourselves but in God who raises the dead* (2 Cor. 1:9). So let us always resort to God with humility, repentance, and confession.

Furthermore, St. Isaac says, "How often do some transgress but then come to heal their souls through repentance, and divine grace receives them! For in all rational nature without exception there is change, and at all times every person is susceptible to alterations, and the discerning person perceives many signs of this. Nevertheless, the trials that come to him every day are able to make him much wiser in these matters as long as he remains watchful, so that by examining himself with the intellect, he will perceive each day how much his mind has strayed from meekness and gentleness, or how it can suddenly slip into agitation from a formerly peaceful state for no apparent reason, or how it can fall into great and unspeakable danger. The blessed Makarios described this with great care and foresight to instruct and remind his brethren, so that they would not fall into despair in the time of alteration caused by reversals, saying that those who are dedicated to purity (τοῖς ἐν τῇ τάξει τῆς καθαρότητος ἱσταμένοις) will always be prone to falls, like temperature drops in the atmosphere, even if they are not guilty of any carelessness or negligence. In fact, even while they are progressing in their way of life (κατὰ τάξιν αὐτῶν), they may fall contrary to their will and intention. St. Isaac explains as follows: "Why is this the case then? 'Changes,' St. Makarios tells us, 'happen to everyone, like cold temperatures in the atmosphere.' Consider the phrase 'to everyone', for nature is one; and do not think that he spoke only of the inferior or the very least, as if the perfect were free from changes and stand unshaken in their condition (ἐν μιᾷ τάξει ἀκλινῶς ἵστανται) without any impassioned thoughts, as the Euchites and Messalian heretics claim. This is why he added the phrase 'to everyone'. And how is that, Makarios? 'Just as it is cold, and then hot after a little while, or after a hailstorm the weather soon clears, there occurs something similar in the ascetical life (ἐν τῇ γυμνασίᾳ ὑμῶν). There is spiritual warfare, and then comes the aid of grace. Sometimes the soul gets caught in stormy weather and the fierce waves threaten it, but again there is a change, and a visitation of grace fills the person's heart with joy and peace from God, and with chaste (σωφρόνων) and peaceful thoughts.' He indicates here that these thoughts are chaste, implying that the ones before were bestial and impure. He further exhorts us, saying, 'If there is ever an assault that follows these chaste and noble thoughts, let us not be sorrowful or fall into despair. And again, at times of rest in grace let us not boast. Rather at times of joy, let us brace ourselves for affliction.' And he continues, saying, 'Understand that all the Saints were engaged in this work. As long as we are in this world, the consolation that abounded in them is also granted to us in a hidden manner, since every day and at every hour we are asked to test our love for God by fighting and struggling against temptations.' And when he says, 'let us not be sorrowful', he means not to grow despondent (μὴ ἀκηδιᾶν) in the struggle. He continues, 'This is how our path becomes straight. But whoever wishes to depart and go astray from these things will become a portion for wolves.' How wonderful is this Saint! How well he has set forth beneficial counsel in a few words, shown it to be full of wisdom, and completely dispelled hesitation (δισταγμός) from the reader's mind. Then he says, 'He who forsakes these things and wishes to stray from the path becomes a portion for wolves. He has fixed in his mind the desire to walk on a path all his own, not to tread in the footsteps of the Fathers.'"

And St. Isaac further writes, "Even apart from works, humility forgives many faults. Works without humility, however, bring no benefit." And a little further, "What salt is to food, humility is to every virtue. It is able to shatter the power of many sins. It is therefore necessary that we be unceasingly sorrowful in our minds, in humbleness and grief with due discernment (cf. 2 Cor. 7:10). When we acquire this humility, it makes us sons of God and even without good works it presents us before God. For without humility, all our works and virtues and labors are in vain. Thus, God desires the transformation of the mind, and through the mind we are fulfilled (βελτιούμεθα). This by itself is sufficient for us to stand before God and give a good account of ourselves, even aside from any other help." And he further reports that one of the Saints once said, "When the thought of pride comes to you, telling you, 'Remember your virtues,' say, 'Old man, behold your own whoredom.'"

On repentance, purity, and perfection.

44. "Perfection in all your ways," St. Isaac says, "is accomplished through these three things: repentance, purity, and perfection. What is repentance? It is to abandon one's former sins and to grieve over them. And what is purity? In short, it is a heart compassionate for all creation. And what is perfection? It is the depth of humility, which means abandoning all things visible and invisible (that is, all sensible and intelligible things), and being free from anxiety about them." Further, "Repentance is voluntarily dying twice to all things. The merciful heart is the heart that burns for all creation, for humans and birds and animals and demons and every creature." And further, "As long as we are in this world and remain in the flesh, even if we are exalted to the vault of the heavens, we cannot be released from labors and toil in a total detachment from cares. Forgive me, but that would be perfection. Having to do anything else beyond that would require care, which would contradict the meaning [of that total 'perfection']." Also, St. Maximos says: "The philosophical life of virtue naturally causes dispassion of will, but in a manner beyond nature (γνώμης ἀπάθειαν ἀλλ' οὐ φύσεως). That is, by means of this dispassion of will the grace of divine pleasure comes upon the intellect." And again, "He who has tasted the sorrow and pleasure of the body may be said to be 'experienced' (δόκιμος) in that he has experienced the comforts and hardships (εὐχερείας καὶ δυσχερείας) of the flesh. But he is perfect who has overcome the pleasure and pain of the flesh by the power of reason, and he is complete who has

preserved the habits of action and contemplation unchanged through ardent yearning for the Divine."

This is why discernment is said to be greater than all the virtues, since those who possess it by God's good pleasure, through illumination by the divine light, are able to discern divine and human things aright, as well as mystical and hidden visions.[35]

Now is the time for us to explain, as promised, the method of beginning holy and deifying *hesychia*, as clearly and succinctly as possible. May God guide us in all that we say.

The five tasks of the first and introductory *hesychia* for beginners: prayer, chanting, reading, meditation, and handiwork.

45. The beginning hesychast should spend his days and nights doing these five tasks in the service of God: 1) Praying, that is, practicing remembrance of the Lord Jesus Christ constantly and in sincere humility, as we have explained: by breathing in calmly through the nose, entering the heart, and leaving the heart by breathing out again, with the lips shut; without any other thought or any imagination (φαντασία), in careful self-control of the belly, sleep, and the other senses, while being enclosed within one's cell. 2) Chanting. 3) Reading from the Holy Psalter, the Apostles, and the Holy Gospels, as well as the writings of the holy and God-bearing Fathers, and especially the chapters on prayer and watchfulness (νῆψις). In addition to reading other things inspired by the Spirit (τῶν λοιπῶν ἐνθέων λογίων τοῦ Πνεύματος), 4) one may remember one's sins with pain of heart and meditate on the judgment of God, or death, or hell, or the delight of Paradise, and the like. 5) Engaging in a small handicraft to prevent despondency (ὡς ἀκηδίας φιμώτρῳ).

And then once again one should return to praying, no matter how much effort it takes (κἂν βίαν ἔχῃ), until the intellect becomes accustomed to avoiding reverie (ρεμβασμός) with ease, to complete concentration on the Lord Jesus Christ, constant remembrance of Him, and dwelling continually in the inner chamber (Matt. 6:6), the hidden place of the heart by constantly returning and firmly rooting itself there. And as St. Isaac writes, "Strive to enter the chamber that is within you,

---

[35] As is made clear from the above, the authors' understanding of *discernment* (διάκρισις) includes *humility* and *perfection*, hence its status of being greater than all the virtues. Humility is required for every virtue, and is said perhaps even to be sufficient for a good judgment before Christ, while perfection is the final goal and aim of all the virtues.

and you will see the heavenly chamber. For they are one and the same, and by going in at one and the same place you will perceive both."

And again, St. Makarios,[36] "The heart rules over the whole person (ἡγεμονεύει ὅλου τοῦ ὀργάνου). And when grace takes possession of the pastures of the heart, then it reigns over all the thoughts and members. For the heart is where the intellect and all the thoughts of the soul reside. Therefore, that is where we must look to see if grace has inscribed the laws of the Holy Spirit [within us]. There. Where? In the ruling faculty, on the throne of grace, where the intellect and all the soul's thoughts reside – in the heart."

Where should those who wish to live the hesychastic life properly and reasonably begin? What is its starting-point, and what is the measure of improvement, progress, and perfection?

46. The first and introductory work of beginners who have chosen to live the hesychastic life correctly proceeds as follows. They begin with the fear of God, the fulfillment of all the deifying commandments according to their strength, freedom from care about either unreasonable or even reasonable affairs, and above all faith, the complete avoidance of sins (τῶν ἐναντίων), and turning oneself in purity toward Him who Truly Is.

Then they grow and increase in undaunted hope. They progress to *the measure of the stature of the fullness of Christ* (Eph. 4:13), with a complete and overflowing eros for God that comes from pure and unwandering prayer of the heart and is perfected by still and motionless spiritual prayer, and by the unmediated ecstasy and rapture of the alone to the Alone – the union with Him who is Ultimately Desirable, which springs from perfect love.

This is unerring progress and resurrection, which proceeds through action to contemplation, and which the forefather of God David suffered when he was transformed by that blessed *change* (cf. Ps 76:11) and declared, *I said in my ecstasy, 'Every man is a liar'* (Ps. 115:2). And as one of the lordly men of the Old Testament says, *Eye has not seen, nor ear heard, nor have entered into the heart of man, the things which God has prepared for those who love Him.*[37] Further, the

[36] In the manuscript the quote is mistakenly attributed to St. Maximos.

[37] St. Paul quotes this from the Old Testament, although it may be a paraphrase or the exact verse may no longer be extant. St. John Chrysostom explains that it could either be a paraphrase of Isaiah 52:15 LXX or in a canonical book that was lost (Homily 7.6 on 1 Corinthians). Cf. Is. 64:3-4.

great Paul concludes by saying, *But God has revealed them to us by His Spirit; for the Spirit searches all things, even the depths of God* (1 Cor. 2:9-10).

The order of *hesychia* for beginners.

47. So then, the beginner, as we have said, should not be continually leaving his cell, should refrain from conversation, or even occupation with any matters, unless it is for certain urgent needs, and even then he should do this only attentively, cautiously, and rarely, as the divine Isaac says: "In everything, keep in mind that the benefit you obtain from precaution is greater than the benefit you derive from works." Indeed, these affairs cause scattering and distraction of mind not only for beginners, but also for those who have already made progress, as Isaac again says: "Rest (ἀνάπαυσις) only harms the young, while laxity (λύσις) harms both young and old. As *hesychia* mortifies the external senses while animating the inner motions, occupation with external affairs does the direct opposite: it stirs the external senses while mortifying the inner motions."

In saying this, St. Isaac indicates the proper way of practicing *hesychia*. John Climacus also describes him who walks and fares well in the way of *hesychia*, writing, "A hesychast is he who strives to confine his incorporeal being within his bodily house, paradoxical as this is."[38] "The hesychast is he who says, *I sleep, but my heart is awake* (Song 5:2)," and then, "Shut the door of your cell to your body, the door of your tongue to speech, and the inner gate to evil spirits."[39]

On prayer of the heart with attention and watchfulness, and how it works.

48. Prayer which is done with attention and watchfulness in the heart, as we have said, that is, without any other thought or imagination of anything whatsoever, works in this manner: through the phrase, "Lord Jesus Christ, Son of God," the intellect is lifted in an entirely immaterial and unspeakable manner to the Lord Jesus Christ Himself as He is being invoked, and through the phrase "Have mercy on me", the intellect returns and comes back to itself, since it cannot help but pray for itself. But when it has attained love through experience, it is simply and wholly lifted up to the Lord Jesus Christ Himself, having received assurance concerning the second part of the prayer.

---

[38] *Ladder* 27.11 (Trans. Moore, with slight modifications), 111.

[39] *Ladder* 27.17-18 (Trans. Moore, with slight modifications), 112.

The different ways that the Holy Fathers passed on to us of saying the Jesus Prayer. What prayer is.

49. For it seems that the Holy Fathers did not describe the Jesus prayer as always being said in its entirety, but one Father handed down the whole prayer, a second Father one half of the prayer, a third Father one part of the prayer, and a fourth Father a different part of the prayer, perhaps depending on the strength and condition of the person praying.

The divine Chrysostom presents the entire prayer, saying, "Brethren, I entreat you never to break or neglect (καταπατήσητε ἢ καταφρονήσητε) the rule of prayer; for I have once heard some fathers saying, 'What is the monk if he breaks or neglects his rule?' Whether he is eating or drinking or sitting or serving or traveling or doing anything else, the monk ought to cry out unceasingly, 'Lord Jesus Christ, Son of God, have mercy on me', so that this remembrance of our Lord Jesus Christ's name might stir up war against the enemy. For the soul that forces itself to pray like this will be able to discover everything by this remembrance, whether it be good or bad. He will first be able to see the evil within his heart, and then the things that are fair. For remembrance is able to rouse the dragon, but it can also humiliate it; the memory is able to reprove *the sin that dwells within us* (Rom. 7:17), and even destroy it (δαπανῆσαι), but it is also capable of rousing all the enemy's power in the heart; but again, the memory is able to overcome and uproot it, in order that the name of the Lord Jesus Christ, by descending into the bottom of the heart, might humiliate the dragon that hoards its pastures, and save and give life to the soul. Therefore abide unceasingly in the name of the Lord Jesus, so that the heart might envelop (καταπίῃ) the Lord, and the Lord the heart, and the two become one. However, this is not the work of a day or two, but takes much time (χρόνου πολλοῦ καὶ καιροῦ). For it requires much struggle and time for the enemy to be cast out and for Christ to come to dwell within."

Again, "We must secure and bridle our intellect, and restrain it along with every thought, and punish every activity of the evil one through the invocation of our Lord Jesus Christ. Moreover, wherever the body stands, let the intellect be there as well, so that between God and the heart nothing else stands as a *middle wall* or *barrier* (cf. Eph. 2:14) darkening the heart and separating the intellect from God. Whenever something arrests the attention of the intellect, one must not dally with thoughts, lest one be guilty of consent to thoughts which lead to sin before the Lord on *the Day* of Judgment, *when God will judge the secrets of men* (Rom. 2:16). Therefore, be still at all times and abide in the Lord our God *until he takes pity on us* (Ps. 122:2); and seek nothing but mercy from the *Lord of glory* (1 Cor. 2:8). As you ask for mercy, seek it with a poor and humble heart; and cry out from morning till evening, and if possible all night, 'Lord Jesus Christ, have mercy on me.' And force your intellect to this work until death. For this labor requires great force, *because narrow is the gate and difficult is the way which leads to life, and there are few who find it* (Mt. 7:14), and only those who apply force enter it, *for the Kingdom of Heaven* is granted to *those who take it by force* (Mt. 11:12). Thus I entreat you not to separate your hearts from God, but abide in Him and guard them, with the remembrance of our Lord Jesus Christ planted in your hearts and thinking of nothing else so that Christ may be magnified in you."

And even before Chrysostom, the great Paul had written the "Lord Jesus" part of the prayer, saying, *If you confess with your mouth, 'Lord Jesus', and believe in your heart that God has raised Him from the dead, you will be saved. For with the heart one believes unto righteousness, and with the mouth confession is made unto salvation.* (Rom. 10:9-10). And again, *No one can say 'Lord Jesus' except by the Holy Spirit* (1 Cor. 12:3).

He adds the phrase *by the Holy Spirit*, indicating the moment the heart receives the energy of the Holy Spirit through whom it prays, and this occurs to those who have made spiritual progress and been richly blessed (πεπλουτηκότων) to have Christ dwell in them manifestly. Similarly, St. Diadochos says, "After we have blocked all its external engagements by means of the remembrance of God, our intellect demands that we provide it with proper work to engage in. Thus it is necessary that we give it the prayer 'Lord Jesus' for the completion of this purpose, for it is written that *no one can say 'Lord Jesus' except by the Holy Spirit* (1 Cor. 12:3). Let the intellect continually and intently contemplate these words within its inner chamber so as not to be distracted by any imaginations. Those who unceasingly meditate on the glorious and precious name of Jesus Christ in the depths of their hearts can sometimes even see the light of their own intellect. For when the mind focuses on this name with great attention one becomes fully aware of how it burns up all the filth covering the soul, because as it is written, *Our God is a consuming fire* (Deut. 4:24). Then the Lord inspires in the soul abundant love for His glory, for when that glorious and precious name abides in the memory of the intellect with heartfelt fervor, it naturally habituates us to love His goodness, there being nothing left to prevent this. Indeed, this is the *pearl of great price* that one may acquire by selling all his possessions so as to cherish the hidden, indescribable joy of discovering it for himself (Mt. 13:46)."[40]

St. Hesychios, recommending prayer with the words "Christ Jesus", writes the following: "As long as the soul has Christ accompanying it, when upon death it

---

[40] *On Spiritual Knowledge* 59, *Philokalia* Vol. 1.

begins to rise to the gates of heaven, it cannot not even be put to shame there by its enemies, but at that time it will speak against them with boldness even as it does at present. Only let it never grow weary of crying out 'Christ Jesus' night and day until the time of its departure, and He will speedily vindicate the soul according to the faithful and divine promise He made when he spoke about the unjust judge (Lk. 18:1-8); and indeed, I venture to say that He will vindicate it both in this present life and after its departure from its body."[41]

At the same time, John Climacus simply mentions "Jesus", saying: "Flog your enemies with the name of Jesus, for there is no stronger weapon in heaven or earth,"[42] and adds nothing else. Again he says, "Let the remembrance of Jesus cling to your every breath, and then you will know the value of stillness."[43]

The words of the sacred and divine prayer have been mystically taught not only by the Holy Fathers, but even by the chiefest Apostles Peter, Paul, and John.

50. One will find these words of the holy prayer not only mystically taught by the aforementioned God-bearing Fathers and those who follow them, but even long before them, by the first and chiefest Apostles Peter, Paul, and John. For Paul, as we have mentioned, says, *No one can say 'Lord Jesus' except by the Holy Spirit* (1 Cor. 12:3). And John says, *Grace and truth came through Jesus Christ* (Jn. 1:17), and, *Every spirit that confesses that Jesus Christ has come in the flesh is of God* (1 Jn. 4:2), and Peter, the chosen (πρόκριτος) of Christ's disciples, in reply to the Savior and Teacher's question to the Apostles, *Who do men say that I am?* made the most blessed confession, *You are the Christ, the Son of the living God* (Mt. 16:16).

Hence, our renowned instructors (παιδοτριβαί) who came after the Apostles, and especially those who lived the monastic,[44] eremitic, and hesychastic life, received these phrases scattered here and there as seeds, foretold in part by these three pillars of the unblemished Church, as divine words prophesied by the revelation of the Holy Spirit and well attested by three trustworthy witnesses; and we know that *through three witnesses every word shall be established* (Deut. 19:15; 2 Cor. 13:1). These heavenly-minded Fathers took these words, and after uniting them most

---

[41] *On Watchfulness and Holiness* 149, *Philokalia* Vol. 1.
[42] *Ladder* 21.7, (Trans. Moore), 72.
[43] *Ladder* 27.61, (Trans. Moore with slight modifications), 116.
[44] ἄζυμον "unleavened" or the emendation ἄζυγον "unyoked, unmarried" could both be understood as referring to the monastic life.

excellently and harmonizing them into one through the Holy Spirit indwelling in them, they declared them to be a bulwark of prayer, and handed them down to those who followed them to keep and guard them in the same manner. Consider now the order and sequence of the words, how exquisite it is, and how much wisdom it contains from above. For Paul says, "Lord Jesus", John "Jesus Christ", Peter "Christ, Son of God"; as if each one were following in the tracks of the other, being closely united to each other in the harmony and bond of the divine words. For you will find that each of them takes the end of the preceding phrase as the beginning, and in this manner the phrase is completed by all three of them. You will notice something similar with the addition of the word "spirit", since it is said by the blessed Paul, *No one can say 'Lord Jesus' except by the Holy Spirit* (1 Cor. 12:3), where the final word, that is, "spirit", is taken as the beginning by the thunder-voiced John, saying, *Every spirit that confesses that Jesus Christ has come in the flesh is of God* (1 Jn. 4:2). And indeed, they prescribed these traditions for all people not on their own authority (οἴκοθεν καὶ παρ' ἑαυτῶν), but because they were moved by the hand of the Holy Spirit. For even the confession of the divine Peter through revelation came about through the energy of the Holy Spirit, for as Scripture says, *One and the same Spirit works all these things, distributing to each one individually as He wills* (1 Cor. 12:11). And so it is that the threefold and unbreakable cord of this deifying prayer is so wisely and cunningly woven, intertwined, and united, and then passed on to us to be preserved in the same manner. At any rate, the addition of the phrase "have mercy on me" was appointed by later divine Fathers and joined to these saving words of the prayer, "Lord Jesus Christ, Son of God", and is meant more for those who are more infantile in virtue – for beginners and those who are not yet mature. But those who have advanced and become perfect in Christ are content with just a part of the sacred prayer, "Lord Jesus Christ, Son of God", and sometimes simply with the name "Jesus", and they take it to heart and embrace it (ἐνστερνίζονται καὶ ἀσπάζονται) as a complete work of prayer, since through it they are filled with an ineffable pleasure and heartfelt joy that *surpasses all intellect* and all manner of sight and sound (cf. Phil. 4:7).

And it is in this manner that the thrice-blessed Saints, as they came to be outside of the flesh and the world, with their senses closed off, mysteriously and blessedly intoxicated and love-stricken through the divine gift and grace that dwells within them, are purified and illumined and perfected, that is, by beholding already in the present time, dimly as in a mirror, the supernatural, beginningless, and uncreated grace of the super-essential Divinity, in part and as a foretaste (cf. 2 Cor. 3:18), and as we have said, they are content simply with the remembrance and meditation on a single part of the above-mentioned names of the God-Man, the Word, and through it they are lifted up and made worthy of inexpressible raptures and knowledge in the Spirit. For our sweetest Lord Jesus Christ, to whom souls are so dear, whose words are acts and whose sayings are, as He says, *spirit and life* (Jn. 6:63), proclaimed aloud: *Without me you can do nothing* (Jn. 15:5), and, *If you ask for something in my name, I will do it* (Jn. 14:14), and again, *Whatever you ask for in my name, I will do it* (Jn. 14:13) and the like, so that we might have full assurance and the clearest confirmation of these matters.

Beginners may sometimes pray with all the words of the prayer, and sometimes with a part of it, but at all times and always in the heart. One should not continually change the words of the prayer.

51. Beginners may at times pray with all the words of the prayer and at other times with only a part of it, but in any case it should always be done in the heart and continually. For as St. Diadochos says, "He who dwells constantly within his own heart is estranged from the charms of this life. For when he *walks in the Spirit* he cannot know *the desires of the flesh* (Gal. 5:16). Such a man then does his rounds in the fortress of virtues, having virtues as gatekeepers guarding his purity, and the devices of the demons are rendered ineffective against him."[45] And St. Isaac writes, "The heart of the person who examines his soul at every hour rejoices in revelations, and he who concentrates his vision within himself beholds the splendor of the Spirit. Whoever has reviled every vain imagination (μετεωρισμός) beholds his Lord within his own heart." However, do not continually change the words of the prayer, lest the intellect become accustomed to any kind of instability or digression through the constant alternation and shifting of the words, and is left rootless and barren, like trees that are continually removed and transplanted.

Much time, struggle, and force are required for one to bear fruit in the heart through prayer. In fact, no good can be achieved except through great toil and after a long period of time.

52. Ceaseless prayer of the heart, along with other spiritual goods, cannot be simply accomplished as it were with a little bit of brief exertion (although you may find this occurring in some rare cases through ineffable divine economy), but they require much time and effort and struggle in body and soul, and great and extensive force to be achieved.

For we must engage in as many struggles as we can and dedicate time proportionate to the share of the divine gift and grace we hope to partake of. This is what the divine teachers call the expulsion of the enemy from the pastures of the heart, and the manifest indwelling of Christ. As St. Isaac says, "He who desires to see the

---

[45] *On Spiritual Knowledge* 57, *Philokalia* Vol. 1.

Lord devises ways to purify his heart through the unceasing remembrance of God, and then in the radiance of his mind he will see the Lord at all times."

Furthermore, St. Barsanuphios writes, "If a man does not profit from inward work by God's grace (μετὰ Θεοῦ), then his outward labor is done in vain. For inward work with pangs of the heart brings purity, and purity brings true stillness of heart; this stillness in turn brings humility, and humility makes man the dwelling place of God, by whose dwelling the demons are banished together with the passions. In this way the person becomes a temple of God, full of holiness, full of illumination, purity, and grace. Therefore, blessed is he who beholds his Lord reflected within the sanctuary (ἐν ἀδύτοις) of his heart and pours out cries and supplications in the presence of His goodness." And again, St. John the Carpathian: "There is need for much time and effort in prayer, so that by means of an untroubled state of mind we might reach that other heaven, the heaven of the heart, where Jesus dwells. As the Apostle says, *Do you not know yourselves, that Jesus Christ is in you?—unless indeed you are disqualified.* (2 Cor. 13:5)."[46] Moreover, the great Chrysostom says, "Abide unceasingly in the name of the Lord Jesus, so that the heart might envelop (καταπίῃ) the Lord, and the Lord the heart, and the two become one. But this is not the work of a day or two, but takes much time (χρόνου πολλοῦ καὶ καιροῦ). For it requires much struggle and time for the enemy to be cast out and for Christ to come to dwell within." But let our discourse now return to the following topics in due sequence.

Prayer of the heart that is not yet pure, and how to enter into pure and unwandering prayer.

53. By persisting in the above-mentioned method of pure and unwandering prayer of the heart, even if one's prayer is perhaps not entirely pure and unwandering (on account of being hindered by passionate notions [προλήψεις] and thoughts), he who struggles will get in the habit of praying truly and purely, without strain or reverie, that is to say, through the intellect's abiding in the heart – not by forcefully descending into the heart while breathing in and then absent-mindedly bringing the intellect back up, but by always abiding there and perpetually praying in this manner. For St. Hesychios says, "He who has not yet acquired prayer that is clear of thoughts has no weapon for spiritual warfare; I mean that prayer which is perpetually at work within the sanctuary of the soul, so that by the invocation of

[46] *Texts for the Monks in India* 52, *Philokalia* Vol. 1.

Jesus Christ we might scourge and scorch the enemy who secretly wars against us."[47]

Again, "Blessed is he who ceaselessly calls on Jesus in the heart and who clings as closely to the Jesus Prayer as air does to our bodies and flames to candle wax." And again, "When the sun rises over the earth it brings about the day, and likewise when the holy and venerable name of the Lord Jesus shines in the mind continually, it will bring forth countless intellections as splendid as the sun."[48]

Pure and unwandering prayer of the heart, and the fervor engendered by it.

54. This is what is and is rightly called "pure and unwandering prayer of the heart", which brings a warmth to the heart, according to the words of the psalm, *My heart has been warmed within me, and a fire will be kindled in my meditation* (Ps. 38:4): the fire which the Lord Jesus Christ came to cast in the fields (εἰς τὰς γαίας) of our hearts, which though they formerly bore thorns through the passions, are now bearing the Spirit through the grace of God, as our Lord Jesus Christ says, *I came to send fire on the earth* (ἐπὶ τὴν γῆν), *and how I wish it were already kindled!* (Lk. 12:49).

This is also the fire that once warmed and kindled the hearts of Cleopas and his companion, such that they cried aloud to one another in ecstasy, *'Did not our heart burn within us as we walked?'* (Lk. 24:32). The great John of Damascus also writes in one of his hymns (τροπαρίῳ) to the most-pure Theotokos: "The fire of chaste (παρθενικοῦ) desire within my heart urges me on to sing hymns." Again, St. Isaac writes, "From this strenuous labor is born an immeasurable fervor, which burns in the heart through the fervent memories that move in the mind in a wondrous manner. Both this labor and this watchfulness refine the intellect through their warmth, and bestow vision upon it." And further, "This fervor, which is brought about by the contemplation that comes from grace, causes tears to flow." And a little further, "From ceaseless tears the soul receives peace in its thoughts; and from peace of thoughts it is raised to purity of intellect; and through purity of intellect man comes to see the mysteries of God." Then, "After these things, the intellect comes to see revelations and signs, like those which the prophet Ezekiel saw." And again, "Tears and the striking of the head during prayer, as well as rolling on the ground with fervor, awaken the warmth of their sweetness within the heart, which takes flight to God in an ecstasy of praise and cries aloud, *My soul has thirsted for*

---

[47] *On Watchfulness and Holiness* 21, *Philokalia* Vol. 1.
[48] *Ibid.* 196, *Philokalia* Vol. 1.

You, the almighty and living God; when shall I come and appear in your presence, Lord? (cf. Ps. 41:3)."

And St. John Climacus says, "When the fire comes to dwell in the heart, it revives prayer; and after its resurrection and ascension to heaven, a descent of fire into the 'upper room' (ἀνωγαίῳ) of the soul takes place."[49] Again, "So who is a faithful and wise monk? He who has kept his fervor unabated, and to the end of his life has not ceased daily to add fire to fire, fervor to fervor, zeal to zeal, love to love."[50]

And St. Elias the Presbyter says, "Whenever the soul takes rest from external things and is joined to prayer, then a kind of flame envelops it, just as fire surrounds iron, and tempers the soul into an incandescent state. The soul remains the same, but it can no longer be touched by outside influences, just as white-hot iron cannot be handled." And further, "Blessed is he who in this life is made worthy of such contemplation that he even sees his own figure, formed of clay, become fiery through grace."[51]

Fervor can be produced by a variety of causes, but the chief kind is that which is brought about by pure prayer of the heart.

55. You should also know that such fervor can be produced and subsist within us in many different ways. This is evident from the various sacred sayings of the Saints that we have put forth, and although we hesitate to speak from our own experience, what seems to be the chiefest among these is the fervor that is brought about through pure prayer of the heart; and through this prayer, the fervor constantly progresses and increases and ultimately reaches a 'Sabbath rest' in the 'enhypostatic illumination', that is, it makes the person in this state enhypostatically illumined, according to the Fathers.

What is the work that follows the warming of the heart.

56. This fervor then keeps away the things that formerly impeded the prayer from being performed with complete purity. For our God is a fire, a *consuming fire* that destroys the wickedness of the demons and our passions (Heb. 12:29). Moreover, St. Diadochos explains, "When a person's heart endures the arrows of the demons

---

[49] *Ladder* 28.45 (Trans. Moore), 122. This is an allusion to Pentecost, Acts 2:1-13, and the word for "upper room" includes the root γῆ, meaning earth, ground ("above the ground"), thus expanding the metaphor of Christ casting fire on the earth.

[50] *Ladder* 1.27 (Trans. Moore), 5.

[51] *Gnomic Anthology* II 105-106, *Philokalia* Vol. 3.

with searing pain, so that it seems like he is being assaulted by actual arrows, then the soul learns to hate the passions through experience, as a beginning of purification. But if it does not suffer greatly from the virulence of sin (ἐπὶ τῇ ἀνδρείᾳ τῆς ἁμαρτίας), it will not be able to rejoice as bountifully in the goodness of righteousness. Thus, let him who wishes to purify his heart always keep it aflame through remembrance of the Lord Jesus, guarding this as his only meditation and never ceasing from this task. For those who desire to cast out corruption (σαπρίαν) from themselves should not just pray from time to time; they should always devote themselves to prayer and keep watch over their intellect, and not only while they are in places of prayer (τῶν εὐκτηρίων δόμων). For in the same way that someone wishing to purify gold will end up with the same hardened material if he allows the furnace fire to cease even for a moment, so someone who remembers God only from time to time loses through laxity all that he seemed to gain through prayer. But the distinguishing mark of the man who truly loves virtue is that he continually burns up the earthy portion of his heart through the remembrance of God, so that evil might gradually be consumed by the fire of the remembrance of the Good and the soul might return to its natural splendor, with even greater glory."[52]

And thus, as the intellect abides in the heart without hindrance, it prays purely and without delusion, according to the Saint who says, "Prayer is true and free from error when the mind guards the heart in prayer." St. Hesychios also writes, "He is a true monk who has achieved watchfulness; and likewise, a truly watchful person is a monk at heart."[53]

On the longing and eros that are born of fervor, attention, and prayer.

57. In this kind of warmth and prayer with attention (σὺν προσοχῇ προσευχῇ), that is, pure prayer, there is born in the heart a longing and divine eros and love towards the Lord Jesus Christ who is constantly being brought to remembrance, as it is written, *Young maidens have loved Me; they have drawn Me* (cf. Song 1:3-4), and, *I am wounded by love* (Song 2:50). Moreover, St. Maximos says, "All the virtues work together with the intellect to inspire divine eros, but none more than pure prayer. For through pure prayer the intellect takes flight towards God and transcends all things."[54]

---

[52] *On Spiritual Knowledge* 97, *Philokalia* Vol. 1.
[53] *On Watchfulness and Holiness* 159, *Philokalia* Vol. 1.
[54] *Centuries on Love* 1.11, *Philokalia* Vol. 2.

On tears of the heart, and more about divine longing and eros.

58. From such a heart there flow abundant tears, which purify and gladden the one who has been enriched with these things through love, yet without either melting him down or drying him out. For the first kind, the tears of divine fear, purify, while the second kind, the tears of divine eros, bring gladness, with intense and irrepressible longing and eros for the Lord Jesus Christ as He is brought to remembrance. And then the enthused heart cries out, "You have captivated me with longing, O Christ, and You have changed me by Your divine eros." And, "Savior, You are all *sweetness,* You are *all desire* and yearning, wholly insatiable; You are Beauty inconceivable (cf. Song 5:16). And together with Paul, the herald of Christ, it cries aloud: *The love of Christ compels us* (2 Cor. 5:14), and, *Who can separate us from the love of Christ? Sorrow or difficulty or persecution or nakedness or danger or sword?* (Rom. 8:35), and, *I am persuaded that neither death nor life, nor angels nor principalities nor powers, nor things present nor things to come, nor height nor depth, nor any other created thing, shall be able to separate us from the love of God which is in Christ Jesus our Lord* (Rom. 8:38-39).

Admonition that one should seek only what is in due measure. Further exhortation concerning the constant remembrance of our Lord Jesus Christ in our hearts.

59. One must strive to be made worthy of such great things and what follows them, about which now is not the proper time to speak, for as it said, "Seek not the fruits of a season (τὰ τοῦ καιροῦ) before their time," and, "Ill-gotten good is no good at all." And as St. Mark says, "It is not beneficial to know what comes after before completing what comes first, for *knowledge* accompanied by laziness *puffs up*, while *love builds up*, since it *endures all things in patience* (1 Cor. 8:1; 13:7)."[55] Instead, one must strive and always struggle, as we have said, to carry about the memory of the Lord Jesus Christ in the depths of the heart at all times, and not outwardly and superficially, as the same blessed Mark says about this: "Unless the secret and true inmost reaches of our heart are opened by a general hope of the intellect, we cannot know with certainty Him who dwells within it, nor can we know whether or not our reasonable sacrifices have been accepted (cf. Rom. 12:1)."

[55] *On the Spiritual Law* 84, Philokalia Vol. 1.

On fervent zeal and the divine manifestation of enhypostatic illumination to us through grace.

60. And thus will one easily turn away not only from both wicked deeds and impassioned thoughts and inappropriate fantasies, as it is written, *Walk in the Spirit, and you shall not fulfill the lust of the flesh* (Gal. 5:16). Even more so, one will completely depart (ἐκστήσεται) from every thought and every fantasy, being aflame with fervent zeal for virtue, extinguishing every wicked deed that had formerly been sensibly or intelligibly at work within him, along with their leaders the demons who rejoice in evil. As St. Isaac says, "He is terrible to demons and dear to God and His angels who roots out with fervent zeal the thorns planted within him by the enemy. And the assurance of God's love for him, and the clear manifestation and indwelling of the enhypostatic and divine illumination of grace will grow within him. And if you wish for me to say more, I say he will return to the original dignity (εὐγένεια) and spiritual adoption as a son, which has already been perfectly accomplished for us from the beginning through the grace of baptism."

Again, St. Isaac says, "This is 'Jerusalem' and the Kingdom of God hidden within us according to the word of the Lord (Lk. 17:21). This country is the cloud of the glory of God, into which only the pure in heart will enter to see the face of their Lord (Mt. 5:8)." However, one should not seek out God's manifestation, lest he mistakenly accept Satan, who is truly darkness but masquerades as the light (cf. 2 Cor. 11:14).

On divine energy and demonic energy.

61. Therefore, when the intellect sees light without seeking it, let it neither accept it nor reject it, as St. Mark says: "On the one hand, there is an energy of grace not easily recognized by spiritual infants, but on the other, there is an energy of evil which only resembles the truth. It is best not to scrutinize these energies, because of the risk of delusion, but neither should one condemn them outright (ἀναθεματίζειν), because of the possibility that they are genuine; in any case one should take refuge in God through hope, for He knows what is profitable in both of them."[56] Moreover, whenever something like this occurs, one should consult a spiritual guide who has the grace and power from God to teach and discern these matters.

---

[56] *No Righteousness by Works* 28, *Philokalia* Vol. 1.

On the illumined and unerring teacher.

62. Now if one has found a spiritual guide who teaches not only what he knows from Holy Scripture, but also according to what he himself has experienced (ἔπαθε) by blessed divine illumination, thanks be to God! But if not, then it is better not to accept [the light one has seen], but rather to take refuge in God in humility, calling oneself unworthy of such an honor and vision and truly considering himself so with a sincere heart, as we have said before, are saying now, and which we will certainly repeat; and all the mysteries we have been mystically taught by the grace of Christ come from guileless mouths, which have moved and spoken by the Holy Spirit, as well as from the God-inspired Scriptures and our small amount of experience.

On true and false illumination – that is, divine light and the light from the evil one.

63. In some of their writings, our renowned Fathers point out certain signs of unerring (ἀπλανής) illumination and certain signs of delusional (τῆς πλάνης) illumination. For example, the thrice-blessed Paul of Latros did so when he was asked about this by his disciple, saying, "The light of the diabolical power is fiery and smoky and similar to sensible fire; and when a self-controlled and purified soul sees it, it feels disgusted and detests it. However, the light of the Good is good, most graceful and pure, and when it comes it sanctifies the soul, fills it with light and joy and gladness, and makes it gentle and loving of other people (φιλάνθρωπον)." And others too have spoken similarly. However, since I have learned these matters through living, oral instruction (διὰ ζώσης ἤκουσα φωνῆς), you shall hear about it in detail elsewhere, since now is not the proper time.

On indecent and decent imaginations, and how one should deal with them.

64. Since we have spoken a little earlier about imagination, and indecent (ἀπρεπής) imagination in particular, we think that it would be most profitable to treat this topic briefly, and to examine the different kinds of imagination as much as we are able. For accursed fantasy strongly opposes pure prayer of the heart and the single and unerring work of the intellect. Hence the divine Fathers describe it and criticize it in many ways.

This imagination that we speak of is shifty (ποικιλόμορφος) like the fabled Daedalus and a beast of many heads (πολυκέφαλος) like the Hydra, and has been called by the Saints a kind of bridge for demons. For by means of it murderous spirits (οἱ φόνιοι ἀλάστορες) pass and cross over to the soul, and they communicate and mingle with it in such a manner as to render it a hive of drones and a dwelling-place of fruitless and impassioned notions. It is therefore imperative that you cast out imagination altogether (ἀποβλητέον τὸ σύνολον). However, an exception can be made when you desire it for the sake of repentance, abasement, mourning, and humility, or else for the study and contemplation of realities (τῶν ὄντων), or even with the goal of opposing and countering an indecent imagination by means of a decent one. That is, by using the one imagination to battle and fight against the other, you may force the indecent and shameless fantasy to cast down its arms in defeat and claim victory over it. Moreover, by doing so you will not only be inflicting damage on the indecent imagination, but will also be bringing profit for yourself, as one who directs his affairs with unfailing judgment, by cancelling out the indecent imagination by means of the decent one, and indeed, using your enemies' weapons again them by striking and slaying them at the right opportunity, as the divine David did against Goliath in ancient times (1 Sam. 17:51).

Both indecent and decent imagination are rejected by the Saints for the purpose of pure prayer and the simple and unified activity of the intellect.

65. At any rate, the above is an exercise for those who are still infants [in virtue], that is, for beginners. But those who are advanced – with the experience that comes with time – entirely reject both indecent and decent imagination and make it vanish (φρούδην ἐργάζονται), incinerating and dissolving it *as wax melts before the fire* (Ps. 67:3), in order to attain pure prayer and to remove and strip the intellect of all things and impressions, for the sake of simple encounter with God, and, if you will, for apprehension of Him and formless and single union with Him. For St. Hesychios says, "Every passionate thought enters into the intellect through the imagination of something sensible; for considering that the enemy (ὁ Ἀσσύριος) is himself an intellect, he is able to deceive us in no way but by making use of the sensible images we are accustomed to."[57] And again, St. Diadochos, "Given that every passionate thought enters the heart through the imagination of specific sensible things, the blessed light of divinity will illumine it once it has become completely liberated (εὐκαιρήσῃ) from all things and free of their shapes and forms. For the divinity's splendor is manifested to the pure mind when it is divested of all notions (νοημάτων)." Also, Basil the Great says, "Just as the Lord *does not dwell in temples made with hands* (Acts 7:48), neither does he dwell in any figures and figments of the mind (νοητοῖς). For these things beset and close off the impure soul, which is incapable of looking clearly into the truth, but is still restricted as it were to dim mirrors and riddles (cf. 1 Cor. 13:12)." Moreover, the divine Evagrios says, "It is said that God presides where He is known. Hence the pure intellect is

---

[57] *On Watchfulness and Holiness* 180, *Philokalia* Vol. 1.

called the throne of God. Thus, the conception (νόημα) of God shall not be found among the conceptions which shape the intellect, but among the conceptions that do not. Hence the one who prays must depart in every way from conceptions that shape the intellect. But the human intellect will be shaped quite differently when it beholds another Intellect, and it will be disposed quite differently when it beholds its Reason." From this we learn that spiritual knowledge removes the intellect from the notions that shape it, and by training it to be free of such impressions (ἀτύπωτον δὲ ἀσκοῦσα) it presents it to God.

Furthermore, in his *Scholia* on the great Dionysios the Areopagite, St. Maximos says, "Imagination is one thing, and intellection – that is, noetic activity – is another; for they come from different faculties and differ as regards their own distinctive movements. Intellection is energy and activity (ποίησις), while imagination is a passion and impression bearing the image of something sensible, or coming about from something sensible. While sensation perceives the form of realities at face value (ἀθρόαν μόρφωσιν), the intellect comes into direct contact with realities, that is to say, perceives them in a different manner, and not as sensation does. So then, while in the corporeal or the spiritual aspect, where the senses are, as we have said before, there is a passive and shaping motion, the faculty of judgment and perception should be attributed to the soul and the intellect; and therefore we must also assign the imaginative faculty to the perceptive faculty of the soul. The imaginative faculty is divided into three parts: first, there is the visual part (εἰκονιστικήν), which visualizes perceptions in such a way as to make the object of perception sensible. Second, there is the representational (ἀνατυπωτικήν) part, which makes representations based on what remains of objects no longer present, without necessarily lending support to its images, and this part is properly called "imagination." Third, there is the part that represents every kind of pleasure and the imagination of what is presumed to be good or bad on the basis of how much grief it causes. At any rate, none of these kinds of imagination, as we have said, has a place in God, for God is wholly and absolutely beyond the conception of all things and transcends them." And again, Basil the Great says, "The intellect which is not scattered towards external things nor dispersed in the world by the sense faculties returns to itself, and through itself ascends to the contemplation of God; and when it is enlightened by that beauty, it even forgets its own nature."[58] Therefore, having come to understand these things yourself, you should strive to pray at all times with the help of God, without imagination, without shapes, without impressions, and with the intellect and soul wholly pure in every way. St. Maximos explains as follows:

[58] *Epistle* 2.2, *To Gregory.*

The purity and perfection of the mind, soul, and heart.

The pure intellect.

66. "A pure intellect is one separated from ignorance and made radiant by the divine light."[59]

The pure soul.

"A pure soul is one liberated from passions and unceasingly delighted by divine love."[60]

The pure heart.

"A pure heart is one which presents the mind (μνήμη) to God wholly free of forms and impressions, and is prepared to receive God's archetypes (τύποι) alone – the ones by which He makes Himself manifest."[61] He then continues and says:

The perfect intellect.

A perfect intellect is one which through true faith has come to know Him who is beyond all knowledge, has beheld the whole scope (τὸ καθόλου) of His creations, and has received from God the comprehensive knowledge of His Providence and Judgment among His creations, that is to say, as far as this is humanly possible (ὡς ἄνθρωπος).

The perfect soul.

A perfect soul is one whose passive power has become wholly inclined toward God.

---

[59] *Centuries on Love* 1.33, Philokalia Vol. 2.
[60] *Centuries on Love* 1.34, *Philokalia* Vol. 2.
[61] *Centuries on Love* 1.82, *Philokalia* Vol. 2.

The perfect heart.

A perfect heart is said perhaps to be the one which has absolutely no natural inclination towards anything whatsoever, but God comes to it and writes His own laws upon it, as upon a tablet polished smooth to the point of utmost simplicity.

On purification.

Moreover, according to St. Diadochos, only the Holy Spirit can purify the intellect. Further, John Climacus says that only the Holy Spirit can still (στῆναι) the intellect. St. Neilos further says, "Whoever wishes to see the tranquil state of his intellect (νοῦ κατάστασιν), let him deprive himself of all thoughts, and then he will see as clear as sapphire." Again: "The stillness of the intellect (νοῦ κατάστασις) is a lofty height of thought resembling the clarity of heaven, and the light of the Holy Trinity comes to rest upon it during prayer." Also St. Isaac says, "When the intellect *takes off the old man* and *puts on the new man* of grace (Col. 3:9-10), then it will see its own purity resembling the clarity of heaven, which was called 'the place of God' by the elders of the sons of Israel, when He appeared to them on Mt. Sinai (Ex. 24:10)." So when you do as we have said – that is, by praying purely, without imagination or impressions – you shall be following in the footsteps of the Saints. Otherwise you will become a daydreamer (φαντασιαστής) instead of a hesychast, and instead of grapes you will harvest thorns – God forbid!

On the manner in which the prophets beheld visions.

67. However, if some people suppose that the visions and shapes and revelations of the prophets came about through their imagination and the natural order, let them know that they are far from the truth or any proper understanding of these matters. For the prophets, like the divine mystics of the present time, did not see or imagine according to the natural order and laws of nature, neither according to their own imagination, but their intellects were formed and received images in a divine and supernatural manner through the ineffable power and grace of the Holy Spirit, as Basil the Great says: "For through some inexpressible power those who have kept their intellect pure and undistracted have received revelations, and have the word of God resounding within them." And again, "The prophets beheld visions when their commanding faculty (ἡγεμονικόν) was formed by the Spirit." Moreover, Gregory the Theologian says, "[The Holy Spirit] was first active among the angelic and heavenly powers," and then, "Later He was active among the patriarchs and the prophets, among whom the former saw (ἐφαντάσθησαν) God or came to know Him, while the latter foresaw the future, since their commanding

faculty was formed by the Spirit, and thus they knew the things to come as though they were present."[62]

More about imaginations and the "many and various visions and contemplations".

68. However if some still doubt this, seeing that they uncritically accept fantasies and many and varied visions, and continue to oppose us, thinking that they are somehow following the Saints by citing, for instance, Gregory the Theologian who says, "God is adumbrated only by the intellect, not according to His essence, but from His attributes, by gathering various images (φαντασίαι) together into some likeness of the truth," and St. Maximos who says, "The intellect cannot become dispassionate by action alone, if it does not also receive many and various contemplations (θεωρίαι)," and likewise other Saints teach the same. However, let these sorts of people know that these words of the blessed Saints do not refer here to spiritual activity and grace "through reception" (κατὰ παραδοχήν), that is to say, the direct knowledge and vision which unites man with God through experience, but they refer to contemplation "through application" (κατ' ἐπιβολήν),[63] that is, the contemplation that is gathered from the wisdom, analogy, proportion, and harmony of created beings and approaches the conception of God somewhat dimly; this conception can be sought out in general and understood by many, or rather by all people. This will be clearly understood by anyone who carefully examines these and other similar passages from the Saints, as it is written: *The Author of creation is understood by analogy to the majesty and beauty of His creations* (Wisd. 13:5); however, this understanding is not derived from secular (κατὰ κόσμον), pagan (θύραθεν), vain, and verbose technical learning. For this learning, like a haughty (ἄσεμνος) handmaid who prides herself on her scientific, sophistical, and analytical opinions, and is not content to live by faith in the Gospel (εὐαγγελικῇ πίστει), humility, and assent to the truth, has been banished far from the sacred door-ways (ἱερῶν προθύρων). But our discourse now concerns the perfect and enhypostatic illumination, which the chief Apostles 'suffered' (ἔπαθον) ineffably, being transformed by the good and truly blessed *change* (Ps. 76:11) when they ascended with Jesus up to Mount Tabor, and they were made worthy to look upon the invisible Kingdom and Divinity even with their sensible eyes, which were transformed into what is more divine, being made spiritual by the right hand of the All-Holy Spirit. And *as far as the east is from the west* (Ps. 102:12), heaven is higher than the earth, and the soul is superior to the body, so to the same degree is

[62] Gregory Nazianzen, *Oration* 41.11 Oration on Pentecost.

[63] Application may be understood in terms of "applying" the intellect or conceptions to God, or as a kind of imperfect "perception". Cf. Dionysios the Areopagite, *Divine Names* 1.5, *PG* 593 B.

spiritual activity and grace "through reception" superior to contemplation "through application".

For contemplation "through application", as we have said, always comes from outside, gathering various images from the well-designed motion, order, and constitution of creation, uniting them into one form of truth so that one can make progress and be raised up to God in faith. But contemplation "through reception" wells up naturally within the heart, directly and hypostatically from God Himself, or sometimes even from outside, and then it communicates to the body manifest participation in its own splendor and most-divine illumination in a manner beyond thought; according to the most-wise Maximos, the heart 'suffers' "unoriginate deification" (ἀγέννητος θέωσις) supernaturally, and does not produce it by itself. Again, St. Maximos explains, "I call 'unoriginate deification' the enhypostatic splendor of the Divinity according to form, which has no beginning, but makes an incomprehensible manifestation to those who are worthy."[64]

In harmony with the above, the great Dionysios the Areopagite says, "It is necessary that we realize that our intellect has, on the one hand, the power to think, through which it sees intelligible realities, but on the other hand, it is also capable of the union which transcends the nature of the intellect, through which it is joined with the realities that are beyond it."[65] Also, the venerable Isaac says, "We possess two eyes of the soul, as the Fathers say, and the two kinds of contemplation that come from each do not have the same function. For with the one eye we see the hidden realities within the natures [of beings], that is the power of God, His wisdom, and His providence for us, which we perceive from the holiness of His reign over us. But with the other eye we contemplate the glory of His holy nature, when God is pleased to lead us into spiritual mysteries."

Furthermore, St. Diadochos says, "Wisdom and knowledge are both gifts of the one Holy Spirit, as are all the divine gifts, but each one has its own particular energy. Hence the Apostle Paul testifies that wisdom is given to one person and knowledge to another by the same Spirit (cf. 1 Cor. 12:8). This knowledge joins the person to God through experience, without necessarily inspiring his soul to articulate the realities he has come to know. Hence, some of those who engage in the philosophy of the solitary life are consciously illuminated by knowledge without attaining the ability to speak about God. But wisdom, when it is granted to someone in *the fear of the Lord* (Prov. 9:10) in unison with knowledge – and

---

[64] *Responses to Thalassios* 61.12 and scholion 14. Cf. *Responses to Thalassios,* (trans. Constas), 443, 447, and 57 in the Introduction.
[65] *Divine Names*, 7.1, *PG* 865CD.

seldom does this occur – makes manifest the inner workings of knowledge; for knowledge is wont to illuminate through spiritual activity (ἐνεργείᾳ), wisdom by word. Prayer and deep stillness in complete freedom from anxiety lead to knowledge, while unpretentious meditation on God-inspired Scriptures and, most importantly, the grace given by God, lead to wisdom."[66]

In addition to this, St. Maximos says in his *Scholia*, "Jacob's well (cf. Jn. 4:6) signifies Scripture; its water is the knowledge found within Scripture; its depth is the difficult contemplation of obscure passages in Scripture; the bucket is instruction through the written letters of the divine word, which the Lord did not require, since He is the Word-Itself_(αὐτολόγος); and hence He does not give to believers a knowledge acquired through education and study, but to those who are worthy He provides from the ever-springing fountain of spiritual grace an ever-flowing wisdom that never ceases. For the bucket – that is, education – draws up only the tiniest amount of knowledge, but leaves the whole, unable to contain it by means of any discourse. By contrast, the knowledge that comes through grace, even apart from study, contains all the wisdom possible to humankind, and it springs up in a variety of ways depending on one's needs."[67]

Again, St. Diadochos says, "Our intellect often has a difficult time with prayer because of the seeming narrowness and restrictiveness of prayerful effort, but when it comes to theology it gives itself over joyfully because of the broad ken of its understanding and the lack of constraint in thoughts about the divine. So then, in order to prevent the intellect from being overly fond of speaking or becoming excessively elated in its joy, let us instead devote most of our time to prayer, psalmody, and the reading of the Holy Scriptures. On the other hand, neither should we neglect the thoughts of prudent men whose faith can be recognized by their words. For by doing this let us train the intellect not to confuse its own words with the words of grace, and prevent it from being dragged down by vainglory and carried away through elation and talkativeness. During the time of contemplation let us preserve the intellect free of all imagination, and take care that whatever thoughts we do have at least bring tears. When it finds itself at rest in times of stillness, and especially when it is delighted by the sweetness of prayer, not only is it free of the faults we have mentioned, but it is constantly renewed in the way it acutely and effortlessly applies divine understanding, as it advances in great humility toward the knowledge of discernment. It is also necessary to know that there is a kind of prayer beyond the ken of human understanding; however, this

---

[66] Diadochos, *On Spiritual Knowledge* 9, *Philokalia* Vol. 1.
[67] *Centuries of Various Texts* 2.29. *Philokalia* Vol. 2.

prayer belongs only to those who have been filled with divine grace in full awareness and complete certainty."[68]

Have you heard and understood? He explains that there is a prayer beyond the ken of human understanding, which is possible only for those who have been supernaturally and enhypostatically filled with the divine illumination of grace in full conscious assurance, and this happens within the heart. St. Isaac calls this 'unstamped remembrance' (μνήμην ἀσφράγιστον), since it is unformed, unshaped, and simple. And other Holy Fathers ascribe other names to it.

On the five powers of the soul; similarly, on imaginations that are natural to the soul and the intellect, and how it is necessary for one to avoid imagination completely, as well as shapes, impressions, and forms while engaged in pure prayer and the simple and unified activity of the intellect.

69. However, as we have clarified, imagining does not only come about from demons, but in fact the soul itself, by its very nature, is capable of imagining, because it possesses five powers, namely intellect (νοῦς), mind (διάνοια), opinion (δόξα), imagination (φαντασία), and sensation (αἴσθησις) (just as the body has the five senses of sight, smell, hearing, taste, and touch). Imagination is one of the powers of the soul, as we have said, and it is by means of this natural faculty that the soul imagines. The soul, therefore, if it desires to order and arrange itself and its capacities aright, must be eager to lift and raise up wholly towards God those powers which unite it most with Him – both in the present age and in the age to come. Regarding the other natural powers, the soul should care for them, make use of them, and be occupied with them only insofar as it is necessary. Let us then examine what the Fathers say about them and what they reveal about the truth.

Thus, St. Maximos says: "Since the soul in-itself (δι' ἑαυτήν), that is, of its own essence, is rational and intelligent, it is necessarily self-existent. And if it is self-existent, it will on account of itself be active by nature, both by itself and together with the body: it will perceive according to nature, and reason, and never cease from the intellectual powers that are naturally proper to it; for the natural properties of any being whatsoever, as long as it has being and exists, are inalienable. The soul, then, since it has always existed in this manner from the moment it came into being, because of God who created it thus, always perceives and reasons and knows – by itself and in unison with the body, on account of itself and its own nature. Therefore, no principle (λόγος) can be found that is able to alienate the soul

---

[68] Diadochos, *On Spiritual Knowledge* 68, *Philokalia* Vol. 1.

from the attributes that are naturally proper to it – not even after the soul's separation from the body."

Since then we recognize and have been mystically taught by the Saints that the intellect and the mind both move toward God and remain active both in the present age and in the future age (while the other powers remain only in the present age, because they are peculiar to it), the soul must therefore choose to act not only for the present, but most of all for the future, like a skilled captain who possesses a natural authority over his whole crew. It must strive in every way to lift and move and unite the intellect and mind toward God during pure prayer – noetic and unified and simple spiritual activity – by completely separating the intellect from the imagination and the other powers of the soul.

For, according to St. Neilos, "The tranquil state of prayer is a dispassionate state that carries the wisdom-loving and spiritual intellect up to a noetic height by uttermost divine eros."[69] For when the soul does so, it will be correctly preserving the precious rank (τίμιον ἀξίωμα) proper to it.

More about the intellect.

70. Likewise, the intellect itself, being an undivided and simple and independent essence, pure and radiant, must guard and keep itself free and separate from the imagination, since it possesses of itself the natural power to do this, and to return to itself, concentrate, and move without hindrance. For this is the stillness of the intellect, which is brought about by divine grace, according to John Climacus who says, "Only the Holy Spirit can still (στῆσαι) the intellect." Indeed, the intellect, even though as a power of the soul it moves and is in a certain manner ruled by it, nevertheless it both is and is called "the eye of the soul," and is moreover endowed, as we mentioned, with a certain natural, simple, and independent power of its own. That is why, when the intellect subsists in being related to the soul and its powers according to nature, then it is intellect *in potential* (δυνάμει), and this state is called the 'natural person'[70] (1 Cor 2:14). But when it takes on its own natural and simple and essential dignity and splendor, which is undivided and independent and self-ruling, that is, liberated from natural relations and motions of both body and soul; and when it is granted to go from being *potential* intellect to being *active* (ἐνεργείᾳ) intellect, that is to say, when it advances to the state of the "spiritual person" beyond nature, then it returns towards itself unceasingly and unwaveringly, and through itself ascends freely and completely unhindered to the shapeless and

[69] Evagrios, *On Prayer* 53, *Philokalia* Vol. 1.
[70] Or: "person who lives in accordance with the soul"

formless and simple contemplation of God, as Basil the Great says: "The intellect which is not scattered towards external things nor dispersed in the world by the sense faculties returns to itself, and through itself ascends to the contemplation of God; and when it is enlightened by that beauty, it even forgets its own nature."[71]

And thus the intellect assumes what is *according to the image and likeness* (Gen. 1:26) and preserves it whole, and for since it is intellect – simply, by itself – it noetically unites and associates with the Divine Intellect, God. This is the activity of circular motion (κατὰ κύκλον κίνησις), that is, the restoration, return, and uniting of the intellect to itself, and then through itself to God, and this motion is alone truly unerring and unfaltering, being unimpeded and unmediated, a union beyond intellection and a vision beyond vision. Moreover, the great Dionysios says, "There is also movement of soul. First, there is circular movement, that is, the motion of entering into itself in departure from external things, and the unifying concentration of its noetic powers, granting it stability, as in a kind of rotation: it turns it from the multiplicity of external things by first gathering it to itself, and then when it has become unified it is united with those powers united in oneness. And in this manner the circular movement guides the soul to the Beautiful and the Good, which is beyond all beings, one and the same, beginningless and endless. But the soul can also move helically (ἑλικοειδῶς) when it is illumined with divine knowledge as far as it is able – not noetically and in unity, but rationally and through discursive reasoning, and by means of compound and mutable activities. Lastly, the soul possesses linear movement (κατ' εὐθεῖαν) when, instead of returning to itself in its own unified intellection (for this, as I said, is circular motion), it proceeds to the things near to it, and is raised up to simple and united contemplations, in departure from external things, which are like many variegated and multifarious symbols."[72]

Furthermore, St. Maximos says, "When the intellect has received unmediated union with God, then the natural power of intellection and perception remains at rest. Therefore, whenever it releases this power and perceives something aside from God (μετὰ Θεόν), it suffers separation from Him, severing that union which is beyond intellection and in which, as long as the intellect is joined to God, it becomes a god by participation in a manner beyond nature, like an immovable mountain, putting aside from itself the law of nature."

Again, he says, "Through its union with the Cause of all beings the pure intellect has entered into a relation beyond intellection, in which it has ceased from its

---

[71] Epistle 2.2, *To Gregory*.
[72] *Divine Names*, 4.9 (*PG* 705 AB).

manifold natural motion and its relation with all that is not God, and in a manner beyond knowledge, it reaches the ineffable end where it encounters only that most-blessed silence beyond all intellection, which reason and perception are completely incapable of making known, and can only be experienced through participation by those who are made worthy to enjoy it beyond intellection. One recognizable and manifest sign of this state is the soul's perfectly serene dispassion (ἀναισθησία) and detachment from the present age."[73] So then, when the intellect is not assisted by the soul in its perpetual motion towards God, and does not accomplish and perform what is proper to it in its own nature, that is, by returning to itself and thus rising unimpeded to the contemplation of God – or rather, when it does not properly avail itself (καρπούμενος) of either of these things, and is instead joined to the imagination – then it inevitably becomes all the more distracted and distant from God."

More about pure prayer.

71. Thus, St. Neilos says, "Strive to make your intellect still (στῆσαι) so that it is deaf and mute during the time of prayer, and then you will be able to pray."[74] Further, "I will repeat a saying of mine that I have told to the young men: Blessed is the intellect that has acquired the habit of being free of forms (τελείαν ἀμορφίαν) during the time of prayer."[75] Moreover, St. Philotheos says, "Rarely does one find people who keep stillness in their mind and reason. This can be found only among those who strive at all times to preserve divine joy and consolation in themselves through the life of hesychasm."[76] And Basil the Great: "The prayer that is good is the one which clearly implants the contemplation (ἔννοιαν) of God in the soul; and this is the indwelling of God in us (2 Cor. 6:16): when one has God in himself through remembrance, with the preservation of the memory uninterrupted by earthly cares and the intellect undisturbed by unexpected passions, and the lover of God flees from all things and departs to God."

That dispassion of intellect is one thing and true prayer another, greater than dispassion.

72. But we must also understand the following, as St. Maximos says: "The intellect cannot become dispassionate by action alone, if it does not also receive many and various contemplations." And again, according to the divine Neilos, it is also possible for someone who has become dispassionate to fail to pray truly, since his

---

[73] *Questions to Thalassios*, 1.1.2.
[74] Evagrios, *On Prayer* 11, Philokalia Vol. 1.
[75] Evagrios, *On Prayer* 117, Philokalia Vol. 1.
[76] *Texts on Watchfulness* 3, Philokalia Vol. 3.

intellect may still be distracted and far from God. This Father explains this as follows: "Until the intellect has moved beyond contemplation of the corporeal world, it has yet to behold the perfect realm of God. For it can easily be distracted by the knowledge of intelligible things and fragmented by their multiplicity."[77] And again, "When someone has achieved dispassion, this does not imply that he has already attained true prayer. For he might still have simple thoughts which keep him distracted and far from God by their information (ἱστορίαις)."[78] Again, "When the intellect no longer spends time pondering simple thoughts about created things, this does not imply that it has already reached the realm of prayer; for it might still be meditating on the *logoi*[79] of these things, since even if these thoughts are stripped of passion (ψιλὰ ῥήματα), the fact that they are ideas (θεωρήματα) of created things means that they can still leave impressions on the intellect and so keep it far from God."[80] St. John Climacus says, "Those whose intellects have learned to pray truly are they who speak face to face with the Lord in a lordly manner (Κυρίῳ κυρίως ἐνώπιοι ἐνωπίῳ) (Ex. 33:11), like ones who speak into the ear of the King."[81]

From these and similar passages, you can understand just how impossible it is to compare the two spiritual conditions and the difference between them, I mean to say, between contemplation "by reception" and contemplation "by application". For the work of the latter involves meditations and many and various contemplations, while the work of the former is true prayer. You will also understand that dispassion of the intellect is one thing and true prayer another, but still that, according to the Saints, the one who has true prayer will naturally and necessarily possess a dispassionate intellect already; however, someone who only has a dispassionate intellect has not yet acquired true prayer.

But let our discourse now return to the topics set before us, and considering that not only the things we have mentioned, but even the remembrance of goods and their contraries tends to leave general imprints on the intellect and lead it to imagination, we must make some notes about this matter as well.

---

[77] Evagrios, *On Prayer* 58, *Philokalia* Vol. 1.
[78] Evagrios, *On Prayer* 56, *Philokalia* Vol. 1.
[79] *Inner principles*.
[80] Evagrios, *On Prayer* 57, *Philokalia* Vol. 1.
[81] *Ladder* 27:21 (Trans. Moore), 112.

More about imaginations and impressions of the intellect and the signs of delusion and truth; what the signs of delusion are.

73. Once you are still and desire to be alone with God Alone (μόνος εἶναι μόνου τοῦ Θεοῦ), never accept anything you see, sensible or intelligible, from inside or outside, even if it is the apparent form of Christ or an angel, or the figure of a saint, or an impression of light appearing to the intellect, but you should rather remain skeptical (ἀπιστῶν) and wary (βαρούμενος) of it, even if it is a good thing, until you consult those who are experienced, as we have told you. For this is what brings the most benefit and is dear and acceptable to God.

Always keep your mind free of color, figures, forms, shapes, qualities and quantities, and attend only to the words of the Jesus prayer, meditating and contemplating them within the motion of the heart, according to John Climacus who says, "The beginning of prayer is to dispel attacking thoughts from the outset by focusing on the words of the prayer alone (μονολογίστως). The middle stage is for the mind to dwell wholly in the words of the prayer. Then the final stage of prayer is rapture towards the Lord."[82]

And again, St. Neilos says, "The supreme prayer of those who are perfected is a kind of rapture of the intellect and a total ecstasy of the senses, with *unspeakable sighs of the Spirit who intercedes for us to God* (Rom. 8:26), who sees the contents of the heart unfolded like a written book, with all its desire inscribed in ineffable letters. This is how Paul was caught up to the third heaven, without knowing whether he was in the body or outside the body (2 Cor. 12:2); this is how Peter came to see the vision of the heavenly sheet when he went up to the roof to pray (Acts 10:11-16). But a second kind of prayer, lesser than the first, is when one says the words of prayer and the intellect attends with compunction (μετὰ κατανύξεως) and understanding to the One to whom it addresses its supplication. However, the prayer that is kneaded through (πεφυρμένη) with interruptions and bodily cares is far removed from the tranquility of the person who prays truly." Therefore, continue to do as we have instructed you, and do not accept anything else that comes to you, at least not until you have an occasion of rest from the passions and consult those who are experienced, as we said before. The things we have warned about above, and others like them, are in short the signs of delusion. But now take note of what the signs of truth are. The signs of the truth, and of the Good and the Life-Giving Spirit, are *love, joy, peace, longsuffering, kindness, goodness,*

[82] *Ladder*, 28.19.

faithfulness, gentleness, self-control, as the divine Paul says, calling them the fruits of the Holy Spirit (Gal. 5:22).

Again he says, *Walk as children of light, for the fruit of the Spirit is in all goodness, righteousness, and truth* (Eph. 5:8-9), while delusion possesses all that is opposed to these things. One of those who are wise in things divine, when asked by someone, said, 'Round about the one truly unerring way of salvation which you have asked about, beloved, are other paths that lead to life, but beware, also many that lead to death.'" And further, "Set before you is one way leading to life: the keeping of Christ's commandments. In these commandments you will find all kinds of virtue, especially these three: humility, love, and mercy. But without these, *no one will see the Lord* (cf. Heb. 12:14)." And shortly after, "These are the three undefeatable (ἀκαταμάχητα) weapons against the devil which the Holy Trinity has granted unto us, namely humility, love, and mercy, and the whole swarm of demons cannot even bear to look upon them. For among them there is no trace of humility, and because of their pride they have become benighted and the eternal fire has been prepared for them (Mt. 25:41). Where is there even a hint of love or mercy among them, who have acquired an implacable enmity (ἄσπονδον τὴν ἔχθραν) against the human race and never cease to wage constant war against it? Therefore, let us arm ourselves (θωρακισθῶμεν) with these weapons, which render the soldier who bears them invincible in the face of his enemies."

And he further says, "We see that this threefold cord, which has been woven and knitted together by the Holy Trinity, is simultaneously three and one. It is three in its names, and, if you will, its 'hypostases', and it is one in its power and activity as well as in its nearness, proclivity, and familiarity with God. In reference to these three virtues the Lord said, *My yoke is easy and My burden is light* (Mt. 11:30), and the beloved Disciple said, *His commandments are not burdensome* (1 Jn. 5:3)."

And a little further, "For this reason the soul that has mingled (ἀνακραθεῖσα) with God through purity of life, the keeping of the commandments, and these three weapons, which are God Himself, has put on God Himself. Indeed, such a person has become a god by adoption, through humility, mercy, and love; and having surpassed the duality of the material realm and ascended to the fulfillment of the law, which is love (Rom. 13:10), he is joined to the super-essential and life-giving Trinity, encountering It directly, receiving light by Its light and exulting in perpetual and everlasting joy." But that is enough about these matters. Since we have mentioned some of the tokens of deception and truth – which, according to the divine Paul, are like fruits – from which we can recognize in a certain manner the spirit of those who act by them, it is also seems reasonable for us to clarify with the aid of the Fathers' sayings the nature of the consolations that come from each, that is, the difference between the consolation that comes from divine and true grace and the false one that comes from the diabolical and opposing power. The divine Diadochos explains this as follows:

On the difference between divine consolation and false consolation.

74. "When our intellect begins to sense the grace of the Holy Spirit, then Satan too pretends to console the soul with a certain sense of false sweetness (ἡδυφανεῖ) in the quiet of the nighttime, when one is drowsy and dozing lightly. But as long as the intellect continues in deeply fervent remembrance of the holy name of the Lord Jesus and avails itself of this holy and glorious name as a weapon against Satan's deceit, the deceiver will abandon this stratagem and from then will try to incite the soul to sin directly. From this the intellect learns to recognize clearly the deceit of the evil one and progresses further in the virtue of discernment by experience."

And again, "The good and divine consolation manifests itself while the body is awake or on the verge of falling asleep, while one is cleaving to God's love in the fervent remembrance of Him. But a delusional consolation comes to the ascetic, as I have said, while he falls into a kind of doze in half-hearted remembrance (μετὰ μέσης μνήμης) of God. True consolation, since it is from God, manifestly consoles the souls of those who struggle in piety and they are drawn to the love of God through a great outpouring of love in the soul. False consolation, on the other hand, tends to buffet the soul with the winds of error, and by means of bodily sleep it attempts to snatch away the experience of spiritual perception from an otherwise healthy intellect, especially while it happens to be lukewarm in its remembrance of God. But as long as the intellect is found in an attentive state of remembering the Lord Jesus, it will be able to scatter the enemy's seductive aura and to engage in spiritual warfare against him undismayed, armed with another weapon alongside divine grace: the confidence derived from experience (τὸ ἐκ πείρας καύχημα).

"Occasionally the soul, free from doubt and fantasies, is kindled and moved toward the love of God, so that it even draws the body into the depths of this ineffable love, which sometimes happens in the way I explained, that is, while the person is awake or beginning to enter a sleep brought on by God's grace, and while the soul is thinking of nothing but the blessed end towards which it is moving. In this case we should know that this is the energy of the Holy Spirit. For when the soul is completely delighted by that inexpressible sweetness, it can bring to mind nothing else, since at that moment it rejoices with an insistent joy. However, if the intellect actively conceives any doubt or impure thought, even while it is availing itself of the holy name of Jesus as a defense against evil and no longer just for the love of God, one must understand that this is false consolation from the deceiver, which comes only in the guise of spiritual joy. This counterfeit joy, which is altogether formless and disordered, is a trick of the enemy used to lead the soul into fornication (μοιχεύεσθαι) with him. For when he sees the intellect proudly boasting in its experience of spiritual perception, that is precisely when he seduces the soul by means of seemingly beneficial consolations, in order for it to be distracted by that spongy and slimy (χαύνης ... καὶ καθύγρου) pleasure and remain unaware of its unholy union with the deceiver. *By this we shall know the spirit of truth and the spirit of error* (1 Jn. 4:6). At any rate, it is impossible for someone to be aware either that he is tasting divine goodness (cf. Ps. 33:9) or that he is being tempted by the bitterness of demons, unless he has full assurance (ἑαυτὸν πληροφορήσει) that divine grace dwells in the depths of his intellect, while wicked spirits can only loiter around the outer parts of his heart. This is what the demons do not want people to discover, lest our intellect come to a clear understanding and we wage war against them with the remembrance of God as our mighty weapon."[83]

Here you have a sufficient treatment of this subject, and this should be enough for you. For, as the saying goes, "Sail not beyond the Pillars of Hercules,"[84] and, *When you find honey, eat a little, lest you gorge yourself and vomit* (Prov. 25:16).

On the divine pleasure that springs from the heart.

75. But now is an especially opportune time to say: Who can describe the sweetness of honey to those who have never tasted it? And as for what is incomparably greater: who can describe the divine pleasure and the supernatural and life-bestowing gladness that springs from pure and true prayer of the heart, which springs up everlastingly? As the God-man Jesus says, *Whoever drinks of the water that I shall give him will never thirst. But the water that I shall give him will become in him a fountain of water welling up into everlasting life* (Jn. 4:14), and again, '*If anyone thirsts, let him come to Me and drink. He who believes in Me, as the Scripture has said, out of his heart will flow rivers of living water.' And this He spoke concerning the Spirit, whom those believing in Him would receive* (Jn. 7:37-39). And the great Paul says, *God has sent forth the Spirit of His Son into your hearts, crying out, 'Abba, Father!'* (Gal. 4:6).

This spiritual delight is signified by many names, but is also unnamable.

76. This spiritual delight has been mystically called a supernatural and life-bestowing and enhypostatic illumination, dazzling darkness (ὑπέρφωτος γνόφος),

---

[83] Diadochos, *On Spiritual Knowledge* 31-33, *Philokalia* Vol. 1.
[84] τὸ γὰρ πέρα Γαδείρων οὐ περατόν. The Straits of Gibraltar - the Western edge of the known world.

inconceivable beauty, the ultimate desire, the sight and vision of God and deification; but even after being expressed it remains inexpressible, after being known, it remains unknowable, and after being understood it remains inconceivable. As the great Dionysios says, "We pray to be found in this superluminous darkness, to see and to know through unseeing and unknowing the One who is beyond all vision and knowledge – for this is done precisely by *not* seeing and *not* knowing (which is truly to see and to know) – and to praise beyond being (οὐσία) the One who is beyond being, through the negation (ἀφαιρέσεως) of all beings (ὄντα)."[85]

Further, "The divine darkness is the unapproachable light in which God is said to dwell (1 Tim. 6:16), which is invisible on account of its surpassing brightness, and unapproachable because of the excess of the super-essential overflow of light. Everyone who is made worthy to see and know God comes to be in this light precisely by neither seeing nor knowing, truly attaining Him who is above vision and knowledge by knowing this: that He is beyond all sensible and intelligible realities."[86]

Moreover, the great Basil says, "The lightning flashes of divine beauty are wholly ineffable and indescribable – word cannot tell, ear cannot hear. And if you were to mention the glow of the morning star, or the brightness of the moon, or the light of the sun, all of these are unworthy to give any idea of that glory, and they are as much inferior in comparison with the true light as deep night and dense darkness (στυγνὴ σκοτομήνη) are inferior to clearest noonday. This beauty cannot be seen by eyes of flesh, but can be perceived only by the soul and the mind, and when it shone on the Saints it left in them the unbearable spur of divine longing. Weary of life here, they would say, *Woe is me, for my sojourn has been lengthened!* (Ps. 119:5), *My soul has thirsted for God, the mighty and living God. When shall I come and stand before the face of my God?* (Ps. 41:3), *To depart and be with Christ is far better* (Phil. 1:23), and, *Now let Your servant, Lord, depart in peace, according to Your word* (Lk. 2:29), since they considered life here to be a prison; and because they could not be satiated with the contemplation of divine beauty, they prayed for the contemplation of the splendor of the Lord to be extended for all of eternal life." Again, Gregory the Theologian says, "Where there is fear of God, there is keeping of the commandments; where there is keeping of the commandments, there is purification of the flesh from the cloud that besets the soul and prevents it from seeing the divine radiance in purity; further, where there is purification, there is illumination, and illumination is the fulfillment of the longing of those who desire

---

[85] *Mystical Theology* 2, *PG* 1025A-B.
[86] *Epistle 5*, 1073A.

the greatest things, or rather the single greatest thing – nay, That which is altogether beyond greatness."[87] Furthermore, the divine Gregory of Nyssa writes, "If you wash away the accumulated filth in your heart by caring for your life, the deiform beauty will shine on you, as happens with iron. When it is stripped of rust with the whetstone, the iron that only slightly before was blackened then glistens with rays in the sun and radiates light. Likewise when the *inner man*, which is what the Lord calls the heart, removes the sullied filth which has been formed over his natural form by the mold of the evil one, then he will again be raised up to a likeness with the Archetype, and will become a good man. For the Good is always pursued by the good that is like unto it." Moreover, St. Neilos says, "Blessed is the person who has acquired the unknowing that is inseparable from prayer." And John Climacus: "The abyss of mourning has seen comfort, and purity of heart has received illumination. Illumination is an ineffable activity which is unknowingly perceived and invisibly seen."[88] Therefore, thrice-blessed are those who, like Mary of old, have *chosen* this *good portion* and way of life, which is spiritual and cannot *be taken away* (Lk. 10:42), and have been made worthy of such godlike happiness that they can be filled with unconcealed enthusiasm with great and ecstatic jubilation and may cry out these words together with the divine Paul: *The kindness and the love of God our Savior toward man has appeared, not by works of righteousness which we have done, but according to His mercy He saved us, through the washing of regeneration and renewing of the Holy Spirit, whom He poured out on us abundantly through Jesus Christ our Savior, that having been justified by His grace we should become heirs according to the hope of eternal life* (Tit. 3:4-7).

And again: *God has anointed us and sealed us and given us the Spirit in our hearts as a pledge* (2 Cor. 1:21-22) and, *We have this treasure in earthen vessels, that the excellence of the power may be of God and not of us* (2 Cor. 4:7). May God grant, by their powerful intercessions to the Lord, that we also may have a part in their inheritance by His mercy and grace.

Anyone who desires to live in perfect stillness must be meek at heart.

77. Child, you must understand at this time, in addition to these things and even in preference to them, that just as he who wishes to learn proper archery does not stretch the bow until he has first set up targets for practice, so he who desires to learn to live in stillness should have constant meekness of heart as his target.

---

[87] *Oration 39*.8, On the Holy Lights.
[88] *Ladder* 7.55 (trans. Moore), 42.

Moreover, St. Isidore says, "Ascesis is not sufficient for one to achieve virtue, but moderation in ascesis is also required. For if we engage in a contest for meekness and thwart it by our tumultuous thinking, that is no different from wanting salvation and yet not being willing to do anything for salvation." And before this, the divine David said, *He shall lead the meek in judgment; He will teach the meek His ways* (Ps. 24:9), and Sirach wrote, *The mysteries are revealed to the meek* (Sir. 3:19).

Again, our dearest Lord Jesus said, *Take My yoke upon you and learn from Me, for I am meek and lowly in heart, and you will find rest for your souls* (Mt. 11:29), and, *Whom shall I look upon, but on the meek and quiet man who trembles at my words?* (Is. 66:2), and, *Blessed are the meek, for they shall inherit the earth* (Mt. 5:5), which signifies the heart that bears fruit *thirtyfold and sixtyfold and a hundredfold* by grace (Mk. 4:20), in proportion to its rank (κατὰ τὴν τάξιν), whether it is found among beginners, the intermediate, or the perfect. The meek person never disturbs anyone, nor is he disturbed, unless it is for reasons of piety.

How we can achieve meekness, and on the three parts of the soul: the irascible, the appetitive, and the rational.

78. You will achieve meekness easily by turning aside from all things and by stirring your soul to love, keeping silent as much as possible, eating in moderation, and always praying, as has been said by the Fathers: "Bridle the irascible part of the soul (θυμικόν) through love, wither its appetitive part (ἐπιθυμητικόν) through self-control, and give wings to the rational part of the soul (λογιστικόν) through prayer, and then the light of the intellect will never grow dim." "Silence in due season is the bridle of anger (θυμός); eating in moderation restrains irrational desire (ἐπιθυμίας); and simple, focused prayer corrects the disordered mind (λογισμός)." And again, "There are three virtues which always bring light to the intellect: paying no attention (μὴ εἰδέναι) to another person's sinfulness, enduring misfortunes unperturbed, and doing good to those who do evil. These three virtues engender three other virtues, even greater than the first: paying no heed to another's sinfulness brings forth love, unperturbed endurance of misfortunes produces meekness, and benevolence towards those who do evil brings peace."

And once again, "There are three basic ethical states (ἠθικαὶ καταστάσεις) among monks: the first is when one does not sin at all in practice (κατ' ἐνέργειαν). The second is when impassioned thoughts no longer linger in the soul. The third is when one is able dispassionately to perceive in his mind the forms of women and of those who have grieved him, without desire or anger."[89]

One must readily repent for any offenses committed, and so be wisely prepared for the future.

79. If you ever happen to be disturbed by something or to slip into some offense by going astray from the right path, you should immediately be reconciled with the one who has grieved you or whom you yourself have grieved, and repent with all your soul – by mourning and weeping and blaming yourself – and in this way you will be careful and wisely prepared for the future, as the Lord Jesus teaches: *Therefore if you bring your gift to the altar, and there remember that your brother has something against you, leave your gift there before the altar, and go your way. First be reconciled to your brother, and then come and offer your gift* (Mt. 5:23-24).

For as the Apostle Paul says, *Let all bitterness, wrath, anger, clamor, and evil speaking be put away from you, with all malice. And be kind to one another, tenderhearted, forgiving one another, even as God in Christ forgave you* (Eph. 4:31-32), and, '*Be angry, and sin not*': *do not let the sun go down on your wrath* (Eph. 4:26; Ps. 4:5), and, *Beloved, do not avenge yourselves, but rather give place to wrath* (Rom. 12:19), and, *Do not be overcome by evil, but overcome evil with good* (Rom. 12:21).

On stumbling and repentance.

80. St. Isaac says about stumbling: "Let us not be grieved when we stumble in some passion, but only when we persist in it. For slips happen often even among the perfect, but to persist in a sin is utter death. The grief we feel for our own faults is reckoned to us by divine grace as a labor in purity. On the other hand, he who falls in hopes of a second chance to repent walks before God with deceitfulness. Death comes upon him when he least expects it, before being able to complete the works of virtue he had intended."

And further, "We should always be mindful that in all twenty-four hours of the night and day we stand in need of repentance. The meaning of the term 'repentance' (μετάνοια), as we have come to know from the very way of things, is the following: devout and unceasing supplication before God for the forgiveness

---

[89] St. Maximos the Confessor, *Centuries on Love* 2.87, *Philokalia* Vol. 2.

of past sins, with prayer full of compunction, and grief so as to guard ourselves from future sins."

And again, "Repentance has been given to human beings as a second grace [after the grace of Baptism] (χάρις μετὰ χάριν), for repentance is a second rebirth from God, and it is through repentance that we anticipate the fulfillment of the pledge we received by faith. Repentance is the door of mercy, opened to all who seek it. By this door we enter into divine mercy, but apart from this entrance we will find no mercy, for we *have all sinned*, as the Holy Scripture says (Rom. 3:23-24), and *are justified freely by His grace*. Repentance is this second grace, and it is born in the heart from faith and fear. Fear is God's paternal rod which guides us until we reach spiritual Paradise, but when we arrive there, it leaves us and departs. Paradise is the love of God, in which is found the delight of all promised blessings."

Further, "Just as it is impossible to cross over the vast sea without a boat or a ship, so no one can pass over to love without fear. The putrid sea of passions that stands between us and the noetic Paradise can be crossed only by the ship of repentance, and it is steered by the rowers of fear. If however these rowers do not guide the ship of repentance by which we pass over the sea of this world to God, we will be engulfed in the putrid sea."

More on repentance, fear, love, mourning, tears, and self-blame.

81. And St. Isaac continues, "Repentance is the ship, fear is its captain, and love is the heavenly port. Fear, therefore, takes us aboard the ship of repentance, carries us over the putrid sea of life and leads us to the heavenly haven of love, where *all who labor and are heavy laden* arrive in repentance (Mt. 11:28). And when we have come to love, we have come unto God – our journey is complete, and we have reached the isle which is beyond the world, where the Father and the Son and the Holy Spirit dwell."

About the mourning that is pleasing to God (cf. 2 Cor. 7:10), the Savior says thus: *Blessed are those who mourn, for they shall be comforted* (Mt. 5:4). And again, about tears, St. Isaac writes, "Tears in prayer are a sign of God's mercy, which the soul has been granted through its repentance; they are a sign that the soul's repentance has been accepted and that through tears it has begun to enter the meadow of purity. For unless the thoughts of transient things are removed, and the soul has cast away the hope of the world, feels disdain for it, and begins to prepare for the journey of departure from the body, and unless the thoughts of the soul begin to stir for what comes after death, the eyes cannot truly weep. For tears come from pure and undistracted meditation and from those many, continuous thoughts which are calmly brought about by a subtle thought in the mind through the memory, and it brings sorrow to the heart by its remembrance. From these thoughts, tears are increased and greatly multiplied."

Furthermore, St. John Climacus says the following: "Just as fire devours stubble, pure tears remove every bodily and spiritual impurity."[90] "Let us acquire for ourselves pure and guileless tears for our death (ἀνάλυσις); for in them there is neither deceit nor conceit, but rather purification, progress in love for God, washing away sins, and dispassion."[91] "Do not put trust in the fountains [of your tears] until you have attained perfect purification; for wine that has been put in a wineskin straight from the wine-press has no guarantee (πίστιν)."[92] And elsewhere, "The tears that spring from fear are possessed of a certain security, whereas the tears of that love which is not yet perfect can be quite easily lost by some (that is, unless the remembrance of the eternal fire intensely kindles the heart, when this is found to be beneficial). And it is amazing how what is humbler also happens to be more secure, so long as it is done at the right time."[93] And again, "Weeping in remembrance of death (ἔξοδος) engenders fear; when fear brings forth fearlessness, joy is revealed; and when inconceivable joy has given way, the blossom of pure love springs forth."[94]

Furthermore, about self-blame, Anthony the Great says, "Man's greatest work consists in doing the following: to take one's error upon oneself before God, and to be prepared for temptation till one's last breath."

And another holy Father, when he was asked, "What have you learned, father, from this way of life?" replied, "To blame myself in everything." The one who asked him praised the answer, saying, "Indeed, there is no other way besides this."

Moreover, Abba Poimen said, "All the virtues have come into this world with heavy sighs. Now think of one virtue which man cannot do without." Then they asked him what virtue he had in mind, and he replied, "For man to always blame himself." Again he said, "He who blames himself has accepted beforehand

---

[90] *Ladder* 7.31.
[91] *Ladder* 7.33.
[92] *Ladder* 7.35.
[93] *Ladder* 7.66.
[94] *Ladder* 7.56.

whatever happens to him, whether it is harm or dishonor or any other affliction; he considers himself worthy of such things and is never perturbed."

On precaution and wise circumspection.

82. Similarly, the divine Paul writes thus about precaution and circumspection: *See that you walk circumspectly, not as fools but as wise, redeeming the time, because the days are evil* (Eph. 5:15-16). And St. Isaac says, "O wisdom, how wondrous you are and how you foresee all things from afar! Blessed is he who has found you, for in doing so he has been freed from youthful indolence. Whoever bargains for the cure of the great passions, so as to acquire it for himself at a cheap price, does very well – for this is what philosophy is, and by means of it a man always remains vigilant even in the least and smallest things that happen to him. In so doing he treasures up for himself abundant rest in the future and does not grow drowsy, lest he fall into any error; rather he cuts off the causes in advance. Through these small matters he suffers a little hardship, but by means of a little hardship he prevents great hardship. Hence, one wise man says, 'Be watchful and vigilant for your life's sake, for the sleep of the mind is akin to actual death, and an image of it.' " Further, the mystical Basil says, "Do not believe that he who is lazy in his own small affairs will be able to excel in those that are great."

The hesychast must strive to do all that we have said, and first and foremost, to be still and meek and devoted to invoking the Lord Jesus Christ purely within the heart.

83. Hence, you should strive to do all that we have said, but first and foremost, to invoke in stillness and meekness and with a pure conscience the Lord Jesus Christ in the depths of your heart, as we have explained. For then, as you proceed along this path, you will have His divine grace resting in your soul.

For John Climacus says, "He who is still hounded (ὀχλούμενος) by anger and conceit, as well as by hypocrisy and the remembrance of wrongs, should never dare set foot on the way of *hesychia*, lest he merely gain distraction (ἔκστασιν) by it. But if anyone is pure from these, he will know what is profitable. (Although I am of the opinion that not even a pure man is always capable of it)."[95]

However, if you continue in this course, you will not only have grace resting in your soul, but will even be able to take perfect respite from the demons and

[95] *Ladder* 27.36.

passions which formerly harassed it. And even if they still harass the soul, they cannot influence it, since it has no dealings with them, nor does it desire the pleasure they have to offer.

On the beautiful and ecstatic eros, and divine beauty.

84. For all of the desire of such a hesychast, his heartfelt and ecstatic eros and entire disposition, are directed towards the exceedingly lovely and most-blessed Beauty, which the Fathers call the Ultimate Desire. And as Basil the Great says, "When the eros of piety takes possession of the soul, she looks upon every kind of war waged against her with contempt, and all the torments that she endures for the sake of the Desired bring gladness to her rather than injury." And again: "What is more wonderful than divine beauty? What conception is lovelier than the majesty of God? What desire of the soul is as sharp and unbearable as that which is caused by God in the soul that has been purified of all evil, and says in all truthfulness, *I am wounded by love* (Song 2:5)."

On spiritual warfare, God's withdrawal for the sake of instruction, and the withdrawal of abandonment.

85. At this point, the hesychast is allowed to be attacked not because God is departing from him to forsake him, but because He instructs him by withdrawal (παραχώρησιν παιδευτικήν). To what end? So that his intellect does not exalt itself because of every good he attains, but by being subject to spiritual warfare and chastised, he always assumes humility; and by this humility alone not only is he able to conquer the demons that proudly wage war against him, but he is also made worthy of continually greater gifts, makes progress as far as this is possible for his human nature – being bound and weighed down as he is with the inescapable chains and burden of the flesh – and so proceeds towards perfection and dispassion in Christ.

Moreover, St. Diadochos says, "The Lord Himself says that Satan fell from heaven like lightning (cf. Luke 10:18), so that the abhorrent one could not look on the dwelling-places of the holy angels. But if he has been wholly deprived of a part in communion among the good servants of God, how could he possibly have a common dwelling-place together with God Himself in the human intellect? But someone might say that this is possible because God withdraws (κατὰ παραχώρησιν) and makes room for him, without any further explanation. Now, on the one hand, there is in fact a kind of withdrawal for the sake of instruction, but by no means does it deprive the soul of divine light. As I have mentioned before, grace often simply hides its presence from the intellect, so that, in facing the bitterness of the demons, the soul is prompted to seek out help from God with great humility and fear, and thus gradually comes to understand the malice of its enemy. A mother does likewise when she sees that her own babe is unruly while breastfeeding: she briefly pushes the child away so that, by being startled by grimy people or some animals that happen to be nearby, it will turn back to her breast in tears and dismay. On the other hand, there is a kind of withdrawal in which God departs from the soul that does not want Him, such that the soul is delivered as a captive to demons. However, we are not children who have become apostates from God – God forbid! Rather we believe ourselves to be true babes of God's grace, which nurses us by briefly withdrawing but always consoling us once again, so that through the goodness of God we may attain *to perfect manhood, to full stature* (cf. Heb. 10:39; Eph. 4:13)."[96]

And he continues: "God's withdrawal for the sake of our instruction brings great sorrow, humility, and even a measure of despair to the soul so that the vainglorious and boastful part of the soul might accordingly be brought to humility; it immediately brings to the heart fear of God, tears of thanksgiving, and abundant desire for beauteous silence. But the withdrawal in which God abandons the soul allows the soul to be filled with despair, disbelief, wrath, and conceit. It is inevitable that we experience both kinds of withdrawal and in either case we must approach God in the appropriate way. In the first case, we ought to offer thanksgiving to Him as we plead our case, knowing that He is correcting the unruly part of our will by the instruction of withdrawal, and as a good Father He wishes to teach us the difference between virtue and vice. In the second case, we should ceaselessly confess our sins, never cease to weep, and depart farther from the world so that by these additional labors we may entreat Him ultimately to make a visitation to our hearts as before. However, we should understand that in the case of God's instructive withdrawal, even when there is a substantial (κατὰ οὐσιώδη συμβολήν) war between Satan and the soul, although grace conceals itself, as I have already explained, it is still actively assisting the soul in a hidden manner, so that the enemies of the soul might be humiliated when it appears to them that this victory is accomplished by the soul alone."[97]

Furthermore, St. Isaac says, "Without experiencing temptations of withdrawal, it is impossible for man to be made wise in spiritual warfare, to come to know his own Provider, to perceive his God, and to become firm in his faith. All of these things occur in a hidden manner and are made possible only by receiving the power of experience. Again, when divine grace sees that conceit has begun to creep into

---

[96] Diadochos, *On Spiritual Knowledge* 86, *Philokalia* Vol. 1.
[97] Diadochos, *On Spiritual Knowledge* 86, *Philokalia* Vol. 1.

his thoughts and he is beginning to have a grand idea about himself, it allows temptations to become stronger and stronger against him until he becomes aware of his weakness and turns back to God with humility. Through these man attains the height of *perfect manhood* (Eph. 4:13) with faith and hope in the Son of God, and is raised up to love. For the love of God is wondrously manifested to man when he occasionally stumbles into things that cut off his hope, and that is where God shows His power for his salvation and deliverance. For man can never learn the divine power in rest and comfort (πλατυσμῷ), and God has never shown His energy manifestly except in places of stillness, in the desert, and in areas free from distractions and the disturbance of people's habitation."

On dispassion. What is human dispassion?

86. Along with the above, we must add here a brief explanation of dispassion and perfection, and so shortly conclude this present treatise. Basil the Great writes, "He who has become a lover of God – who yearns to acquire if only the smallest portion of His dispassion, and desires to taste of His spiritual sanctity, serenity, peacefulness, and tranquility, as well as the gladness and joy that spring from them – has striven to ward off thoughts of any material passion that darkens the soul, and looks upon the divine with pure and unclouded eyes, insatiably filling himself with its light. And after exercising his soul in this state and condition, he becomes familiar with God to the extent that he has become like Him, becoming beloved and most dear to Him because he has accomplished such a great and difficult feat (μέγα τε ἆθλον καὶ δυσήνυτον ἀνατλάς), and by transcending his mixture with matter, he has been able to approach (ὁμιλῆσαι) God with a mind clear and in a certain manner separated from the confusion of bodily passions."

Now this is said in reference to dispassion. But regarding the question of what human dispassion is, St. Isaac writes, "Dispassion is by no means an inability to feel (αἰσθηθῆναι) the passions; rather it is a matter of not accepting (δεξάσασθαι) them. Through the many different visible and hidden virtues which one acquires, the passions grow weaker and cannot easily revolt against the soul. And then the mind does not always need to pay attention to them, since at all times and in all its thoughts it is filled with meditation on those ways that are best, which move within the intellect with prudence, and it clings to them. Then, whenever the passions begin to move and stir, the mind is immediately wrested away from them through a certain prudence in the intellect, and accordingly the passions remain inactive, just as the blessed Mark says: 'The intellect which performs the deeds of virtue by the grace of God and has drawn near to knowledge seldom pays attention to the evil and foolish part of the soul; for its knowledge seizes it away up to spiritual heights and removes it from all things in the world.' And because of their purity, the subtlety, lightness, and acuity of their intellect, and their ascetical labor, their intellects are purified and made radiant, since their flesh has been dried up through the stillness of *hesychia* (ἐκ τῆς σχολῆς τῆς ἡσυχίας) and their great perseverance in it. Thanks to this, their inner contemplation calmly and quickly comes over them and leads to further ecstasy. Hence their contemplations are multiplied, their mind never lacks material for understanding, nor do they ever live without the benefits brought to them by the fruit of the Holy Spirit. Moreover, long-standing habit blots out (ἐξαλείφονται) of the heart both the memories that rouse the passions of the soul and the power of the devil's rule. For as long as the soul is neither compromised by the passions nor complicit through meditation on them by constant preoccupation with earthly cares, the grasp of the passions' claws cannot take possession of its spiritual senses." And again, the divine Diadochos says, "Dispassion does not mean to be immune from assault by demons, *since then* we *would need to go out of the world*, as the Apostle says (1 Cor. 5:10); rather, it is to remain unconquered (ἀπολεμήτους) when they assault us (πολεμουμένους). For when adversaries shoot arrows at soldiers clad in armor, they hear the sound of the bow and even see most of the arrows being fired at them, yet they remain unharmed because of the firmness of their armor. And if they remain invincible (τὸ ἀπολέμητον ἔχουσιν) simply by being ironclad, let us cut through the dark ranks of demons by bearing the armor of divine light and the helmet of salvation through every kind of good work (cf. Eph. 6:11-17). For ceasing from evil is not sufficient to bring purity, but we must also overthrow evil by striving for what is good."[98]

Furthermore, St. Maximos divides dispassion into four kinds, stating: "I define the first kind of dispassion as refraining from the body's inclination to actively (κατ' ἐνέργειαν) commit sin. The second kind is the complete rejection of impassioned thoughts in the soul, and it withers the impulsiveness of the passions which are still present in the first kind of dispassion, since it no longer has impassioned thoughts which incite it to action. The third kind is complete stillness of passionate desire, and it tends to bring about the second kind, which arises from purity in one's thoughts. The fourth kind of dispassion is the complete rejection of all sensible representations in the mind, and the third kind arises from it, because the mind no longer possesses the representations of sensible things which provoke imagination of the passions in it." He also says, "Dispassion is a peaceful state of the soul in which it hardly inclines towards evil."[99]

---

[98] Diadochos, *On Spiritual Knowledge* 98, *Philokalia* Vol. 1.

[99] Maximos, *Centuries of Various Texts* 3.52, 36, *Philokalia* Vol. 2.

More about dispassion and perfection.

87. St. Ephraim too speaks of dispassion and perfection as follows: "Those who are dispassionate stretch out insatiably towards the ultimate desire, and make perfection endless, since there is no limit to eternal goods." Further, "Perfection is perfect in terms of human capability, but it is endless in that it always transcends itself with daily increases and is constantly being elevated in its ascents to God."

Likewise, St. Neilos says of perfection, "Two perfections must be understood; there is one that is temporal and another that is eternal, about which the Apostle Paul writes, *When that which is perfect has come, then that which is in part will be done away* (1 Cor. 13:10). The phrase 'when that which is perfect comes' means that we cannot receive divine perfection here."

Further, "The divine Paul knows two perfections. He recognizes the same person as both perfect and not perfect. He calls such a person perfect in regard to the present life, but says he is not perfect in regard to *that which is* truly *perfect*. For he says, *Not that I have already attained this or am already perfected*, and a little further he says, *Therefore let us, as many as are perfect, have this mind* (Phil. 3:12, 15).

On passionate desire, the passion of pleasure-seeking, passionate sensuality, and dispassion.

88. And St. Elias the Presbyter says: "Passionate desire (ἐμπάθεια) is the evil matter of the body; the passion of pleasure-seeking (ἡδυπάθεια), that of the soul; and passionate sensuality (προσπάθεια), that of the intellect. Physical touch is to blame for passionate desire, the rest of the senses for the passion of pleasure-seeking, and a stubbornly perverse disposition for passionate sensuality."[100] Further, "The pleasure-seeker is close to the impassioned man, and the sensualist is close to the pleasure-seeker. But the man of dispassion is far from all three."[101]

---

[100] Elias, *Gnomic Anthology* 1.71, *Philokalia* Vol. 3.
[101] *Ibid.* 1.72, *Philokalia* Vol. 3.

What is the character of the impassioned man, the pleasure-seeker, the sensualist, and the man of dispassion, and what is the therapy for each kind of passion?

89. "The impassioned man has an inclination to sin (τὸ ἁμαρτητικόν) stronger than his reasoning faculty, even if he does not sin outwardly for the time being. The pleasure-seeker has a tendency to commit sin, but this tendency is weaker than his reasoning faculty, even though he is still prone to external passions. The passionate sensualist has freely resigned himself to several ways of sinning, or rather, he has become enslaved to them. But the man of dispassion keeps far away from all these different forms of passion."[102] And regarding their therapy, he explains, "Passionate desire is eradicated from the soul through fasting and prayer, the passion of pleasure-seeking through vigil and silence, and passionate sensuality through stillness and attentiveness, while dispassion is established through the remembrance of God."[103]

On faith, hope, and love.

90. But considering how the threefold and God-woven cord of faith, hope, and love are the beginning, middle, and end, and one might say, the provider and ruler, of all goods – and above all love, since God truly is, and is named, love (1 Jn. 4:8) – , it would not be right to complete this treatise without filling in this gap. Moreover, since according to St. Isaac one receives the perfection of the abundant fruits of the Spirit once he is made worthy of perfect love, let us then briefly discuss this.

As John Climacus writes, "And now, finally, after all that we have said, *there remain these three* that bind and secure the union of all: *faith, hope, love; and the greatest of these is love* (1 Cor. 13), for God Himself is so called. And (as far as I can make out) I see the one as a ray, the second as a light, the third as a circle; and in all, one radiance and one splendor. The first can do and bring about all things; the divine mercy surrounds the second and makes it immune to disappointment (ἀκαταίσχυτον) (Rom. 5:5); the third does not fail, does not stop in its course, and allows no respite to him who is wounded by its blessed rapture (μανία)."[104]

Further, "The angels know how to speak about love, and even they can only do this according to the degree of their illumination. *God is love* (1 Jn. 4:8). Thus whoever wishes to define this tries with bleary eyes to measure the sand in the

[102] *Ibid.* 1.73, *Philokalia* Vol. 3.
[103] *Ibid.* 1.74, *Philokalia* Vol. 3.
[104] *Ladder* 30.1-3 (trans. Moore, with modifications), 126.

ocean. Love, by reason of its nature, is a resemblance to God, as far as that is possible for mortals; in its activity it is inebriation of the soul; and by its distinctive property it is a fountain of faith, an abyss of patience, a sea of humility. Love is essentially the banishment of every kind of contrary thought (παντοίας ἐναντίας ἐννοίας), for *love thinks no evil* (1 Cor. 13:5). Love, dispassion, and adoption are distinguished from one another only in name. Just as light, fire, and flame combine to form one energy, it is the same with love, dispassion and adoption."[105]

And St. Diadochos: "Let faith, hope, and love – and especially love – govern all spiritual vision (θεωρίας). For faith and hope teach us to disdain attractive sights, while love unites the soul with the virtues of God by searching out the Invisible God through noetic perception."[106] And again, "The soul's natural love is one thing, while the love that comes to the soul from the Holy Spirit is another. The love that comes from our own soul occurs when we desire and according to how much it is stirred by our will and desire. Hence it is easily taken over by wicked spirits when we do not have a firm hold of our free will. In contrast, the love from the Holy Spirit inflames the soul in the love of God to such a degree that at that time all its parts cleave to His unspeakable goodness with divine yearning, in an infinitely simple inclination. For it is as if the intellect then becomes pregnant through the energy of the Spirit, and there gushes forth from it a spring of love and joy."[107]

Moreover, St. Isaac says, "The love that comes from some things is like a little lamp that feeds on its oil, and so keeps its light, or it is like a torrent swollen by a heavy rain, which stops flowing as soon as the rain ceases. But love that has God as its cause is like a fountain that springs up and its currents never cease, for He alone is the fountain of love, with a flowing source that never fails." And again, when he was asked, "What is the perfection of the abundant fruits of the Spirit?", he responded, "It is reached when one is made worthy of the perfect love of God." And again when he was asked, "How might someone know that he has attained perfect love?", he replied, "When the remembrance of God comes to his mind, his heart is immediately moved in love for Him, and tears profusely stream from his eyes. For love is wont to bring forth tears at the remembrance of loved ones; and a person who has attained such love never lacks tears, since he is never deprived of the source that perpetually leads him to the remembrance of God, so that even in

---

[105] *Ladder* 30.5-9 (trans. Moore, with modifications), 127.
[106] Diadochos, *On Spiritual Knowledge* 1, *Philokalia* Vol. 1.
[107] Diadochos, *On Spiritual Knowledge* 34, *Philokalia* Vol. 1.

his sleep he may converse with God. It is indeed a habit of love to do such things, and this is the perfection of human beings in this life."

He also said, "The love of God is fervent by nature, and when it comes to anybody beyond measure, it makes that soul ecstatic. That is why the heart of the one who feels it cannot contain or endure it, but depending on the quality and the degree of love that has come upon him, one can observe in him an unusual alteration. And these are the perceptible signs of this change: the person's face becomes rosy, full of gladness, and the body grows warm. Fear and shame are removed from him, and he becomes ecstatic. The power that gathers the intellect is released and he is filled with a divine madness. He thinks of dreadful death as a joy, and the contemplation of his intellect is never interrupted while he studies heavenly things. While absent he speaks as though he were present, without being seen by anybody. His natural knowledge and vision depart from him, and he does not perceive with his senses his bodily motion while he goes about things; even if he does anything practical, he does not sense it at all because his intellect is elevated in contemplation, and it is as if his mind were always conversing with someone. The Apostles and Martyrs were inebriated with this spiritual drunkenness: the former went all over the world *laboring and suffering reproach* (1 Tim. 4:10), and the latter, while being crushed in their limbs, poured out their blood like water, and even while suffering the most terrible torments, never did they lose their courage but endured bravely; and though they were wise, they were reckoned as fools (2 Cor. 11:16). Others *wandered in deserts and mountains, in dens and caves of the earth* (Heb. 11:38), living in apparent disorder, but all the while ordering themselves well before God (ἐν ἀταξίαις, εὔτακτοι ὄντες). May God grant that we also attain such foolishness! (cf. 1 Cor. 4:9-13)"

On the Holy Eucharist, and all the benefits that are granted to us through frequent communion with a clean conscience.

91. Now concerning the purification of the soul, the illumination of the intellect, the sanctification of the body, and indeed the divine transformation (μεταστοιχείωσις) and immortality of the whole person (not to mention the overthrowal of passions and demons, and even more so, our divine and supernatural union, whereby we are joined and mingled [συνάφειαν καὶ ἀνάκρασιν] with God), there is nothing that contributes so much to these as continual reception and communion of the holy, immaculate, immortal, and life-giving Mysteries of the precious Body and Blood of our Lord and God and Savior Jesus, as long as this is done with as much sincerity and purity of heart as possible. Hence it is especially important to say something about this subject and to incorporate into the conclusion of our discourse. And the truth of what we say will

become evident not only from what the Saints say, but how much more from the very words of Life-Itself (αὐτοζωή) and Truth-Itself (αὐτοαλήθεια). For He says:

> I am the bread of life. This is the bread which comes down from heaven, that one may eat of it and not die. I am the living bread which came down from heaven. If anyone eats of this bread, he will live forever; and the bread that I shall give is My flesh, which I shall give for the life of the world. Unless you eat the flesh of the Son of Man and drink His blood, you have no life in you. Whoever eats My flesh and drinks My blood has eternal life. For My flesh is food indeed, and My blood is drink indeed. He who eats My flesh and drinks My blood abides in Me, and I in him. As the living Father sent Me, and I live because of the Father, so he who feeds on Me will live because of Me. This is the bread which came down from heaven, and he who eats this bread will live forever (Jn. 6:48, 50-51, 53-58).

And the Christ-bearing Paul says the following:

> For I received from the Lord that which I also delivered to you: that the Lord Jesus on the same night in which He was betrayed took bread; and when He had given thanks, He broke it and said, "Take, eat; this is My body which is broken for you; do this in remembrance of Me." In the same manner He also took the cup after supper, saying, "This cup is the new covenant in My blood. This do, as often as you drink it, in remembrance of Me." For as often as you eat this bread and drink this cup, you proclaim the Lord's death till He comes. Therefore whoever eats this bread or drinks this cup of the Lord in an unworthy manner will be guilty of the body and blood of the Lord. But let a man examine himself, and so let him eat of the bread and drink of the cup. For he who eats and drinks in an unworthy manner eats and drinks judgment to himself, not discerning the Lord's body. For this reason many are weak and sick among you, and many sleep. For if we would judge ourselves, we would not be judged. But when we are judged, we are chastened by the Lord, that we may not be condemned with the world. (1 Cor. 11:23-32).

It is necessary to understand the miracle of the Holy Mysteries: what they are, why they were given, and what their benefits are.

92. St. John Chrysostom writes, "It is necessary to learn the miracle of the Mysteries: what are they, why were they given, and what are their benefits. We are all one body and members of the flesh of our Lord Jesus Christ, and of His bones (Rom. 12:5; Eph. 5:30; cf. Gen. 2:23). Now let those who have been initiated into the mysteries attend to what is said. Christ did not only want us to become His body spiritually through love, but also wished for us to be actually mingled with His flesh, which takes place through eating the flesh He has given, and it is in this way that he wishes to show His love (πόθος) for us. Hence He has mixed Himself with us and mingled His body with ours, so that we might become one, just as a body is joined to its head. For this is a characteristic of those who are exceedingly affectionate. It was also intimated by Job when he said of his servants, who loved him exceedingly, how they used to say in a display of their affection, *Who will grant us to be satisfied with his flesh?* (Job 31:31). And so Christ has done just this, in order to lead us to a greater friendship with Himself and to demonstrate His affection for us, granting to those who desire Him not only that they might see Him, but that they might touch and eat and plant Him deep in their flesh and embrace Him and satisfy all their desire."

And again, "Those who partake of the all-holy Body and precious Blood stand alongside the angels and archangels and the hosts on high, vested in Christ's royal garment and armed with spiritual weapons. But even this is not saying enough, for they have *put on* the King Himself as their *garment* (Gal 3:27). Now considering how great and dreadful and wonderful this Mystery is, know that as long as you draw near in purity, you will have drawn near to your salvation; however, if you draw near with an evil conscience, you will be subject to torment and punishment. *For he who eats and drinks in an unworthy manner eats and drinks judgment to himself* (1 Cor. 11:29). For just as those who defile a king's robe are punished in the same way as those who have the audacity to tear it apart, likewise it is not at all unreasonable that those who receive the Body of the Lord with an impure mind are liable to the same punishment as those who have rent it and nailed it to the cross. Consider how terrible a punishment was described by Paul when he said, *Anyone who has rejected Moses' law dies without mercy on the testimony of two or three witnesses. Of how much worse punishment, do you suppose, will he be thought worthy who has trampled the Son of God underfoot, counted the blood of the covenant by which he sanctified a common thing, and insulted the Spirit of grace?* (Heb. 11:28-29). So then, for all of us who partake of this Body, and all who taste this Blood, let it be understood that we are receiving a taste of Him who is enthroned on high, worshiped by the angels, seated next to the inviolate Power of the Most High. But woe to us! For how many ways have been given to us for our salvation? After all, He has made us His body, has given us part in His very own body, and yet do none of these things dissuade us from evil? What blatant indifference on our part! What insensitivity!" And again, "An admirable elder once told me one of the things he was granted to see and hear in a vision: that those who are preparing to depart from this life, as long as they have partaken of the Mysteries with a pure conscience when they are about to die, are accompanied by angels and taken away for the sake of the Body and Blood that they have received."

Furthermore, the divine John of Damascus says, "Because we are twofold and composite beings, it follows that our birth must also be double, and likewise that our food be composite. Thus, birth is given to us *through water and the Spirit* (Jn. 3:5), and our food is the very Bread of Life, our Lord Jesus Christ, descended from heaven. And as in the case of Baptism He joined the oil and water with the grace of the Spirit, making this the bath of regeneration, because it is a custom of people to bathe in water and then to anoint themselves with oil, so in accordance with our custom of eating bread and drinking water and wine, He joined His divinity with them and has made them His Body and Blood, so that we can reach the supernatural through what is ordinary and natural. This Body is truly united with divinity; it is the very Body that was born of the Holy Virgin. That is not so to say that His Body, which has ascended, physically comes down from the heavens, but rather that the bread and wine are transformed (μεταποιεῖται) into the Body and Blood of God. But if you seek to know the manner in which this happens, it is sufficient to know, *through the Holy Spirit*; it is similar to the way in which the Lord established (ὑπεστήσατο) flesh for Himself from the Holy Theotokos *through the Holy Spirit*, and we know nothing more, but only that the Word of God is true and active and all-powerful, while the manner of activity is inscrutable. So then, to those who receive communion worthily and with faith it brings the remission of sins, eternal life, and protection of soul and body. But to those who receive communion unworthily and in disbelief it brings punishment and condemnation, just as the Lord's death. Moreover, the bread and wine are not a mere representation (τύπος) of the Body and Blood of Christ – God forbid! They are indeed the very deified Body of Christ, and His very blood. *For My flesh*, He says, *is food indeed, and My blood is drink indeed* (Jn. 6:55). They are the Body and Blood of Christ, which unite our souls and bodies, and can be neither consumed nor corrupted; they are not ultimately expelled like food, but constitute the essence and preservation of our being, and cleanse us of every impurity. We are received like debased gold in a crucible, and it purifies us with a trying fire, *so that we may not be condemned along with the world* in the age to come (1 Cor. 11:32). Being purified through it, we are united to the Body of Christ and to His Spirit, and we ourselves become Christ's Body. This bread is the beginning of the future bread, which is *the bread that is to come* or *the essential bread* (Mt. 6:11). For *epiousion*[108] signifies either the future bread, namely the bread of the age to come, or the bread we receive for the preservation of our essence (*ousia*). The flesh of the Lord is *a life-giving spirit* because it was conceived through the *Life-Giving Spirit*, and *that which is born of the Spirit is spirit* (1 Cor. 14:45; Jn 6:63; Jn. 3:60). Of course I say this not to undermine the physical nature of the body, but because I wish to indicate its life-giving and divine quality. Hence the Mysteries are called the *copies* or *antitypes* of things to come not as though they were not truly the Body and Blood of Christ, but because through them we participate in Christ's divinity at the present time, while in the future we shall participate in a fully noetic manner, simply through Divine Vision."

Moreover, the divine Makarios says, "Just as wine is diffused (κριvᾶται) into all the body parts of him who drinks it, and the wine becomes part of him, and he part of the wine, likewise the Spirit of Divinity is poured into him who drinks the Blood of Christ; the Spirit is mingled with the perfect soul, and the soul with Him, and in this way the soul is sanctified and made worthy of the Lord. For as the Scripture says, *we have all been made to drink of one* and the same *Spirit* (1 Cor. 12:13). Furthermore, through the Bread of the Eucharist, those who receive communion in truth are granted to become participants in the Holy Spirit, and these worthy souls are made capable of living forever. Again, just as the life of the body is not self-sustaining (ἐξ ἑαυτοῦ), but is sustained by matter external to it – from the earth – so God has been pleased to provide the soul with food, drink, and clothing not from its own nature, but from His divinity – from His own Spirit and Light, which are the true life of the soul. For the Divine Nature possesses *the bread of life* (the very One who said, *I am the bread of life* [Jn. 6:48]) and *the living water* (Jn. 4:10) and *the wine that delights* (Ps. 103:15) and *the oil of gladness* (Ps. 44:8)."

Again, St. Isidore says, "Partaking of the Divine Mysteries is called communion, because it bestows on us union with Christ and makes us communicants of His Kingdom." And the blessed Neilos says, "It is impossible for the believer to be saved, receive forgiveness of his trespasses, and obtain the Kingdom of Heaven unless he receives communion of the mystical and spotless Body and Blood of Christ with fear and faith and longing (πόθος)."

---

[108] The rare Greek phrase *arton epiousion*, which is usually translated "daily bread" in the phrase, "Give us this day our daily bread", of the Our Father, is understood by St. John of Damascus to mean either "bread that is to come" (cf. Gk. verb *epieinai*, meaning "to be upon", "to come"), or the bread that is "substantial" and "essential" for our being.

Also, Basil the Great writes the following in his letter to the patrician lady Caesarea: "Communing and partaking of the Holy Body and Blood of Christ is good and beneficial, for He says clearly, *He who eats My flesh and drinks My blood abides in Me, and I in him, and has eternal life* (Jn. 6:56, 54). For who would doubt that constantly partaking of Life is anything other than living life in abundance (πολλαχῶς)? As for us, we receive communion four times a week, on Sundays, Wednesdays, Fridays, and Saturdays, and also on other feast days in commemoration of a Saint."[109] (I suppose that it was on these days that St. Basil served the Divine Liturgy, since he could not officiate every day, busy as he was with pastoral cares.)

Furthermore, St. Apollo once said, "The monk must, if possible, receive communion of the Mysteries of Christ every day. For he that removes himself from them, is removed from God, whereas the one who constantly communes receives Christ's flesh continually. For the Savior's voice proclaims: *He who eats My flesh and drinks My blood abides in Me, and I in him* (Jn. 6:56). Therefore it is of the greatest benefit for monks to do this in constant remembrance of the saving Passion. Every day the monk must be ready and prepare himself so that he will always be worthy to receive the Holy Mysteries, for through it we are also granted the remission of our sins."

Moreover, John Climacus says: "If a body is changed in its energy when it comes into contact with another body, how can someone not be changed when he touches the Body of God with innocent hands?"[110]

Again, the following story is written in the *Gerontikon*: "John Vostrinos, a holy man who also possessed authority against unclean spirits, once put a question to the demons who had been dwelling in girls who suffered from madness and were wickedly influenced by them, saying, 'What is it you fear about Christians?' and they said, 'You do in fact possess three great things; one is that thing you wear around your neck, another is that thing you bathe in at Church, and another is that thing you eat at the Liturgy.' And again he asked, 'Which of these three things do you fear the most?' and they replied, 'If you all guarded well that thing you receive at communion, none of us would be able to harm a Christian.' So then, what the hostile spirits fear more than anything else is the Cross, Baptism, and Holy Communion."

---

[109] Letter 93.
[110] *Ladder* 28.52.

Conclusion of all the topics that were discussed in detail, and a short exhortation to the inquirer.

93. So then, dearest child, your request has been granted with the help of God. Whether it has been completed in the way that you had in mind or intended, of this we cannot be certain. At any rate, we have completed it to the best of our abilities and with an effort pleasing to God. Therefore, make sure that your studiousness and diligence do not stop here, but that you prove to be studious and earnest in works also. For as the renowned Brother of God says: *My dear brethren, be doers of the word, and not hearers only, deceiving yourselves. For if anyone is a hearer of the word and not a doer, he is like a man observing his natural face in a mirror; for he observes himself, goes away, and immediately forgets what kind of man he was. But he who looks into the perfect law of liberty and continues in it, and is not a forgetful hearer but a doer of the work, this one will be blessed in what he does* (Jas. 1:22-26).

One must obey and follow the spiritual tenets of the Fathers.

94. Most importantly, it is essential that you obey and receive the divine and spiritual precepts (θεσπίσματα) of the Fathers faithfully and with due reverence. For as St. Makarios says, "Spiritual realities cannot be touched by the inexperienced; but the communion of the Holy Spirit comes to the holy and faithful soul and leads it to a comprehension of them. Moreover, the heavenly treasures of the Spirit become manifest only to the person who has experienced them. The uninitiated cannot even conceive of them. Therefore give reverent attention to what the Saints say about these matters until you too are made worthy to obtain them by your faith. For then you will know through experience, by seeing with the eyes of your own soul, the spiritual goods and mysteries that Christian souls can participate in even in this life. With this knowledge you will quickly reap the fruits and benefits of what you have read or heard in the Scriptures; and by learning and doing them, you will make progress and even be able to exhort others through your own experience, guiding them to divine realities hidden (ἀμύητα) from most people. May this be granted to you by the support and guidance of the almighty hand of Christ. Amen." So then, considering how a surfeit of words is harmful to hearing (κόρος λόγου πολέμιος ἀκοαῖς), as eating in excess brings harm to the body, and "everything is best in moderation" (πᾶν μέτρον ἄριστον), we intend to avoid excess and embrace moderation as what is best. Therefore, now is a suitable time for us to drop the anchor of our discourse by elaborating just a little further with a brief recapitulation of the present treatise.

Recapitulation. How one should pray. On true illumination and divine power.

95. The Fathers say that whoever wishes to be sober in mind (ἐν λόγῳ) should always strive to pray with his heart purely and without rambling – breathing in through the nose – contemplating, ruminating, and concentrating on the words of the Jesus prayer alone: "Lord Jesus Christ, Son of God, have mercy on me". This should be done until the moment of the intellect's illumination in the heart, as St. Diadochos says: "Those who unceasingly meditate on the glorious and precious name of Jesus Christ in the depths of their hearts can sometimes even see the light of their own intellect."[111] From such an illumination, and with God's guidance, we will be able to continue the remaining journey of a God-pleasing life without error, delusion, or obstacles, walking in the light, and even as *sons of light*, as the Light-Giver Jesus says: *While you have the light, believe in the light, that you may become sons of light* (Jn. 12:36), and, *I am the light of the world. He who follows Me shall not walk in darkness, but have the light of life* (Jn. 8:12). Moreover, David cries out to the Lord, *In Your light shall we see light* (Ps. 35:10), and the divine Paul says, *For it is the God who commanded light to shine out of darkness, who has shone in our hearts* (2 Cor. 4:6). Then true believers are guided by this illumination, as by an inextinguishable and radiant lamp, and come to see clearly realities which lie beyond the senses. Further, the heavenly gate of the entire lofty and angelic way of life is opened to them because they are *pure in heart* (Mt. 5:8). Indeed, like the rising sun there dawns on them the gifts of examination, discernment, clairvoyance, foresight, and the like. And, in general, through this illumination all the manifestation and revelation of the invisible mysteries shine upon them, and they are overwhelmed by supernatural and divine power in the Spirit, and through such supernatural power their earthy matter (ὁ χοῦς αὐτῶν) is made lighter, and the heaviness of their flesh is refined, elevated, and takes flight. Through this illuminating power in the Holy Spirit some of the holy Fathers, while they were still in the flesh, walked over impassable rivers and vast seas without even getting their feet wet, as though they were immaterial and incorporeal; they traversed lengthy and wearisome roads in but a moment, and performed other great wonders in heaven and on earth, over the sun and the sea, in deserts and in cities, in every place and country, over beasts and reptiles, and throughout the length and breadth of all creation and over all the elements of nature, and through all of these things they were glorified. While they stood in prayer, their holy and venerable bodies were lifted up from the earth as if by wings, as the consuming, divine, and immaterial fire of grace incinerated their bodily thickness (πάχος) and even their physical weight, and caused them to levitate – a wondrous miracle! –, and they were transformed, tempered, and transfigured into what is more divine by the

---

[111] Diadochos, *On Spiritual Knowledge* 59, *Philokalia* Vol. 1.

deifying hand of strength and grace that resided within them. After death some of their venerable bodies have remained incorrupt, a clear testimony of the supernatural grace and power that dwells within them to all those who have true faith. At last, after the general and universal Resurrection, through the same illuminating power of the Spirit they will put forth wings, as it were, and *shall be caught up in the clouds to meet the Lord in the air*, as that initiate in ineffable mysteries, the divine Paul, says, *And thus they shall always be with the Lord* (1 Thess. 4:17).

In addition to these things, David, singing in the Spirit, states: *Lord, they will walk in the light of Your countenance, and shall rejoice in Your name all the day long* – that is, for eternity – *and in Your righteousness they will be exalted. For You are the boast of their power, and by your good pleasure will their horn be exalted* (Ps. 88:16, 18), and, *The mighty ones of God have been greatly exalted over the earth* (Ps. 46:10). Likewise, Isaiah with a majestic voice proclaims, *Those who wait on the Lord shall put forth wings* and *they shall renew their strength* (Isa. 40:31).

Moreover, St. Makarios says, "Every soul, which through faith and diligence in all the virtues has been granted to *put on Christ* perfectly with power and full assurance (πληροφορία) even here on earth, and been united with the heavenly light of the incorrupt image, is granted to receive hypostatic knowledge of heavenly mysteries forever. At last, on the Day of Resurrection, when the body has been glorified together with the soul – the heavenly image of glory itself – and been *caught up* by the Spirit into heaven, as it is written, *to meet the Lord in the air* (1 Thess. 4:17), and been made worthy to be *conformed to His glorified body* (Phil. 3:21), then they shall reign together with Christ in both soul and body for eternity."

Another recapitulation.

96. The beginning and cause of these new and wondrous realities of which we speak, though they are beyond speech, is the *hesychia* we have described: stillness, attentiveness, and prayer in complete freedom from anxiety. They serve as a sort of foundation and solid, impregnable bulwark for ensuring the fulfillment of all the deifying commandments according to one's strength. For freedom from anxiety, stillness, attentiveness, and prayer kindle that stirring and warmth in the heart which scorches passions and demons, and purifies the heart as in a crucible. This fervor in turn enkindles desire and unceasing eros for the Lord Jesus Christ, from which pours a sweet stream of heartfelt tears by which the soul and body are cleansed and cheered through repentance, love, thanksgiving, and confession, as with hyssop (cf. Ps. 50:9). These then give rise to serenity and a peace of mind that

has no end (Is. 9:7) and *surpasses all understanding* (Phil. 4:7), which in turn bring an illumination as bright and shining as snow (χιονοφεγγόφωτος). And finally there comes dispassion (as much as it is possible for humankind); the resurrection (ἐξανάστασις) of the soul before the body;[112] restoration and return to being *in the image and likeness of God*, through practice and contemplation, through faith, hope, and love; complete ascent towards God, as well as immediate union, ecstasy, rest, and repose in Him. This occurs in the present age as *through a glass, darkly*, and as a *foretaste*, but in the age to come it shall be the most utterly perfect participation in God and the eternal enjoyment of Him *face to face* (1 Cor. 13:12; cf. Eph. 1:14).

Hesychia with obedience is truly the unerring and true and God-pleasing way of life which has been handed down by the Fathers, and the Saints have wisely called it _the life hidden in Christ_ (Col. 3:3).

97. This is the way that is pleasing to God (κατὰ Θεόν), the noetic way of life, and sacred work of true Christians; it is the true and unerring and genuine life, *the life hidden in Christ* made manifest (Col. 3:3). It is the path that the God-man and dearest Jesus laid down and in which he led the way as in a mystagogy; it was tread by the divine Apostles, and then followed by those who came after them, our renowned guides and teachers, who shone like *beacons of light in the world* (Phil. 2:15) through the rays of their life-giving words and their wondrous deeds, from the time of Christ's First Coming on earth up to the present day. These Saints passed on to each other, down to our own generation, the good seed (Mt. 13:24), the sacred yeast (Mt. 13:33), the holy first-fruits (Rom. 11:16), the secure deposit (1 Tim. 6:20), divine grace, the power from on high (Lk. 24:49), the precious pearl (Mt. 13:46), the divine inheritance of the Father, the treasure hidden in the field (Mt. 13:44), the pledge of the Spirit (2 Cor. 1:22), the royal sign, the living, springing water (Jn. 4:14), the divine fire, the praiseworthy salt, the gift, the seal, the light, and the like, which will continue in the inheritance and the mystical succession (διαπορθμευόμενον) from generation to generation until the Second Coming of Christ. For He does not lie who promised this: *Behold, I am with you always, to the end of the age. Amen* (Mt. 28:20).

Although there are also other ways leading to salvation, this is the chief and royal highway and leads to our adoption as sons.

98. Now, there are certainly other paths, ways of life, and good labors (ἐργασίαι χρησταί) which lead the person who pursues them to salvation and give him rest

---

[112] See Step 29 in John Climacus' *Ladder of Divine Ascent.*

(καταπαύειν), taking him by the hand, as it were, and bringing him either to the state of servitude or that of a wage-earner, for as the Savior says, *In my Father's house there are many mansions* (Jn. 14:2). However, this way is indeed the chief and royal highway, and it exceeds and surpasses all other spiritual labors to the same extent that the soul surpasses the body, since it re-creates from *earth and ash* the person who follows it dutifully, leading him to adoption as a son of God (cf. Gen. 18:27), and paradoxically makes him a god through the Holy Spirit, as Basil the Great says: "When the Holy Spirit comes upon a person's soul, He gives him life, grants immortality, raises him from his fallen state; and the one who has been animated by the eternal animation (τὸ δὲ κινηθὲν κίνησιν ἀίδιον) of the Holy Spirit becomes a holy living being (ζῷον ἅγιον). And when the Holy Spirit has taken up His dwelling in him, a man who was formerly *earth and ash* receives the dignity of a prophet, an apostle, an angel, a god."

This way of life is called by several names because of its sublimity.

99. Hence the divine Fathers have extolled this way with a wide variety of splendid appellations. For they have called it the way of knowledge, laudable practice, and consummate contemplation, prayer beyond the ken of understanding, watchfulness of the intellect, noetic activity, the work of the age to come, the angelic state, the heavenly life, the God-inspired way of life, the land of the living, mystical vision (μυστικὴ ἐποψία), an abundant spiritual banquet, a divinizing Paradise, heaven itself, the heavenly kingdom, the Kingdom of Heaven, the dazzling darkness beyond light (γνόφος ὑπέρφωτος), the *life hidden in Christ* (Col. 3:3), the vision of God and deification (θεοπτία καὶ θέωσις), the supremely supernatural reality (τὸ ὑπερφυέστατον), and so on. By following these Holy Fathers ourselves, though we are still yoked to evil and unclean thoughts, words, and deeds, and weighed down *in clay and in brick-making* (cf. Ex. 1:14), we diligently set out to fulfill your request in writing, dear one. Indeed, in accordance with what you requested, we did not even shrink back from speaking beyond our capacities (ὑπὲρ τὸ μέτρον ἡμῶν) out of love for you and deference to the commandment of our fathers, as we explained in the introduction of the discourse. This is the angelic life that has been established by the wondrous and ineffable economy and Incarnation of the Word and Son of God, the good pleasure of the Unbegotten Father, and the synergy of the Holy Spirit.

ETHICAL EXHORTATION

Along with the help and grace of God, it is also necessary that we strive and struggle with all our effort to become worthy of such great and supernatural

gifts, starting from this present time, as a partial pledge, lest we fail to attain them for want of a little care – God forbid!

100. Dear ones, considering then how we have such great goods set before us, let us not be content merely with hopes and promises for the future, but let us eagerly strive in truth and in deed, starting from this present moment while we still have time. Let us race and struggle that we too may be made worthy of these things through but a little temporary diligence and brief exertion on our part, and even more so, through the gift and grace of God. Let us heed what the divine herald Paul proclaims: *For the sufferings of this present time are not worthy to be compared with the glory which shall be revealed in us* (Rom 8:18). And indeed, by striving we will be able to attain these things even from this present time, as first-fruits and a partial pledge of what is to come (Rom. 8:23; Eph. 1:14). For people of the lower classes, if they could but be summoned up to royal kinship and society, would be willing to do absolutely anything for the sake of such unstable (ῥευστῆς) and temporary glory and honor, by means of all sorts of deeds, words, and designs. For this goal they do the impossible and are sometimes disdainful of their very life, although this often leads to nothing profitable, but only to total destruction. If this is so, how much more should we who have been called by God make our journey and hasten to communion, marriage, and union with Him, the King of all kings, the Creator, the only Incorruptible One, who eternally distributes and provides illustrious and everlasting glory and honor to those who belong to Him. Not only does He do this, but He has even granted us the *right to become children of God*. For *as many as received Him, to them He gave the right to become children of God, to those who believe in His name* (Jn 1:12). He gives us the right (ἐξουσία); he does not tyrannically drag us or force us against our will (παρὰ πρόθεσιν ἡμετέραν). For tyranny always arms the tyrannized against the tyrant, such that evil is redressed by evil (ἵνα κακῷ τὸν κακὸν ἐξιάσηται). In contrast, God honors the ancient dignity of our freedom (τὸ ἀρχαῖον τοῦ αὐτεξουσίου ἀξίωμα), such that the good, even though it is accomplished entirely by His own good pleasure and grace, might also be reckoned to us as an achievement of our own effort and diligence. And He, while being God and Lord, has done all that He has done – both creating all and dying on behalf of all – so that He might save us all. It remains for us to draw near to Him, to believe, to endear ourselves to Him, to worship with fear, earnestness, and love the Friend of Man, our Lord and Protector who so genuinely loved us that He willed to endure death voluntarily for our sakes, and a shameful death at that. This He did to liberate us from the tyranny of the devil, the enemy and author of evil (ἀρχέκακος), and to reconcile us to God the Father, to present us as *heirs of God and co-heirs with Himself* (Rom. 8:17), a mystery paradoxical and supremely blessed. Therefore, let us not deprive ourselves of such an abundance of goods, precious gifts, and delights by preferring to indulge in momentary laziness, carelessness, and counterfeit pleasure. Rather, let us do

everything for Him and make a good transaction, even laying down our life for His sake if necessary. For although He is very God, He did this for us that we might be made worthy of all manner of gifts and crowns even at the present time. May we all be granted to obtain these things by the good pleasure and grace of our exceedingly good and merciful Lord and God and Savior Jesus Christ, who so humbled Himself on our behalf, and who rewards to those who are likewise humble His supernatural and deifying grace actively and abundantly starting from the present. For to Him be all glory, honor, and worship, together with His Unbegotten, All-Pure Father, and His Co-eternal, All-Holy, Good, and Life-Giving Spirit, now and forever and to the endless ages of ages. Amen.

Saint Kallistos Angelikoudes

CHAPTERS

Chapters on Prayer

1. If you wish to learn the truth, take the lute player as a model for imitation; while seated, he inclines his head and hearkens intently to the song, and strums the strings with his plectrum. And as soon as he skillfully strikes the strings the lute produces a harmony, and the musician springs up with joy (ἅλλεται) from the sweetness of the melody.

2. Let this be a clear example to you, O diligent worker of the vineyard, and do not fall into disbelief. When you become as watchful as the lute player in the depths of your heart, you will easily find what you seek after. For the soul that is completely captivated (ἁλοῦσα) by divine eros is unable to turn back, and hence the godly David says: *My soul has clung to You* (Ps. 62:9).

3. Beloved, understand (νόει) the lute to be the heart, the strings the senses, and the plectrum the mind (διάνοια) – that is, the mind constantly moves the 'plectrum' through reason (τὸ λογικόν), and this is the constant remembrance of God, which gives rise to an ineffable pleasure in the soul and reflects divine rays to the pure intellect.

4. If we do not shut off (μύσωμεν) the senses of the body, there will not gush forth within us that *fountain of water springing up* (ἀλλόμενον) which the Lord granted to the Samaritan woman; for although she was seeking sensible water, it was ultimately within herself that she found the water of life springing up (Jn. 4:14). Again, just as the earth by nature contains water and overflows with it, likewise the 'earth' of the heart by nature possesses this water welling up and ready to spring forth (ἀλλόμενον καὶ πηγάζον) from within it. And such was the light possessed by our forefather Adam before he lost it through disobedience.[113]

5. The living and welling water gushes up from the soul perpetually, much like how water from a spring does not cease to flow. Indeed, this is the water that resided in the soul of Ignatios the God-bearer and moved him to say: "There is no

---

[113] Possibly a reference to Gen. 2:6, where it is mentioned that there was no rain before the Fall, but *a spring came up from the earth and watered the whole face of the earth.*

fire of love for material things (φιλόυλον) within me, but there is water that is active and speaking."[114]

6. This blessed – or rather thrice-blessed – noetic watchfulness of the soul is like water welling and springing up from the depths of the heart. The water that gushes up from the spring causes it to overflow, while the water that springs up from within the heart and moves, so to speak, with perpetual motion through the Spirit, causes the whole inner man to overflow with divine dew and spirit, even making the outer man fiery in appearance.

7. The intellect that has been purified from external things and fully subdued the senses through practical virtue remains as unmoved as the celestial axis; it directs its vision to the depth of the heart as to a center, and taking command of the head, it gazes within, the beams of the mind like rays drawing out divine perceptions (νοήματα) from within, and thus it subdues all the senses of the body.[115]

8. Let no one who is uninitiated (ἀμύητος) or who still needs milk (1 Cor. 3:2) touch these things, since they are forbidden before their due season. For the Holy Fathers judged that the only thing it brings about is confusion of mind when people prematurely seek to obtain things before their due time, as if recklessly aiming to enter the harbor of dispassion without the proper equipment. For it is impossible for someone who does not know how to read to study books.

9. That which is moved within the soul by the Holy Spirit as a result of spiritual struggle calms the heart and cries out to God, *Abba, Father!* (Gal. 4:6). And while it has neither figure nor form (ἀσχημάτιστον ἢ καὶ ἄμορφον), it nevertheless transfigures (μετασχηματίζει) us by the radiant glory of divine light, and rightly forms (μορφοποιεῖ) us by the flame of the divine Spirit. However, it alters and transforms us in a manner that only God knows, by His divine power.

10. The mind that is purified through watchfulness is easily darkened if it does not completely wean itself away from external matters through the constant remembrance of Jesus. But the person who has successfully united practice with contemplation as a secure guard of the intellect no longer even needs to reject

---

[114] *Epistle to the Romans* 7.

[115] Angelikoudes is possibly alluding to theories of medieval optics, in which the eyes were understood to emit rays of light that retrieved sensory information from surrounding objects. In this scheme, the gaze of the intellect is directed to the heart within to collect divine perceptions for the head to rule, as it were, the external senses.

disturbances or repulse distracting sounds, either distinct or indistinct ones. For when the soul is wounded by the divine eros of Christ, it follows after Him as her Beloved (cf. Song 5:8).

11. For those who live in the world, stilling (στῆσαι) the passions and impulses of the flesh, or even practicing stillness (σχολάζειν) with reason, according to the verse, *Be still and know [that I am God]* (Ps. 45:11), can reasonably be done. However, it is impossible to obliterate and eliminate them while living in the world. On the other hand, the solitary life can eradicate them completely.

12. When water flows it may be observed how one stream moves more rapidly, while another flows with a slower, tranquil motion. The first does not easily become muddied owing to its rapid motion, and even if it does for a short while, it is easily purified again because of the current. But if the flow of water slows to a crawl, then not only does it become muddied but often even stagnates. Then it requires a kind of repurification and return to motion.

13. The devil assaults beginners (εἰσαγωγικοῖς) and those who engage in the ethical and practical path by distracting them with distinct or indistinct sounds. But to those engaged in contemplation, he projects imaginary forms (εἰδωλοποιεῖ) as if painting the air to make it resemble light, or sometimes fire, in order to mislead the athlete of Christ by employing deceitful wiles contrary to his goal.

14. If you wish to learn how to pray, look to the end-goal of your attention and your prayer, and do not be deceived. For this is its purpose, beloved: unceasing compunction, a contrite heart, and love for your neighbor. Again, the things that are contrary to these are obvious: thoughts of desire, slanderous backbiting, hatred for your neighbor, and the like.

The Paradise described in Scripture is an Image of Man.

15. Visible things are images (εἰκόνες) depicting the invisible things of man, and thus the exceedingly beautiful garden of Paradise planted with all wisdom by God in the East, in Eden (Gen. 2:8), is an image of the inner man: his heart is the 'earth' and soil, and the plants are the things freely (βουλόμενος) planted by the intellect created *according to the image of God* (Gen. 1:27), which is to say, the many and various contemplations relating to God, as well as divine perceptions and even divine manifestations; these contain variety and all sorts of forms and spiritual fragrances, and they further provide nourishment, contentment, and of course pleasure. This is precisely what the garden of Eden signifies, that is, the heart that

is naturally cultivated and takes conscious enjoyment and pleasure in things divine. Furthermore, in the East the sensible sun dawns on the sensible Paradise, while the noetic Paradise within man is illuminated by the knowledge of the Noetic Sun. For according to the Fathers, the heart that is deprived (ἀμοιροῦσα) of the light of knowledge cannot receive divine perceptions, contemplations, and manifestations of God, nor, in general, can it be be filled with divine conceptions – either the simpler or more perfect ones – so as to manifest anew a transcendent Paradise. Again, no garden can have the lush plants and fruit trees that it should have without water. For this reason a streaming fountain appears in the midst of the garden of Eden, dividing into *four principal rivers* (εἰς ἀρχὰς τέτταρας) and indeed *watering the whole face of the earth*, as it is written (Gen. 2:6-10). Thus, within man the fountain of living water is the life-giving motion of the Holy Spirit, about which the Lord Himself said, *The water that I shall give him will become in him a fountain of water* (Jn. 4:14), springing miraculously from the heart as from Eden and dividing into prudence, temperance, justice, and courage, the four cardinal virtues (ἀρχὰς τέτταρας) upon which all godly virtue depends. Hence, it further says that it waters *the whole face of the earth*, which signifies, if you like, 'the face of the heart', or better, the energy that produces increase and growth, and the fruit-bearing of the choice fruits of godly virtues.

How wonderful, pleasant, and lovely it is for us to reflect on the nature (ἅπερ ἔνεστι) of this spring, which is an image of the supernatural motion and energy of the Life-Giving Spirit from the midst of the heart, as I mentioned above. Now, the spring is not of the same nature as the plants or the soil since, unlike the one single spring, they are all quite different from each other. Nevertheless, the water, being *one*, is sufficient to water, nourish, and irrigate without measure all the plants, which are *many* and can hardly be counted; and this the water does despite the fact that the plants differ so vastly from one another, even to the point that they are often contrary to each other in terms of composition (κράσεως): while some need an arid climate, others need humidity, and while some are mild, others are hardy. So then, just as the spring moves out towards all these diverse varieties, as I have mentioned, likewise the One and Unique (μονοειδές) is distributed, granting perfect assistance (συνεργοῦν) by 'splitting into four principles' so as to contribute to each plant what it requires. Again, the divine supernatural illumination of the Life-Giving Spirit and His ever-flowing motion and energy is not of the same nature as our own activities – either virtue, knowledge, or spiritual contemplation – and neither is it of the same nature as our heart. Rather it is bestowed as a gift of grace to the faithful and ceaselessly streams from the heart in a strange manner, and similarly to how the spring divides into four rivers, it is clearly distributed into the four virtues and perfectly assists them, as well as all the remaining virtues in succession, all the while being *one* 'water'. Hence, as spirit, it cooperates with prudence (φρόνησις), and as knowledge it assists the participant in justice (δικαιοσύνη); again it is called *a spirit of a sound mind* (σωφρονισμός) and *power* (δύναμις) (2 Tim. 1:7), since it manifests the energy to bring about temperance (σωφροσύνη) even to those afar off, and brings about true courage (ἀνδρεία) as well. Furthermore, Paul and Isaiah are excellent witnesses to the fact that it has [the nature of] love and wisdom. St. Paul distinctly proclaims, *The love of God has been poured out in our hearts by the Holy Spirit who was given to us* (Rom. 5:5), and Isaiah clearly indicates this by numbering the *spirit of wisdom* amongst the seven energies of the Spirit (Is. 11:2). However, the Spirit does not only assist in love, but also becomes the spirit of zeal, which might seem to be diametrically opposed to love, since *love covers a multitude of sins*, as it is written (1 Pet. 4:8), but zeal, for the sake of putting restraints on evil (πρὸς ἐλέγχους), occasionally even allowed for killing [the body]; this is shown by Elijah, the great prophet and friend of God, who slaughtered so many shameful priests by resorting to the sword (cf. 3 King. 18:40), and earlier by Phineas, who slew a Midianite woman together with an Israelite with a spear (cf. Num. 25:8), and even before them the most-holy bestower of the old Law, Moses himself, often delivered men to death out of zeal, to be slain by their own people (ἐμφυλίων). Again, for those who engage in the practical life, the best thing is knowledge, while for those who engage in contemplation the unknowing beyond intellect (ἡ ὑπὲρ νοῦν ἄγνοια) is best. In any case, it is impossible to do what we must if we do not possess the Spirit of Truth and of Knowledge in our soul. Furthermore, heartfelt joy and its exact opposite, sorrow, are clearly both operations (ἐνεργήματα) of the Spirit. For you hear it said in Scripture that joy is a *fruit of the Spirit* (Gal. 5:22), but also that God gives *a spirit of contrition*[116] to some (Rom. 11:8). And in short, according to the Fathers, the Holy and Life-Giving Spirit is able to assist (συνεργεῖν) to such a degree in everything that works towards virtue, and even in conditions seemingly opposed to one another, as previously mentioned, that Scripture calls Him both 'fire' and 'water' – the most antithetical elements – and this is because of the Spirit's assistance and energy which enables all good and beautiful things pertaining to the soul. For this reason the energy of the Holy Spirit is referred to in both the singular and plural in Scripture, and the Savior calls it a "fountain" and "rivers". In this way, it divides into four principles, proceeds to all the virtues, and wholly renews the nature of the soul that participates in the Spirit, granting life (ψυχή) to it supernaturally, moving it towards all that is good and right, and bringing about its proper perfection (τελεσιουργοῦσα).

I understand that rock which was struck (πληγεῖσαν) by the lawgiver Moses's rod and supernaturally streamed forth (πηγάσασαν) waters (Ex. 17:1-7) to be the heart

---

[116] κατάνυξις. Usually translated "stupor" in the context of Romans 11:8, but often with the meaning of "contrition", "compunction", "sorrow on account of sin" in ascetical literature.

of stone which has become hardened out of stubbornness, and when God strikes it at the perfect moment, with His Word instead of a rod, it becomes contrite (καιρίως πλήξῃ καὶ κατανύξῃ), and the power of the Spirit springs forth freely. It then moves supernaturally like life-giving streams, assists in everything magnificently and vivifies, as it were, all the many and innumerable partakers of it in a way proper to each, while being one 'water' with respect to its nature. Furthermore, it is truly extraordinary how that rock that was carried on a single carriage (ἅμαξα) streamed forth water sufficient to fill a countless multitude of carriages.[117] Whence did it receive this power, and such a great power at that? And from what source did it gush forth while being transported? But then again, what is even more extraordinary to those who rightly consider the matter is that the vessel of the heart – such a small organ carried within such a small body – is able to receive a constant and boundless stream of *spirits* from the Holy Spirit, sufficient to give life to the innumerable bodies of the faithful.

Where does the heart receive a power so abundant, even immeasurable? Truly, as the Truth-Itself (αὐταλήθεια) has said, *The Spirit blows where He wills, and you hear the sound of Him, but cannot tell where He comes from and where He goes* (Jn. 3:8), yet He blows perpetually.

We have been granted to plant within ourselves a divine Paradise in imitation of God Himself (θεομιμήτως), one that cannot, indeed, be grasped by the external senses, but is intelligible and far superior, which brings abundant happiness and transcends every conception of anyone who has yet to experience this sacred dignity. Having received so great an honor from God, let us give ourselves fully to Christ God and the Holy Trinity, with reverence and true uprightness in faith, in perfect stillness and obedience to the commandments. By abiding in that condition, with our contemplation recollecting the aforementioned visions and divine perceptions (συλλεγούσης τὰ πρὶν εἰρημένα θεωρήματα και θεῖα νοήματα) and, as it were, insights in theology (θεολογήματα), and by 'planting' these in the heart by God's grace, let us persuade God with prayer that is fitting (ἐν προσευχῇ προσηκούσῃ), and with all our hearts, to grant the Holy Spirit to abide in us, causing divine and transcendent perceptions, or 'rivers', to stream forth. For as the Lord said, *He who believes in Me, as the Scripture has said, out of his heart will flow rivers of living water* (Jn. 7:38), and as the Beloved Disciple explains, *This He spoke concerning the Spirit, whom those believing in Him would receive* (Jn.

[117] This passage suggests that the rock in the wilderness was transported by the Israelites through the desert. Cf. 1 Cor. 10:4, where St. Paul mentions how the rock "followed" them, and Num. 20:1-13.

7:39). Now to Him who bestows gifts beyond understanding be the glory unto the ages.

On spiritual gifts.

16. Behold the generous gifts and graces that God has irrevocably and incomparably bestowed, and rejoice in the latter miracle that He has wrought, considering (ἀναλογιζόμενος) both the great things God did for that first-formed human Adam, and the things He afterwards did for us which exceed them. *He breathed the breath of life* (πνοὴν ζωῆς) – the grace of the Life-Giving Spirit (ζωοποιοῦ Πνεύματος)[118] – into Adam, and thus did Adam become a perfect man, for *man became a living soul* (Gen. 2:7), and not merely 'a soul'. For the Spirit of God is, of course, not the soul of man, but man becomes a 'living soul' through the Spirit. That is to say, the Holy and Life-Giving Spirit truly becomes life for the soul that lives as a rational and deiform (θεοειδής) soul should live. But if the Spirit of God does not coexist with the soul, or if He has woefully fled from it, then the divine form (τὸ θεοειδές) and the life befitting the rational soul is lost and replaced by a cattle-like or even a savage, bestial state. Indeed, when we are wholly apart from the Spirit of God and Christ *we can do nothing* of what we should, as the Savior has said (Jn. 15:5). Hence, Adam became a man lacking in nothing (ἀνελλιπής), that is, complete; not simply 'a soul', but *a living soul*, because God *breathed into him breath*, which is life for rational souls. And, as I mentioned before, this breath breathed into Adam, for as long as it was present in him, provided him with no small measure of glory and godlike brilliance (θεοείκελον εὔκλειαν), and as he participated in it, it granted him the power to perceive things with insight (διορατικῶς) and prophecy, and to be a true creator together with God, as a second god by grace, so that even the supremely-wise Creator of All was well pleased with Adam's exceedingly radiant visions and prophecies. Yet when he bent his knee and fell into error through the most wicked disobedience, then alas! the Life-Giving and Illuminating Holy Spirit fled far away, for Adam *did not understand* that he must guard so great an *honor*, and *he was made comparable to the senseless cattle, and became like them* (Ps. 48:13). Hence, he walked in a wholly ignorant and wayward manner, far from his divine purpose, and as if immersed in terrible darkness, he could not so much as raise his head since he was now left altogether desolate because of the departure of that divine and supernatural gift of breath which God had breathed into him.

---

[118] Note the similarity of the Greek Septuagint terms πνοή, "breath", and πνεῦμα, "Spirit", which can likewise be translated "breath"; noting this relation, St. Kallistos explains how the Holy Spirit is the Divine Person who uniquely provides the *breath of life* to man.

But later the time for God's compassion came, and He even *sent us His Word to heal us from our corruptions* (Ps. 106:20), and the Word contains the Spirit who bears witness to Him in Their shared nature, and thus the Spirit illuminates and reveals the divinity of the Word, or one might say, His power. The prophet spoke about these things, as in a confession to God on behalf of all mankind: *Send out Your light and Your truth; they have guided me and led me to Your holy mountain,* that is, ' up to Your simple and most high knowledge', *and to the tabernacles* (Ps. 42:3) of Your glory, that is, 'contemplations', to which the intellect is borne up by God to ascend and encamp, as it were, in these 'tabernacles', rising beyond visible things, and approaching in a wondrous manner the Most High God Himself. And since, as we mentioned, the True Word of our God came to us, naturally bearing with Him the Holy Spirit of God, since He Himself is the Holy Logos of God, it follows that all who have truly received the Word of God through faith simultaneously receive the Holy Spirit of God, who is eternally present with the Word without division. Again, not only do they receive Him externally, as Adam did in the beginning from God the Father, or as Christ's disciples later did when Christ breathed upon them (cf. Jn. 20:22), but invisibly and *suddenly,* as a *breath of wind* (πνοή) (cf. Acts 2:2), since this is of the Spirit (Πνεῦμα), and the Spirit's grace was blowing (πνέουσα) manifestly; and those who partake of this grace noetically behold the Spirit bursting forth from the heart as from an ever-flowing spring and indeed, as He illuminates, He gives the intellect the power to see the marvels of spiritual rebirth and divine glory, as far as this is possible. And in sum, when the intellect supernaturally participates in the Spirit through grace, it accordingly becomes a mystical contemplator of magnificent realities, and as it makes further progress by the abiding support and attraction of grace, it attains insights and foreknowledge by the illumination of the Spirit, and thus reascends to the rank of god (εἰς θεοῦ τάξιν); it sees how the hypostatic union of the divine nature with human nature has been realized in a manner beyond all understanding, as well as the outpouring of the Holy Spirit for all; this is a gift Adam did not see, nor was he made a *partaker of the divine nature* (2 Pet. 1:4) and a true adopted son of God (Θεοῦ θετός).

On divine and human energy, and on peace.

17. Let us now examine, to the best of our ability, the energy of the Holy Spirit and its effects, as well as our own natural energy and the things pertaining to it, and how it is hardly possible for us to acquire any peace through our own natural energy. For peace is truly a fruit of the Spirit's energy, and it is to this energy that true love and joy also belong (Gal. 5:22), as well as forbearance, kindness, and abundance of goodness and generosity towards one's neighbors through participation in the Spirit. Now, it is plain that none of our natural energies are

separated from the soul's own initiative (ὁρμή), which is clearly a certain part of the irascible part (θυμικόν) of the soul, and neither does any natural energy move without our will (θέλησις).[119] Moreover, the will naturally depends on appetite (ἐπιθυμία) for the practitioner, just as it depends on yearning (ἔφεσις) for the contemplative. Hence, no natural energy of ours can keep appetite and irascibility completely extinguished as long as it remains active, as is only natural. However, the supernatural energy of the Holy Spirit within the heart, which by no means owes its existence to nature, but rather manifests itself incomprehensibly to those who have received mercy,[120] and it moves and blazes forth quite independently of the will of man. That is why nothing is required of us for this energy – that is to say, the illumination or manifestation of the Spirit – other than for the partaker to look within the heart without commotion and to delight in it supernaturally. So then, since the divine energy has absolutely no need of our will or natural impulse in order to move, it is plain that appetite and anger will have to remain inactive and idle. And in short, the part of the soul subject to passions (τὸ παθητικόν) is set aside and rendered inactive when the supernatural inspiration of the Life-Giving Spirit is working (ἐνεργεῖν) within the heart, but then the intellect feels joy (εὐθυμεῖν) and life.[121] And in this way, with peace, tranquility, and all the dispassion (ἀπάθεια) befitting it, the soul truly contemplates God – thus acquiring a wondrous relation to Him[122] – and attains illumination and ascent by the Spirit, of whom it has become a partaker through the grace of God. It then sees that it has reached knowledge of the inexpressible and dazzling beauty of divine loveliness (ὡραιότης), and so loves the surpassingly beautiful God, and speechlessly rejoices in so great and infinite and limitless and incomprehensible a Father of our Lord, and knows Him even from the present time as its inheritance by His unspeakable divine mercy. And then it enjoys a wonderful peace, since it sees that, through the grace of God, it is by no means deprived of the Ultimate Beauty beyond intellect. And because, as we mentioned, anger is made inactive through the self-moving activity (αὐτοκίνητον ἐνέργεια) of the Comforter, the soul's constitution is thus filled with forbearance and kindness and greater goodness – these being the fruit of the Holy Spirit (Gal. 5:22) – and those who have received mercy partake of Him. But, in contrast, the spirit of delusion and falsehood, even if it seems to move in

---

[119] θέλησις does not just mean "will", but also "desire"; i.e. the whole human being is characterized by the desire for life.

[120] τοῖς ἠλεημένοις. Perhaps an allusion to the Jesus Prayer, in which the faithful pray for, and receive, Jesus' mercy.

[121] There is a subtle wordplay in the Greek: when ἐπιθυμία "appetite" and θυμός "irascibility", the two lower parts of Plato's model of the tripartite soul are made inactive, then the intellect feels joy (εὐθυμεῖ).

[122] Note how the phrase πρὸς Θεὸν θεωρεῖ is immediately followed by the clause σχοῦσα θαυμαστῶς σχέσιν πρὸς Θεόν. According to Kataphygiotes *On Union with God*, 2, 19, contemplation (θεωρία) is the activity that God (Θεός) is named after, and so the intellect that seeks likeness with Him must be contemplative.

the soul apart from the will and initiative of the person who possesses it, brings neither calmness nor gives the passible (παθητικόν) part of the soul any peace, but instead agitates it all the more, and does not produce (ἐνεργεῖ) love for God, nor joy, nor peace. For falsehood is disorderly and incoherent and completely alien to the peace and serenity of God.

18. O Lord, I stand in awe of the gladsome light of this wonderful peace.[123] It brings a supremely restful repose, is dearly beloved, exquisite by nature, most graceful, and exceedingly radiant; this light alone is the perfect life of the intellect. O almighty Holy Sovereign, I marvel that man, to whom You have reached out by Your ineffable touch in Your infinite goodness, still lives wholly for himself and not for You (cf. 2 Cor. 5:15), the super-essential and Life-Giving Life and Source of all goodness and beauty. Indeed, if the woman who simply touched You, and not Your body but just Your garment, O Savior, and not even Your whole garment but merely its hem – despite the fact that this was done in secret – was immediately relieved from such a grievous illness and her health was restored beyond hope (cf. Mt. 9:21-2), then, O my King, what miracle will occur to the person to whom You in Your goodness have reached out by Your divine inexpressible touch, O Savior, and to whom You have manifested and shown Your wondrous mercy? Indeed, what life will this person live, and to whom will they dedicate such a life? We know that when you touched the hand of Peter's mother-in-law, her fever was suddenly extinguished, and she became perfectly healthy, immediately arose, and began serving You with great amazement and eagerness (cf. Mk. 1:30-31). But first, this woman was touched only once, and second, this occurred outwardly, through her hand. If she became completely whole in this way, then what miracle will be worked in those whom You ineffably touch, not just once, but constantly, by day and by night, and not just outwardly, but in the innermost chamber of the heart, O dearest Lover of Souls, and of course those whom You strengthen in trials, exhort to do what is right, and grant myriads of good and beautiful things? How then, O Most High, can such people live for themselves rather than living with all their hearts for You, as is right? Or again, how could those who live for You alone not consider themselves wretched and bow down with humility, in seeing how they have failed to earn even the slightest reward despite the exceedingly great and extraordinary assistance of Your grace?

Glory to You, O truly Glorified One, who glorifies the humble-minded, and by glorifying them makes them all the humbler, since they are indebted to You for Your many, infinite, and ineffable gifts unto them. And hence, bestowing Your

---

[123] An allusion to the evening hymn Φῶς Ἱλαρόν "O Gladsome Light" chanted at vespers in the Orthodox Church.

grace on them because of their humility, by some miracle they find You firmly rooted in their hearts, as they are glorified. For You, O Wisdom of God, have said clearly in the books of Solomon, that *I have rooted Myself in a glorified people*, in a manner beyond all understanding. And further, *Like a cedar in Lebanon I was raised high* (ὑψώθην) (Sir. 24:12-13) – in the heart, that is. And this means, You utterly transcend lowly and earthly things, and by manifesting Yourself from a divine height (ὕψος), or *mountain*, that is, from the height of divine perceptions, You say, *I have stretched out My branches like a terebinth tree*, extending them to those in whom You have been rooted through the grace of the Spirit; *And My branches are branches of glory and grace* (Sir. 24:16). This is of course perfectly true, O Lord, who are the Truth-Itself; for this reason the pure soul which has chosen to become Your bride *has desired You* with such great chastity and *sat under Your shade*; and as soon as she sits in Your shade she realizes how *sweet Your fruit is*, and not just in point of fact, but by having tasted it *on her tongue* (Song 2:3); for all have not attained the sensation (αἴσθησις) of the sweetness of God – on the contrary, as is clear when He says, *I gave a scent as of cinnamon and aspalathus, and I spread a sweet fragrance as choice myrrh*, that is, He does not grant this experience to everyone.[124] And Paul would go on to express this by saying that he, while being one and the same person, became *to some the aroma of death leading to death, and to others the aroma of life leading to life* (2 Cor. 2:16). So likewise, both the divine "sweetness", if you like, as well as the glory of God, are not manifested to everyone, but only to those few who are endowed with noetic senses (αἰσθήσεις νοεραί), that is to say, to those who practice stillness and who have consciously attained, by God's goodwill, participation in the Life-Giving and Illuminating Spirit, and generally to those *who have been purified in heart* as far as this is possible (cf. Mt. 5:8). For, as is only reasonable, a tumultuous and impure life without any manifest participation in the Spirit is far from being worthy of the glory of God, and especially from receiving the sensation of His *scent* and *sweetness* in the soul. Indeed, it is far from that. Hence the need for flight from the world, and seclusion and stillness: to be cloistered, to engage in a proper virtuous life, and to practice watchfulness, prayer with attention, and all else that is practiced by those who are truly repentant; these things are done so as to give space to the unsurpassable goodness of divine compassion, that it may incline with love towards mankind as it desires, and dwell within the soul that diligently seeks it; all so that this wondrous mercy may be shown, and – O God, what grace! – that it may become one spirit with the soul, rooted in the depths of the heart, shining from within miraculously, and forming, as it were, a tree that rises to a lofty height, broadens the branches of the intellect, and bears spiritual fruits, such as *love, joy, peace, long-suffering, goodness, and gentleness* (Gal. 5:22), and brings forth myriads of other good and beautiful things that nourish the partaker of the Spirit.

---

[124] The word *choice* (ἐκλεκτή) here also means *elect*, in the sense of the spiritually *chosen* people.

How great will you understand this glory to be when you have judged these things aright; how delightful a fragrance and sensation of sweetness do these pure fruits of the Life-Giving and Illuminating Spirit bring to the tongue of the soul! Therefore, truly *blessed are* those who are *pure in heart* through knowledge and practice of the virtues, *for they shall see God* (Mt. 5:8), in a more complete and manifest way in the life to come, but even in the present as a *foretaste* (Eph. 1:14), according to the Scriptures, which indicate not only that they see and *shall see*, but also that they will experience (πάσχειν) supernatural things in a manner appropriate to each, just as they even now experience and enjoy them in part by the grace of Christ.

On the contemplative life, and what the contemplative requires; prayer is an aspect of contemplation; the Fathers count contemplation as prayer.

19. The contemplative life is the co-dweller and constant companion of sacred prayer, and they are two divinely favored (θεοχαρίτωτοι) and deifying (θεοποιοί) blossoms of the noetic part of the soul. Hence these works are truly inseparable from the soul that is divinely borne up (θεοφορουμένης) and rightly (ἐν θεσμῷ) divinized (θεουργουμένης) by God.[125] And indeed, for this reason contemplation and prayer are so closely united that the Fathers refer to them both by the single term, "the action (πρᾶξις) and contemplation (θεωρία) of the intellect." And so, as St. Isaac says, "The action of the intellect is found in its work of refinement, in continual meditation on God, in unceasing prayer, and the like. This is performed in the desiring part (ἐπιθυμητικόν) of the soul, and it is called contemplation." Can you think of any indication of unity that better shows the union of prayer and contemplation? This is why he also adds that this contemplation purifies the soul's energy of love, which is a natural yearning (ἐπιπόθησις) that refines the noetic part of the soul. You may understand this as one single energy of the contemplative part of the soul, that is, of both prayer and contemplation. Hence, St. Maximos also explains this by saying, "The intellect cannot be purified without contemplation of God and fellowship (ὁμιλίας) with Him in prayer." And also, "Departure from the world, contemplation, and prayer diminish desire and then eradicate it." Again, "The rational part of the soul moves properly when it is drawn toward God through spiritual contemplation and prayer." Furthermore, "Give wings to the rational part of the soul through reading, contemplation, and prayer." Thus, contemplation is altogether necessary and is a companion of prayer, and both belong to the intellect, or rather, they are the natural and proper energy of the rational part of the soul, and are inseparable from each other; the intellect performs this activity as long as it is healthy, and action and contemplation assist each other when the rational part of

---

[125] This profusion of words beginning with θεο- is likely related to the association of contemplation (θεωρία) with God (Θεός).

the soul is sound and engaged in the practice of stillness with knowledge and experience. This is why the Fathers refer to the intellect that prays without the contemplative faculty as "a bird without wings" (ὄρνις ἄπτερος), since it cannot truly ascend to God with its entire disposition, nor can it wholly abandon earthly things to approach heavenly ones with all the strength of the soul. According to St. Maximos, "Contemplation purifies the intellect, while the perfect state of prayer presents it stripped before God." And it is clear that the latter occurs through the purification bestowed by contemplation, which the intellect cannot acquire unless it rises to the contemplation of God as it ought. For, he says, the intellect is rendered pure through the revelation of mysteries. Then, the purity of the intellect is perfection in the returning motion (ἐν τῇ ἀναστροφῇ) of heavenly contemplation, which moves beyond the senses by the spiritual power of the world above, which is filled with unfathomable wonders. From this we see that the contemplative prays in a manner that is quite sublime and becomes pure in mind through the practice and knowledge of contemplation; and because of this purity, he sees God without his mortal eyes (ἀνομμάτως), inasmuch as this is possible, and is made truly blessed in prayer.

On the verse, "God is Spirit, and those who worship Him must worship in spirit and truth" (Jn. 4:24).

20. The Scripture says, *God is Spirit, and those who worship Him must worship in spirit and truth* (Jn. 4:24); Christ says '*those* who worship Him' in the plural, and not the singular, '*he* who worships Him.' And this is most fitting to Him who *desires that all men be saved and come to the knowledge of the truth* (1 Tim. 2:4), who has prepared many different *mansions* for our residence (Jn. 14:2) to be eternally enjoyed by those who shall be justified, who is the *Messenger of Great Counsel* (Is. 9:5-6), the Savior, who out of His great love for mankind opens His hands to the wise, the unwise, the weak in speech (cf. Ex. 4:10), and the more dull-witted of us. And accordingly He explains all at once the one salvation to all human beings, how it is brought about in a variety of manners and completed in many different ways, that is, depending on the condition (ἕξις) and free will (προαίρεσις) of each person, and, I might add, in accordance with their strength; and of course they must follow the teaching of a guide, someone who is himself drawing near to God and has chosen to worship Him as I have said. For oftentimes a person who does not have a teacher, despite having a good nature, fails to achieve his perfect purpose in God. On the other hand, some are prevented from reaching perfection because of their lack of a good disposition, despite having a teacher experienced in divine and spiritual things. Nevertheless, both the latter and the former, and in short, everyone, can *worship God in spirit and truth* if they wish, according to their own particular station (τάξις) and strength, and one must say, according to the gifts

which they have received from the God of all. And so, even someone who is uneducated, as long as he walks according to the commandments and faith, and humbly follows experienced leaders, it is clear that such a person truly *worships God in spirit and truth.* For faith is indeed spirit, since it speaks clearly about God and divine and invisible realities. For Christ says, *The words that I speak to you are spirit, and they are life* (Jn. 6:63). These are the marvellous and deifying commandments of Truth-Itself, and I think no one is so dull of mind as to wish to set these apart from the truth even in the slightest. So then, the person who follows the faith, as mentioned, in truth and in spirit, and teaches about matters of faith in God, is called a practitioner and a contemplator. Again, like the others, the person who is occupied with the knowledge of creation and Holy Scripture, and then is gathered to God, proceeds in a certain manner from the visible and verbal to the noetic – as it were, from *the flesh* to *the Spirit* – and thence directly ascends to what is beyond intellect, and even beyond all truth, to God; it is obvious that such a person *worships God in spirit and truth.* Again, as for those who chant and pray, as long as they pay attention to the meaning of the words they chant and pray, and feel them as much as possible, then they also altogether *worship God in truth and in spirit.* For it is clear that the sacred words of the Psalms, chants, and prayers are *spirit and truth.* Again, the person who through manifest participation and assistance in the Spirit sees God in a concentrated manner, that is, simply and without eyesight, by the light of knowledge, *worships God in truth and in spirit* even more sublimely. Moreover, in addition to these examples, the person who reflects the light of the glory and economy[126] of Christ within himself as far as possible, and subsequently experiences the outpouring of the Holy Spirit through Christ from the Father which inspires and comforts the faithful, truly *worships God in truth and in spirit*, in Christ Jesus.

On prayer.

21. God is *He that teaches man knowledge*, as it is written (Ps. 93:10). But how does He teach? By *granting prayer to him who prays* by the Spirit's holy inspiration, which blows unstintingly and manifestly (cf. 1 King. 2:9). For indeed this sacred prayer, being a great gift of such exceedingly generous grace, becomes a teacher to him who has acquired it, rendering him a wholly pure mirror for the face of the soul, as it were, by which the intellect may clearly see the deviation, wandering, captivity, negligence, and deception it is prone to; but not only these, for it also sees the air of purity, the radiance of contemplation, the spirit of divine and godly ascent to God, the fiery flame of divine eros, noetic simplicity and formlessness, and subsequently a silence away from all things and an immensely

[126] οἰκονομία. Jesus Christ's Incarnation and the plan of salvation.

joyful wonderment. To summarize, by prayer the intellect comes to see and surely know the different states of the soul and the influence of the passions, and it is initiated into a clear understanding of the primary causes of the motivating principles of the soul; it mends some and carefully tends to others, depending on which of them require his care or repair. And hence it attains the experienced monastic life, having learning from experience acquired through discipline (ἄσκησις), and not only by using the intellect and reason, as well as mind and sense as it should, but also by acquiring discernment to provide what is needful to the irascible and appetitive parts of the soul, and generally it will learn to unite the melodic and graceful harmony of the soul's faculties well and truly with the indispensable knowledge of the mind, and to raise through practice and contemplation a noetic melody more delightful than any other. For this reason the much-desired peace of God, the grace-filled joy that accompanies it, and holy love come to dwell in the initiate of true prayer who is arrayed with the fruits of the Spirit. Hence, the person who has resolved to *pray* by all means and in every manner and *without ceasing*, as the Apostle Paul says (1 Thess. 5:17), and has applied the greatest effort to accomplish this, will be ranked among the disciples of Christ, since he has followed their instructions regarding sacred prayer; such a person has been made a child of grace in Christ.

On the things necessary for prayer and how it is worthy of such great honor.

22. If sacred spiritual prayer were simply a teacher and instructor in the obligations pertaining to virtue, as we have mentioned above, would it not still be worthy of great praise? But seeing now that it not only teaches and instructs but also naturally exhorts towards all that is good, what praises and honors will not fall short of it and fail to reach its lofty height? Furthermore, considering that both teaching and exhortation can be ineffectual because of the weakness of the person who is being taught or exhorted, and hence strength is needed to counteract this, *seek and you will find* that only prayer can empower the soul to be spiritually active – such and so great is the power of prayer among the virtuous, and understandably so. For inspired and, I might say, "living" (ζῶσα) prayer moves and gushes unceasingly from the heart through the manifest participation and energy of the Life-Giving Spirit, and hence it has the following three crucial aspects: instruction in the virtues that are befitting to spiritual people, exhortation and comfort for those who put them into practice amidst their struggles, and above all, the power that makes these commandments light (ἐξευμαρίζουσαν), even when they are difficult. Therefore our Lord, the Giver of the Spirit, says, *You shall receive power when the Holy Spirit has come upon you* (Acts 1:8). Again He literally calls this power

"comforting"[127] (παράκλητον) when He says, *But the Comforter, the Holy Spirit, whom the Father will send in My name, He will teach you all things, and bring to your remembrance all things that I said to you* (Jn. 14:26). The teaching of St. Paul moreover expresses clearly that the manifestation of the Spirit is granted to each person through prayer for the sake of spiritual benefit, and that to one is given the spirit of wisdom, to another knowledge, to yet another healings, along with the other gifts mentioned by the Apostle; *and one and the same Spirit works all these things, distributing to each one uniquely as He wills* (1 Cor. 12:11). Again, it becomes clear from the sacred words of the Lord mentioned above that to him who has in any way become a partaker of the gift of the Spirit, there must follow these three things, namely, power beyond nature, teaching beyond this world, and divine consolation. Besides, when the Lord says, *Without Me you can do nothing* (Jn. 15:5), it shows beyond any doubt that divine power is needed for whatever action we are required to fulfill. Moreover, when He says, *Do not call anyone on earth your Teacher; for One is your Teacher and Guide, the Christ* (Mt. 23:7-10), it makes it clear to all that man requires divine instruction concerning the deeds that are proper and pleasing to God. And when He consoles and strengthens the disciples by saying, *I will pray to the Father, and He will send you another Comforter, that He may abide with you forever* (Jn. 14:9), remember that this consolation is completely necessary and inseparable from grace. It has thus been demonstrated that there are many differences within the one distribution of spiritual gifts; for wisdom is one kind of gift, while knowledge is another; prophecy is not the same as the first two, while the gifts of healing are yet another kind, and to put it briefly, all the gifts of the Holy Spirit, as the Apostle lists them (1 Cor. 12:8-9), are distinguished from each other. Nevertheless, every kind of grace of the Spirit is adorned by the three aforementioned energies of the Life-Giving Spirit. For how can a created intellect, bound to the body, become a communicant of noetic things and virtue if it has not received a power beyond heaven, to participate in a reality that not even the angels have reached? Without the initiation of the Spirit, how can it participate in transcendent realities? It is clear that it will grow dizzy (ἰλλιγιάσει) trying to attain such a great height of divine generosity and applying itself in the severe strain of virtue, unless it receives the sacred consolation of the Good. What should we then conclude about prayer which, through the empowerment of the Holy Spirit, procures every manner of spiritual gift for the soul, bearing within itself the power and teaching and comfort of the Holy Spirit? Of what praises is such prayer not supremely worthy, and how greatly should it be honored by those who have acquired it through grace? How

---

127 Παράκλητος can be translated "exhorter," "comforter", "advocate", "helper", and the verb παρακαλέω brings out an even richer array of meanings: "console," "exhort", "appeal", "entreat", etc. Hence, the activity of the Holy Spirit, the Comforter, provides assistance to the Christian in every way.

much should it be sought after by those who are still bereft of it, for it binds the intellect to God with sacred bonds, in Christ Jesus, the true Son of God!

On prayer.

23. When by grace the intellect acquires a clear conception of God, through proper study of the things around God (τῶν περὶ Θεόν) and the aid and inspiration of the Life-Giving Spirit, let it examine itself and its own weakness: how far short it falls of what is right owing to its negligence, its forgetfulness of duties, and consequently its ignorance of the things that are truly befitting to it. And thus, after you have engaged justly and honestly in the work of self-condemnation and become humble in spirit, let the intellect then approach God through prayer, with a humble mind and with conviction and hope founded upon God's incomprehensible love for man in His ineffable goodness; it is because of this exceeding love that we are taught by St. Paul to *approach the throne of grace with boldness* (Heb. 4:16). For God is not wont to do things as we do them, but rather does them according to His own infinite mercy. Thus, at the time of prayer let us not turn towards ourselves, but rather towards the long-suffering and most-compassionate power of our exceedingly good God and Father, that we may thus easily acquire in ourselves His divine and truly saving eros.

On the verse, "'God said to Abram, "Depart from your land"'" (Gen. 12:1); on contemplation.

24. *God said to Abram*, that is, 'the migrant' (τῷ περάτῃ),[128] "*Depart from your country, and from your kindred, and from your father's house, and come to the land that I will show you* (Gen. 12:1), *a land flowing with milk and honey*" (Ex. 33:3). Here God is also speaking with a more sublime meaning to the intellect that has become a migrant and passes from sensible things to intelligible ones: "Depart from your sense-perception, from sensible things, and from the whole visible world completely, and come to the land that I will show you"; and this is undoubtedly similar to what the Lord says: *Sell all your possessions and give to the poor*, and *take up your cross,* that is, "be crucified from the senses and sensible things and the whole world", *and come, follow Me* (Mk. 10:21), "as I ascend to the Father, not without the *guiding Spirit*" (cf. Ps. 50:14). For indeed in that passage it also says, *God said to Abram,* meaning that the Father spoke to him through the Word, that is, the Son. And further, *and come to the land that I will show you,* and we are

---

[128] Abram is called a "migrant" (Gen. 14:13), lit. "someone from the other side", possibly referring to the land on the other side of the Euphrates River, which he crossed when he came to the land of Canaan. The LXX renders the Hebrew term literally as περάτης, the term used by St. Kallistos here.

accustomed to showing things by pointing with the finger; and the Spirit of God has been called 'the finger of God', according to which it says, *But if I cast out demons by the finger of God* (Lk. 11:20), while in another gospel it says, *by the Spirit of God* (Mt. 12:28). Hence this is what the wise men among the Egyptians called the activity of the Spirit, saying, *This is the finger of God* (Ex. 8:15). He says, *To the land that I will show you*, as if to say, "to the place I shall lead you by My Word and Spirit;" and, *To a land flowing with milk and honey*, that is, to the understanding of God and to the proper knowledge of Him, to which the intellect cannot arrive in any other way, unless its path is brightened and it is enlightened by the illumination of the Life-Giving Spirit, reflected through the Son. For after the intellect has become accustomed to turning from evils and striving for intelligible things, God who loves mankind draws it, like another Abram, to pass (διαπεραιοῦσθαι) from sensible things to noetic ones and beyond, where there is the unified vision and contemplation of the Divinity in three Hypostases, and God of course causes and manifests this by the triune power and energy of the Divine Monarchy. For the God and Father Himself is precisely that Promised Land which *the meek shall inherit* (Mt. 5:5), together with those who are upright in heart, according to the promise we received from the Holy Spirit, and they will become inheritors by striving for it in hope. *A land flowing with milk and honey*, that is, the primal Lights (τὰ πρωινὰ φῶτα), the twin Rays, the life and delight and purification of the whole world. For, on the one hand, the Son who is begotten of the Father and inseparable from Him, could in a way be called 'honey' because His Incarnation is like a honeycomb by which the whole human race is sweetened, and indeed wondrously is it delighted – or how might this be expressed? – by His sublime teachings and graces, and all His other goods and countless beauties. On the other hand, the Holy Spirit is 'milk', being simple in form, not begotten, but proceeding from the Father, luminously bright like the whiteness of milk and nourishing infants to become rational by divine nourishment, since to such belongs the entrance into the Kingdom of Heaven, as the Lord has said (cf. Mt. 18:3; Lk. 10:21). Hence 'the land flowing with milk and honey' can be quite reasonably contemplated as the Father and the Son and the Holy Spirit – the land to which the intellect is really transported, having become a "migrant", according to Scripture, through the guidance, power, and energy of the Trihypostatic Divinity. For just as, according to St. Paul, *No one can say that Jesus is Lord except by the Holy Spirit* (1 Cor. 12:3), likewise no one can concentrate the noetic power of his soul on the simple glory and magnificence of the Triadic Unity and gaze upon It without the power, energy, and grace of the Trinity, by rejecting the sensible things that enter through the senses – ultimately even by transcending the intelligible things contemplated in Scripture – and by departing from all earthly things. For indeed in this way, *In Your light* – God's light, that is to say, "In Your unique radiance" – *we shall see light* (Ps. 35:10), that is, "we shall see You, who illumine our hearts and intellects"; and once we have experienced contemplation, we will come to know "Thine own of Thine own" (τὰ σά ... ἐκ τῶν σῶν),[129] so that *no flesh may boast* that it has achieved this by itself (cf. 1 Cor. 1:29). And hence he who was previously called 'Abram' – which signifies that he was a 'migrant' – after he left his country when he heard [the voice of God], forsook everything as commanded, and moved to the land flowing with milk and honey, was renamed 'Abraham', which means 'father of many nations'. Likewise, the intellect which is worthy to be called a 'migrant' because, by the power and energy of the Trihypostatic Divinity, it has transported itself from sensible things, sensation, and the entire world to the unified radiance, contemplation, and vision of the Holy Trinity, also becomes a father and producer (προβολεύς) of many great and ineffable and mystical conceptions, like *many nations*, and other such extraordinary things are revealed and born to it. Then it rejoices, exults, and delights in these, just as a father in his children, and thus acquires peace in Christ.

On humility and contemplation.

25. Wonderful are Your works, O Lord, and my soul becomes ecstatic in comprehending them. The cause of the exaltation of the intellect becomes the ultimate motivation for humility, and that which infinitely exalts the soul is precisely what exceedingly humbles it. For the beginning of contemplation is humility, and the perfection of humility is contemplation. Even if one knows all the wisdom of this world, without humility it is impossible for him to acquire the contemplation which exalts (ὑψοποιὸν θεωρίαν). I call it "contemplation which exalts" to distinguish it from the contemplation that the Greeks had, which did not exalt. Without contemplation which exalts, it is impossible for man to humble himself, even if he *bends down his neck like a ring* (Is. 58:5).

O the ineffable wisdom of Him who created us so wisely! Who could ever conceive of such a thing before having seen it, that is, how the highest exaltation arises from humility, and how supreme humility comes from the highest exaltation? One might perhaps even say regarding the godlike (θεοειδής) intellect that *he who has descended is also the one who ascended*, and to add to this that he who has ascended is also the one who descended (cf. Eph. 4:10). For when with understanding and humility the intellect attains the highest things through grace, exulting and rejoicing in realities beyond reason as if they were its own, it then lowers itself beneath all things in its humility. For as David says, *O Lord, my heart would not have been exalted or my eyes raised high, neither would I have been brought to things great or wonderful for me, unless I had been humble-minded* (Ps.

[129] Divine Liturgy of St. John Chrysostom.

130:1-2).[130] And in addition to this, the intellect might also possibly say the reverse: "O Lord I would not have humbled myself, or afflicted and called myself '*earth and ashes*,' (Gen. 18:27) unless my heart had been exalted and my eyes raised high and I had been brought to things great and so wonderful for me." O wondrous Creator and King! You fill my heart with ecstasy when I consider the work of Your wisdom, the intellect, and how it has been created to be so wise by Your providence.

On the same.

26. At first, when the intellect returns to God with the help of grace, it is possessed by a state of self-blame (κατέχεται καταστάσει καταγνώσεως). This is also why the person who possesses this intellect grieves in mourning and cries out with laments, afflicting his heart as much as he can bear, purifying its impassioned condition all the day long, and humbling himself as is proper, not without great sorrow; and when by the gift of Christ he has achieved purification by means of the stillness proper to him, noetically perceives intelligible realities, is raised up to God and His glory and steadfastly looks to it, he then reaches a second self-blame of the intellect that comes after the first; this self-blame is abundant and inevitable, great, continuous, and constant. Moreover, from this state he acquires a humility that is truly more secure and pure, so much so that even if it were possible for all men publicly to pronounce blessings upon him, he would still genuinely see himself in the conscience of his soul as lower than every one of them, or rather, not just lower than everyone, but even as less than nothing, for even that which does not exist at least does not sin, while he, on the other hand, perceives himself sinning continually. And although he is in this state and consequently continues to humble himself, he nevertheless greatly rejoices and exults, not of course in himself (for how could such a thing be possible for someone who constantly blames himself for sinning?), but rather in the Most-Compassionate God who is nearer to him than his very breath (μᾶλλον τῆς σφετέρας πνοῆς ἐγγίζοντι αὐτῷ), or to put it more clearly, to Him who produces in his heart flowing streams of heavenly light and unceasing rivers of the wonders of the Spirit, who illumines the intellect, and all but says to him outright, *I am with you* (Jer. 1:8). Thus God manifestly reveals mysteries to him as to a friend, and fills him with joy. Indeed, it then occurs to him to proclaim the words of David: *He has not dealt with us according to our iniquities, nor rewarded us according to our sins* (Ps. 102:10), and so on, and the words of Paul, *By grace we are saved* (Eph. 2:5), even if he truly carries out all the divine commandments to the best of his ability, and hates

[130] This passage from the LXX Psalms poses some difficulties for translation, but our rendering reflects the exegesis of Angelikoudes, who emphasizes how spiritual exaltation and humility compliment each other.

every unrighteous path with all his might, and altogether strives not to neglect any of the things that lead to salvation, insofar as this is possible. He who has not consciously perceived himself to be discerning and experiencing the above has not yet touched upon true contemplation or wept unceasing tears; nor has he beheld *the unity of faith* (Eph. 2:13) and *the understanding of the truth* (1 Tim. 2:4); he does not truly see divine glory, nor indeed what lies beyond human affairs; or rather, simply put, he does not have knowledge of the divine and human reasons (λόγοι) underlying reality.

On contemplation.

27. Creation with its intelligible realities and Scripture with its spiritual realities bear witness to the glory, kingdom, wisdom, power, and the overall magnificence of God. But to what extent does each of these things bear witness, and to what exactly do they witness? In fact, their testimony is remarkably small, like a drop in the ocean (ἐκ πελάγους ῥανίδα). For God does not, if I may say so, manifest Himself absolutely and activate all His power, or wisdom, or glory and magnificence in all the things He has made, even if they appear to us magnificent and glorious, full of wisdom and power. Anything but! He did not consider His own, but provided exactly what was necessary out of the abundance of His goodness. He decided to what extent [creation would be filled], and precisely as He decided he let it come to be, in an exceedingly harmonious and well-proportioned manner, and to the degree that was necessary for man to dwell, live, and flourish therein, so that it would be commensurate to man's use and enjoyment. When He formed the one Adam, He did so contemplating the whole multitude of human beings. And even now it is possible to see that the earth is neither lacking in resources, nor is there any shortage of human beings who dwell upon it. For the earth has maintained its proportion for those things which exist below, just as the sky, the sun, the air, and the sea come to be in balanced proportion to the earth. And indeed these things maintain amongst themselves the due proportion given to them by God, who knew all things before they existed and disposed all things with the order and power proper to everything, granting proportion and harmony to each of them. For indeed, had the Creator not caused the creation of beings only for the sake of what was needed, but according to His own power, wisdom, glory, and magnificence, then perhaps rather than one world, you would see an infinite number of them. Or perhaps not worlds such as the one we see now, but ones which are strange, supernatural, and beyond comprehension, and their beauty and brilliant complexity would be such that the soul could hardly bear their glory and brilliance, but would forsake the body in astonishment.

God willed to make one work – the human being – the king of everything on earth, even as another god set over the creations of God, and He produced this world easily and instantaneously for man's needs.[131] For instance, as one of the prophets says, *He who has made the earth as nothing, and hangs the earth upon nothing* (cf. Is. 40:23; Job 26:7). And another says, *He stretches out the heavens in the highest like a curtain* (Ps. 103:2). And the fact that He simply *looks upon the earth* and it is shaken with trembling (Ps. 103:32) – what great abundance of power does this show! Hence He brought all visible things into being by His word alone, while the more glorious and sublime things are reserved for a later age, those things which in order for the soul to bear to see them, it is poured at death into the crucible (διὰ χωνείας) of the tomb and is made a new man for new realities, delights, and visions, while the things we now see are like a kind of shadow and, one might say, a long, drawn-out dream. And should you wish to be assured of this, look to the splendid noetic order of angels if you have such strength, and you shall certainly behold there beauty, glory, wisdom, and power such that are not only impossible to describe, but cannot even be conceived of; even though that angelic world was arranged just by a single conception of God, with all the immense complexity and marvellous realities that exist there. If such things came to be by a single thought, what would possibly happen if the entire will, wisdom, and power of God were brought to bear? But again, how could we even have access to such a thing, that is, how would it be possible for us to conceive of the infinite? For there is no end to the infinite, and for that which has no end, there is no movement, but rather the overabundance, so to speak (and this only in part), of the energy that comes from the power that proceeds from God's essence. And therefore, even all the testimony that creation and Scripture present to us concerning God, when compared to His power, is like a dim and tiny drop in the fathomless and boundless sea. Nevertheless, I still consider it worthy for us to attain knowledge of this spiritual drop of water, and thus, by spreading our intellect from the beauty, glory, and delight of the contemplation of this droplet out to the infinite, and worthily praising Him who is infinitely beyond infinity infinitely many times, as far as we are able, let us be united to Him in unity beyond the world, becoming ourselves simple, infinite, and invisible intellects in imitation of the angels, with ineffable gladness and joy of heart and exultation, by the energy and grace of the Spirit. Amen.

On the practitioner and the contemplative.

28. He who engages in the practical life cannot help but chant while taking care to cultivate the meekness and vigilance suited to practitioners. But the contemplative

---

[131] According to patristic interpretations of Gen. 1:1, the whole universe was created instantaneously *ex nihilo* before being formed in various ways in the six days of creation. Cf. Gregory Palamas, *Topics of Natural and Theological Science*, 21 (Philokalia Vol. 4).

cannot chant, or, at any rate, he has no desire to. He cannot do so when he has received the energy of divine grace and is utterly filled with divine delight in silence, rejoicing in the quietness and stillness of his heart. Again, he has no wish to chant when he contemplates one single thing and moves the noetic aspect of his soul to activity among unmoving (ἀμεταβάτοις) and peaceful perceptions in deep tranquillity. Hence, it is necessary for the contemplative to carry out the act of divine vision in contemplative silence, and if he ever appears to be occupied with reading something, this should come as no surprise to those who consider the mutability of the intellect and the complexity and changeableness of our nature. Yet we must understand this, that the interruption of the contemplation that comes through grace, that is, reading, is inferior to the act of contemplation, whether it is done for its own sake (καθ' ἑαυτήν) or for the sake of liberating the intellect, since the intellect cannot avoid being divided while engaging in any kind of reading. However, with the noetic freedom that is celebrated mystically in silence, the intellect sees, for the most part, in a unified manner – a state completely different from that of division. And is it not true even regarding sensible things that it is far superior to see something than to hear it? For as everyone says and admits, "The eyes are more trustworthy than the ears" (ὀφθαλμοί … ὠτίων πιστότεροι). And so, what applies to the case of sensible things, applies to that of intelligible ones as well: to see, that is to say, to contemplate an intelligible thing, is far superior to hearing about it, which is what readers do. Again, the Samaritan woman, after conversing with the True Word, proclaimed His divinity to her fellow citizens, but afterwards, when the Word went to their city out of the exceeding abundance of His goodness and deemed its inhabitants worthy to meet Him, they said they no longer required the testimony of the woman to recognize the divinity of the Word (cf. Jn. 4:42).

It is quite similar when the mind externally gives evidence regarding divinity to the soul and its powers through the discourse of reason; but when the soul, along with all of its powers, receives the vision of the divinity of the Word through grace, then the soul no longer requires external evidence. For everyone who hears needs to confirm what he hears by seeing it too; yet he who sees has no need for someone to teach him about what he sees, as long as he is truly reckoned to be one of those *who have eyes to see* (cf. Mt. 13:16). We can see this in the case of Thomas as well, who heard, yet did not believe, but rather said, *Unless I see, I will not believe* (Jn. 20:25). However, as soon as he saw Jesus, he immediately proclaimed as *Lord and God* (Jn. 20:28) the very One whom he did not believe before seeing Him, and confessed this truth of his own accord. And that which Thomas did not possess in hearing, that is, faith, this did he acquire as soon as he beheld Him. Hence, from this we must discern how contemplation is as superior to practice as the intellect is superior to sense perception.

On the same.

29. Both the infant (νήπιος) and the one who is mature (ἐνακμάζων) in age drink milk, but the infant does so to be nourished, while the adult does so for pleasure. Likewise, the practitioner engages in reading psalms, and the contemplative seems to do the same. However, the former does so to strengthen and fortify his soul, while the contemplative does so for the joy of his heart, and also to provide rest to the fire-bearing, tear-streaming, striving motion of his heart up to God. For even if the spirit in him leaps up and is made *willing* by the rays of divine splendor and *is transfigured from glory to glory* (2 Cor. 3:18) and grows stronger, nevertheless, the composite [nature] of the flesh and the earthen clay of the heart are *weak* (Mt. 26:41), hence, for the sake of knowledge and the instruction and understanding that derive from it, the practitioner engages in the study of divine words. But the things that the contemplative comes to know in silence, as well as those he is taught ineffably, are beheld in contemplation, and word and reason cannot express them. For as Scripture has it, *the ear* of stillness *shall hear extraordinary things* (cf. Job 4:12). It said *extraordinary things,* but what kind of extraordinary things it could not say. Hence it has left unexpressed that which is beyond speech and beyond reason. For this reason I am compelled to call blessed those whom the Divine Word first blessed because they believed before seeing (Jn. 20:29), that is to say, those who engage in the practical life. At the same time, I believe those who engage in contemplation to be *beyond* blessed. For if the practitioner, despite not having seen, possesses a blessed condition simply out of faith, what might one conclude about the contemplative who, in addition to the fact that he *walks by faith* that is far superior to practice (2 Cor. 5:7), has also beheld great and extraordinary things, and experienced (πάσχοντος) ascents in his heart (cf. Ps. 83:6), and has even grown accustomed to behold such things daily?

30. The Orderer and Maker of all things granted to each part of the dual mixture of man the enjoyment (εὐπάθεια) and the life proper to each. He produced the whole visible creation for the visible part of man, while for the intelligible part, that is, the soul, He produced all that is intelligible in the sensible creation. For just as the noetic part of man is united to the sensible part, likewise throughout all of the visible creation noetic beauty can be seen underlying everything that exists; and it is impossible for any of the things that appear, even the least of them, to be deprived of noetic affinity (συναφή). And this is quite reasonable, since it was altogether necessary that none of what was created for man by the divine Word of the Almighty could be perceived as absurd, and this would be the case if the intelligible did not coincide with the phenomenal part of creation. For then, even if the body could delight in the cooperation of visible things, the Christian soul would remain empty; in consequence, the body would prove to be superior to the

soul, which is absurd.[132] Or at what other starting-point could the soul begin to enjoy the life that is proper to it (πρώτως)? In God? Yet this would be contrary to the order set forth by the Word of the Creator of All. For then incomposite beings would prove to be inferior to composite ones, if, that is, we directly had the power they possess whereby they move towards God of their own accord. But would it not then follow that we must ascend directly from simple intelligible things and procure the delight of divine vision in this manner? But again, this would give us an order on par with the angels', when this is contrary to nature, namely, for material intellects to be raised up to the Good in the same manner as immaterial intellects. For they do not receive their own proper life and their ascent towards the First Good from outside themselves, but beginning from themselves they delight in the unified rays of divine splendor. On the other hand, we who have a lesser nature and are second to the angels, are gathered and drawn to God and His beauty in a manner that is, I might say, lesser and subsequent to the angelic order, and by order of degrees we are gathered up to God and His beauty, and do not take our beginning from incomposite essences or absolutely intelligible realities. For this is a property of angels, namely, to begin their ascent to God of their own accord. On the other hand, by setting out from composite things in accordance with reason and concluding with simple created ones, we pass over to uncreated realities, in a mode consistent with our nature, just as I have explained; and in this manner we are gathered in unity with ourselves and with God. Hence, in order to make us familiar with the intellect's proper enjoyment and life and ascent to Him, God implanted in all sensible things intelligible truths which are perceived by contemplation; these, however, remain invisible to the practitioner, either because he cannot see them or does not wish to. He cannot if he has no spiritual guide or Scripture to show these things to him; or else he does not wish to see them and, despite having both these means at his disposal, out of baseness and conceit he distrusts his neighbor and believes only in himself, and so remains inexperienced in instruction concerning these matters, considering the letter of Scripture to be a sufficient guide for himself, while making feeble use of creation, only for the service of the body, and regards this as piety, contenting himself with these things without seeking anything more. In contrast, the contemplative, by garnering invisible realities from the visible creation and finding them according to the spirit of Scripture, he swiftly and gladly proceeds to non-composite essences, and having beheld the comeliness of their splendor, he joyfully passes beyond them through grace and moves onto the uncreated intelligible realities of God. And after taking delight in their infinitude and contemplating them, as much as this is possible, he then silently draws near to the radiance of divine beauty in a unity beyond nature. Once he has ecstatically enjoyed, as is right, that inexpressible transcendent

---

[132] This argument is related to the opening premise that body and soul are each endowed with their own proper capacity to enjoy.

loveliness and most-luminous splendor in a unified and unique condition, he knows not what will become of him for joy and wonder. Indeed, he receives the unending stream of divine jubilation and then ungrudgingly guides the practitioner, by means of words and letters, to the way that leads to the truth.

On participation in the Holy Spirit.

31. Do you know what is poured into the hearts of believers and what the sign of this outpouring is? It is, in fact, the very Holy Spirit who proceeds from the Father through the Son (ἐκ Πατρὸς δι' Υἱοῦ), and who fills the universe. He is present absolutely everywhere and wholly fills every believer, being distributed without suffering change (ἀπαθῶς) and partaken of without limitation (ἀσχέτως). A sign of participation in Him, or of His outpouring within us, is the humble desire for poverty, the effortless and unceasing stream of tears, complete and untainted love for God and neighbor, joy of heart and exultation in God, long-suffering in the midst of all our trials, kindness towards all; and again, it is generally indicated by goodness; the unity, contemplation, and light of the intellect; the ever-stirring and fervent power of prayer; and to summarize, the freedom from care for temporal things through remembrance of eternal ones. *O how wondrous are Your works, Lord!* (Ps. 103:24); and indeed, *glorious things have been spoken of you, O City of God* (Ps. 86:3), and this city signifies the faithful heart.

32. If you have understood the *great counsel* of our God, referred to in Scripture, which is wrought by the inconceivable goodwill of the Father's supernatural love for mankind, of which Jesus became the *Messenger* (ἄγγελος) for us (Is. 9:6), delivering it in exceeding holiness beyond understanding, goodness, and love for the human race, by which all the *purposes* (λόγοι)[133] of visible things are gathered into one *overall purpose* (λόγον συντετμημένον) that God has promised to accomplish for us (cf. Is. 10:23), then you will never cease to be astonished, rejoice, and be assured with peace.

33. If you know the purpose that the divine majesty has for us, and what will subsequently be accomplished between God and us in accordance with this plan, then you will understand what God desires from us, and the purpose for which our affairs are destined, and how far we fall short of what is right. But the ignorance

---

[133] *Logoi*: "words", reasons, or principles of creation. Is. 10:23 LXX, λόγον συντετμημένον "brief word", "brief work", in the sense of a royal decree or divine word that is said and perfectly accomplished.

of this purpose gives us much reason to grieve with sorrow that is pleasing to God and full of sincere humility.

On contemplation.

34. He who meditates on all that has been set out by the love of God by means of noetic visions through spiritual discernment (κατ' ἐπιβολήν) [134] shall no doubt find three things rise up in his soul about which all the sacred books and Scriptures speak vigorously in order to rouse people to acquire them by all means; I of course mean faith, hope, and love, which are the end, or rather, the foundation of absolutely all practical and contemplative virtues. This is indeed a "holy trinity" within us, by which we are united to *the* Holy Trinity, approaching God like other angels.

On contemplation.

35. The healthy intellect generally contemplates three triadic orders of mysteries around God: the personal (προσωπικήν), the natural (φυσικήν), and that which follows the natural (ἑπομένην τῇ φυσικῇ).[135] The first triad discloses itself to the intellect primarily through the sacred writings. Then, the natural is contemplated through the apprehension of existing realities. Next, that which follows the natural is gathered from the perception of the truth in the *Logos*.[136] Furthermore, when the intellect enters into the first triadic order, or to speak more precisely, when the intellect gazes upon it, it encounters the Unapproachable One, but not with as much simplicity. But in the second order it finds ecstatic joy in wisdom. And when it enters the third triad, it is then that the intellect truly *enters into the darkness where God is* (Ex. 20:21), becoming altogether and utterly simple, infinite, invisible in a formless and shapeless condition. At last, when it contemplates by means of these three triads, or rather, when it beholds a kind of tenth order together with them, within which, as the heralds of truth say, *all the fullness of divinity has come to*

---

[134] Cf. Kallistos and Ignatios Xanthopoulos, *Exact Rule and Canon* 68, 72.

[135] These three triadic orders are related to the statement in ch. 34 that we approach God like "other angels" with the trinity of faith, hope, and love. According to the *Celestial Hierarchy* of St. Dionysios the Areopagite, the hierarchy of angels is arranged into three triadic orders. Cf. ch. 57.

[136] It is not perfectly clear what these triadic orders consist of, or what are the three parts that make up each triad, but the key Greek words in each triad are as follows: 1) personal: χωρηγεῖ, ἔκφανσις, ἱερὰ γράμματα 2) natural: θεωρεῖται, κατανόησις, τὰ ὄντα, 3) following the natural (ἑπομένη τῇ φυσικῇ): συνάγεται, ἀληθείας, λογικῆς. The description of each triad mentions how and by what means one ascends to it, but does not describe the content of the mysteries, perhaps precisely because they are *mysteries*. This difficult passage may be better understood in the light of Angelikoudes' other explanations of anagogical ascent through Scripture, creation, and the Divine Logos, as well as the writings of Dionysios the Areopagite and Maximos the Confessor.

dwell bodily (Col. 2:9), that is when it truly sees the *peace which surpasses understanding* (Phil. 4:7) in the perfection and consummation of the grace of contemplation.

On contemplation.

36. And then, by continuing to apply the same subdivisions in this manner, the intellect mystically contemplates three states of the dispensation of spiritual grace in Christ's gift, from which peace streams forth. These states are: beyond the world (ὑπερκόσμιον), around the world (περικόσμιον), and within oneself (ἐν ἑαυτῷ). And thus, within this triadic unit – or perhaps "decade", or else perfection of contemplation – the spurs of divine love are put to the soul by God's good grace, and through this love the intellect is initiated into mysteries, illuminated thereby, and thus made glad and radiant with joy. And further, by the grace of the Spirit the man directs the true loving power of his soul toward God and kindles it as much as he can to divine eros; thus he begins to love God quite naturally, and is further lifted up, making progress in this love, directing all his gaze, attention, and diligence to the commandments. And he is industrious in the commandments so that, with the help of grace, divine love may rightly be increased in him, and even reach the perfection that befits him. Then God and the intellect become *one spirit* in a paradoxical manner, when God enters the intellect spiritually through reception (κατὰ παραδοχήν), and the intellect attains to God through perception (κατ' ἐπιβολήν). And then he clearly witnesses what Paul says: *He who is joined to the Lord becomes one spirit with Him* (1 Cor. 6:17). God then becomes illumination and light and divine eros for the intellect, and the intellect in turn is gladdened by the presence of God and exults with wonder at the One Illumination of the Triadic Light, and is assured with ecstatic peace and joy in Christ.

On contemplation.

37. The contemplative intellect gathers (λέγει), as one might say, or knows (νοεῖ) and clearly sees, five general principles (λόγους)[137] regarding Jesus who became man (cf. 1 Cor. 14:19): glory, love, grace, as well as peace and rest. It sees the principle of glory reflected from the creation of all things that have come to be, both visible and intelligible. For *all things were made through Him, and without Him nothing was made that was made* (Jn. 1:3), including the ages and all that exists throughout all eternity, including the entire super-celestial order, and hence

---

[137] This chapter, which has to do with the mystical contemplation of *logoi* through God the *Logos*, opens up with a playful use of the word λόγος and its cognate verb λέγειν ("speak", "gather"): Πέντε λόγους, εἴτε λέγει τις λέγειν ἐθέλοι, εἴτε νοεῖ.

all the more everything that exists in time. And what is even greater than this is the fact that Christ shares the throne and His nature with God the Father and the Spirit, being *the image of the invisible God* (Col. 1:15), *the radiance of His glory* (Heb. 1:3), and *having all that the Father has* by nature (Jn. 16:15). Thus *He is in the Father and the Father in Him* (Jn. 14:10). Then, the principle of love is seen from the fact that *the Word became flesh* from our own flesh *and dwelt among us* (Jn. 1:14). The principle of grace is seen from the gift and outpouring of the Life-Giving Spirit into us, for *from His fullness we have all received, and grace for grace* (Jn 1:16). The principle of peace is seen from how Christ became *the preacher of the gospel of peace to those who were near and to those who were far* (Eph. 2:17), *brought about peace* (Eph. 2:15), and *reconciled things on earth with those in heaven* (Col. 1:15). And thus the Father *raised us up and seated us with Himself in heavenly places together with Christ* (Eph. 2:6). Lastly, the principle of rest is seen from how we have become uncontested heirs of God through Christ. Not only is there nothing superior to this dignity, but neither is there anything equal, for it is exceedingly and infinitely beyond comprehension. Hence, by the grace of the Unique Trinity, the intellect contemplates three principles (λόγοι)[138] united into the extraordinary end of the singular mystical purpose (σκοπός), towards which it is led by contemplating these five principles *in Spirit and truth.* And thus, through love, self-control, vigilance, reading, and prayer, with a humble and obedient spirit and practical deeds of righteousness according to one's strength, the intellect accordingly progresses to the contemplation of manifestations of God and divine perceptions, and lives alone with God, without however losing any due reverence or fear. In this way does man delight in the many and exceedingly splendid gifts of the Spirit, in holy love, joy of heart, supernatural peace, and those other truly blessed things that come after these; and he is even made a temple of God, a new heir, and indeed a god by grace and adoption (χάριτι θετὸς θεός).

On the passage, "God said to Abraham, 'I will abundantly multiply your seed'" (Gen. 22:17).

38. Thus, when I look to the Lord and God-Man with the tranquil eye of my soul by the life-giving and illuminating power of the Spirit, and I meditate on the five *logoi* regarding Him that I have mentioned above, I distinctly see the miraculous fulfillment of that promise given to Abraham long ago by the Incarnate *Logos*, when He enlightened us with the words: *I will abundantly multiply your seed as the stars of heaven, and as the sand by the shore of the sea* (Gen. 22:17). For when God says, *In your seed all the nations of the earth shall be blessed*, St. Paul infers

---

[138] It is unclear what these three principles are.

that the meaning of 'seed' (σπέρμα) is found in Jesus; thus it is with good reason that we can understand 'the seed of Abraham that is multiplied' to be the Lord Jesus, since He alone is exceedingly abundant on account of the unity and energy of His divinity. For He is infinite in greatness, unsearchable in magnitude, and truly 'multiplied' as the God of all graces, *as the stars of heaven, and as the sand by the shore of the sea*. Again, Christ is of the race of Abraham and nobody denies that He is a descendent of him. Now, then, it is unreasonable to suppose that God would say this about Ishmael. For he was not the *son of a free woman* (cf. Gen. 16; Gal. 4:21-31), and Scripture says that, *Through Isaac shall your seed be named* (Heb. 11:18). But neither does it refer to Israel, for this nation did not reach so great a number, and neither for that matter could all the human beings of the earth attain the greatness of Christ the Lord, who, being God the Word, assumed the seed of Abraham, and is one Person, both Man and God; His *peace* alone *knows no bounds* (cf. Is. 9:7), and His *judgments are unfathomable* and His *ways inscrutable* (Ps. 35:7; Rom. 11:33). Moreover, His power and wisdom, and all his divine attributes are infinitely infinite. In Him even nations that had not yet come into existence acquired a blessing beyond expectation, and it is clear that so great a 'multiplication' was fulfilled in the manner we have said. Besides, it would neither be fitting nor by any account necessary for God to do a favor for the Patriarch by literally undertaking to multiply multitudes of people from his seed. For taking joy in such things is altogether pagan (ἐθνικόν) and vulgar (βάναυσον); but for a man who considered excellent things and was a friend of God to the degree that the Patriarch Abraham was, what is fitting is to love and rejoice with all one's soul in the knowledge and contemplation of God as far as this is possible (cf. Jn. 8:56), and in so doing to receive a multitude of divine perceptions, contemplations, and illuminations, and hence to be 'multiplied' by God in a manner appropriate to Him. In this way Moses became a worthy supplicant when he begged to see and know God when He appeared to him (Ex. 33:13). Furthermore, when he saw God, to the degree that he was made worthy to see Him, he was also made great, and was given such abundance of divine knowledge that no one can describe it.

Solomon too was given such an abundance and multitude of wisdom and knowledge of existing things, that it was like the *sand by the shore of the sea*, and hence he was magnified beyond all his contemporaries. Whoever gives thought to the matter shall understand quite easily how it is that God multiplies a person dedicated to Him, or the 'seed' of that person. For, of course, God does not rejoice in the sheer number (ἐπὶ πλήθει οὕτως ἁπλῶς) of people, but rather in the wisdom and spiritual knowledge of the soul and the other innumerable divine virtues, all of which were perfected and possessed in abundance by the Lord Jesus Christ, the seed of Abraham, in whom all the *fullness of divinity dwelt bodily*, and this fullness transcends any conception of multitude by infinite measure. From it comes every existing thing and every multitude, and together with them *the treasures of knowledge and wisdom* that are *hidden in Christ* (Col. 2:3). And this is the gift that is truly worthy of God and most excellent; it is the gift which was rightly promised to so excellent a friend of God as Abraham. Consider, furthermore, the abundance found in Christ Jesus, divine and boundless as it is, from the five principles I have mentioned: first, from the glory surrounding Him are manifested the splendors of the divine nature, all of which He possesses by nature as True God. These splendors are said to be infinite in magnitude and unsearchable in multitude. In addition to these, there are the properties of His sonship from the Father, the true tokens of His consubstantiality with Him, as well as the characteristics of His unity with the Spirit, and even the outpouring of gifts, which myriads of human beings partake of – and even if the entire universe were to partake of them, they could never be diminished; and furthermore, among these are also the truths of His Incarnate economy, which are ineffable and innumerable. In short, whoever examines, as far as possible, all that springs from His glory, love, and grace – and from our peace and rest in Him – shall see the hidden meaning of how Jesus Christ, the seed of Abraham, has been multiplied beyond *the stars of heaven* and *the sand of the seashore*. And he will give God due praise, delighting in so great a promise – sublime, wondrous, and mystical – worthy of God alone, who is the Source of all graces. For this is the promise bestowed on His elect and most faithful friend for the exceeding universal happiness of the human race, especially of believers. Glory to Him who was well pleased to bring about this multiplication. Amen.

On the passage, "Praise the Lord, O my soul" (Ps. 145:1).

39. *Praise the Lord, O my soul* (Ps. 145:1), for the heavens of heaven, whose essence is light! Praise Him in the highest, among *all his angels and their hosts* (Ps. 148:2)! His power and wisdom are greatly to be praised, and blessed be His holy name! Praise the Lord for the waters above the firmament and the light which is above them; for the firmament of heaven, its marvellous order and swirling winds, and for the burning ether; for the glory and loveliness of the sun and moon and stars, for their variations, positions, and movements, that burn by nature without fuel and are truly awesome; for the light of day and the change in the length thereof, by which the things of the world are balanced in abundant wisdom. Praise the Lord, O my soul, for the perfect equilibrium of the four greatest elements of the universe: water, fire, air, and earth, which preserve a marvellous peace and stability despite their mutual oppositions and incompatibilities; for the vigorous flight and flocking (φορᾶς καὶ διαφορᾶς) of the birds and His providence for their life and their sustenance; for the sea and the might of its dominion, bridled by a barrier of porous sand, and for all the creatures that dwell therein, innumerable

beings with myriads of diverse forms, sizes, qualities, characters, and habits, as well as proclivities, powers, and activities. O praise the Lord in peace and amazement for each and every harvest of the sea, by which the things needful for human life are swiftly retrieved. Praise the Lord with joy for the earth and the animals that move thereabout, even the creeping things innumerable in all their diverse and sundry species. And again, for the trees that grow therein, those that bear fruit and those that do not, with their countless visible variations even among trees of the same species, as strange as these appear to be; and again, for the herbs and gourds, the grains and legumes, and those plants that are mixed together for scenting, heating, cooling, wetting, and drying, which all differ from one another in uncountable, unthinkable ways; for the waters divided into all shapes and sizes, rain, snow, hail, and storms with thunder and lightning. And so for all these things and their like, O my soul, praise and bless the Lord; for His inconceivable power, ineffable wisdom, and indescribable glory; and consider especially that all these things were made for you by such a Creator, out of His inexpressible love for you, that you might dwell uprightly among these bright glories as a rational being and see the majesty, wisdom, and power of your Maker mirrored in them. *For He so loves you that He gave His only-begotten Son* to become man on our behalf (Jn. 3:16), in a mystery wondrous beyond comprehension.

On Contemplation.

40. What was the plan conceived, if I may put it thus, by the omnipotent power of Your dominion, O transcendent Lord? And what was Your design, O all-wise King, if I may be so bold? What did You desire in Your inconceivable good will, O truly good God? And what is it You have done for us out of Your infinite Love, O Lord Almighty, O most glorious One, in the inexpressible providence of Your goodness towards us? Glory to Your infinite goodness, which You have shown to be just as limitless as You are, through Your providence for us in all wisdom and incomprehensible power, O You who are in all things wholly boundless! And so I might join with the Righteous David in saying, *How magnificent are Your works, O Lord, Your thoughts are exceedingly deep* (Ps. 91:6). For I see just as he did in the Spirit and in truth, and behold! *the house of the Lord is full of glory* (see Is. 6:1). And indeed, when I see in this way, I also see myself within the house of the glory of the Lord, being filled up with glory and grace, in ineffable repose and inexpressible, everlasting peace. And how could I help but be astonished, struck and *wounded* by the arrows of divine *love* (Song 2:5)? Yea, I am set aflame with fervent eros, with spiritual joy and gladness and exultation beyond this world. Through divine grace, I am filled up from the depths of my heart with sacred light through the inextinguishable guiding-torch of the Spirit (if I may say so). And so I am guided into the *logoi* of all things, all united in one mystical *Logos*, and I see

the words of the Scriptures all culminating in that Word (Λόγος). And many such mysteries are revealed to me as leading up to that one Word, and through that one Word they are made manifest to those who see in truth and in Spirit.[139]

That Word is the great counsel of God, and upon seeing it David sang, *The counsel of the Lord abides forever, the thoughts of His heart from generation to generation* (Ps. 32:11). *For no one will frustrate the counsel of God* (cf. Is. 14:26-27). This counsel cannot be discerned or imparted by erudition, but only by manifest (ἐνυπόστατος) spiritual grace, which gives true light to the intellect and enables it to see things beyond this world. Scripture has said, *Who knows the power of Your wrath, O Lord, and who knows how to number his days because of the fear of Your wrath?* (Ps. 89:11). However, the spiritual wisdom within me says, "Who knows the power of Your love, and who can number the workings of Your eros?" *Marvellous are the works* of Your love, O Lord. My soul knows this full well, and the knowledge of Your divine eros *is too wonderful for me* (Ps. 138:14, 6). Who can gaze fully upon it? Not only does the quality of this knowledge extend to endless infinity, but it inexpressibly proceeds in diverse processions hither and thither with boundless wisdom and commensurate power, O ineffable Lord: You are one in essence, power, and energy, yet three in hypostases and in the unique properties of personhood.[140] Blessed are You, who have *blessed us with every spiritual blessing* (Eph. 1:3) in the person of our Christ Jesus, in whom You have also *raised us up together, and made us sit together in the heavenly places* (Eph. 2:6), *far above all principality and power and might and dominion, and every name that is named, not only in this age but also in that which is to come* (Eph. 1:21), making us *joint heirs with Christ* (Rom. 8:17) and full heirs of You, the Godhead three in one. You have committed all the wonders in heaven and on earth to our authority, and again through Christ Jesus, through whom we, who are but sons of earth, have been justified both by nature (λόγῳ πεφυκότι) and by grace. What divine love and all-surpassing, transcendent eros, O triune God, that we might truly partake of the gift of God the Word! Glory to You, O Lord, for thus imparting to us Your natural glory, which surpasses understanding! You are truly indescribable and Your deeds inconceivable; Your eros toward us cannot be expressed!

41. Blessed is the man whose noetic sense (νοερὰ αἴσθησις) has blossomed afresh (ἀνέθηλε) through contemplative stillness[141] and has, as it were, recovered

---

[139] Cf. Maximos the Confessor, *Ambiguum* 7.2 (Blowers, 54-5).

[140] According to some Church Fathers, such as St. Gregory the Theologian, the unique properties of personhood refer to the Father's unbegottenness, the Son's begottenness, and the Holy Spirit's procession from the Father.

[141] ἐλλόγιμος ἡσυχία, "contemplative stillness" with the additional paradoxical meaning of "silence through the word", or "eloquent silence". Such verbal paradoxes are a favorite in hesychastic

(ἐπανῆλθε) its true nature and now lives by the breath and power of the Spirit. This is the fruit of a mind made whole by grace; it restores the dispositions of the soul, rouses the intellect as well and effortlessly transforms the heart, as the mind takes flight in pursuit of divine things. It is easier for a man to swim through the air than for his noetic sense to recover its true nature without meditative stillness and purity of intellect. And with it, the remembrance of God and the contemplation of Him become both possible (ἀνύσιμον) and profitable (ὀνήσιμον). But without this noetic sense, it is as if the remembrance of God becomes forgetfulness, and the knowledge and vision of God become ignorance and blindness. One might say that he who has found this divine sense by God's grace has found God Himself. Such a person has no need for words; he prefers rather to stand in God's presence and minister (λειτουργεῖν) to Him. He embraces silence, or rather, keeps silent without effort. The Spirit of God dwells in him, and love and peace and spiritual joy take their rise from Him. The life he lives is different from the customary, common life. He rejoices in God and his eyes see the noetic light, for they themselves are noetic. His heart bears fire. To his astonishment, simplicity and immutability, infinity and limitlessness, beginninglessness and endlessness come to dwell with him. Constant tears flow from his eyes, and likewise a spring of spiritual living water gushes forth from his heart. He is wholly united in one accord with intelligible realities and is enlightened by the radiance of the One; he delights in a delight beyond this world, is inspired and gladdened in awe and marvels at the inner change that directs him toward God (ἐντρέψει τῇ περὶ Θεοῦ). He who has tasted these things will understand and sing due praise unto God, the super-essential and exalted One, without form or figure, ageless, immeasurable, simple, shapeless, infinite, limitless, incomprehensible, intangible, invisible, ineffable, unexplainable, without beginning or end, uncreated, incorruptible, inconceivable, unsearchable, beyond being, beyond power, beyond goodness, and beyond beauty. To Him be glory and praise unto the ages.

On divine illumination.

42. *To those in need of understanding*, O Lord and Wisdom, You have said, *Come, eat of My bread and drink the wine I have mingled for you* (Prov. 9:4-5). So I come, Lord, as one truly *in need* (ἐνδεής) *of understanding* because of my sinful deeds, but trusting in Your ineffable love for mankind. And so I entreat (δέομαι) You, I entreat You: grant me the gift of Your mercy, the spiritual food and drink of Your Spirit, for that Spirit is assuredly Light as well. That is why Your children say that those who bear spirit also bear light. And when the Light shines its ineffable, supernatural rays within me, then I will know indeed that You are with me as my

---

literature. Here we have translated it "contemplative stillness", as it relates to the method of contemplation through the Word outlined in ch. 40.

own garment, and as my very life, holy and blessed. For those who bear Your light, O Christ, as Your people say, are thereafter *clothed* in You (Gal. 3:27), *the brightness of the Father's glory* (Heb. 1:3), the true and undefiled life. And again, according to Your saints, they are clothed in the Father as well. And so they become glorious dwellings, resting places and temples of the thrice-brilliant and supremely-praised Godhead. They go beyond visible things and rest from all their noetic efforts and find repose in You by the Spirit, O God beyond divinity.

How divine eros is imparted to the soul.

43. Divine eros is naturally brought to the soul through keeping the commandments and divine doctrines and through the spiritual rekindling of the Life-Giving Spirit in the heart, where He flares up like a flame. It is like a life (ψυχή) of pure, eternal, and ever-flowing divine prayer, movement, energy, unity and insight, ecstasy and vision, and the illumination that yields true holy pleasure. It is the unerring path towards a perfect and supernatural union with God and the sure starting-point of the following: 'enhypostatic noetic illumination' beyond nature, as the Fathers teach, the gift of deification, *the guarantee* of the future *inheritance* of the saints (Eph. 1:14), the pledge of the glory of Christ, and the garment of joy that surpasses heaven and earth; the sacred seal of adoption, and in a word, the radiance that presents us conformed to Christ and participants in Him, and through Him, in His own ineffable deification.[142] For He calls us His brothers and heirs of God and His own joint heirs, and – what is still more wonderful – we truly are! Therefore he is blessed who, through diligent study of these things, makes the unspeakable love of God his possession and is devoted to Him in holy prayer and the way of stillness. For he shall truly be bound to God and undergo a deifying transformation beyond intellect, even *considering sufferings* for the sake of Christ *as joy* (Col. 1:24), and *delighting greatly in His commandments* (Ps. 111:1), to whom be glory unto the ages. Amen.

More on divine eros.

44. God is by nature immeasurably and infinitely removed from all contemplation, even that of the Cherubim. However, the eros of His infinite goodness can nevertheless be contemplated, since from it originated those things that are intelligible and created (νοεῖται δήπου κτιστά), as well as the visible things which have clearly come into being for the sake of intelligible ones – and all for the sake

---

[142] The deification of Christ's humanity is precisely what causes the deification of man. Christ was deified according to His human nature, so that human beings might be deified through Him (cf. Rom 8:29, Phil. 3:21).

of eros (ἐρωτικῶς). This is why divine eros first manifests itself by being poured out on intelligent beings (that is, angels and souls), for they are closer and more intimate with God. For the noetic natures have a property [namely, intellect] which is closer to divinity, and it is clearly for their sake that God created all the others, because of His love (ἀγαπητικῶς) and, I might say, the "nobleness of soul" which so befits Him, or rather His "generosity of intellect."[143] And so it is possible to behold the love of the One who is Himself altogether invisible, and indeed one does behold His noetic and transcendent eros most brilliantly, that is, through the manifestations around Him, like so many divine wedding gifts.

For a great multitude of gifts are given by the Loving God (ἐραστοῦ Θεοῦ) to the beloved human person (ἐρωμένου ἀνθρώπου), which by their nature manifestly and manifoldly proclaim His divine eros. And indeed, when the intellect found in an illumined heart attains stability and receives the energy of spiritual vision, it then bursts into flame when the soul receives the pledge of spiritual life in the heart, that is, through the conscious experience of energy in the intellect; indeed, it is at this point, through divine illumination, that the soul supernaturally begins to contemplate the "wedding gifts" of her Lover and to remember Him without wandering or wavering; at once she is enraptured and desires to meditate constantly on these gifts. Then the soul happily beholds the face of her Lover and is filled with awesome wonder and grows faint before the eros of God, leaving behind her all sense and thought of anything else, and she marvels and knows not what will become of her for all the abundance of this vision. And after experiencing all these things, the soul leaps for joy and ceases to worry, and from there she makes a kind of ascent and begins to love God in return and experiences a joyful flame of eros, full of the mysteries of God and kindled (ἐνεργουμένη) by the All-Holy and Life-Giving Spirit, who sets the heart ablaze. And thus a kind of sacred circle of divine eros (ἱερός τις ἐράσμιος κύκλος), exquisitely delightful and wonderful, is set in motion (ἐνεργεῖσθαι) when first God manifests His divine eros to us through His deeds, and whereby God appears as our Lover and at the same time raises us up to love Him in turn, so that God becomes our Beloved and what once began with God now also ends with Him. And then when we have attained the likeness of God by imaging Him forth (θείας ὁμοιώσεως) in the jubilation and enjoyment of His divine ravishment (θείας ἐρωτοληψίας), we are made good through wisdom; that is, we become practicers of good works through

---

[143] In Greek μεγαλοψυχία "greatness of soul" and μεγαλόνοια "greatness of mind" are both synonym meaning "magnanimity, generosity", but because μεγαλοψυχία includes the root ψυχή "soul", Angelikoudes here deems μεγαλόνοια to be more appropriate, especially in the context of explaining how God created *intelligent, noetic beings* (who are "closer" to God by possessing intellect). Moreover, *intellect* (νοῦς) is often ascribed to God (especially God the Father) in devotional and theological literature.

contemplation, beloved by God and lovers of God, experiencing the ecstasy and mysteries of this divine and life-giving union and 'suffering' blessed passions (μακάρια πάσχοντες πάθη) in Christ our Lord, from the resplendent light of knowledge.[144]

On the fear that is preserved in love.

45. Once you have been caught up into the love of God and the spiritual rest of His mystical eros and have consciously enjoyed the taste of His divine cup, you will rejoice beyond words and take undeniable delight in beholding the depths of transcendent mysteries, delighting in unspeakable wonders and resting in profound peace; yet still you should fear, pay due attention unto God, and pray in all humility, heeding the clear voice of the godly David when he called out to God: O *You who are my joy, deliver me from them that have compassed me about* (Ps. 31:7). And teaching most brilliantly, or rather by the inspiration of the Spirit, he says, *Serve the Lord with fear, and rejoice in Him with trembling* (Ps. 2:11). Also consider Paul, *the chosen vessel* (Ac. 9:15), who was caught up to the third heaven, entered sacred Paradise and *heard inexpressible words, which it is not lawful for a man to utter* (2 Cor. 12:2); and yet after all these things, he still feared *lest, when he had preached to others, he himself should become disqualified* (1 Cor. 9:27). And if David, the divine teacher of all the earth, says: *You that love the Lord, hate evil* (Ps. 96:10), then he is clearly implying that those who love the Lord ought to fear. For he discerned that even after one attains love for God, evil will still try to contend with it and ensnare the soul however it can. And so he exhorts those who love the Lord and have reached this state to continue to beware of evil and hate it. And if you are taught to hate something, then it is still a thing to be feared. For if it were not worth fearing, the prophet would not have exhorted those who love Christ to hate it.

Although it is indeed a noble, godlike, and truly grace-filled condition to rejoice and exult in God as we behold supernatural mysteries, the soul is still by nature subject to change and is by no means removed from earthly matter and the body that enfolds it;[145] perhaps this is so that the soul might have a little fear in the midst

---

[144] While the verb πάσχειν can be understood in the original sense as "experience, feel", Angelikoudes employs the word somewhat paradoxically. While "blameworthy passions" prevent the soul from union with God and cause it suffering, this situation is reversed when the soul "suffers blessed passions" through union with God; moreover, these are experienced "in Christ", who showed divine eros through the sufferings of His Passion. "Blessed passions" does not refer to physical or emotional sufferings, but comes from "the resplendent light of knowledge."

[145] βρύω, here translated as "enfold", has the connotation of both natural union with the body but also swelling motion.

of its perpetual struggle against backsliding[146]. And thus, the soul is wondrously bound to the body and shares, as it were, the very same breath (whether it wishes to or not), and suffers together with it, and in some instances it is so altered from its own nature that one might think it no longer holds authority. The body on the other hand is the soul's unyielding opponent and throws it off balance in all sorts of ways. And so the fear that occurs shows the soul its need to struggle and pray; however, the amount of fear and trembling that a soul needs in its ascent to God, and what kind of attention and prayer, is something I leave for the more sagacious readers to examine and discern. The soul can of course contemplate these things by the illuminating grace of the Spirit and accordingly experience the realities of divine love.

If Adam had had fear in proportion to the surpassing greatness of the gift of prophecy he enjoyed in imitation of God, then alas! he would not have suffered such an ignoble defeat. The same can be said of Samson, the son of a divine promise (cf. Jdg. 13:3), and David the God-bearer, and many others, including the marvellous Solomon. And if such people had need of fear, struggle, and attentiveness with prayer, then what shall we conclude about those who have not yet received the supernatural gift and energy of the Spirit, and have not yet ascended to the ecstatic ardors of divine eros and to the mad ravishment of the visible beauty of God? How much fear and trembling, pious vigilance, and prayer in Christ Jesus do they require, both at all times and in a humble spirit?

How the form of love is threefold.

46. Experience knows that the principle of love is threefold, and accordingly its primary objects are also of three kinds, and its causes three. There is sensible (αἰσθητική) love (that is, of the senses), towards such things as can be apprehended by the senses. It is a passionate craving for some desirable thing; and hence it is through this love that even irrational animals feel love. Another love is the rational desire (ἔφεσις λογική) of the soul for that which is considered as good, for the sake of attaining that good. The third kind is noetic, and it originates from the Life-Giving Spirit. It is a supernatural ravishment (θέλξις) that compels the good into the heart apart from the will; it burns and works through the contemplation of the ultimate Beauty,[147] namely, God. Just as God is not contemplated as good and infinitely more beautiful than all things because the soul wills it, but because of His nature, so likewise, His divine eros does not burn by the will of man, for it is the ever-moving natural energy of the Life-Giving Spirit working within the heart;

---

146 νεύσις "backsliding, nodding" denotes a descent towards the material. Cf. Greg. Naz. 45.7.
147 τὸ ἄκρον καλόν. The highest good or beauty; *summum bonum*.

in fact, it is so far from being moved by man's will (θέλησις) that, on the contrary, by its own nature it moves the will.[148] That is why it is, and is rightly designated, divine 'consolation' (παράκλησις), because that is precisely what it is: it is, on the one hand, the energy of God imparted to the soul through the Spirit's inspiration and visitation and, on the other hand, it constitutes the relation (σχέσις) of the life-giving soul to God.[149] This is the only true and wondrous union and affinity which, through a noetic desire for good things, attracts the whole intellect, including all the faculties of the soul and all its vitality, into union with the Divine Beauty. This is why none of the aforementioned things – neither the appetite for some desirable thing nor even the desire for good – can properly be called 'consolation', but only the noetic love of beauty achieved by contemplation, that desire which is manifestly set in motion in the heart by the Holy Spirit: only that love can be called 'consolation'. The Holy Spirit who enables this (which is indeed the true love – the other two are merely images of it) is called the 'Comforter' (Παράκλητος); or rather, the love of the soul which pursues the good through reason is the proper image of divine and spiritual love, while sensible love is, in turn, an image of the soul's natural love.

This is why a man can know almost nothing of love, sweetness of heart and consolation (which is to know nothing of love at all), before he receives the ever-flowing and manifest life-giving power of the Holy Spirit within his heart. For rationality clearly does not possess the natural power to animate the throne of the soul's faculties – that is, the heart – from within, but only from without; how much less, then, do the outward senses have any power to do this! So these kinds of love are just a fragment, an image, a shadow of real love. But the power and energy of the Holy and Life-Giving Spirit wholly takes possession of this abode of the soul from within, and thus wholly moves it (as we have said) by enticing the faculties of the soul in noetic contemplation of the supreme Beauty; thus it supremely and truly ravishes the soul away to divine beauty with real love and rapture beyond this world. And so only he who is moved by God and receives these divine energies can truly know in the secret place of his soul what proper love is and how it is enjoyed, and that no man can truly love any of these things, nor indeed God Himself, before partaking of the Life-Giving Spirit, even if he loves with all his might. In fact, he does not even know what real love is, nor the ineffable pleasure

---

[148] In Greek, "will" (θέλησις) is intrinsically related to "desire", and hence the beauty and love manifested by the Holy Spirit are ontologically prior to man's will and do not depend on it. So this of course does not imply that the Holy Spirit moves the will against man's will, but draws it to Himself and supernaturally fulfills it.

[149] *relation* perhaps in the sense of closeness, likeness, relatedness. For divine παράκλησις "consolation, comfort, intercession, exhortation", cf. Jn. 14:16,26; 15:26; 16:7; Acts 9:31; 2 Cor. 1:5-6; for "life-giving soul", cf. 1 Cor. 15:45; for the Holy Spirit's energy in prayer, cf. Rom. 8:26-7; 1 Cor. 12:11;

that arises from it, in Christ Jesus our Lord, to whom is due all glory, honor, and worship.

The intellect proceeds to the contemplation of God in three ways, etc.

47. Just as bodily movement requires something in addition to its own constitution, (I mean the eyes), and something beyond its own nature (that is, light), in the same way the movement of the intellect needs eyes in addition to its own constitution and a light beyond its own nature. This is why not every movement of the intellect is advantageous, but only when it moves by these eyes and this light of grace. The eyes of the intellect within me refer to the opening of my heart (καρδιακὸν ἄνοιγμα) by faith, while the light is God Himself working in my heart through His Spirit. And just as physical light does not move a blind man in the right direction unless he is led by someone who can see, so too the Noetic Light, God, does not move the mind of one whose heart is closed except through one whose heart is open. Just as our own eyes do not work without light, so neither does open-heartedness (ἄνοιγμα καρδίας) occur without God, or rather it is impossible for the heart to even open unless God operates and manifests Himself to it.

On the participation of vision.

48. After the noetic union of the heart through grace, the intellect sees unerringly by a spiritual light, and reaches out to the object of its desire, which is God, going completely beyond the senses and unconscious of color, quality, or the impressions of the senses. Our intellect is a kind of divine vessel, which has poured into it as much unapproachable radiance of the divine beauty as it can hold. And indeed, this vessel is miraculous because it expands in proportion to the amount of the Divine Spirit that flows into it. When the inflow is greater, it itself becomes greater, and when the inflow is less, it also becomes smaller. Moreover, it waxes stronger the greater the flow, and grows weaker when the flow abates. And no matter how much is poured into it, the vessel seals itself up and spills not a drop of what it has received, but if little is poured into it, it shrivels up at once and grows slack and cannot even hold what little it has. And when it receives more, it becomes lighter, while when it receives less than its capacity, it becomes heavier and collapses inward. Moreover, it is easier for it to contain more than less, contrary to how physical vessels work: for they can better contain a smaller amount than a greater one. I believe this is why John, the 'Son of Thunder', says at the beginning of his Gospel, *In the beginning was the Word, and the Word was with God, and the Word*

was God (Jn. 1:1), so that by the magnitude (μεγέθει) of the Word[150] he may stretch out the intellect to accommodate It, and by granting gradually increasing illumination of the matter he may provide it with greater capacity, and by the weight of the utterance, render the intellect solid, capable in itself, and more fit to ascend to the contemplation of God and become a container of God's supreme wisdom. And when Jesus tells Ananias that Paul *is a chosen vessel of Mine* (Acts 9:15), Paul is chosen according to his noetic 'inner man', which is also how he was taken up to the third heaven (as he himself writes), where he *received* (ἐδέξατο) *inexpressible words, which it is not lawful for a man to utter* (2 Cor. 12:4).

On contemplation.

49. Our intellect is like a place that receives (παραδεχόμενος) the radiance of divine revelation, and its peculiar nature, about which I shall speak, is a marvel and works opposite to what we see in physical space. For the more area a physical space covers, the more it can hold, but with the intellect it is the other way around: The more the intellect draws itself in in concentration (συμπτύσσεται), the more it can receive, and when it limits and ceases all movement, rational or noetic or whatever else, it is then that it perceives that which is great[151] beyond all things, God. It beholds Him in proportion to the grace imparted by the All-Holy Spirit, and insofar as the nature of a created being enmeshed in matter is able to see beyond the physical world. These are no idle fancies, nor does it simply conjure up its own thoughts, as in a dream, but by the ineffable power of the Holy Spirit the heart receives energy in light and 'suffers' a transformation beyond nature (πασχούσης ὑπὲρ φύσιν ἀλλοίωσιν), which it receives by grace. And even while the man is asleep and at rest, his *heart is awake* (Song 5:2), and one could more easily forget the fact that he is a man than mistake that energy for anything other than divine and spiritual. For at that time, his heart is caught in a fervent, life-streaming, spiritual, perpetual motion, which usually yields gentle tears. This energy not only puts the heart at peace with itself, but also with all people. It brings forth purity, sweetness, quiet utterances of supplication, an open heart, gladness, and ineffable pleasure. He whose happy lot this is will truly and genuinely avoid even hearing of any bodily pleasure, any joy or riches or glory, for they are outward and hold no more allure for him.

50. For the man has received and now possesses all of these things divinely and spiritually, in heart and intellect; it is not merely a figment of his imagination

---

[150] This seems to carry a double meaning, referring to both the majesty of God the Word and the magnitude which gradually unfolds in the opening *words* of John's Gospel.

[151] μέγα, just like the English "great", has connotations of size, which Angelikoudes employs in his illustration here.

(λογισμός), but he is certain of it and no longer even cherishes the sensible light. For such distraction of the senses only dulls the divine noetic and truly desirable light, and for this reason he only ever seems to need a little of it, just enough to comfort his small 'outer man'. He *bears all things, endures all things* (see 1 Cor. 13:7), is secure in all things, because of his inner disposition of divine love and contemplation. No affliction can grieve him, except for sin. The great David toiled with great diligence to find this 'place' (that is, an intellect filled with divine eros), and he teaches us his desire and shares his labor with us all, saying that he would not give sleep to his eyes, nor slumber to his eyelids, nor rest to his temples, *until*, he says, *I have found a place for the Lord* (Ps. 131:4-5). Solomon the Wise also commands us, *If the spirit of the ruler rises up against your heart, leave not your place* (Eccl. 10:4). And when the Savior tells His disciples, *Arise, let us go from here* (Jn. 14:31) and performs the spiritual Passover[152] in the 'Upper Room' (Mk. 14:15), this is the 'place' to which He was referring as well. This is why I think He said, *Blessed are the poor in spirit* (Mt. 5:3), indicating that poverty of spirit is the drawing in (συστολήν) of the intellect; a kind of stripping bare and concentration in oneself. For then the intellect not only beholds the kingdom of God, but also experiences and acquires immortal joy in peace.

On the practitioner and the contemplative.

51. When the contemplative practices silence and contemplates Jesus, he reaps that pleasure which is the *good portion* of true contemplation. But the practitioner does not know this pleasure, for he has never tasted it, but is *anxious and troubled about many things* (Lk. 10:41), such as chanting, reading, and disciplining his body. Sometimes he will even censure as lazy and remiss in their duties those who extend their noetic faculty unto intelligible realities that cannot be perceived by the senses – for engagement in these things is ineffable pleasure and rest in them is unspeakable joy. He seems not to have brought to mind that the benevolence of the true Word of God, who is Himself in need of nothing, also gives rest to us, for He dearly loves mankind. This generally comes from contemplating Him, though He Himself is supremely perfect and has no need of our rest. This must be why Mary garners His praise and acceptance by sitting at His feet and hosting Him through the contemplation of His words and rousing her inner person to understand them (cf. Lk. 10:42), while Martha receives no such adulation, even though she was *anxious and troubled about many things* (Lk. 10:41), as the Gospel account states.

---

[152] τυπικὸν … Πάσχα. Could be referring specifically to the spiritual fulfillment of the Jewish Passover, to the basis of the Christian Pascha/Easter, or to the Last Supper as a type of this 'place'. These symbols or "types" by no means contradict the historical meaning of the biblical narratives, and Angelikoudes uses verbs with the suffix ὑπο- "sub-, under-" (ὑπογράφειν, ὑπεμφαίνω) when referring to additional hidden meanings.

The Lord was not only admonishing them that one time about what is better, but also teaching everyone who came after them not only to refrain from accusing of laziness those who wish to contemplate and have leisure for this purpose, but even to praise them and to try to imitate them as much as possible.

How contemplatives contemplate.

52. Amidst things that are present and currently happening, contemplatives behold the condition of the future age and the things that will come to be as *in a mirror, dimly* (1 Cor. 13:12). And although a mirror cannot reflect the real depth of whatever it shows, yet it still does show something. For whoever loves the truth must agree that what is perceived in the mirror is a perfectly clear image of something. Likewise, things that exist and come to be, display no depth or substance beyond their own, and yet they undoubtedly show images of real things to those who have received the power to contemplate them and lead them safely to the truth itself. So when you hear Paul say, *We walk by faith, not by 'form'* (2 Cor. 5:7),[153] do not think that he is talking about a purely rational faith that comes from mere hearsay. For how could he then say, *Now I know in part, but then I shall know just as I am also known* (1 Cor. 13:12) and, *When that which is perfect has come, then that which is in part will be done away* (1 Cor. 13:10)? Do you not see that knowledge in the present enables us to contemplate what shall come about in the future age, and that the difference between the future knowledge and the present knowledge that is being perfected is just the same as the difference between an action that is completed and the [same action] which is still ongoing, and so 'imperfect'?[154] Moreover, the same Apostle who says, *We walk by faith, not by 'form'* (2 Cor. 5:7), says in another place, *I run thus: not with uncertainty. Thus I fight: not as one who beats the air* (1 Cor. 9:26); that is how certain he is of the things of the future age! And this is not simply inconsistency on Paul's part (God forbid!). That is only the impression it makes, because the word 'faith' (just like the word 'form') has two meanings: There is faith that requires demonstration based on pure reason, and there is faith that needs no demonstration, but persuades the believer by the realities manifested to him; this is called 'enhypostatic faith' (ἐνυπόστατος πίστις).[155] An example might help you to understand this more clearly: Suppose that I told you that I have seen a brilliant weaver who can weave

---

[153] In this verse εἶδος is usually translated "sight", but Angelikoudes reads it specifically as "form".
[154] In Greek, the same word τελεῖν is used to mean both "to perfect" and "to complete". This could be compared to the grammatical tenses in English: the action has been completed or will be completed in the perfect and future tense, but is still ongoing in the imperfect and present tenses. But regardless of the different tenses, the verb can signify the same *action*, e.g. contemplation.
[155] Or "substantive". Cf. Maximos the Confessor, *Responses to Thalassios* 25.3 (trans. Constas), 164. For the relation between *hypostasis* and faith in the NT, cf. Heb. 11:1, and for other instances of *hypostasis*, cf. Heb. 1:3; 3:14.

winged beasts and the shapes of lions and the forms of birds of prey, horses, chariots, and battle scenes and so on, all out of thread. If you have never seen this with your own eyes, then for you to give it assent, your faith must be based on pure reason. But if you happen to see this woven fabric, but not the weaver, then you would certainly not need anyone explaining it to you to know that it is a human contrivance. For it is not in the fabric's nature to be thus woven by itself, nor could it have been woven by any other animal. So then, another faith which differs greatly from the former begins to take shape within your soul.

Moreover, as I mentioned, the word 'form' has the same double meaning as 'faith'. Now suppose you saw a blond or dark-haired man, tall in stature, and (let us say) well-proportioned in all other aspects: his eyes, the flush of his cheek, his nose, lips, and all other visible facial features by which his personal form is seen (εἶδος προσωπικόν). [From all the above you see] the enhypostatic form. But if someone asked you about the form of that weaver whom you have never seen, then judging by the look of the fabric, you would be able to deduce very generally that he is a human being. You would certainly not claim to know his enhypostatic form since you have never seen him with your own eyes, but you would not deny that the one who wove this masterpiece is a human being and human in form. This then is the form seen un-hypostatically, which you would wholly take for granted as if you had seen it yourself, even if you never have.[156]

So in summary, there is a purely rational faith that comes through hearing, and there is also an enhypostatic faith that comes through undeniable substantive evidence. Likewise, there is a form contemplated in some specific substance, which could be called enhypostatic; and there is a form not attached to a specific object, which can be rationally contemplated in a generic class, but cannot be universally predicated of each of the specimens, which all greatly differ amongst themselves. Thus, all who engage in contemplation possess, on the one hand, enhypostatic faith; on the other hand, they see the form, but no one sees the enhypostatic form.[157] For if God were not an intelligible form, how could God be

[156] It may be noted that in this visual analogy the verb "to see" is in many cases θεωρεῖν, which also means "to perceive cognitively, to contemplate."

[157] The following exegesis of 2 Cor. 5:7 is a subtle expression of Hesychastic apophatic theology. Angelikoudes shows how enhypostatic faith can have manifest certainty but can never attain the vision of God according to essence, substance, or hypostasis, but only to the noetic/intelligible manifestation of His form (through the glory *around* Him, which is often identified with the uncreated energies of God in hesychastic literature). Angelikoudes' doctrine of the distinction between the aspect of God's form which can be contemplated by the intellect (and hence "intelligible") and the absolutely invisible underlying substance of the form may be compared to St. Gregory Palamas' defense of the real distinction between God' essence and energies. It may be further noted that

called 'beauty'? Again, that beauty of God that is intelligible but not contemplated in hypostasis, you must come to know (νόει) it in the same way as His intelligible form: as majestic, supremely wondrous, most glorious, which brings astonishment to the soul and floods the intellect with noetic light and illumination and overwhelms with great and brilliant splendor (πολλῆς καὶ ποικίλης αἴγλης) and imparts to it the contemplation of God (Θεοῦ ἔννοιαν). When Manoah received the manifestation of this form, he said to his wife, *We are lost, for we have seen God* (cf. Jud. 13:22). And, indeed, everyone who has beheld that form recognizes it to be the manifestation of God's very presence. Moses the Great also saw God in this way, as it is written, God appeared to Moses *in His form, and not in riddles* (Num. 12:8; cf. Ex. 3:2). If God had been entirely devoid of divine form, then He would have remained completely unseen. Beauty is a symmetry[158] and in a certain manner is an aspect of form.[159] But if we may not attribute a divine form to God, then neither may we attribute beauty to Him, or even less so, a countenance (πρόσωπον), which includes both form and beauty. But in fact, when the Prophets say, *We saw Him, and He had no form nor beauty; but His form was ignoble* (Is. 53:2-3), this is referring to the divinity of the Word when He was hung on a tree and reckoned as one of the malefactors (cf. Lk. 23:33) and bore no recognizable feature of divine nature. This is because, according to His humanity, even though He had no beauty in death, He nevertheless had form, that is, the form of a dead man. And when David extols Him as *lovely in beauty* (Ps. 44:3), he is certainly not referring specifically to His humanity, for he adds, *grace is poured out from Your lips* (Ps. 44:3), and this 'grace' is clearly proper to His divinity, as is His 'beauty'. Moreover, David often mentions God's countenance: *You turned away Your countenance, and I was troubled* (Ps. 29:8) and again, *Do not turn away Your countenance from me* (Ps. 26:9) and again, *Turn Your countenance away from my sins* (Ps. 50:11), and in many other places.

And if he does not shrink from ascribing to God a 'countenance' and 'beauty' (inasmuch as such things can be said of God) – that is, without shape and without being seen in substance (ὑποκείμενον) – then just as he speaks of 'countenance' and 'beauty', one could of course justifiably speak of His 'form', which is what Paul had in mind when he said, *I run thus: not with uncertainty. Thus I fight: not as one who beats the air* (1 Cor. 9:26). For even though God cannot be seen or participated in in His essence (καθ' αὑτόν), He who is incomprehensible can still be seen and apprehended in another manner. This is why David calls us to *seek the face of the Lord always* (Ps. 104:4), so that we might find a great, unspeakable

---

Angelikoudes chooses this particular terminology to expand his *visual* analogy for contemplation (θεωρεῖν means both "to see" and "to contemplate") and how faith relates to the real vision of God.

[158] συμμετρία. That is, it implies form, and perhaps the "multiplicity" inherent in form.

[159] The Greek is somewhat obscure at this point.

grace, divine delight, and pleasure by reaching the manifestation of His Divinity. As he says to God concerning himself, *I shall be satisfied when Your glory appears to me* (Ps. 16:15). For God's resplendent, infinite glory shines from the radiance of the divine countenance upon those who contemplate Him *in truth and in Spirit*. And the delight and joy which proceed from it are inexhaustible to those who experience them and almost unbearable on account of their superabundance; while for those who have never beheld nor experienced this it can neither be described nor conceived of. For if no words can tell the sweetness of honey to those who have never tasted it, how could one ever illustrate what surpasses intellect to them that have no experience of it and have never received the divine delight and pleasure that come from these things? But enough on this subject.

The most holy Paul, because he had enhypostatic faith in God and in God's majestic and supremely-beautiful, albeit non-hypostatic, form, said he *walks by faith* (2 Cor 5:7) (that is, of course, "by enhypostatic faith"); he does not see *by form*, that is, not by the form contemplated according to substance (ὑποκειμένῳ), which does not produce 'unoriginate deification'.[160] For as St. Maximos puts it: "I call 'unoriginate deification' the enhypostatic illumination of the Divinity *according to [Its] form*: it has no beginning, but makes an incomprehensible manifestation in those who are worthy."[161]

Again, beauty can only be seen through form, and concerning this beauty, Basil the Great explains, "What is more desirable than divine beauty?" Again he says, "The beauty around the divine and blessed nature is true and desirable and can be contemplated (θεωρητόν) only by the purified intellect." This is why Paul testifies that, although he was *untrained in speech* (λόγῳ), he was not *in knowledge* (2 Cor. 11:6). And because he was great in spiritual knowledge, he could know *in part* the God who surpasses all conception (ὑπὲρ ἔννοιαν), in the intelligible form proper to God. This partial knowledge was also shared by Moses the God-seer, for when he contemplated the divine form and beauty which cannot be seen according to substance (τὸ μὴ ἐν ὑποκειμένῳ ὁρώμενον), he said, *If then I have found grace in Your sight, reveal Yourself to me, that I may see You in knowledge* (Ex. 33:13). For because he had already received the divine manifestation and the glorious appearance of beauty, and not according to substance (οὐκ ἐν ὑποκειμένῳ), he entreats Him for that which is more perfect. But God did not grant this, since it is

[160] Cf. Kallistos and Ignatios Xanthopoulos, *Exact Rule and Canon* 68.
[161] ἀγέννητον λέγω θέωσιν τὴν κατ' εἶδος ἐνύποστατον τῆς θεότητος ἔλλαμψιν, ἥτις οὐκ ἔχει γένεσιν, ἀλλ' ἀνεπινόητον ἐν τοῖς ἀξίοις φανέρωσιν. *Responses to Thalassios* 61.12 and scholion 14. Cf. *Responses to Thalassios,* (trans. Constas), 443, 447, and 57 in the Introduction. See also *Exact Rule and Canon* 68.

impossible for every intelligent soul, even for the eyes of angels, and it transcends the boundaries of all knowledge.

Moses is indeed the 'God-seer' and beheld God in darkness (ἐν γνόφῳ); but not according to hypostasis, but rather in intelligible form and beauty different from substance. This is how God's nature reveals itself, as Moses and Elijah and all the company of the prophets who were made worthy of divine vision would attest with one voice. And if *we walk by* enhypostatic *faith* which is based on the realities we contemplate about God, confirmed by the glory which flashes forth from the beauty of His countenance, and attested by the form of the manifestation of His dazzling light, which is not a faith of pure reason contrived by hearing, then we *walk by* enhypostatic *faith* and *not by* contemplating the *form* according to substance (2 Cor. 5:7).

There is no need for faith in the age to come, and that is why we now have enhypostatic faith. For then we will see the magnificent form of God's beauty in all its clarity; and so for now we behold only a shadow. And just as Gregory the Theologian speaks of "various visions (φαντασίας) gathered together into some likeness (ἴνδαλμα) of the truth," so the form, according to him, is a shadow. But on that day we shall see *face to face* (cf. 1 Cor 13:12) and, *When that which is perfect has come, then that which is in part will be done away* (cf. 1 Cor 13:10). But for now, as St. Augustine says, this partial vision of God's form (εἶδος) is what enthralls every rational soul in the divine eros of His glory. Through it the soul becomes unified (ἑνοειδής) and gazes in unity at the unique (μονοειδές) and hidden and transcendent Oneness of God. This enlightens and adorns and illuminates every intellect in form and beauty and countenance, with all-surpassing enlightenment and adornment and illumination of the Spirit. This is how the intellect is made simple, exalted, and filled with wonder. This is how the soul receives hidden illumination and is filled with divine pleasure and jubilation. And in a word, this is how those who love to contemplate and hearken to God's rule are glorified and deified and become friends and followers and seers of God,[162] even while they are still bound to this fleshly condition. In this way they discern and see with their noetic eyes as in a mirror the joy of the good things to come and a partial image of the coming age which *eye has not seen, nor ear heard, nor has entered into the heart of man* (1 Cor. 2:9).

[162] θεοῦνται οἱ τῆς θεαρχίας φιλοθεάμονες καὶ φιλήκοοι καὶ Θεοῦ γίνονται φίλοι.

On the passage, "Jerusalem is being built as a city, whose fellowship is complete; for there the tribes ascended, the tribes of the Lord, a testimony to Israel" (Ps. 121:3-4).

53. 'Jerusalem' means 'place of peace' and is a type of the place of God, that is, of the soul that is at peace in Christ. Not every soul is at peace in Christ and bears the name of 'peace' in itself, but only the one that *is being built as a city*, which rests on the cornerstone that God has laid in Zion, just as he promised, *a precious stone* (cf. Is. 28:16). Now, Zion is the watchtower that stands high over Jerusalem and is a type of the contemplative intellect of a soul at peace. For if you seek an uplifted mind which looks down from on high and contemplates the truth, you will find it nowhere else but in the heart which has embraced the peace of Christ and has been fully transformed by the pattern of a life of deep and abiding peace. Now, a soul that has the peace of God has *the choice cornerstone* (Is. 28:16) and the words of the Holy Scriptures as precious stones tumbling down, which crash into the wild beasts as they race up the mountain of God, and the bitumen (that is, humility) that is wrought by the Holy Spirit, who melts the stony hardness of the heart with divine fire and breaks it down into a repentant and contrite spirit (cf. Ps. 50:19); it is watered by the downpours which the Saviour causes to flow from the streams of our hearts, and has beams of wood that never rot (that is, thoughts of genuine good works), and nails and the mighty augur that is fear of God's commandments; moreover, it has the Word of God as its architect, together with His workmen. These workmen are the ones who govern the faculties of the soul under His supervision, and the builder's simple tools: fasting, vigilance, psalmody, reading and all the rest; to put it briefly, all things that are given to us as instruments in the path of virtue, including the *scarlet cord* (cf. Jos. 2:18), the sacred laws of God in the Scriptures, a noetic light that is brighter than the sun and reflects back into the life of the soul. So in a word, this is that spiritual Jerusalem: the soul that has been outfitted with all the physical, divine and spiritual equipment for building a city. This is the city being built as the dwelling place of the God who is above all, the life-giving and eternal Trinity. *I and my Father will come to him* (spiritually, that is) *and make Our home with him* (cf. Jn. 14:23), says Christ. It is as if He were saying, "We shall make him a city, a city of wonders that stretches into eternity." This is why the verse says 'Jerusalem is *being* built' and not just 'is built'. For it is a dwelling place, and He who dwells in it is uncontainable, so it is only natural that it as well should stretch into eternity. This must be why it does not say 'Jerusalem is a city being built', but 'Jerusalem is being built *as* a city'. For Jerusalem is being built by many different parts coming together that all contribute to completing the one objective, including the height, length, and width of the construction and the palace of the eternal King; so it could indeed rightly be called a city. But this construction will never have an end, for it is built to house the Endless One, and that is quite unlike any city ever built. Therefore the Holy

Scriptures were right not to say it is 'a city that has been built', but 'being built as a city', for its inhabitants (that is, the soul's faculties) all live together and do not break apart or wander or roam, but live in perfect peace and fellowship in Christ.

Then, as if in conclusion, he adds another feature to the unity of the city's inhabitants: *There the tribes ascended, the tribes of the Lord, a testimony to Israel* (Ps. 121:4). Those whom the passage above considered inhabitants of the city, it now calls 'tribes' (φυλάς). For the faculties of the soul are nothing but its own tribes (οὐ … ἔκφυλαι), and those who were simply 'tribes of the soul' become the 'tribes of the Lord' by ascending serenely through the peaceful soul to otherworldly realms, which is a 'testimony' and confirmation to Israel (the intellect that beholds God), and so they all become fellow builders of God's single design, which is the knowledge of God. So all of these spiritual tribes labor in unison to build the peaceful and holy city of God Almighty.

For there the powers of the soul truly have ascended to the heights and made the intellect that beholds God to be caught up and carried by Him. For when the soul is splintered and racked by strife and division, its faculties are no longer in unity and it becomes impossible to make ascents and build up the soul. For there is no 'place of peace' there, and neither is Jerusalem being built, so that one could see where the noetic place is. And thus, when they have congregated together, they cannot help but rise up in spiritual and glorious ascents to the Lord, lending their voices and protection to the intellect that gazes on God. And so the soul certainly is built in peace and serenity like a spiritual city, *whose fellowship* (that is, the fellowship of its faculties) *is complete*; there the spiritual powers make ascents to the Lord and in perfect concord and harmony lend their skillful aid to the one who contemplates God. And so now you as well must join in singing, *Jerusalem is being built as a city, whose fellowship is complete; for there the tribes ascended, the tribes of the Lord, a testimony to Israel*, in Christ Jesus our Lord.

On the same subject.

54. It might not be amiss to add a word to what has already been said. If you wish to know whether the divine light of peace has begun to overshadow your soul; if you wish to ascertain whether your soul is 'being built as the city of Jerusalem' and whether its fellowship is complete, then take heed: If all of your soul's thoughts and powers have united in one heart and one mind to love each other and themselves and to build not a loose, sprawling city, but a city tightly knit together; if the tribes of the Lord ascend there up to Jerusalem which is being built as a city, (that is, more broadly, the divine faculties of the soul that meet together in spirit to make the ascents); if you perceive these things at work within you, then do not stop

building! Consider how the Tower of Babel[163] was built and the languages were confused (cf. Gen. 11:1-9), and recognize that not every good building looks good to those on the outside. Broadly speaking, there are two types of buildings and ascents that are visible to our eyes. One is God's good dwelling place, and the mark of this is that its inhabitants hold firm concord and the tribes that ascend there are tribes of the Lord, who preach great and mighty wonders of peace, love and holiness to the soul they are building up. The other, however, is evil and ruinous to the soul, and the clear sign of this is the division of the tongues of the mind and the raucous confusion, and it ultimately becomes a dwelling place for the passions, like the many-legged beasts[164] at the Tower of Babel. So consider the difference between these two buildings and you should easily be able to choose the better one. If your heart does not occasionally (or frequently) feel a profound peace and single-minded devotion and spiritual light; if your heart does not have an unspeakable pleasure rise up within it at the contemplation of God; if you are not moved by a rekindling of the eternal, enhypostatic power of the Spirit in the innermost place of your heart, so that you might often think it enveloped even the members of your body above the heart with gladness, brilliance, and deep mystical vision; if your soul does not know the taste of the unutterable mysteries; if there is no inexpressible joy and inconceivable wonder being wrought together harmoniously within you; if you do not apprehend the sanctification (ἁγιασμός) of Christ rising up within you, then you can be sure that your soul is not Jerusalem and is not being built as a city; its fellowship (that is, its thoughts) is not complete, nor do its tribes (that is, the whole host of the soul's faculties) belong to Jesus, or ascend and work wonders, initiating the intellect into the mysteries and proclaiming to it what *eye has not seen, nor ear heard, nor has entered into the heart* of any man who does not share in the Spirit (cf. 1 Cor. 2:9). So take care not to build another spiritual Tower of Babel, doomed to destruction and the division and confusion of tongues and utter ruin, as I have described. I should like to discuss the reason why the souls of some are being built as the city of Jerusalem, and what causes the Tower of Babel to be built and torn down, and what it means for the fellowship of the soul to be complete, and the tongues to be divided into many at the Tower of Babel. But in deference to my hearers' wishes, I have omitted this for the sake of brevity.

---

[163] ὁ Χαλάνης πύργος "the Tower of Chalane" or "Calneh", i.e. the region where the Tower of Babel was built (cf. Gen. 10:10, Is. 10:9). All mentions of "the Tower of Babel" in this section refer to it as this.

[164] Σκολοπένδρον "Skolopendron/Skolopendra" was a hideous sea monster of Greek mythology that later became associated with the millipede.

On "those who were noble men from the East."[165]

55. Noble men from the East – the rising of the sun – (Job 1:3) would be men of the dawning rays of the sun, men who have received illuminations and enlightening rays from the Noetic Sun of Righteousness (Mal. 4:2),[166] ennobled and made virtuous by contemplating and beholding God and by reason (διάνοια), *who were born, not of blood, nor of the will of the flesh, nor of the will of man, but of God* (Jn. 1:13). Their heart and intellect cherish their dwelling place in divine palaces in the heavens, and they have been made worthy to converse with God and to receive the divine and ineffable mysteries of the kingdom.

Having become the body of Christ the Son of God and His individual members (1 Cor. 12:27), united into one body with Him, becoming His joint heirs and fellow partakers (Eph. 3:6), having Him as an inheritance and the Most High God and Father, becoming *partakers of the divine nature* (2 Pet. 1:4) which is beyond comprehension, and sealed by the Holy and Life-Giving Spirit in whom they partake and by whom they live and see. They are clothed in the whitest of garments that belong to the Spirit (cf. Rev. 4:4), and tunics both embroidered with gold and bedecked with precious stones and pearls. Set upon their heads are garlands and crowns bejeweled with Parian marble and rubies and every type of choice stone, and they eat and drink at the royal banquet. This food is inexhaustible (οὐκ ἔχει κόρον ἡ βρῶσις ἐκείνη), and the nectar is ever-abundant, for everything is spirit and they receive it spiritually.

There are exceedingly many marvellous wonders performed in those royal courts: Fire which refreshes (δροσίζον) and invigorates and moves the spurs of love in the heart, "living water that speaks" and gushes forth rivers of eternal life;[167] sweet-smelling air (εὐωδόπνους), and the Life-Giving Spirit (Πνεῦμα), and a shining, pure, supernatural light. Therefore, as spectators and beneficiaries of such delights, they separate themselves from things below and are joined to things above. They have disregarded things visible and devoted themselves to those of the intellect. They have run past (παρέδραμον) that which is passing away (παρατρέχοντα) and taken their rest among things that abide. They lie below and yet their conversation is in heaven; they are bound and drawn down by the body, but at a nod from the Spirit (νεύει τὸ Πνεῦμα) their fetters catch fire and burst. And at once they are set

---

[165] This is a reference to the noble men of the East described in Job 1:3 LXX. The original verse is, *That man [Job] was a noble man from the East.* Cf. Rev. 16:12.

[166] In Job 1:3 LXX, ἀφ' ἡλίου ἀνατολῶν, which is translated "from the East". In this spiritual exegesis, Angelikoudes pays special attention to Scripture's use of the plural form of ἀνατολή (lit. "risings").

[167] Ignatios of Antioch, *Epistle to the Romans* 7. Cf. ch. 5.

free and fly beyond the heavens with such swiftness and delight! They are of one mind in their unified vision of God. They have separated themselves from all things in single-minded contemplation of Him, being carried away *from glory to* greater *glory* of spirit (2 Cor. 3:18), and moreover they pass from riches to greater riches and enjoy ineffable things. They said unto themselves, "How great is this wealth of glory and delight!" And yet every time they beheld greater sights then before, they were astounded and only seemed to themselves to be naked and impoverished in all things. They were petrified (πεπήγασι), or perhaps it is more suitable to say they stood with mouths agape (χεχήνασι) in their ecstasy and their hearts were transfixed with joy. They became attendants and conversants with the King of Hosts and joined in the chorus of the angels, amazed at the outpouring of such grace, exceedingly glad in that inexpressible inheritance and His unspeakable love for mankind. Such are, as far as I can tell, the noble of the men of the East in Christ Jesus our Lord, to whom be glory and dominion unto the ages. Amen.

When the intellect sets its gaze solely upon the divine truth in Christ, then it is *a time to be silent* (Eccl. 3:7). For then is a time to drink of the divine nectar, a time for jubilation and spiritual exultation; a time for mystical visions and the enjoyment of supernatural goods. For it is then that the intellect clearly sees the *cup full of unmixed wine in the Lord's hand*, and when the Lord *tilts it from side to side*, the intellect manifestly beholds and fully realizes that *it has not been emptied to the dregs* (Ps. 74:9). For the last draught of the divine goodness poured out for us (which is to say the depth of the wealth and the extent of His grace) is never shown to be empty in the present life, indeed even if one attains the highest ascent toward God and deification. For the end and the 'perfect' are reserved for all to enjoy in the age to come. According to the beloved disciple of Christ, *It has not yet been revealed what we shall be* (1 Jn. 3:2). And according to St. Paul, *now we know in part* (1 Cor. 13:9), but then the perfect shall come; when all the sinners together with the righteous will drink, so to speak, of the mystical cup of God, when the reflections as in a mirror will have fulfilled their purpose, and the truth of that which is now hidden and shrouded in mystery shall be plainly revealed to those have come to experience it. The righteous, in order to exult more perfectly, shall have the reward of hope in God and shall reap the fruits of their virtuous deeds for which it was written, *They shall become intoxicated with the fatness of Your house, And You will give them drink from the abundance of Your delight* (Ps. 35:9). And the Lord has said unto them that He shall recline at the table in the Kingdom of the Father and shall serve them (cf. Lk. 12:37), to whom He also promised that together they would drink from the new cup in His Kingdom and rejoice.

But the sinners shall drink in bitter gall and eternal sorrow. And they drink so as to see that, because of their folly (ἀβουλία), they are miserably deprived of that sweetest nectar which the divine David commends to us now, saying, *Taste and see that the Lord is good* (Ps. 33:9); yet sinners do not turn to it. However, those who do turn to it and obey the commandment as they should, those who see the cup and have perceived it tilt from side to side and drink from it wherever it turns, enjoying it with heartfelt gratitude; they truly do taste its sweet sensation in their soul, and rightly do they sing songs of thanksgiving to God, crying, *Your cup intoxicates us like the best wine* (cf. Ps. 22:5), *and Your mercy* – which is beyond conception, and now hidden as the dregs at the bottom of the cup – *shall pursue us all the days of our life* (cf. Ps. 22:6), which shall be ever-lasting and deathless. For having received the divine blessings of the age to come, we shall nevermore be parted from them. Indeed, those who taste that which is poured out from every side of the life-giving and renewing (καινουργοῦ) cup in the hand of the Lord and drink from it day by day, they even come to know from what they already see that which is still hidden. And thus from the drippings (προχεόμενον) they sound out the dregs (ὑποκείμενον), and as a foretaste they reckon at what is to come.

For this reason, it is obvious that there the righteous shall partake richly and more fully of that which they already partially share in while still enmeshed in the thickness of the flesh and this nether gloom (τῷ κάτω ζόφῳ) here below; David did not say (and it is clear why) that all the righteous and sinners would drink; but having mentioned that which was perhaps ambiguous (that is, whether or not sinners would drink), he omitted as self-evident that which is commonly acknowledged (that is, that the righteous would drink as well). For if even sinners would drink, then it is unnecessary to say whether the righteous would or not (which is self-evident), for they are already so filled with the wine that they are gladdened and shout, *You, O Lord, have made me glad with Your work: and in the workings* (ἔργα) *of Your hands will I exult* (Ps. 91:5), and by saying 'the workings of His hands,' David means the holding, and the extending of the cup full of unmixed wine of the drink offering and the tilting back and forth out of His love for mankind and the reserving of the dregs in it for what is to come. But they, once more, are full to overflowing and shout to God, *Your cup intoxicates us like the best wine* (Ps. 22:5) in Christ Jesus, and so on.

I shall sing unto my Creator and praise You, O Most High God, whose merciful grace is poured out unto me; Your sacred finger pierces (νύττει)[168] me in the depths of my heart, O Lover of souls and Supremely Good King, for truly *You alone do wonders* (Ps. 71:18). And having exalted me and prepared me rightly to behold the

[168] Cf. κατάνυξις, "compunction".

writings of Your holy hand in the book of life, inspired by Your Most Divine Spirit and the awesome beauty wrought by Your hands, and to apprehend aright with my noetic sense all the fullness of gladness and hidden joy in Christ Jesus our Lord.

There is a peace, more apparent than real (μᾶλλον δοκοῦσα ἢ οὖσα), in an indulgent body, which does great mischief to the soul, even though for a time it will profess to be tranquility. And there is a peace of the senses which comes from seclusion and flight from all things in the pursuit of stillness. But this also, though it is incomparably better than the first, is by nature fleeting; for the body and the whole man are naturally disturbed and suffer together with the soul when it is hounded by distracting thoughts. There is also a third peace superior to these which is a peace of the senses and of the soul, when the powers of the soul and of the inner man come to rest, which follows instruction and refined study; this causes one both to pray more purely and to mourn more sweetly, and to converse with the word of God with pleasure. But this is not yet the perfection of peace. For as one who plays the flute or the lyre cannot continue playing his instruments forever, but rather he will surely either suffer fatigue of the hands or some weariness will befall him, or some other afflicting circumstance that causes the flutist to cease playing and the lyrist to break the harmony. Likewise the soul which puts its own essential powers in harmonious order cannot forever remain at perfect peace, but slackens, willingly or unwillingly, either out of anger at something that has befallen it, or by its own capriciousness (φιλοτρεπότης) and boredom (ἀκηδία), since it too is a created thing and somehow paradoxically co-natural with the body, despite its thickness and unruliness. And yet when by grace the soul receives the presence of the Uncreated Creator of all things and partakes of the Unchanging and Life-Giving Spirit, it is then wondrously transformed and takes on a new kind of life. And having been given life according to the nature of the Spirit, it enjoys a life that is not of this earth and is truly unchanging. And as it lives by this life-giving power, then it also sees that this Life-Giver is also light, and it greatly rejoices at seeing the supernatural things of the One who transcends nature, it has a *peace which transcends all understanding* (Phil. 4:7); this is because the Life-Giver's gift of life (ζωοποιοῦ ζωοποίησιν) also transcends all understanding, as does the illumination, vision, and joy of those who see the hidden things. It does not change at all, nor is it subject to fatigue, nor does it pay attention to the snares and assaults of the enemy, but it fixes its gaze on God and the things of God, without the slightest exertion of willpower (θέλησις), but with power and motion, and one might add, with the will (θέλησις) of the tireless Spirit (ἀκάματον) working manifestly (ἐνυποστάτως) in the heart, not as one might imagine, but as only the Spirit knows how, who searches out and knows *the deep things of God* (1 Cor. 2:10) and initiates those who commune with Him through the senses of the soul. So inasmuch as we take care to kindle the Spirit's grace within us by hesychastic training and holiness and not mistakenly quench it (1 Thess. 5:19, we shall be full of ineffable and supernatural peace in God the Trinity, and then we shall have the true peace that we have described, of body, spirit, and soul in tireless humility, love, and prayer. For the peace won by toil (μετὰ κόπου) is not yet perfect peace, but leads to perfection. And perfection, as we have said, is made perfect in the complete absence of toil, in the perfect Sabbath rest and repose in Christ.

Consider then, O reader, that you came into existence out of non-existence, and eagerly acknowledge your Maker and Creator, and mark well the cause of your existence where once you were nothing; and if you are wise, you will offer up in divine eros all that you are with all of your faculties to the sweetest Jesus your God, your Fashioner and Creator, both in action (πρᾶξιν), but also in the contemplation of His countenance (πρόσωπον). For when you live this life both in practice and in contemplation, you will receive abundant gifts from God and become a god yourself, like unto Him both in spirit and in all other ways (you, the creature, unto your Creator!), rejoicing together eternally with your Lord and Father, resting in the divine eros and reposing in God through Jesus Christ unto the ages of ages, enraptured away from all visible things. Amen.

56. When I behold (that is, by discerning with my noetic eyes) from whence I so wondrously came and second, whither I am bound, and thirdly, when I consider Him who brought me forth and carries me and shall lay me to rest, I perceive the Indescribable Father and begin to get an idea of His love. And thus I catch a glimpse of the mysterious purpose of my own existence as if in a mirror; and indeed, I am more delighted by these three visions than words can say. But an equal sorrow often follows this great gladness, when I perceive how my conduct is so clearly unworthy of my calling (κλήσεως). And then, when I thus contemplate how You manifest Your unapproachable glory to me through creation and Your unutterable love for me through the incarnation of Your only-begotten Son, and when I perceive how You show Yourself to me and recognize Your ineffable and supernatural union with me, as You offer it to me in ever-flowing, unspeakable spiritual communion; then I am awestruck at Your glory and am astonished at Your strange and wondrous mercy towards me, and how You thus draw me away from all visible things, give me rest from all musings, and give me repose and unspeakable gladness in You, O Holy Trinity who transcends all being.

God in His exceeding wisdom desired to create man as a second angel upon the earth, a heavenly creature, in the form and likeness of God,[169] and so for this reason

[169] We must quote this sublime statement in full: ἄγγελον ἄλλον ἐπὶ γῆς, ζῷον οὐράνιον, θεοειδές τε καὶ θεοείκελον, θέλων ὁ θεὸς ποιῆσαι σοφῶς ὡς λίαν τὸν ἄνθρωπον,

He placed a noetic and intellectual soul of divine knowledge and understanding within him. And so He declared concerning those things, *I said, 'You are all gods and sons of the Most High* by grace' (cf. Ps. 81:6), that is, as another order of angels, silently contemplating God and being lifted up to Him in divine eros and spiritual light. And it would clearly be impossible for earthborn man to ascend to an angelic state if he did not first become spirit, like the angels. For through faith the faithful believer is made spirit by the almighty and infinitely gracious God, refashioned after the likeness of the mystical form of God, as the Savior declares, saying, *That which is born of the flesh is flesh, and that which is born of the Spirit is spirit* (Jn. 3:6);[170] and that those with bodies together with their souls will also be born of the Spirit, the faithful John bears witness saying, *to them He gave the right to become children of God, to those who believe in His name: who were born, not of blood, nor of the will of the flesh, nor of the will of man, but of God* (Jn. 1:12-13), in the inner man (that is to say, who had been made in the image of God his Creator). And because this birth is not by natural means, but by grace, those who are born of the Spirit are born through a reception beyond the conditions of nature (κατὰ παραδοχὴν ἄσχετον). Therefore it is only right that the participant intellect should become the throne of the Holy Spirit. For just as iron heated by fire becomes fire itself as long as it is with the fire, not changing into fire by nature, but by transference and through its participation in the fire, so it also becomes a "throne" for the fire and the fire comes to rest in the iron, as it were. So also in the same way, the intellect, through its birth or union and reception of the Spirit, also becomes spirit itself and the throne of the Spirit, who encompasses and indwells it in glory, as it were God resting on the throne of the intellect.

This is the extraordinary beginning of the soul's progress; not unto a lower order of Angels in the heavenly hosts, but unto the order of God the Most High. Only then does it proceed to the order of the Thrones, and afterward that of the Cherubim, then to that of the Seraphim, and so it continues until it becomes an Angel (that is, the more lowly order),[171] proclaiming (ἀναγγέλων) to its neighbors the renowned and mystical things of God in the Spirit. For if, as the wise men of God say, communion (μετοχή) must precede communication (μετάδοσις), how is it not obvious that one must clearly first participate in the Spirit by having one's intellect become His Throne, and thus pass on the things of the Spirit, so as to become Cherubim in the Spirit (which indicates an outpouring and an abundance of spiritual wisdom) and to want to make others wise, then to become like the

---

[170] *On Union with God and the Contemplative Life* 2.

[171] Dionysios the Areopagite, *Celestial Hierarchy* 6-7. According to St. Dionysios, the Thrones (or "Seats of God"), Cherubim, and Seraphim are the highest order of celestial beings, while the "Angels" are in the lower order, as "messengers" who proclaim (ἀναγγέλων τοῖς πλησίον). One might say that the intellect ascends to descend, that is, for the sake of love of neighbor and divine eros.

Seraphim in knowledge of wisdom and to drink from their cup, to attain a burning and stirring love (ἀγάπαι) for God (for this is what 'Seraphim' indicates)?[172] And then they may kindle the divine eros (ἔρωτες) in others, and thus fan them into flame to walk the path until they, in turn, may reach the order wherein they teach their neighbor; for this is what it means to be an Angel (τοῦτο γὰρ ἄγγελος). Therefore, before becoming gods in Spirit and Thrones of God, Cherubim and Seraphim and the other lower spiritual orders, they would not be steadfast Angels nor could they *worship God*, nor teach what is needful *in truth and in Spirit* (Jn. 4:24). So the true progress of the soul has its beginning in participation in the Most High God and proceeds in Jesus Christ, our Lord, by the steps we have described.

I will praise You, O Ineffable Triune Lord, not according to Your worth, O Master, but according to my ability. For You, O Inexpressible One, and Your virtues are infinite beyond measure, soaring high above all word and thought of any that seek to comprehend or speak to You. You have created me out of nothing by Your magnificent design. Your hands have fashioned me as they have fashioned no other thing (ὡς οὐδὲν ἕτερον); according to Your image and likeness You have created me (cf. Gen. 1:26). And yet I am a fool in the midst of neighbors of such glory and honor; I have been willfully blind to Your commandments, though these are holy and full of peace, true joy and divine power. And what is most marvellous is that before You brought me into being, for the sake of me, that I might live and look upon You and know You and for the irresistible spiritual pleasure thereof, You created the world with all its magnificent beauty and glory, its power and creative wisdom, so richly adorned in every way. Without these things I could not exist for even an hour, while with them I live in this body, enjoying their comforts and being nourished by them, and I understand them in my soul's contemplation and I am awestruck at the deep wisdom and the almighty ocean of Your providence and love. This is who You are, O Ineffable One, while I, the fool, have lived my whole life until now as a prodigal in opposition to Your commandments, alas! the very commandments which are truly pleasing and dear to the prudent. Alas, my callous soul! Alas, its hardness! O foul soul, do you not see how just to preserve his physical life the poor man will become the rich man's slave and at once submit to his master's commands, even if some of them are harsh and are not given for the slave's sake, but obviously for the sake of the master? My foolish soul, how then do you so ungraciously reject and turn against the commandments of such a Creator, Benefactor, and Caretaker, even though they are given for your own sake and for your immortal glory? O the thanklessness, and the eternal evil that awaits you!

---

[172] In Hebrew *seraphim* denotes "the burning ones".

O Lord, I had spoken to my poor and truly sinful soul (Your creation, O Lover of Souls), when I turned towards You, O Most Good One – of my pleasure beyond words, saying, "*O soul, you have many* spiritual *things. Eat, drink, and be merry*" (cf. Lk. 12:19). And when some sinner rose up against me, I had said, *I am afflicted and greatly humbled* (Ps. 37:9). O, but how great are the riches of your goodness, O Most Merciful One? For when I erred and strayed from the good and straight path, You then hastened quickly to bring me back through Your unsurpassable gifts. But having indeed eaten and drunk and spiritually rejoiced in Your mercy and compassion, I have still wandered away again and have been cast out many times, whether because of the wicked scheming of some demon or my own heedlessness, or perhaps both, I do not know. Or perhaps there was also some more profound judgment of Yours which sometimes allows for withdrawal, forsaking, and chastisement.[173] Many times I was also *stuck fast in deep mire, and there is no standing* (Ps. 68:3), and truly I was troubled and downcast and pierced by a thorn (cf. Ps. 31:4), (or the deathly sting of sin), and in short, by all the evil things of the enemy mischievously conspired against my soul through my own terrible negligence and grievous folly. But You, O Most Good One, would never overlook my distress in the end, but You cried out with a spiritual voice into the innermost reaches of my heart, and You said to my reviled soul, "*I am your salvation* (Ps. 34:3), fear not; but return to your rest, and wander no more." And so You comforted me, O Long-Suffering Jesus, and You became the bright shield of my salvation and as the Right Hand of the Lord the Father, You helped me mightily, and Your instruction (παιδεία) has set me upright many times in the utmost gladness of Your ineffable mysteries. Come then, O Word of God, as a firm seal over my heart, that I might contemplate (θεωρία) Your unutterable and extraordinary beauty. Come into my arms, that I might carry out (πρᾶξις) Your holy and life-giving commandments, O King Jesus Christ, exalted above the heavens. Come that I might live spiritually in You. Draw near unto me that I might sense you, as I turn to You with all my soul. You are gladness beyond this world, surrounded by unutterable mysteries; *send forth Your lightning*, O Infinitely Wise One (Ps. 143:6),[174] so that my noetic soul might be drawn together in itself and then drawn together in You, and so that *those who hate me without cause* and persecute me for naught and injure me mercilessly might *be scattered* and dwell in destruction (cf. Ps. 3:8). O Lord, I beseech You to keep me ever *as the apple of Your eye* (Ps. 16:8), that I might ever be with You and contemplate You, O Ineffable Lord beyond glory!

57. O Uncreated Lord, what am I but *earth and ash* (Gen. 18:27)? And what is my time but *a passing shadow* (cf. Ps. 143:4), or a fleeting dream, O Unoriginate,

---

[173] παραχωρήσεις, ἐγκαταλείψεις, παιδεῖαι.

[174] ἄστραψον ἀστραπήν σου, ἀπειρόσοφε.

before You in whose eyes *a thousand years pass like yesterday or as a watch in the night* (Ps. 89:4)? And what is my understanding before You? For You *made the heavens with understanding* (Ps. 135:5) and the earth and the universe in wisdom, indeed altogether and immediately, so that in every way, O Lover of Souls, I stand before You as my Judge. Spare me, O Master, I fervently beseech You, for parents do not call their little children to account for the things they do, nor do they demand any work from them, but easily and kindly and with goodwill they care for everything they need as they need it, nourishing and aiding them as much as they can. This is why, O Holy One (for You are truly our dear eternal Parent (γονεύς), who created all things out of nothing), I ask You not to be vexed at my mistakes and iniquities, not to demand works from me, O Lover of Mankind, according to Your grace. Forbear, O Good One, forbear (μή, ἀγαθέ, μή)! But as with a little child (or indeed, much more!) never stop pardoning me and increase Your immaculate gift in me, a feeble and foolish man begging for your help. Yes, O Supremely Praised One, You created and fashioned (πλάσας) and re-fashioned (ἀναπλάσας) me for a supremely good end; to shape me most skillfully and to adorn me with the beauty of divinization (θεουργικοῖς κάλλεσι κατακοσμήσας), as Your true image, and to glorify me in a manner just as pure and noble. For You came *not to judge, but to save the world* (Jn. 3:17). Amen.[175]

58. I am self-condemned, as You, O Lord, who know the inner parts of my heart, can see. I need no other judge, O Most Wise One. For it is only right to judge doubtful cases, O Most Good One, but when the defendant stands rightfully condemned aforetime and he sees and plainly confesses himself to be not just a sinner, but continually sinning every day, every hour – spare me, O Lover of Mankind, from the penalty! I seek for mercy and I beg for grace, O bounteous Spring of Mercy and Grace. In Your good pleasure You became man for me, and because of Your abundant goodness and overwhelming love for us, You do not punish us according to our iniquity nor repay us for our sins (cf. Ps. 102:12). But rather Your innate love masters You (ἀγάπῃ νικώμενον πεφυκυίᾳ) and You take away our sins from us *as far as the East is from the West* (Ps. 102:10). I beg you therefore, long-suffering Lord Jesus Christ, merciful Lord, I beg you, though I am unworthy, to overlook all my iniquity and all my sins, and to place on my heart the perfect seal of Your most holy Spirit, the truly holy gift, by your power and wisdom. Thus will I do what is pleasing in Your sight, with wisdom and spiritual prudence through the power of Your grace, such as I am able. And hereafter the spiritual rivers of Your immaculate wisdom shall again flow from my heart in knowledge of the truth and pure light; and thus will I be with You, a communicant

[175] Wordplay: "adorn" (κατακοσμήσας) and "world" (κόσμος).

of Your mysteries, unto ages of ages, illuminated by Your glorious light from henceforth, through Your incomparable mercy and inexpressible grace. Amen.

59. No one fully understands the schemes (ἐπιβουλήν) – or let us rather call them the assaults (προσβολήν), since they are literally diabolic (διαβολική)[176] – as well as the one who has escaped the demons and is free for a time from their assaults. And no one escapes and is thus set free from them unless God renders him aid by breathing His ever-flowing and enhypostatic breath into his heart. This comes of faith, humility and active love toward God and people, and the quiet (φιλησύχῳ) way of life with alertness and reading, at times practical, at times contemplative and at times theological and prayerful. Active love naturally means fulfilling God's holy commandments as best you can. And that leads to not only a clearer and more acute knowledge of God, but also a precise understanding and a better discernment of the crafty devices of the demons and their attacks against the soul. But then the struggles become greater and so we strive in proportion to the spiteful demons; they rush headlong at us, trying furiously to do whatever harm and mischief they can to the God-bearing soul. And if the true Savior of His people did not lovingly safeguard us, and Christ did not fight on behalf of the faithful, surely no human being, not even a Saint, would be saved.

60. I know full well and confess to you (ἐξομολογοῦμαι), Lord, that I, a rational creature (λογικός), am worse off than the irrational beasts (ἄλογα ζῷα) because of my carelessness, folly and vanity (ἀλογοπραγία). For they conform to their nature and live according to it, while I have never even for one hour known the pure and true nobility of my nature. For it is polluted by unclean passions and is entangled with and clings to the things of this world. Thus I play the fool (ἀνοηταίνων) and do not even know what my nature really is. Indeed I have outstripped the hordes of demons in wickedness and my desires are even worse than theirs. For if I were immune to illness like they, and immortal and needed nothing to live, then this poor wretch would surely be single-minded in his wickedness and wholly devoted to perverse appetites. As it is though, I am not only mortal, but also given to frequent and long-standing illnesses; yet still I flout the law (παρανομῶ) and revel in and cleave to my sins. And worst of all, I am not inclined towards just one evil, shunning all the others, as each of the demons does; one produces avarice, another vainglory, another sensuality and yet another some other passion, or rather aids and abets those who succumb to it; but I alone am such a passionate lover and perpetrator of all the passions that I do not even need the demons to urge me or assault me from without, for I follow my passions of my own free will, or rather stumble miserably into them. That is why I have not done the evil from which I

[176] διαβολική is etymologically related to προσβολή.

have refrained, not because I willingly avoided it or resolved against it, but because I was unable to do it. How justly and fairly then I am judged so much worse than the demons? For they are immortal, immune to illness and need nothing to live, yet each one of them tends towards only to one type of sin; whereas I – whose days are not only short, but as I have said, full of disease and sickness and suffering – I am swift to sin and willing, alas, eager to commit it. Therefore, I am really much worse than the demons. But Lord, Lord! Your mercy is all-surpassing, and salvation is in Your nature, for You would freely grant repentance even to the demons, if they wished; support me with wisdom and all that is necessary for me to repent properly for my sins and to propitiate Your most holy countenance. You are the wonderful and blessed life and the everlasting, heavenly enjoyment of the just; you are unfathomable Love itself and unutterable charity and compassion, Lord. Show Your great and wonderful mercy to my soul, for it cries to you, "Have mercy on me, Forgiving One!" Let those who hear it understand that if even the demons would come back to You as they are and plead the mercy of Your infinite goodness, You would not turn them away from Your grace, nor would You reject them, for You are the Fountain of Grace. If then you pardon me, though I am worse than the demons and baser than the mindless beasts, then there is truly none guilty of sin, no man nor demon, who will fall down before You and cry out "Have mercy on me!" and will not at once find Your infinite goodness and Your most abundant and most wonderful mercy above every expectation. Have mercy on me, Jesus, and our Father by nature, and the Fountain of Mercy.

61. Many things come to my mind that I should like to know (νοούμενα), Lord, but there is nothing that I can be sure I fully understand (κατανοῶ), and there is nothing at all that does not eventually exceed my knowledge. And so it is only natural that I clearly lack both simple and general knowledge. Of course, I can certainly see the sky above and the earth below, but I have no idea what they are and on what foundation they stand and how they hold together and many other things about them and their nature. I can easily procure air and water and fire for anyone who wishes, but if someone asks what the nature of each is, and why the one sinks and the other rises and yet air goes in all directions, I cannot even open my mouth to stutter an answer. But I quickly give up on this, realizing that I have nothing to say. And a single hair, which seems so insignificant, we barely notice it; nothing of where it came from and how, or when or in what order, or what in fact hairs even are.

That is why I beg you, Sovereign, to deliver me from my intellectual conceit, which causes me to judge and condemn the motives of my neighbor and everyone else. And take me under the shelter of Your powerful arm, because I am simpleminded and very slow in perception. Who knows the extent of the sky and the mass and weight of the earth and the swift and tireless track that the sun describes with marvellous art and precision? Who could ever comprehend the power that so wisely directs all this? How can a man know this, who does not even have the knowledge of a gnat? And where could he find it out? I am too foolish and feeble to understand the might of Your wisdom; and I make bold to speak of Your grace in deification or the supernatural union with God, which God Himself performs and we can understand only in part.

62. Only those who have received spiritual discernment through grace-given insight (διόρασις) can utterly and truly understand those who have not acquired spiritual discernment, but are led naturally by outward, visible signs. For, as the divine Paul teaches, such a man *can discern all things, though he himself cannot be judged by anyone else* (1 Cor. 2:15). But whoever the others might be, not only can they not distinguish the one who is devoid of the Spirit of God, but will often out of ignorance praise those who should actually be objects of pity, because they have not received the grace-given spiritual discernment, but are governed by a worldly spirit and are "natural" (ψυχικούς), as the word of God calls them (1 Cor. 2:14). Those who have spiritual discernment and have been joined to the likeness of God never judge things rashly nor by outward appearances, as most do, but by the unwavering and constant truth within them; for they have been initiated by the Spirit who gives life and light, who gives to those whom He manifestly indwells a different kind of life than the ordinary, a supernatural life, and light and knowledge, quite unlike what most people see. Such was the Patriarch Jacob, who traveled to many places, but in this one place he remained fixed, and saw many things with the eye of discernment and prophesied many marvellous things of his sons (Gen. 49:1). In the same way Isaiah, the thundering prophet, saw Jesus being *led as a sheep to the slaughter* (Is. 53:7), yet was neither seized by His passion nor scandalized (προσκεκρουκώς) by the manner of His humiliation, but with spiritual eyes he saw the secret glory that was, of course, hidden in all of this (μυστικῶς); he was such that while he saw the stately *form* and *beauty depart* from Jesus (Is. 53:3), and all His other sufferings, he nonetheless confessed His divinity.

In a word, such were all the prophets, who by their intellect pondered the things of the intellect, in the light of the Spirit. But anyone who wishes can easily see those who bear the spirit of the world, or rather, to be more precise, those who are borne by the worldly spirit; he need only remember that faction of the Scribes and the Pharisees mentioned in the Gospels, how wholesome they seemed on the outside and how addicted they were to appearances, and how they desired with all their soul, with reverence and decorum and pomp, to be called Israel's teachers, and did nothing but put on a hollow show and falsely bless the virtuous life (Mt. 23:3ss). And thus they so despicably condemned Jesus the Christ to death (what dreadful blindness!), the very Son of God Almighty, the divine and true Life, because of the envy which the worldly spirit had given birth to within them. For if the Holy Spirit does not speak to us *out of envy*,[177] as it is written (Jas. 4:5), then clearly the spirit of the world will speak out of envy, and its ensuing judgment is unjust and dark. Therefore, as it is written, *they will beat their breasts* (Rev. 1:7) when the time comes for God to judge the world, and they will rightly deplore themselves for *they will see the one whom they have pierced* (Jn. 19:37) and they will say in despair: *Is He not the One whom we thought of no account and whose life we considered madness? How then is He counted among the sons of God* (Wis. 5:4-5)? For in their darkened understanding they were deceived by the worldly spirit and stumbled grievously; and naturally they could not see the real truth and thus walk by it, in which those led by the straight (εὐθές) and Light-Giving Spirit walk. Paul says somewhere about those of the Spirit: *Do you not know that we will judge angels? How much more the things of this life!* (1 Cor. 6:3). Thus, he who has the Spirit *can discern all things* (1 Cor. 2:15); but, as the Lord says, the world cannot *receive* nor *comprehend* Him (Jn. 14:17). So those who have not put on the super-celestial Holy Spirit with true discernment of the soul and do not have him working unspeakable mysteries within them and saying that which words cannot express – it is clear that their spirit is of the world. *You, however*, Paul says, *are not in the realm of the flesh but are in the realm of the Spirit, if indeed the Spirit of God lives in you. And if anyone does not have the Spirit of Christ, they do not belong to Christ* (Rom. 8:9).

So do you see that those who have the Spirit within are not carnal? And those who, alas, are destitute of Him, that they not only cannot discern the things of God aright, but they do not even belong to Christ? The Apostle elsewhere more subtly illustrates the opposition of the worldly spirit to the Spirit of God, saying: *What we have received is not the spirit of the world, but the Spirit who is from God, so that we may understand what God has freely given us* (1 Cor. 2:12). Do you see how only those who have received the Spirit of God can understand the things of God and the truth? As the Lord said: *However, when He, the Spirit of truth, has come, He will guide you into all truth* (Jn. 16:13). Do you see how the whole truth is gifted to the intellect, so that discernment is easy and free of any grave errors (διαμαρτίας)? That is why the Holy Spirit is called Spirit of counsel, Spirit of knowledge, of understanding, of wisdom (Is. 11:12), directing Spirit (ἡγεμονικόν) (Ps. 50:14), right Spirit (εὐθές) (Ps. 50:12), Spirit of truth (Jn. 14:17). Isaiah also calls Him the Spirit of judgment (Is. 4:4), because by Him the soul is directed unerringly to what has been spoken, and by His working through it, the soul can discern these things aright, for it participates in Him, and without the Spirit all is

---

[177] Or "out of jealousy" (πρὸς φθόνον), "begrudgingly".

filled with darkness devoid of truth. The one devoid of the Spirit of truth and the other things we have mentioned, when he tries to exercise discernment, will draw false conclusions and misrepresent the truth. *No one knows the things of another except the spirit which is in him* (cf. 1 Cor. 2:11), *for the Spirit searches all things* (1 Cor. 2:10). And if it were possible to find the truth without Him, the Holy Spirit would not be called 'the Spirit of truth' and 'the Spirit of judgment' and the things we have mentioned.

If anyone claims to judge without the Spirit of truth, he will be advocating falsehood by guessing at what is not so, and in a word he will depart from the truth (the Spirit is also called 'the Spirit of judgment') and of his own accord (ἑκών) be cast out and cut off from God and the glory of God; and rightly so, for he has judged against the truth and rendered a hasty verdict (προπετῶς), in his ignorance betraying justice like a second Judas. For he is truly thrice-accursed and condemned on account of this: he has shamefully and wrongfully betrayed Righteousness and Truth, our Lord Jesus Christ, the Righteousness sent to us by the Father (cf. 1 Cor. 1:30), who referred to Himself as *the Truth* (Jn. 14:6). Wretched, blind Pharisee – you go about devoid of the Spirit that gives light to the noetic eyes of the soul and are quick to pass false judgment on the inward man based on his outward appearance, just as those Pharisees saw (if indeed they *did* see) wondrous resurrections from the dead and many other miracles, performed at a single nod from Jesus, the true God; and while they should have honored Him and praised Him and put their faith in Him, instead they were indignant and incensed that, in His great wisdom and love for humanity, He would break the Sabbath, and that the disciples of the Bridegroom would not fast (cf. Mt. 9:15) and ate without washing their hands (cf. Mk. 7:2). O foolish, senseless Pharisee, full of darkness! Would you call to account the Wellspring of wisdom and unspeakable miracles, and close your eyes to works of such great power, while yet scrutinizing the most insignificant things that for you are truly inscrutable? How twisted, unfeeling, and senseless you are! And even if you did take offence (as you have no right to) at these "nothings" (οὐδέσι), how could you help but marvel at the greatest works that He had done, and not give due glory and praise to the One who had done them? And why did you not then go to Him humbly and with sincerity ask Him to explain to you the reason (λόγος) for these breaches of custom, as they seemed to you? But it seems that conceit (οἴησις) is the worst and most terrible thing of all, as is the wickedness (πονηρία) that follows it. It is darkest when it flaunts its knowledge, and most foolish when it knows not its own folly.

Again, blind Pharisee, you do not check whether the inside of the cup is clean, but you would rather look at and cleanse the outside of the cup (cf. Mt. 23:26) and the dish; have you not heard what Christ, the true Wisdom, commands about judgment? *Do not judge according to appearance, but judge with righteous judgment* (Jn. 7:24). Do you not understand that righteous judgment and fair rulings are not based on outward appearances? This is what "according to appearance" (κατ' ὄψιν) means: that which can be clearly seen. How then, you fool, do you not fear the Father's commandment and seemingly not understand that the outward appearance is not the true man? How do you not hide in mortification, feeling no shame at judging based on what you see? Yet that is only natural, since you live deprived of real life, light, wisdom, truth and knowledge of the truth, and so many other blessings that are poured out in communion with the Spirit, without which you not only cannot judge other things aright, but you cannot even see your own abysmal state. Take my advice (εἴτε ἐμοὶ πείθῃ) and remove the plank (δοκόν) from your eye (I mean the appearance [δόκησιν] or the conceit from your intellect), and once you can see clearly, you should then easily be able to remove the speck (cf. Mt. 7:5) (that is, the sin) that has somehow landed unexpectedly in your neighbor's eye without his knowing it. But if your own inner eye cannot see the noetic light, then of course it is the plank sticking out of it that is causing the darkness.

So only after searching yourself as best you can and removing evil far away from you, together with the demons' deception and the effects of your own ignorance, should you presume to do that which belongs only to the enlightened; the undertaking is dubious in the extreme, and the attempt is fraught with danger. Let the redeemed of the Lord speak and let them then render judgment, as the holy David advises; that is, those the Lord has redeemed from the hand of their enemies (cf. Ps. 106:2), (that is, spiritual enemies) and gathered from the nations (that is, the various and sundry passions in which they were living), uniting them with each other and with His glory. So those who are gathered and united and enlightened, let them speak and judge as the redeemed and the saved. But you who are not filled with spiritual light, as I said, remain safe and remain silent; do not be at all ashamed of learning new things and confessing your own ignorance, giving heed to any word (λόγος) (any word of salvation of course, not perdition). How does Christ not put you to shame when he says, *I judge no one* (Jn. 8:15)? And what do you say? "I will judge everyone!" But how senseless and deluded! Christ says, *The Father has committed all judgment to the Son* (Jn. 5:22). The Son has been given authority to judge by the Father; but who has given it to you? Does the Trinity truly dwell within you and walk for all to see (ἐμπεριπατεῖ ἐμφανῶς), as God has promised (cf. 2 Cor. 6:16)? Do you see yourself in God the Word, and God the Word in you? Are you in God? Are the rivers of the Holy Spirit flowing and gushing forth in unapproachable light from within your heart? Do you have all the other manifest signs of God's working in His saints? Or are you far removed from this?

So then, keep your tongue from evil and your lips from speaking guile (cf. Ps. 33:14). Ask thoughtful questions of others, be inquisitive and teachable; do not presume to teach and give your opinion; let others judge you, and do not pass judgment yourself. It is great folly for a blind man to think he can read, and an even greater folly to think that you can know your neighbor's thoughts without having the living Spirit. In fact, you cannot even know your own thoughts with clarity. But these are the arts and decoys of an evil, spiteful demon that hates the good; these move against us when we are ruled by conceit and when we wrongly undertake to pass judgment, so that with such ignorance we stumble and sadly misrepresent the truth. And instead of coming and learning, we remain helpless and cause ourselves and our neighbors to stumble and come to harm; we thus fall under the dreadful judgment of God. But one day we will see the demon's intrigue for what it is, in obedience to the great Paul's command: *Judge nothing before the time* (cf. 1 Cor. 4:5). Then our Lord will indeed come among us and by the Spirit will illuminate and thus reveal to us the depths of divine visions and knowledge of hidden things and revelations. And He will teach us in truth and show us those who are indeed spiritual and God-bearers (or rather gods themselves), and He will raise us up to glory and restore us with the grace of discernment; and then we will know full well what an evil it is for those to sit in judgment who have not the gift of Christ. And then we will judge aright and with equity (ἀνεπισφαλῶς ἐν εὐθύτητι).

63. From the beginning God had lavished salvation and care on Israel and proclaimed it to be *the line of His inheritance* out of all other peoples (cf. Dt. 32:9). But the spectacular and marvelous displays of God's care and salvation to those who believe in Christ are so far superior to what He did for Israel as the soul is superior to the body; and they so outshine the others as the sun outshines the stars; and the works He has wrought among the Christians so surpass those of the Israelites as the body surpasses its own shadow. For upon closer inspection, we see that those things were truly a shadow of what has come to pass for us. There Pharaoh, a bitter and ruthless ruler, and his cruel taskmasters (cf. Ex. 1:8-11) are images of Satan and his company, who do not afflict our bodies, but tirelessly and relentlessly oppress our very soul. There Moses led the people of God (cf. Ex. 3:10), but we (how far better it is!) have the true Son and the enhypostatic Word of God Himself (cf. Jn. 1:14), so superior, so infinitely superior to the letter of the Law! They had a rod (cf. Ex. 7:9, 20; 8:2; etc.), we have the cross (cf. Mt. 27:32); the staff miraculously transformed and swallowed up the serpents (cf. Ex. 7:12), and the cross, an instrument of evil, also underwent a kind of transformation and brought about such goodness, proving to be the bane of the demons (ὀλετὴρ τῶν δαιμόνων). Was Egypt spoiled of its gold and silver and costly apparel (cf. Ex. 12:35-36)? We also see how we secretly do the same in our minds, transferring the allure of pleasure from sin to God. Israel had a fiery pillar of cloud leading them

directly to the sea (cf. Ex. 13:21-22); we have the vision of God and His fiery eros, when the faithful and contemplative mind attains unceasing tears, in which all enmity is lost and dies, and then the mind passes on from there, as the Israelites passed through the sea, but Pharaoh and his army were spectacularly destroyed (cf. Ex. 14:28). In a word, if you consider and meditate on what happened to the Jews then, you will see that it is all a shadow and type of what has now come to pass for true Christians.

Now, if you wish to determine the difference between us and the Jews more briefly and to the point, then merely consider the teaching of the old Law and that which belongs to the Christians, and your inquiry (διαγνώσεως) will not go amiss. For the old Law tells us that creation, meaning visible creation, was made by God: *In the beginning God made* (ἐποίησεν) *heaven and earth* (Gen. 1:1), and so on. But Christianity teaches not only about sensible creations, but also about intelligible creations (and even more so about *uncreated* intelligible realities):[178] *In the beginning was the Word, and the Word was with God, and the Word was God* (Jn. 1:1). Judaism teaches, *God said, Let Us make man according to Our image and likeness* (Gen. 1:26), while Christianity teaches, *The Word became flesh and dwelt among us* (Jn. 1:14). They teach, *Let them have dominion over the fish of the sea, and over the flying creatures of heaven, and over the cattle and all the earth* (Gen. 1:26). We teach, *Of His fullness we have all received* (Jn. 1:16). They say, *God said, Let there be light* (Gen. 1:3). We say, *It is the God who commanded light to shine out of darkness, who has shone in our hearts* (2 Cor. 4:6).

So then, once you have examined both of these teachings we have described, you can see how incomparably superior are the blessings that the Christians have received from God than those of the Jews; and you will surely agree that these things are a shadow and a type of our supernatural reality as Christians, or rather of Christ. And you will give praise and due glory to the divine grace and providence that has gently lifted up mankind out of the shadow and the type to the supernatural mercy of transcendent things, in Christ Jesus, our Lord.

God, by His charity, can be apprehended by every noetic faculty.

64. O most holy enhypostatic Wisdom, Power, and Word of God (1 Cor. 1:24)! How can I praise Your essence and glory, O Lord, for it is unapproachable? How can I praise Your infinite goodness, for I am human and my intellect is finite? And

[178] About sensible creation, intelligible creation, and the intelligible uncreated realities (which could be identified as the knowable aspects of God's uncreated energies), cf. *On Union with God and the Contemplative Life* 35, 91.

yet I will praise You and exalt You as I am able. And perhaps in this way I shall attain some sense of Your glory and Your goodness, that my soul may strive with all its might to cleave after you (cf. Ps. 62:9), and when I hear you I may fear you as I ought and so stand amazed at all that is within You, as the prophet said, *Lord, I have heard Your report, and was afraid: I considered Your works, and was amazed* (Hab. 3:1). O Highest Word, Unfathomable One, You knocked at the door, and the bride from the Song of the Songs heard You, and her heart leapt for You (cf. Song. 5:4); she was transported by delight and desperately sought to find you, and even shouted, *Show me Your face, and cause me to hear Your voice; for Your voice is sweet, and Your countenance is beautiful* (Song 2:14). For indeed she wished to say, as Job did, *I have heard the report of You by the ear before; but now my eye has seen You* (Job 42:5). As the Word and the Wisdom, so also *the true Light which gives light to every man coming into the world* (Jn. 1:9), a Light that gives some light when it is first seen shining, and then gives light to see by, for it is the Sun of noetic Righteousness; with it a man can, by his virtues (ἐξ ἀρετῶν), gaze enraptured upon the wonders of God and behold with divine eros the unspeakable marvels of the One God.

That is why John plainly teaches that, *We beheld His glory, the glory as of the only begotten of the Father, full of grace and truth* (Jn. 1:14). For you are the true God, and truly the Light, as John again testifies, and those who from Your fullness have received the unspeakable, inexpressible gift (cf. Jn. 1:16) cry aloud that You are *the God who commanded light to shine out of darkness, who has shone in our hearts* (2 Cor. 4:6). Words cannot express Your brilliance and how brightly You shine, to enable us to see supernatural and unearthly things of supercelestial grace and truth and to take such marvellous delight in them. For not only can we apprehend You (ληπτός) (by Your charity [φιλανθρώπως]) through sound and sight, but also through touch (ἁφή); as the bosom-friend (ἐπιστήθιος) of Christ says, *that which we have heard, which we have seen with our eyes, which we have looked upon, and our hands have handled, concerning the Word of life* (1 Jn. 1:1). And since You also become a garment for the faithful, giving abiding rest to those who belong to You, then clearly You must somehow come into contact (ἐπαφή) with the intellect, O Good One. For those who were baptized into You and into glad belief in You have yet more gladly *put You on* as a garment, Generous One, as Paul writes, that most holy herald of the truth (cf. Gal. 3:27).

So Isaiah, the thundering prophetic trumpet, whose soul rejoiced in God the Father and Lord because He had clothed him magnificently with You, Lord, and the Father had girded him wondrously *with the robe of his salvation and the garment of his joy* (Is. 61:10). For how much joy and true gladness does it bring a man, when he is taken by God and sees You, the sacred[179] and supernatural Light, enveloping him? And how much more when he recognizes that it is his salvation, for You are the Salvation? And in Your infinite love, You even become perceptible to the noses of the intellect (νοεροῖς μυκτῆρσιν), when they are strong in faith; and this is where You give wondrous rest to those who belong to You, who sing heartily and praise You, for *Your name is ointment poured forth* (Song 2:3), and recount to their neighbors that, *As beautiful as an apple*" (that is, to the sight, and pleasing to the smell, and sweet to the taste) *is my kinsman, and my nard gave forth the smell of Your unctions* (Song 1:12). That is how Paul, who was clothed in You, could say that we are the fragrance of Christ (2 Cor. 2:15). But You are also the taste and meal of the faithful, the true food and drink (Jn. 6:55) of the soul; You give us life and feed us miraculously, You grow us as well and give us joy in communion, as the holy prophet David experienced when, by Your grace, he tasted You, calling his neighbors to *taste and see that the Lord is good* (Ps. 33:9). For though You appear as an 'apple', yet the *poor in spirit* (Mt. 5:3) and the humble will eat of you as of the richest, choicest food and will be filled; and they will praise You, Lord, for the abundance of your goodly taste (Ps. 21:27), those who ever seek You to find You and eat of You. Because out of the abundance of Your life-giving power is poured holy food and drink, and the souls of those who have You as their food will live forever. Since You are eternal and incorruptible, You make incorruptible those who eat of You, and You guide them forevermore with the boundless energy of Your nature. That is why, by Your infinite goodness which brings forth all fair things and is a boon to all (καλλιεργός … εὐεργέτις), You call and exhort those who can understand (καλεῖς καὶ παρακαλεῖς λογικούς), saying, *Come, eat of my bread and drink wine which I have mingled for you* (Prov. 9:5). Thus You call Yourself 'holy bread', because elsewhere You say, *I am the bread of lif*e (Jn. 6:35) and *they have forsaken Me, the fountain of water of life* (Jer. 2:13). And You even offer Your most holy body and blood for them to eat and drink (cf. Mt. 26:26, etc.). And so You feed and delight all the noetic senses (αἰσθητήρια νοερά) of Your people, charitable Lord, and become for them light and life and every kind of enjoyment of all things supremely good and beautiful. You are the blessed spiritual manna from heaven, Jesus, who feeds the countless multitudes. Glory to Your unspeakable love for us, O Master, and Your inexpressible compassion and forbearance! Amen.

The Spirit of God dwells within the faithful.

65. How truly and wholly wonderful it is to the noetic sense or 'spirit' (πνοή): the outpouring of the Life-Giving Spirit from God the Father upon carnal hearts, once

---

[179] ἄδυτον. This word usually refers to the inner sanctum of pagan temples which was "off-limits" to most worshipers, but it could also possibly describe clothing that "cannot be put on".

they have received sound faith in the incarnate economy of the Word. That this gift and divine power and energy should be so poured out (wonder of wonders!), by the uncreated and transcendent Godhead, and that it should be joined with the heart in constant motion – this is indeed wondrous and never ceases to amaze it.

66. How truly and exceedingly wonderful it is that the Father, in the Spirit, and through the divine Word of God, through whom He created all things visible and invisible, that this Trinity should together indwell a human mind and walk about therein (2 Cor. 6:16)[180] and make its dwelling there; what a miracle that the Triune Godhead should send an emissary (ἄγγελος) to every pious believer; and that the all-powerful and life-giving Trinity should look on man with favor and strengthen and work in him divinely and spiritually, is truly beyond miraculous.

67. It is indeed truly and wholly wonderful that an ever-faithful heart should bear the holy radiance of the Most High God, who is over all. And that God should make the mind to shed its own light from the outside (ἔξωθεν) is sweet succor and a miracle of love, but that He should truly and surely give Himself – what joy! – as Light to the believer, and this within his heart, not outwardly, and forever, not just for a time, this clearly defies comprehension or even wonder.

68. It is truly and wholly marvelous that He whom the Seraphim and all the heavenly host together bear aloft with joyful reverence, is carried also in the believer's heart; this is fully incomprehensible. And not only to carry, but also to be united and mingled together (ἀνακρινᾶσθαι) with Him, how does this not surpass all wonder?

69. It is truly no ordinary miracle that through grace the soul should be made the throne and resting place and chariot of the infinitely wise and powerful God who sits enthroned in heaven. But that such a One should love the soul so much as to become one with it in spirit, and to share with it supercelestial things and entrust to it such mysteries – who can worthily praise Him in wonder?

70. It is truly marvellous and astonishing that God, who has *no resting place* (Is. 66:1), should take up His royal residence in the heart. For think, if a king (even an earthborn, local sovereign) embraces someone (even a nobleman) warmly or takes him by the hand, how much glory and honor he bestows and how much he

---

[180] Ἐνοικήσω ἐν αὐτοῖς καὶ ἐμπεριπατήσω. This can either be translated, "I will dwell *among* them and walk *in their midst*", or, as Angelikoudes takes it, "I will dwell *within* them and walk *inside of* them".

increases the standing of the one whom he has embraced or whose hand he has taken, and what gladness and joy that one feels. But no mere mortal king, but the eternal and uncreated God, the Creator and Lord of all things, before whom *thousands upon thousands of angels stand*, and to whom *ten thousands of ten thousands minister* in due reverence (Dan. 7:10), deigns not only to touch a pardoned sinner, but touches him within his heart; or rather resides in him not just for a time, but forever, in order to be with him and to glorify him mightily and by His power to deify him (θεοποιεῖν) wondrously and to bestow on him countless hidden treasures, and to fill him with grace; what glory and honor and gladness and joy does this bring him, O inconceivable wonder! Have mercy, Triune Lord.

71. It is remarkable that God, who created all things and thus governs all things, should appear so fully and abidingly enclosed within a faithful heart. For if a mortal king, whose reign is but fleeting, were to come knocking at someone's house and went in and ate and drank with him, sharing his food and his table, this would of course be a great enough distinction and honor, a mighty cause for joy and delight and comfort. But if the everlasting King and Lord and Creator of all things visible and invisible were to come not to the home, but to the heart of a sinner who has received mercy (ἠλεημμένος), not knocking at the door and not to share in enjoying the good things in his heart, but to impart to him the strength of heaven and otherworldly consolation and a wondrous, incorruptible glory, how do you think the one who received Him would feel? How greatly would he rejoice, what gladness and delight and all-encompassing joy would be his! How utterly and totally wondrous! What an unlooked-for miracle, that He who fills all things (ὁ πάντα πληρῶν) and is above all things, should make the human heart His home and His eternal temple.

72. *The God who said, Let light shine out of darkness* (2 Cor. 4:6) shines radiantly in the hearts of the faithful. *The love of God has been poured out in their hearts by the Holy Spirit who was given to them* (cf. Rom. 5:5). God sends the Spirit of His Son into their hearts, crying: *"Abba, Father!* (Gal. 4:6). The faithful who are thus joined with the Lord (what a wondrous union!) *become one spirit* with God (1 Cor. 6:17). What else could come close to moving us as much as the grace of these things?

73. Believers thus become *heirs of God, co-heirs with Christ* (Rom. 8:17), a kind of second christs (χριστοὶ δεύτεροι), *partakers of the divine nature* (cf. 2 Pet. 1:4) (which surpasses all thought and transcends every intellect), and so they are publicly proclaimed (χρηματίζουσιν) to be sons of God and gods by status and grace (θεοὶ θέσει καὶ χάριτι). And they truly do see (θεωροῦνται) supernatural wonders and 'suffer' – or rather, enjoy naturally (οἰκειότερον) – those things that

eye has not seen, nor ear heard, nor have entered into the heart of man (1 Cor. 2:9). Glory to the inestimable love of God the Father, to the Trinity, who has truly loved us with unspeakable, supercelestial, and supreme goodness.

Every believer has been richly honored by God

74. Christ has said, *That which is born of the Spirit is spirit* (Jn. 3:6). What amazing grace! What an unspeakable gift that God should create man with so many marvellous graces! Now, that which is created (τὸ κτισθέν) is by nature a creature (κτίσμα). But the all-merciful Lord, the supreme and omnipotent Trinity, in His abundant generosity, has graced the creature, I say, with the uncreated Spirit, and fully (none will ever comprehend how) united him with Himself, rendering him god, son, and spirit.[181] For He says, *I have said, You are gods; and all of you children of the Most High* (Ps. 81:16). And it is written of God, *He has made an ordinance, and it shall not pass away* (Ps. 148:6), and, *All that the Lord willed, He has done* (Ps. 134:6), and, *The counsel of the Lord endures forever, the thoughts of His heart from generation to generation* (Ps. 32:11); for His nature is fixed and unchanging. For this reason His enhypostatic Word came and brought to us His word and His ordinance and His will and His counsel, acting as a *angel* (ἄγγελος χρηματίσας) of this surpassingly *great* and *wonderful counsel* (Is. 9:6). He breathed the Spirit onto the disciples (cf. Jn. 21:11), and with this spiritual rebirth He proclaimed them in a mystery to be spirit and thus made them sons of God: *For as many as are led by the Spirit of God, these are sons of God* (Rom. 8:14). And if they are sons of God, then they must be gods themselves as well; for whatever is born must bear the nature of the one who gave birth to it.[182] This is why the Savior teaches His disciples to call God 'Father' (cf. Mt. 6:9), for they are in communion with the Spirit. And in this way, the Holy Trinity makes the faithful into gods and sons and spirits, far overshadowing any other glorious gift imaginable. Amen.

On the passage, "He receives them having spread His wings, and takes them up on His back" (Dt. 32:11).

75. Apply your noetic sense and pay heed to what I tell you now; for I am sure that if you do, you will be astounded and filled with spiritual joy and a kind of divine delight. The Holy Spirit says through David, *You who sit upon the Cherubim, manifest Yourself* (Ps. 79:2), and elsewhere, *You who see the abyss, who sit on the Cherubim* (cf. Ps. 98:1), and again, *And He mounted on Cherub*im (Ps. 17:1). So what about the faithful? They could not be more different from the Cherubim! God

---

[181] ἑνοποιῶν τὸν ἄνθρωπον ἑαυτῷ, θεοποιῶν αὐτὸν καὶ υἱοποιῶν καὶ πνεῦμα ἀποτελῶν.

[182] Cf. *On Union with God and the Contemplative Life* 2.

does not just stand over the faithful, like a bird over her brood, protecting, caring for and sheltering us and taking wondrous delight in us. But (O what astonishing love He feels for us!) He even takes us on His back, in the unfathomable, infinite abundance of His love making Himself a kind of spectacular vehicle (ὄχημα) for us. And He keeps us safe and mightily bears us forth into untold heavenly secrets of the supercelestial life. Thus He makes us ride in all-surpassing ease, in peace and deepest rest, overjoyed and delighted in His Spirit and rightly glad and content. For the holy Moses also says in the Spirit, *He* (meaning God) *receives them having spread His wings, and takes them up on His back* (Dt. 32:11). What ineffable love! Merely spreading His wings and receiving the faithful and thus becoming their glorious carriage truly exceeds the honor accorded to Cherubim and is cause for unspeakable joy. But to take them up and set them on His back, hiding them there under His shadow, as the divine David says (Ps. 90:4), not even the intellect of a Cherub can consider this thing and praise it accordingly. Surely Your mercy is as unfathomable as Your greatness, Holy Trinity. Glory to You.

76. The *schema* of the monks and its attendant vows and the monastic (μοναχικός) life require a solitary (μοναδικόν)[183] intellect. Only God can accomplish this, and He brings it to pass through the diligent efforts and the rules of the monks. This He does by imparting His life-giving grace and by the single and solitary vision of His almighty dominion and glory. For He alone is supreme, unparalleled anywhere, unmatched and peerless in His perfections, the only truly almighty One, in whose power all things are possible, the only truly wise One, who bestows on the wise their wisdom as a gift; the only true and eternal Father and Creator of all things. Thus it is right and good to say, *For from Him and through Him and to Him are all things, to whom be glory forever* (Rom. 11:36).

So if this is as we have said, and literally every good and beautiful thing whatsoever owes its existence to God and is upheld and maintained by Him and finds its end in Him, so to speak; and if these things unite and bind all who use them rightly to God, for He is the Father of all such things: goodness, love, prudence, wisdom, knowledge, contemplation, proper conduct, deification, and even divine pleasure, holy joy and supercelestial peace, likewise reverent fear, strength and counsel, the way of piety and knowledge, and all things that comport with rational nature and bring us joy and glory and gladness, making us more godlike and gods ourselves. If then every good and beautiful thing comes from God alone, then he is truly a vain fool who loves the good and beautiful, but at the same time separates and cuts himself off from God, the source and root of all that is good and beautiful. For he will neither have any share in the Creator and Sustainer of all that is good and

---

[183] Or "unique".

beautiful, since he has so ungraciously turned away from Him who is the Foundation of everything good or beautiful, nor will the good and beautiful that he thinks he has turn out to be truly good and beautiful; but rather a deception and a cruel trick (χλεύη δεινή). But we must abide wholeheartedly with God alone and diligently study and cleave to His Law only. This is the only way to achieve real glory and unadulterated pleasure and unending, incorruptible riches, and all this host of other things that we have mentioned; but (O the wonder!) we will have God Himself as well, *dwelling within us* and *walking therein* (2 Cor. 6:16), and we shall enjoy seeing and hearing transcendent things truly invisible and inaudible to the outward senses, and thus we shall live in unity and solitude (μοναχικῶς) in Christ Jesus our Lord.

77. When the heart that has the Spirit is filled with humility in a quiet (ἥσυχος) life and has received the energy of grace, the intellect which has been happily joined with the truth of God witnesses[184] many divine visions and becomes an initiate into transcendent and indescribable mysteries. He considers himself a newcomer and a visitor passing through this world, he delights and enjoys in the Spirit those things that utterly surpass his intellect and ability to conceive. He often sees God mystically and 'suffers' ecstatic visions of God and silently rushes upward to deification, itself a kind of 'blessed passion', inflamed and enraptured with wondrous eros, driven by the force and power of the Spirit who gives life and light, in Christ Jesus our Lord. Amen.

78. He who is diligent to attend only to God and in a way to make Him his dwelling place, who likewise sees God in the Spirit walking about and dwelling in himself, behold! he has proven that he has kept the divine commandment of the Lord Jesus, saying: *Abide in Me and I in you* (Jn. 15:4). He has been mysteriously united with God and at the same time has miraculously died, much to his joy, and thus become an unfailing doer of all of the Savior's commandments. For the Savior says, *He who abides in Me, and I in him, bears much fruit* (Jn. 15:5) (that is, many virtues). So whoever wishes to grow in godly virtue, let him strive with all his might to abide and remain in God, through contemplation, prayer and higher study, so that God may see his holy struggle of the soul and incline the heavens (what a miracle!) and against all hope may come and dwell and walk about within his soul; by this communion he will enjoy all things good and beautiful and please the Lord by keeping all His holy commandments. For it is He who said, *Without Me you can do nothing* (Jn. 15:5), even though you might think that you can.

---

[184] Following the emendation from θεούς to θεατής.

79. If it is wrong to conceal treasure or wisdom from the common good, then love would clearly dictate that we should not keep our noetic labors for God and our contemplation and exertion pent up in the mind without writing it down, but rather love should drive us to commit it to writing and make a record of it for the good of all. For since man is a thinking creature (λογικὸν ζῶον), he is certainly receptive to intellectual reflection and knowledge. This is why, when he meditates on God and those things that follow out of faith in Him, he will of necessity acquire a divine and appropriate intellect, progressing boldly with knowledge into the realm of the holy commandments. He then needs God as a helper in these things and an aid (συλλήπτορος), or to put it more aptly, a supporter (ἀντιλήπτορος), so he prays often and with tears and asks God to make His commandments easy for him. And when God is pleased to pity this petitioner, as a father pities his son (Ps. 102:13), He suddenly pours out His Spirit into his heart (O what a miracle!), and so moves the man who has received this gift to warm and loving affection for Him. And as a father lets his son be free about him, so He too pours out the Spirit's inexpressible life-giving power on the communicant as a pledge, and makes the man truly kind and good and humble. He exalts him then again in glory and honor through union with Himself and draws him into the fiery ardors of divine eros, so that whatever the man sees of God he counts as his very own. And moreover all of the Father's possessions, the wealth and glory and power and beauty and wisdom and dominion and all the brilliance and all the good and beautiful things, the glory and praise, are naturally a pleasure and a source of pride and joy to the son. So when the soul in its natural contemplations enters into communion with the Spirit, that is, when it meditates on God the Trinity, as Basil the Great explains, then the man truly does see God as one who loves him deeply and as his true Father; and the things of God are likewise his own, as we have said, and he is content simply to behold God and rejoices exceedingly and is glad in Christ Jesus our Lord.

What proper pleasure is.

80. I do not think that anyone who has given the matter careful thought will be unaware that what is properly called "pleasure" (ἡδονή) is not condemned by nature and reason, has the longest effect and fills the heart with joy and gladness, even after it has been fulfilled; this is far from the so-called "pleasure" of the flesh, which is only outward and not proper pleasure at all. So anyone who desires the pure and lasting intellectual and spiritual pleasure should ask for it, and he will not go wrong; on the contrary, with all the more ease his intellect will progress from earthly things to heavenly, and his whole soul will then follow after. Because this is the true and proper pleasure of the heart: It is irrevocable and sincere to an intellectual, immortal soul, it abides eternally, is luminous, ever-flowing, guiltless, or rather prayerful and blessed, a steady companion to the saints of all ages,

peaceful, kind, courageous, brilliant, fair, godly, clear, consoling, and full of joy, both in the moment and after. If you have ever experienced this pleasure of the intellect and spirit, then you will certainly agree with what we have written. If you have not yet, then hold in faith what we have said until you do.

On carnal pleasure.

81. That carnal pleasure which is not of the mind and spirit should not even be called "pleasure". For it brings with it bitter regret once the thing is done; clearly pleasure is a false name for it. It is spurious and alien to the soul endowed with reason, thoughtless, base, slothful, filled with dark delight, chaotic, pestilent, transient and subject to swift decay. And once the body has grown old, it departs unwillingly and full of shame. Guilty, miserable, unkind, captive, reproachful, filthy-minded, foolish, ugly, hopeless, reckless; it leaves its perpetrator or agent with only black regret (λύπην ἠμαυρομένην) once it is done. If you have ever experienced it, you will surely know the truth of what I have written. If you have been protected from it by God's hand, believe my words as true and know that you will reap the glorious harvest of life.

82. I possess an ever-shining spiritual light and transcendent life, both sustenance (τροφήν) and satisfaction (τρυφήν) divine, the ascents and behests and unions and pleasures of the inexplicable Triune Godhead, and unutterable motions of love toward Jesus Christ, the Lord of all. But alas, my misery and my senselessness! Alas, my wicked folly! My mind, that has thus by grace traversed the heavens, is still led astray and inclines toward false things, things of earth and filth, all rotten and reeking, alas! Who would not wonder and mourn at my predicament, and would not beg for mercy on my behalf of God who bears such unspeakable love for mankind, to grant me greater divine power through the Spirit, the Giver of life and light, so that I might more easily reject the devil, that wicked enemy who conspires against this sacred and wondrous life of mine! All you most holy angels and all you souls of the righteous, pray and entreat God for my sake, for my mind is base and calloused.

83. My God, my God! There is nothing greater than You, for you are incomprehensible. You are everything (ὁ τὸ πᾶν),[185] for You are the Maker of everything, and are infinite times infinitely beyond everything (ὑπὲρ τὸ πᾶν), for You transcend being itself (ὑπερούσιος). O Lord, my Lord! What unspeakable, holy union, and unutterable concord (σύμπνοια) among us Christians on whom Your mercy rests! Glory to You. When I behold You, Sovereign, shining in my

---

[185] St. Porphyrios of Kavsokalyvia would say a similar phrase: "Christ is everything", ὁ Χριστὸς εἶναι τὸ πᾶν.

heart both night and day and evermore, how do I not lose myself in rapture at the abundance of Your grace? But rather I disregard and am senseless of such a great gift, Almighty One. Alas, how sinful a man am I!

If you knew the One who has captivated me and unto whom He has bound me and wherewith, you would swiftly sing enraptured praises to the transcendence of God and thank Him profusely for the glorious things He has done out of His goodness.

If you understood how far short I fall of the dignity of the mystery of Christ, quicker than thought (θᾶττον ἢ λόγος) you would be caught up in wonder, condemning my indifference, sloth, and negligence, not to mention my obvious hardness of heart and dullness of mind.

At that time Jesus answered and said, 'I thank You, Father, Lord of heaven and earth, that You have hidden these things from the wise and prudent and have revealed them to babes. Even so, Father, for so it seemed good in Your sight" (Mt. 11:25-26). Ask for us and pray that, amid the sorrows of life, nothing alien to the faith may befall us, nor anything unworthy of both God and ourselves; and forgive me.

Saint Kallistos Telikoudes

ON THE PRACTICE OF HESYCHASM

There is no repentance without stillness.[186] Neither is it possible to achieve purity without retreat from the world. Nor, by associating with and seeing people, can one be made worthy of association with God and vision of Him. Hence those who have diligently managed to repent of their errors and to be purified of their passions and to attain association with God and the contemplation of Him – which is the end and purpose of those who live in a manner pleasing to God and, one might say, the pledge of God and His eternal inheritance – such people pursue stillness by all means possible and consider it necessary and most beneficial to depart from the world and to flee from people with all their souls' desire. And then in stillness, they begin by practicing disciplines such as mourning, self-blame and self-condemnation – which make mourning even purer – vigils, standing in prayer, self-control, and bodily labor, all of which contribute to the goal of weeping with tears that flow from the eyes of those who think humbly of themselves in heartfelt compunction. This is how they devote themselves to purification and achieve it through practical virtue (πρᾶξις). Again, the goal of these latter virtues is peace of mind, just as we said that the goal of all the former virtues was the flowing of tears. Then the intellect naturally begins to carefully examine the nature of beings, to strive to understand the handiwork of God, and to conceive divine notions. It assumes the work of contemplating the power, wisdom, glory, goodness, and other attributes of God, and penetrates into the secrets of Scripture; it tastes supernatural goods, delights in beauties beyond this world, and is made a vessel of God's love. In this way the person is seized with divine eros, and rejoices and is gladdened when it has ascended to the goal of the virtues, to the love of the Creator of all, while avoiding any fall into spiritual delusion whatsoever, even in the slightest way. He will naturally be susceptible as a mutable human being to stumbling, sinful impulses, and indecent promptings which arise from various causes, but in dealing with these, he must repeatedly correct himself and stand far off from despair. Such a one takes wings from hope in God's love for man, engages in tears and prayer and the other aforementioned virtues, and takes delight, as far as possible, in the divine Paradise of love; he sees and visualizes nothing, neither form, nor matter, nor any shape – in short, absolutely nothing – but only attends to tears, peace in his thoughts, and God's love. For by means of these the danger of error and delusion is avoided and salvation is rewarded to the soul that is modest, watchful, and prays in Jesus Christ, our Lord.

---

[186] *Hesychia.*

While you are sitting in your cell, let your intellect have boldness before God in all humility: humility because of your own unworthiness and nothingness, and boldness on account of God's insurpassable love and forbearance towards man. For in this manner the soul honors God, when for all its consciousness of its sinfulness it nevertheless has confidence in God's love for man and surrenders itself to Him. That is why St. Paul enjoins us, saying, *Let us come with boldness before the throne of grace* (Heb. 4:16). And indeed, boldness before God is truly the eye of prayer, or its wings, and is a strangely wondrous relation. Not that anyone should ever be bold because he thinks he is good – flee from such a thought, and keep yourself far from it! – but rather one should take wings from pondering the ineffable compassion, love, and forbearance of God in an ascent to divine hopes. Therefore, pray with an emboldened spirit and a humble mind, cherishing good hopes in God, in accordance with what we have said, in Jesus Christ, our Lord.

You should always diligently seek the things that calm the body and release the intellect from disturbances. These are: moderation in food and drink, short sleep, standing and kneeling in prayer according to your strength, in humble *schema*; poor attire, reticence in speech, depending only on necessities, sleeping on the ground, and other practices that tame the body. Along with these practices, you should seek to do all the disciplines that awaken the intellect and help it to cling to God. These are: reading the Holy Scriptures and the Saints who explain them (and this too in moderation), chanting with understanding, meditation on the words of the Scriptures and the wonders we see in creation, and praying with the mouth until the holy grace of the Spirit manifestly causes prayer in the heart; for then there comes a different kind of feast and the occasion for another, [greater] celebration, not spoken by the mouth, but activated in the heart by the Spirit. Strive to do these things as follows: Kneel as often as you can, and sit and pray. When you grow weary from praying, go read, as we said, and then return to prayer. And if you become despondent in prayer again, get up and chant for a while and then come back to prayer. If you continue to feel despondent, engage moderately in the meditation we mentioned above, and then continue the prayer. Moreover, make use of a small handicraft as an obstacle to despondency, just as you have heard from the Fathers, O most devout one. In all of your God-pleasing work, from day to day, let prayer take precedence. Indeed, the other practices we have mentioned are done to get rid of despondency, all for the sake of prayer; for when mercy visits the soul and the grace of the Spirit causes prayer to flow from the heart as a spring, from that moment onwards the intellect engages only in prayer and contemplation, removing itself from all things and delighting only in prayer and contemplation in the Paradise of divine love.

Prayer is superior to all good works. It begets tears of repentance, greatly contributes to peace in one's thoughts, leads one to think only of God, who is the ultimate Peace, and brings forth the love of God. Prayer alone purifies the rational part of the soul through the vision of God, who causes the purification of the angels; it also preserves the desiring part of the soul in purity before God, for by associating and conversing with God, who is infinitely and supernaturally good and beautiful by nature, it joins all desire to God; prayer also soothes irascibility inasmuch as it causes it to fall down before God in beseeching and supplication, and humbles the soul through this dependence on God. For no one who beseeches and supplicates God can bear a haughty or irascible spirit.[187] Hence, virtually all the powers of the soul and all its energies, both practical and noetic, are purified and restored by pure prayer, and all the more so when it is accompanied by both the contemplation of God and the subsequent divine eros within the life and practice of stillness, as we have described above. Let your mind turn its thought and gaze within, to the place of the heart from whence weeping springs while you calmly breathe in during prayer, and let it remain there for as long as it can. For this is greatly beneficial and induces constant and profuse weeping, abolishes the captivity of the intellect, brings about noetic peace, becomes an incentive to prayer, and helps you to find prayer of the heart with the help of God and the grace of the Life-Giving Spirit in the name of our Lord Christ Jesus.

As one who contemplates and beholds mystical realities and delights in them, you should know that corresponding to the divine nature, on the one hand, and human nature, on the other, are two different kinds of mourning, and consequently two kinds of tears, which differ, if you like, in genus or in form. They are quite different from each other, although they are both good and God-given and they bring divine favor and, accordingly, divine inheritance. The former have their origin in divine fear and causes of grief, the latter in divine love and God. The former do not bring so much joy, while the latter bring abundant and wondrous gladness. The first kind of weeping is proper to beginners, the second to those who have attained perfection through grace.

There are five works of stillness: Prayer, that is, the constant remembrance of Jesus introduced into the heart while breathing, without any kind of thought, and this is attained through complete self-control in regard to eating, sleeping, and the other senses while you are enclosed within your cell with humility; chanting and psalmody at intervals; reading from the Holy Gospels, the divine Fathers, and chapters on prayer, especially by Symeon the New Theologian, Hesychios, and Nikephoros; meditation on the judgment of God or the remembrance of death, and

[187] See Sts. Kallistos and Ignatios, *Exact Rule and Canon* 78.

similar practices; and lastly, some handiwork. Then, after doing these, return to prayer, even if the task requires exertion, until the intellect becomes accustomed to cease wandering through the remembrance of the Lord and continual descent into the work of the heart. This is the work of novice monks who wish to practice hesychasm. Such a person then should not come out of his cell often and should avoid seeing or conversing with anyone, unless it is for some great need, and even then only rarely, with care and caution. For this sort of engagement causes distraction not only to beginners, but even to those who have already made spiritual progress.

Prayer with attention, that is to say, without any thought, is performed as follows: through the phrase "Lord Jesus Christ, Son of God", the intellect, in complete silence and without any material conception, raises itself up to the Lord in remembrance of Him, and then, through the phrase "Have mercy on me", it comes back to itself, since it cannot help but pray for itself. But when it has attained love through experience, it is simply and wholly lifted up to the Lord Jesus Christ Himself, having received assurance concerning the second part of the prayer.

For it seems that the Holy Fathers did not describe the Jesus prayer as always being said in its entirety, but some mention the whole prayer, such as John Chrysostom, while others mention just the "Lord Jesus", like St. Paul who adds the phrase "*by the Holy Spirit*" (1 Cor. 12:3), indicating when the heart receives the energy of the Holy Spirit by whom it prays, and this occurs to those who have made spiritual progress, even if they have not yet reached perfection; this is the state of illumination. Again, St. John Climacus says, "Flog your enemies with the name of Jesus,"[188] and, "Let the remembrance of Jesus cling to your every breath,"[189] and adds nothing more than the name "Jesus". Beginners may sometimes pray with all the words of the prayer, and sometimes with a part of it, as we have mentioned; but do not continually change the words of the prayer, lest the intellect become distracted by this. By persisting in the above-mentioned method of pure prayer of the heart (even if one's prayer is perhaps not entirely pure because it is still hindered by preoccupations and thoughts), he who struggles will get in the habit of praying effortlessly, by keeping the intellect in the heart – not by forcefully descending into the heart while breathing in and then carelessly bringing the intellect back up, but rather by letting the intellect abide there of its own accord. This is, and is properly called, "prayer of the heart". It is preceded by a certain warmth in the heart, which removes the obstacles that had formerly prevented the prayer from being performed in a wholly pure manner, and the intellect then

[188] *Ladder* 21.7, (Trans. Moore), 72.
[189] *Ladder* 27.61 (Trans. Moore), 116.

remains in the heart and prays unhindered. From this warmth and prayer the love for the Lord Jesus is born in the heart, and from this love in turn flow sweet tears in abundance out of yearning for Jesus as He is brought to remembrance.

For someone to be made worthy of these things and what follows them, although it is not the proper time to mention these, he must strive to keep the fear of God before his eyes, as we explained, with the remembrance of Jesus in the heart, and not only superficially, simply to avoid wicked deeds, but also to avoid impassioned thoughts, to make spiritual progress, and to receive full assurance of God's love for him even in this life. Only let him not seek out His manifestation, lest he mistakenly accept the devil, who is truly darkness but pretends to be light. Again, when his intellect sees light without seeking it, he should neither accept it nor reject it; instead he should consult someone who has the power from God to explain it to him so as to learn what is genuine. Now if one has found a spiritual guide who teaches not only what he knows from Holy Scripture, but also because he himself has suffered the blessed divine illumination, thanks be to God! But if not, then it is better not to accept the light one has seen, but rather to take refuge in God in humility, calling oneself unworthy of such a vision, since this is what we were taught in practice by the Fathers. Indeed, in other writings they explain the signs of undeluded illumination and that which is a product of delusion, but in the same way that I have told you about the above-mentioned matters through living oral tradition, you will be able to hear more about this matter in due season; but now is not the proper time. At this time what one must understand, in addition to the things we have said and even in preference to them, is that just as he who wishes to learn proper archery does not stretch the bow until he has first set up targets for practice, so he who desires to learn to live in stillness should have constant meekness of heart as his target. The meek person never disturbs anyone, nor is he ever disturbed, unless it is for reasons of piety.

This meekness can easily be achieved by turning aside from all things and keeping silent as much as possible. However, if the hesychast ever happens to be disturbed by something, he should immediately repent and blame himself, and from then on be more careful, so that he may make a new beginning in the invocation of Jesus with stillness and a clear conscience, as we have explained, and then he will have His divine grace resting in his soul as he moves along this path. Not only that, but grace will even provide to his soul perfect rest from the demons and passions that formerly harassed it, and will gladden the soul with ineffable joy; and even if they do still bother the soul, they cannot influence it, since it has no association with them, nor does it desire the pleasure they have to offer. For all of the desire of such a hesychast has been lifted up to the Lord who has given him His grace. At this point, God allows him to be attacked, but not because He has forsaken him. Why then? So as to prevent his intellect from becoming puffed up because of the good he has attained, and so that, by being subject to spiritual warfare, he always assumes humility; by this humility alone not only is he able to conquer the demons that proudly wage war against him, but is also made worthy of continually greater gifts. May we also be made worthy of such gifts from Christ, who humbled Himself for our sake (Phil. 2:8) and provides His grace in abundance to those who are likewise humble (Jam. 4:6), now and forever and to the ages of ages. Amen.

Selection from the Holy Fathers on Prayer and Attention[190]

All the ascetic's care should be dedicated to the humbling of the soul's pride, which is brought about by the insurrection of pleasures. For how will the soul be able to look up with a free gaze to the noetic light that befits it as long as it is nailed down to the pleasure of the flesh? That is why it is necessary first of all to exercise self-control, which is a safeguard of prudence, and not to allow the commanding intellect to meditate on impure thoughts. Thus, we must take care of the *inner man*, so as to keep the intellect undistracted, with its concentration intent on the glory of God, in order to avoid judgment by the Lord who said, *Woe to you, for you are like whitewashed tombs which indeed appear beautiful outwardly, but inside are full of dead men's bones and all uncleanness. Even so you also outwardly appear righteous to men, but inside you are full of hypocrisy and lawlessness* (Mt. 23:27-28). Hence, a great struggle is required, and one which is done *according to the rules* (2 Tim 2:5), in heart, in speech, and in practice, so that we do *not receive the grace of God in vain* (2 Cor. 6:1), but that we may mold ourselves in the *inner man* by the teaching of our Lord Jesus Christ, as wax is molded by an emblem, and practically fulfill what St. Paul said: *Put off the old man with his deeds, and put on the new man who is renewed in knowledge according to the image of Him who created him* (Col. 3:9-10). He calls all the different (κατὰ μέρος) sins and impurities *the old man*. Let us be formed together in the *inner man* to *newness of life* until the day we die, as Paul says (Rom. 6:4), so that we may be made worthy to say truly: *It is no longer I who live, but Christ lives in me* (Gal. 2:20). Hence we need great diligence and vigilant care, not only to avoid falling short of so great a reward by setting out to perform a commandment contrary to the rules we have mentioned, but also to escape falling under such dire threats. When the devil attempts to contrive against the soul, even when he does this with great intensity, and shoots his own thoughts like flaming arrows (Eph. 6:16) into the soul that is trying to keep still and calm, and suddenly he inflames it and makes memories that had entered it just once permanent and inextinguishable, we must then resist these schemes with watchfulness and greater attention, just as an athlete dodges his adversaries' strikes with the utmost caution and bodily agility; we must further dedicate everything to prayer and the invocation of help from above to overcome this assault and repel the bombardment of arrows. For this is what St. Paul taught us, saying, *In all things take up the shield of faith, by which you may extinguish the flaming arrows of the evil one* (Eph. 6:16). But when the soul relaxes the concentration and intensity of the intellect and accepts random memories of random things, then the mind drifts in an uneducated and ignorant manner towards these things, and the more it becomes occupied with them, the more it exchanges

---

190 The *Selection from the Holy Fathers on Prayer and Attention* is possibly a work written by St. Kallistos Angelikoudes.

one delusion for another until it often ends up in the most wretched and absurd state of mind. But this negligence and distracted state of the soul must be corrected and restored through greater focus and mental concentration, and by constant engagement in the study of good things.

For the attentive philosopher, having his body as a monastery and safe haven for the soul, whether he happens to be at a marketplace, at a festival, on a mountain, in a field, or in the midst of a great multitude of people, is established in his own natural monastery by concentrating his intellect within and meditating on the things that befit him. For it is possible for an indolent man who is sitting still at home to be wandering outside in his thoughts, and for another man who is in the marketplace to be watchful as if he were in the desert, concentrating within on God alone, without accepting by means of his senses any of the confusion that enters the soul through sensible things. Moreover, he who comes to partake of the Body and Blood of Christ in remembrance of Him who died and rose again for our sake (Lk. 22:19), should not only keep himself *pure from all defilement of flesh and spirit* (2 Cor. 7:1), so as not to eat and drink judgment to himself (cf. 1 Cor. 11:29); but also that he might manifestly show [in himself] the mind of Him who died and rose for our sake, not only by cleansing himself from all sin, but by dying to sin, to the world, and to himself, and *living for God* (Rom. 6:11).

Some evil thoughts cannot even touch the soul at all as long as we guard ourselves circumspectly and safely, while others are born and grow within us when we are careless; however, as long as these are removed immediately, they are quickly cut off and buried away. Others are born and increase and lead to evil deeds, and they corrupt all the health of our souls when we are found to be in a state of great carelessness. So then, the first and blessed state is to refuse completely the acceptance of any evil thought. The second is to expel the thoughts as soon as they enter, and to prevent them from tarrying there any further and to leave no pasture within yourself for their malice. But even if we have been careless up to this point, there is still, by God's love for man, a cure for this sluggishness, and His ineffable kindness has prepared many medicines for such wounds. So I beseech you, as long as you are in the body, do not release your heart. For just as a farmer cannot feel complete security about the crop growing in his field, since he never knows what may happen until he has stored it in his barn, likewise no man should release his heart as long as he has breath; and just as a man knows not what manner of misfortune may befall him until his last breath, so the monk cannot release his heart as long as he is still breathing, but must constantly cry out to God for His kingdom and His mercy.

Hence, the evil one, knowing well that the greatest things can be accomplished by anyone who prays undistractedly to God, attempts by means of any kind of distraction, whether it be reasonable or unreasonable, to make the intellect wander. But since we are well aware of this trickery, let us withstand our enemy. And when we stand or kneel in prayer, let us allow no thought whatsoever to enter the heart, whether it be white or black, from the right or left, written or unwritten, except for supplication to God and the illumination and radiance that comes from heaven into the commanding faculty of the soul. "It takes much time and effort in prayer for us to reach an untroubled state of mind – that other heaven, the heaven of the heart, where Jesus dwells. As the Apostle says, *Do you not know yourselves, that Jesus Christ dwells within you?* (2 Cor. 13:5)."[191] Whoever wishes to see the tranquil state of his intellect, let him keep himself from all thoughts, and the intellect will see itself with a quality almost like the sapphire transparency of heaven. The intellect will not see 'the place of God' within itself, unless it first rises above all conceptions about created things. And it will not rise beyond them until it has stripped itself of the passions that bind it to sensible things by means of thoughts. The passions are removed by means of the virtues, dispassionate thoughts are overcome by means of spiritual contemplation, and lastly even contemplation is surpassed when the divine light is made manifest to the intellect.[192]

---

[191] Cf. *Texts for the Monks in India* 52, *Philokalia* Vol. 1.
[192] *Exact Rule and Canon* 66.

Saint Kallistos Kataphygiotes

ON UNION WITH GOD AND THE CONTEMPLATIVE LIFE

Biographical Note

Concerning our holiest father Kallistos, called Kataphygiotes (whose name is perhaps taken from the Church of the Theotokos Kataphyge, or "Refuge"), who he was and where he came from, and where he fulfilled the anchoritic life, we know nothing apart from anecdotes. But as far as we can tell from the chapters of his that follow, he was a man with profound philosophical knowledge in both secular and spiritual learning, and indeed, more capable than any other of traversing the noetic heights and depths, lengths, and breadths of contemplations. For this blessed man raised himself up to the transcendent hidden Unity of the super-essential Trinity by the aid of grace to such a degree that he attained the vision of God, immediate union with Him, noetic silence, and the unknowing that surpasses all ignorance, and having been completely liberated from created things, he was exalted for his exceeding purity, so that he truly appeared as 'another angel' and 'a god by grace upon the earth.'[193]

Some have claimed that he is the same Kallistos who is called Xanthopoulos, the Patriarch of Constantinople, who wrote the other collection of one hundred chapters, basing their opinion on two pieces of evidence: the other century of chapters mostly explain the practical life, while these chapters refer only to theory and the contemplative life. Now since practice and theory are united to each other, it reasonably follows that the author should be one and the same. In addition to this, many of the points of the first treatise are similar to those presented here, namely those that relate to the application and reception of the intellect, divine union, the energy of the heart, and illumination. But there are others who think that this Kallistos is a different author because of the differences in the style of writing. However, we have thought it best to agree with the former, without having qualms concerning the differences in style. For it is possible, and indeed easy, for the wise to adapt their manner of communicating to be appropriate to each subject matter, expressing humble things in a humble way and lofty ones in a lofty manner. But what is truly grievous is that, even though the chapters explaining the contemplative life should presumably be about one hundred in number, only the following chapters have been preserved in our manuscript, and, in my opinion, these are the loftiest and most perfect texts both in terms of their conceptions, the

[193] These are favorite terms used by St. Kallistos throughout the treatise to describe the Saints.

grandeur and overall elegance of their expression, and in the compelling development of their syllogisms.

ON UNION WITH GOD AND THE CONTEMPLATIVE LIFE

1. By nature every living being receives both rest and a commensurate pleasure by means of the highest activity (ἐνεργείᾳ) natural to it, and in this way it both strives for these goals and rejoices in them. So then, surely man too, because he possesses intellect and the activity of intellection as his life by nature,[194] experiences the greatest pleasure and truly receives rest when he knows the highest things pertaining to himself – which one might call 'the good' or 'the beautiful'. Now this truly occurs when he has God in his intellect and meditates on the virtues of Him who is verily the ultimate Reality to be known, although He surpasses intellect (ὑπὲρ νοῦν νοητός), who supremely loves man in a manner beyond intellect (ὑπὲρ νοῦν), and who prepares for His own people supreme rewards and good and beautiful things that transcend the intellect (ὑπὲρ νοῦν); and He grants these to be enjoyed for all eternity.

2. Every birth brings forth offspring that resembles its parent, just as the Lord said, *That which is born of the flesh is flesh, and that which is born of the Spirit is spirit* (Jn. 3:6).[195] If then he who is born of the Spirit is spirit, it is clear that he will also be a god, like unto the Spirit that begot him, for the Spirit is true God, and it is from Him that the partaker of the Spirit is born by grace. And if this man is a god, he will evidently be contemplative as well, as is only reasonable, since God is called *Theos* because He contemplates and beholds (*theorein*) all things.[196] Thus he who does not contemplate has either not yet received spiritual birth and participation,[197] or else he has received it but since he has never learned better, he shuts off his power of vision, and since he has never been taught, he diverts his gaze from the intelligible divine rays radiating from the Noetic Sun of Righteousness (Mal. 4:2); and although he has became a participant in the *potential*

---

[194] νοῦν ἔχων καὶ τὸ νοεῖν πεφυκότως ζωήν. As explained in the Translator's Introduction, νοῦς is consistently translated as "intellect." Nevertheless, νοῦς and its several cognates in Byzantine theology have a vast array of meanings and uses. In *On Union with God and the Contemplative Life*, the characteristic activity of the νοῦς, τὸ νοεῖν/νόησις are translated "intellection" and "knowing", in the sense of understanding, direct noetic perception, and cognition, especially of an intelligible/spiritual reality.

[195] In Greek, the verb γεννάω means both "to give birth" and "to beget". Hence, there is no distinction made between "generation" and "birth", or between being "begotten" and "born" of the Spirit.

[196] Cf. *That There are not Three Gods*, Gregory of Nyssa (Jaeger 3-I:44).

[197] I.e. Holy Baptism and Chrismation.

of contemplation, he remains woefully deprived of its *activity*, even if he truly is striving for holiness.

3. All things have received their motion and natural property from Him who created them by word and reason (λόγος), and this applies to the intellect as well. However, the motion of the intellect has the property of eternality, and eternality is infinite and unlimited. Thus it would be contrary to its proper dignity and what is truly natural to it for the intellect to be confined or limited in its motion. This, however, will be seen to be the case as long as it moves amidst finite and limited things. For if the thing itself is finite and limited, then the motion of the intellect towards it or around it cannot proceed to the infinite. Hence the perpetual motion of the intellect requires something infinite and unlimited towards which it may move in accordance with reason and its own nature. And yet, there is nothing infinite and truly unlimited but God, who is in His nature One in the proper sense of the word. Therefore, the intellect must strive and direct its gaze upwards, and move towards the truly infinite One, God. This is, after all, what is truly natural to the intellect.

4. The realities contemplated around God are infinite and limitless. But not even these realities can be experienced with perfect joy by the intellect, which seeks the One from whom they proceed. For since each thing naturally rejoices in what is like unto it, and the intellect is one in nature (albeit many in intellections [νοήσεις]), so when it strives upwards and, as it were, moves towards God, who is One in nature and many in energy, it is impossible for it fully to rejoice until it has attained through the Spirit the One whose unique nature has no limits, after having 'passed beyond the many', so to speak. Therefore, the intellect by its very nature can only fully rejoice in God. But surely each thing that exists chiefly rejoices in its own natural property; and the chief natural property of the intellect is surely to move, ascend, attain, and fully rejoice in God alone, who is simply and illimitably One.

5. All the motion of every kind of created thing, including that of the intellect itself, strives and tends toward stability (στάσις) and tranquility (ἠρεμία), and to become stable and tranquil through its motion is the purpose and proper rest of any given created thing. Nevertheless, the intellect, although it is one of the created things, is unable to partake of stability and tranquility by means of motion amidst created things. For since creation has of course received finitude, since it has a beginning, the intellect will inevitably be left in perpetual motion and thus constantly seek to move elsewhere. Thus, either the intellect will never find tranquility nor achieve its purpose, or else it will cease from its innate perpetual motion, as we have described, by being enclosed within the limited and the finite, in a condition far

from its natural state, which is manifestly ever-moving. It is therefore unreasonable to presume that the intellect may find tranquility or stability in created things. But where, then, may the intellect make proper use of its motion (that is, by becoming stable through motion), and so find tranquility and peace and receive a secure sense of repose, unless it attains what is uncreated and uncircumscribable? And thus, only in God, who is truly and transcendently One. He is the uncircumscribable One whom the intellect must attain through motion, in order to find the tranquility natural to it in its proper noetic rest. For that is where [one may find] stability through the Spirit, a paradoxical state of rest, and the boundless beyond all things. And there is no lack of motion for any intellect that has attained the One, since it has reached the unlimited, boundless, uncircumscribable, formless, shapeless, and absolutely simple. For such is That which we call the One, that is, God.

6. Now if God, according to David, *makes spirits His Angels* (Ps. 103:4; Heb. 1:7), and those among men who are born of the Spirit He makes *spirit*, as the Lord said (Jn. 3:6), then the man who is born of the Spirit through conscious participation in Him is made an angel. Now, since the work of the angels is to contemplate constantly the face of our heavenly Father, as the Lord said (Mt. 18:10), then surely the conscious participant in the Holy Spirit must raise himself up to contemplate the face of God. This is presumably why David also teaches: *Seek the Lord and be strengthened; seek His face continually* (Ps. 104:4). Therefore, whoever has become a participant in the Holy, Life-Giving, Illuminating, and Love-Inspiring Spirit, has experienced the ineffable birth of the Spirit, and has ascended to the dignity of an angel, does not take proper care of his new condition if he shuts off his noetic perception (νοερὰν αἴσθησιν) of God and does not desire to lift himself up to God and divine realities out of excessive pious fear; for these things are in fact commanded by the Savior, who told us to *abide in Him, as He also abides in us* (Jn. 15:4). Moreover, David says, *Draw near to Him and be illumined* (Ps. 33:6), and indeed if we intend to do what is proper and consonant with them, then in the Light of God the Father, that is to say, in the Holy Spirit, *we shall see the light* around God, that is, the divine truth (Ps. 35:10); unless, that is, we prefer in our ignorance to turn away from the divine rays.

7. There are three ways in which the intellect mounts up to the contemplation of God: through intrinsic motion (αὐτοκινήτως), derived motion (ἑτεροκινήτως), or a combination of the two. The mode of intrinsic motion is performed simply by the nature of the intellect by exerting its will through the conceptual faculty

(φαντασία);[198] its end is contemplation of the realities around God (τὰ περὶ Θεὸν θεωρία), which the sons of Greece were able to conceptualize (φαντάζεσθαι) after a fashion. The second mode is supernatural and is brought about by the will and illumination of God alone; then the intellect comes wholly under divine influence (κατοχή), is seized with divine revelations, tastes the ineffable mysteries of God, and beholds future events. The combined mode is made up of aspects of the first two; for inasmuch as it operates by means of one's own will and conceptual faculty, it conforms to intrinsic motion; but it participates in derived motion inasmuch as it is united with itself through divine illumination and ineffably beholds God even beyond its own noetic union. At that point the intellect goes beyond all the realities beheld around God and said of Him, seeing neither "benevolence" nor "deifying power", neither "wisdom" nor "empowering rule", neither "providence" nor any other divine attribute, but is filled to the brim with noetic light and great joy, kindled by divine fire and mingled with love.

8. The intellect that employs its own conceptual faculty (φαντασία) to contemplate invisible things is guided by faith, and when it is illumined by grace, it is assured of hope; when it is flooded with divine light, it becomes a treasure trove of love for people and even more so for God. Thus the threefold order and movement of the intellect in faith, hope, and love becomes perfect and deifying, sure and steadfast. Again, one might say that when it has reached this spacious citadel it is secured in the fortress of love. This is why St. Paul said: *Love shelters all things* and *endures all things* for the good of faith and hope; he further says, *love never fails*, on account of its blazing union and ineffable affinity with God (1 Cor. 13:7-8).

9. The *One* cannot be abstracted from any *one* created thing. Of course, all created things differ from one another in respect to some mode of *unique* particularity (ἰδιότης), as we well know, but inasmuch as they are all created, they do not differ from one another by all having a beginning, being finite, fulfilling their end in nature, and not a single one of them being absolutely *one* in the true sense of the word. For only the Uncreated is truly *One*, being simple, beginningless, endless, limitless, and therefore infinite, that is to say, God. If the intellect gazes at It

[198] We have translated φαντασία here as "conceptual faculty" so as to avoid the misleading term "imagination". While φαντασία as "visualization, imagination" is considered a hindrance to prayer in other hesychastic texts, Kataphygiotes uses this word differently, either in the higher sense of "receptivity to divine manifestation" of something, the general sense of "conceptual or contemplative faculty", or the lower sense of "speculation, reasoning". Thus, while the mode of intrinsic motion is produced by the human will "through the conceptual faculty", the second mode corresponds to this as a product of the divine will and the illumination of God. The fact that the intellect can undertake to contemplate God by φαντασία alone is indicated by the reference to Greek philosophers who were able to "conceptualize" or "imagine" a certain conception of deity.

through participation in the Life-Giving Spirit and empowerment by Him, it daily receives the increase it needs and is united, made simple, and possessed of a divinized state. The intellect recognizes with complete certainty that apart from the One, and without its gaze directed towards It in the Spirit, it is impossible to attain fulfillment (νοῦν βέλτιον ἔχειν). This is because the intellect is scattered by being subjected to the fragmented world and the passions. Consequently, it stands in need of a transcendent power, that is, the supernatural One to which it must turn its gaze, so that by being seized away from the things that divide it, it may overcome the passions and discord and thus attain likeness to God (τὸ θεοειδές). It is for this reason that the Lord prays to the Father that we the faithful *may be one* in the Father and Himself, the Son, through the Spirit, and even *that we may be one as They are One* (Jn. 17:22) (although not as Sabellius falsely taught when he called Them "one"):[199] so that we may be made perfect as we should be, both by the grace of the Spirit who unites us and through unifying contemplation in the One God. This is clearly our true fulfillment (βελτίωσις); it is our perfect purpose (τέλος) and our only true rest. Moreover, this is why the envious and misanthropic ranks of demons perversely scattered our veneration among many gods, sowing the seeds of deception over the unity of the intellect and preventing it from receiving the manifestation (φαντασία) of the transcendent One, so that by the worship, disorientation, and division among the many, as well as by seducing the intellect to move against its own nature, they might make it desire all manner of passions and falsehood instead of truth and virtue. Thus the Holy Spirit exhorts us through the prophet, *Draw near to Him*, that is, to the One, *and be illumined* (Ps. 33:6). And elsewhere, *I am God, the first, and I am hereafter; beside Me there is no God* (Is. 41:4; 44:6). And again the Spirit says, *Hear, O Israel: The Lord your God, the Lord is One* (Deut. 6:4). For the three hypostases of the one Deity do not divide the one lordship, and while the persons are three, They are no less One in essence and power, in will and energy, and in all the other essential attributes of Their goodness. Therefore, to worship the One God, to look to Him, and to be gathered to Him from the many with all our concentration:[200] this is God's will for us and constitutes the fulfillment (βελτίωσις) of the intellect; it is the discovery of truth and divine eros and is the product of deification.

10. If falsehood is fragmented, while the truth is one, then the intellect that ascends to the One in the Spirit – to the transcendent, to that which is beyond all things and

---

[199] Sabellius taught a form of the Modalist heresy, which claims that the Father, Son, and Holy Spirit of the Trinity are just three different "modes" or manifestations of a single divine person, in contrast to the Orthodox belief in three distinct consubstantial eternal hypostases/persons perfectly united in the One Godhead.

[200] συνάγεσθαι, ὅση δύναμις, πρὸς αὐτὸ ἀπὸ τῶν πολλῶν. "to be gathered to God" is an idea expressed by Dionysios the Areopagite, and συνάγεσθαι can also be read as "to concentrate". Cf. Ch. 17.

from which come the many – ascends to the truth itself. However, the intellect cannot be free of the passions unless *the truth sets it free* (Jn. 8:32). Thus, the intellect is set free once it has shifted its gaze[201] and raises itself in unity towards the transcendent One. Moreover, freedom is most befitting to the dispassion, deiform condition, and spiritual adoption of the intellect, while servitude is anything but.[202] For as Scripture says, *The servant does not know what his lord is doing* (Jn. 15:15). And while ignorance is a trait of the servant, it is clear that the person who has gained his freedom knows the mysteries of the Father, and has thus succeeded in ascending to the excellent dignity of an adopted son. For just as ignorance is obviously the opposite of knowledge, so clearly we may presume that the servant's rank is the opposite of the son's. Furthermore, if whoever *does not know* is a servant, then whoever *knows* is by no means a servant, but free, or as I would say, he is a son; for indeed, the Spirit of Truth truly sets free those to whom He comes, and this is precisely what makes them sons of God, as the Apostle says: *All who are led by the Spirit of God are sons of God* (Rom. 8:14). So then, if contemplation of the super-essential One is the essence (εἶναι) of truth,[203] and the truth grants freedom to the intellect, and if freedom is moreover a sure sign of divine adoption (and there is certainly nothing greater than the gift of adoption, nor anything more befitting to rational nature), then it is the most reasonable course of action and, in fact, an utter necessity for the intellect to strive and look upward, being borne up by the Spirit (πνευματοφορήτως), and to concentrate with all its strength on the transcendent One – God.

11. The Holy Spirit says, *The Lord your God, the Lord is One* (Deut. 6:4), so it is our duty to lift up the intellect to the transcendent One by the grace of the Divine Spirit; moreover, it is surely not right for someone to proclaim (κηρύττειν) the One while feeling no desire for the intellect to turn to It and behold It. For what the Holy Spirit says is precisely what He wills for the intellect to know (νοεῖσθαι), and what is known is also that to which the intellect must turn. As a matter of fact, if the intellect were not designed to turn towards an intelligible reality, then the reality that the intellect could potentially know would not exist either;[204] and this

[201] Literally "once it has nodded its head" or "inclined" (νενευκώς).

[202] ἡ δουλεία, can also be rendered "slavery". In the Greek of this passage there is no distinction between "slave" and "servant".

[203] The Greek word for truth is ἀλήθεια, which means "not-forgetting", or "unconcealed reality". Hence, defining the essence of truth as a kind of contemplation is quite appropriate in Greek.

[204] This reflects the basic Aristotelian understanding that "nature does nothing in vain. Everything either exists *for* something or else it is an accessory to something that exists *for* something" (μηθὲν μάτην ποιεῖ ἡ φύσις. ἕνεκά του γὰρ πάντα ὑπάρχει τὰ φύσει, ἢ συμπτώματα ἔσται τῶν ἕνεκάτου, *De Anima* 434a.31-32). Therefore the most basic needs and desires within man must have their counterpart in the outside world. Thirst implies the existence of water; eyes imply the existence of light and a world full of visible objects; and in the same way, the ability of the intellect to contemplate means that there must also be intelligible realities for it to contemplate.

would of necessity alter our proclamation of the One and thereby our faith as well.[205] If, then, this is absurd, then it is absurd not to think actively of the One by turning and raising the intellect to It.

12. It is natural for caused realities, especially rational beings, to ascend and look to their cause in a motion of return (ἐπιστρεπτικῶς), and moreover all things, including the intellect, have God as their cause, God being the supreme and absolute One. It is therefore natural for the intellect to ascend and look to the supreme and absolute One, thereby returning to its cause.

13. If *all things are from Him and through Him and to Him* (Rom. 11:36), and the intellect is, of course, one of *all things*, then the intellect exists *from Him* and *through Him*; and this is especially true of the intellect because of its resemblance to God (διὰ τὸ θεοείκελον). Hence the intellect ought more than anything else to look back *to Him*. Now the expression *to Him* indicates that one must redirect one's gaze to the manifestation of the transcendent One in a motion of return; in conclusion, the intellect ought to direct its gaze to the One.

14. The many proceed (προιέναι) from the One, not the One from the many. Furthermore, creation is many, and hence it is quite clear that creation came from the One. Moreover, this One stands above creation as its Creator and Maker. So then, he who contemplates creation rightly will inevitably be led to the transcendent One at the conclusion of his contemplation. After all, amidst the things that are caused there are, as it were, infinitely many echoes (πάμπολλα [...] ἀπηχήματα) of the Cause, and by means of these is He recognized who produced all things according to His will and providence, in artistry and in wisdom, in power and in goodness. For this reason Isaiah, inspired by the Spirit, says, *Lift up your eyes, and see, Who has shown forth all these things* (Is. 40:26). He says *all these things* about the many things that are caused, and *Who* in order to raise [206] our intellects to Him from whom all these things exist, and who is by nature absolutely One.

15. Creation, too, is gathered (συνάγεσθαι) into one, but this unity is composite and manifold and not unoriginate (ἄναρχος), since it is created. In contrast, the Creator is One, and not only One in terms of producing the harmonization of many

[205] The word for "not exist" is ἀπεῖναι ("to be absent"), which does not necessarily imply complete non-existence, but at least total inaccessibility and non-intelligibility.
[206] "To raise" (ἀνάγειν) can also be used in the sense of logic, as Kataphygiotes employs in his syllogisms, i.e. taking logical premises about the nature of being as starting-points to direct the intellect to God. Thus, the Scriptural exegesis based on this method is called *anagogical interpretation.*

and various things into an organic universal unity[207] for one purpose, but also simply because He is Uncreated as the Preoriginate Cause (προκαταρκτικὸν αἴτιον). When the intellect ascends to what is prior, it will eventually reach a One that both designs visible order (τακτικόν τάξεως) and originates the genesis of created beings (ἀρκτικόν γενέσεως), fusing them into an organic unity (σύμπνοια) and harmonizing them into one; otherwise it would have to continue *ad infinitum*, which is absurd. Indeed, for each thing that moves and becomes there must be a time when it was not; and inasmuch as it did not yet exist, it began. Again, if it has begun, it has also been set in motion. We must then seek That which set it in motion and brought it into existence, and This will have to be unmoved insofar as It causes things to move. For if It is not unmoved, then what could possibly move It, considering that It exists under no other principle (ἀρχή), being Itself Unoriginate (ἄναρχον)? But if It is indeed unmoved, then It is also immutable, and if this is the case, then it follows that It will also be simple, since the composite is subject to change, while we have already shown that It is immutable; for composition is the beginning of division, and division the beginning of dissolution, which is the last phase of motion. Surely then there is no composition in It, lest there also be division; no division, lest there also be dissolution; no dissolution, lest there appear any change or motion pertaining to That which is immutable and unmoved; for It causes to move without being moved and It brings into existence without coming into existence or becoming. If, then, It is immutable and unmoved, it follows that It is not composite and hence is utterly simple, transcendent, and absolutely One. The intellect that ascends to It goes beyond all things so that by all means it might look to That which is supremely lovely and pursue That which is above all, or rather, to the One *from whom* everything exists and *to whom* all things naturally ascend. Furthermore, when the intellect rightly does this according to reason, then it goes beyond the passions. For the intellect that wholly extends itself and even reaches beyond supreme beauties would hardly stay behind to languish in the shame of the passions. Hence, the sacred Law states, *Him alone shall you worship*, that is, the One (Deut. 6:13). So then, we must lift ourselves up to the supreme One if we wish to fulfill the Law of God and overcome the passions.

16. *The Lord alone was leading them, and there was no foreign god with them* (Deut. 32:12). Do you not see the power of the One and Only, how there was no foreign god with them since the Lord alone was leading them? However, the Lord leads those who follow, not those who turn back. Now, that which someone follows is that towards which he directs his attention (ἐπιστρέφεσθαι). If then we would have no other god with us, whether it be a demon or a passion, let us follow the One and Only by directing our intellect to Him, that it may rightly be said about

[207] Literally "shared breathing" (σύμπνοια); perfect, living unison.

us, too, that *the Lord alone was leading them, and there was no foreign god with them.*

17. Although the many come (εἰσὶν) from the One, each of them comes from the One in a different manner, since realities proceed from the first Unity in various modes. Some of these "many" have a beginning and are created, while others are uncreated and outside of the principle of beginning in time (τὸν τῆς χρονικῆς ἀρχῆς λόγον). Now, the One beyond reality (ὑπερούσιον) is the Cause of absolutely all of these realities, but It is the Cause of the former according to the mode of creation and of the latter according to the mode of nature. And for this reason we ought not to approach and engage with all these realities in the same way or to an equal extent, but the things that exist under the principle of beginning and creaturehood should be approached for the sake of something else and not for their own sake, as in the way we approach a mirror not for the mirror's sake, but to see the form and image reflected by it. In fact, we can receive no fulfillment (βελτίωσις) by approaching creation for any other reason than for the sake of the ultimate One manifested within it. On the other hand, we approach the beginningless (ἄναρχα) and natural [properties] of God not for the sake of something else, but both for their own sake and for the sake of the One from whom they proceed (τὸ ἐξ οὗ). For these are the realities that should truly be approached for their own sake, and the supreme One belongs to them in an immediate and natural mode; or rather, they belong to the ultimate and supreme One in an immediate and, again, natural mode. So then, we must not only approach them, but also cling to them, and hasten by means of them to imitate and receive the imprint of (ἀποτυποῦσθαι) the One Primal Beauty, so that by the assistance and help of grace we may obtain the dignity of being *in the image and likeness* of God's glory. Hence, when we examine aright the caused realities that are created (δημιουργικῶς), we are naturally drawn to raise our intellects in contemplation to the reflection of the One and to unite them to the undifferentiated perception (ἔννοια) of the transcendent One in an absolute and simple manner; that is, of course, as long as our intellect contemplates them properly. In the case of those realities that come naturally from the Cause, when the intellect operates in accordance with them for the sake of the Cause, or conforms to their likeness,[208] it can be united through them with That which is truly One in Itself. Therefore, starting out from all the various caused realities – whether they are caused naturally or by being created in time – the intellect has the natural habit of being gathered back to the One in a variety of ways, either practically or, of course, contemplatively. And when the intellect makes use of "one" or "many", whether it be natural [to God] or created [in time], as long as it does not make use of it for the sake of the One, or to concentrate itself on the primal One, or to strive for It (by the empowerment of the illumining Spirit

[208] οἷς δὲ φύσει τὸ αἴτιον καὶ πρακτικευόμενον τὸν νοῦν διὰ τοῦτον ἢ κατ' αὐτὰ μορφαζόμενον

and holy participation in Him in a simple, unifying, and unique manner), this is reckoned to the intellect as sin, even if the use seems to it to have a certain appearance of good. For all things from the One naturally lead to the One when we make proper use of them, as the great Dionysios the Areopagite says: "Every procession of light sent and kindly bestowed on us by the Father uplifts and fulfills us as a uniting power (Jas. 1:17), and brings us back to the unity and deifying simplicity of the gathering Father; *for from Him and to Him are all things* (Rom. 11:36)."[209] But if they do not lead the intellect up to the One, then this is contrary to nature, and as long as it does not use them in the way we have said, it does not make proper use of them.

18. There is a kind of action (πρᾶξις) that precedes contemplation (θεωρία) and a kind of action that follows contemplation. The first kind of action is performed in the body so that by bridling the body's impulses and gradually training it to comport itself well, it might thereby enable the intellect to pass over freely to the things proper to it, that is, to intelligible realities (νοητά), and thereby properly achieve its own distinctive virtue (διαφέρον καλῶς ἐργάζοιτο). The second kind of action begins with the intellect and the act of knowing in the Spirit, and it concentrates (συνάγεσθαι) on that which is beyond intellect, that is, God. When the intellect approaches Him, it encounters the One, for God is the One. And then even the intellect is united with itself into one and becomes undivided. For when we contemplate the One it brings about oneness and deiform simplicity, since it would be incompatible for the intellect to contemplate the One without it becoming one and simple itself. But when the intellect sees things divided and composite, it inevitably becomes divided and varied itself. Again, I have called "absolutely One" that which exists as Simple in Itself. For since the being of the intellect is subject to changes in energy,[210] while [in essence] it remains simple, the intellect must also become one in energy when it beholds the One. If, however, the intellect beholds the One, but is itself divided, even if it is only split into duality, what will be the activity of the part that is separated from the part that sees the One? Either it will be seeing something else, or not be seeing at all; and this state of duality (τοῦτο διssῶς) will either be because the one part does not desire vision, or because it is dimmed, or perhaps because it is focused on an action of another nature, and not on the activity of vision. However, if we assume that the intellect sees something else, then it is obvious that it does not see the One in simplicity, but is seeing double contrary to reason (παρὰ τὸν λόγον) – and while it is seeing double, it cannot itself be one, because it is torn between the things it contemplates, as we have shown. Let us now consider the possibility that one part of the intellect does not see, either because it does not desire to, or because it is made dull, or because it is focused on

[209] *On the Celestial Hierarchy* 1.1. Also quoted in ch. 81.

[210] ὅ,τι πέρ ἐστιν ὁ νοῦς τὰς ἀλλοιώσεις πάσχει κατ' ἐνέργειαν

another kind of action. The first is impossible, because it is not possible for the rational intellect to stand idle even for the briefest moment; neither is the second case possible, because if one part of the intellect were made dull and the other acute, the intellect would be composite and not simple, since it would be composed of disparate parts; the same thing will be seen to be the case if one part sees, while the other is engaged in another form of activity, since this is a predicate of composites, but it is quite unacceptable to posit this of the intellect which is simple. For these reasons it is clear that if the single and simple aspect of the intellect contemplates the absolute One, it will also itself be one in energy; and if it is simply one, then it will behold the simple One. It follows then that every kind of action or contemplation should be directed towards the One who is beyond intellect. Otherwise, it will achieve nothing, and all the intellect's action and contemplation will prove to be in vain. For the intellect will be engaged in the passions, subject to division, unable to move in consciousness of soul toward unifying union with the One beyond intellect. And this union is precisely what has the power to purify and cleanse the contemplative faculty of the intellect, as it is lifted up and looks to the One, clinging to Him *from whom and through whom and in whom are all things* (Rom. 11:36), and for whom it has come into being, exists, and subsists.

19. The most ultimate desire of all (τῶν πάντων ἐφετῶν ἄκρον) is the union of the soul with God beyond intellect. This union with God requires likeness to God; likeness to God requires noetic activity, that is, contemplation (*theorein*). For such is the Divine (*theion)*, and hence the name '*Theos*' has been ascribed to Him. And indeed, contemplation proceeds directly to the perception (ἔννοια) of God. For everywhere and in all things, God presents certain rays of light to the contemplative intellect. Now, the contemplative intellect has God as its object, and God is the transcendent One. Again, the nature of the intellect is such that it becomes like in energy to what it sees, as the divine Theologian Gregory makes clear when he refers to the phrase "seeing and 'suffering' (πάσχειν) the splendor of God."[211] For what the intellect has seen, it has also 'suffered' – that is to say, it becomes like it. And hence Peter of Damascus says that the intellect is saturated by the things it contemplates, and as when it sees divided and varied things it becomes varied and divided, likewise when it has ascended to the vision of the transcendent and absolute One, it accordingly becomes one, as I have mentioned before. Then, when it reaches the One, it beholds the beginningless and infinite

[211] λαμπρότητα Θεοῦ καὶ ἰδεῖν καὶ παθεῖν. *Oration* 45.7, On Holy Pascha. This quote from St. Gregory Nazianzen served as one of the most foundational texts for describing union with God in Byzantine mystical theology, and is one of the reasons we have often translated it "suffer" (for St. Gregory's works were exegeted in ways similar to Scriptural texts, and accepted as authoritative). It is often found in conjunction with ἀλλοίωσις (change or transformation), cf. Ps. 76:11. See also *paschein* in Glossary.

and formless and simple, for such is the One; and thus the intellect is made beginningless, infinite, unformed, simple according to its energy, and after it has 'suffered' this transformation, it attains a kind of assimilation to the Divine as far as possible. From there it soars aloft to the most ultimate desire of all: divine and ineffable union beyond intellect, which is the ultimate purpose of the life dedicated to God. We must therefore make every effort to lift up our intellects and strive by the grace of the Spirit for the contemplation and vision of the transcendent One.

20. When the intellect is split into many or even just two parts, it is quite clear that it cannot behold the simple One. That is why it is limited and finite and indistinct, because such is the nature of things that are not absolutely simple. But when it comes into intangible contact with the true One, and in the Spirit gazes upon It beyond sight, then it too is made beginningless, infinite, limitless, without shape or form; it is immersed in speechlessness and keeps silent in astonishment; it is filled with sheer delight and 'suffers' (πάσχειν) the ineffable. However, do not think that I am saying that the intellect becomes beginningless, infinite, and limitless according to its essence; no, this occurs according to energy, because what changes in the intellect is not its *essence* but its *energy*. For if it were to be transformed in essence by 'seeing and suffering' deification, that is to say, to become god by contemplating God, it would be God in essence. But this is of course impossible, and not even the angels are able to be God in essence, for this belongs to the One and Only and Supreme God alone. So then, if it is absurd to say that the intellect can be deified in essence, the only possibility that remains is to say that it 'suffers' this through the very act of beholding God. Hence the intellect by nature cannot be transformed in its essence, but in energy. Moreover, if the intellect naturally changes in accordance with the things it contemplates, as we have said, and because it can by no means contemplate the divine essence, but only the divine energy, this also implies that the intellect will not be transformed according to essence, but according to energy.

21. All things, after having shone forth, so to speak, from the transcendent One, were not removed from the One by whom they were made (in whichever mode of being), but just as they came to be in Him, so are they held together and perfected in Him. There exists not a single thing that does not have a kind of effluence and scent, as it were, of that Creative and True One.[212] And all the things that participate in being not only send forth their voice announcing the transcendent One (cf. Ps. 18:4) (for It is established above all forms of contemplation and intellection), but also set forth rays of Its transcendent radiance, so to speak.

[212] οὐδέν ἐστιν ἐν οὐδενὶ τῶν ἁπάντων, ἐν ᾧ οὐκ ἔστιν ἀπόρροια καὶ ὡσανεί τις ὀσμὴ ἐκείνου τοῦ ποιητικοῦ καὶ ὄντως ἑνός.

Hence, because the One is loudly proclaimed by all and all incline towards the One – and this transcendent One manifests Itself to the intellect through all things – so the intellect must be directed and guided and led to the transcendent One. On the one hand, it is compelled by the persuasive voice of the multitude of things; on the other hand, the creative One about whom we have been speaking also desires for the intellect to behold It in the abundance of Its goodness, so that the intellect may experience true life in It, as the ineffable One Himself says: *I am the life* (Jn. 11:25), and, *This is eternal life, that they may know You, the only true God* (Jn. 17:3), and elsewhere in Scripture, *Seek God and your soul shall live* (Ps. 68:33); for from seeking comes vision, and from vision comes life; and again, this is so that the intellect may be gladdened, illumined, and delighted, as David says: *All who rejoice have their dwelling in You* (Ps. 86:7), and, *In Your light shall we see light* (Ps. 35:10). Why else would He have created the intellect as a contemplator and sown signs of Himself throughout all created things, manifesting Himself through them to the intellect like a flash of noetic radiance bursting through windows, except to enrapture it by drawing it to Himself in illumination?

22. All that God – who is the One Triadic Good – has made, He has made by His will. But again, all that God wills is utterly good, for goodness is His nature. Thus He has made the intellect a contemplator of Himself and of His attributes, which lead the contemplator to the One. Therefore, God *wills* for the intellect to be His contemplator, and so this is in and of itself the highest good. God is properly and absolutely One, and gazing and concentrating single-mindedly on Him is the ultimate good, as we have shown.

23. If absolute eros is *one* and is felt with single-minded devotion (συνεπτυγμένος), according to the instruction of those wise in divine matters, then the object of that eros[213] must be *one* also. For even if there were at least two objects of eros, then there would either be two kinds of eros, or the one eros would be divided into two and could hardly be said to be one and single-minded. But now, since absolute eros is said to be one and to be felt with single-minded devotion, then we can clearly understand that there is also one beloved. But of course the beloved must exist prior to the eros felt for it, and there is no way for someone to experience eros of the beloved before first catching sight of the beloved. Eros is intense love (ἀγάπη), and this is the kind of love that the natural and written law of God demands that we have towards God. That is, the natural law wholly persuades the intellect that loves beauty (φιλόκαλος) to seek the Superior, that is, God, while the written law says: *You shall love the Lord your God with all your soul and with all*

---

[213] Greek thought draws a sharp distinction between the active giver of eros, the lover (ὁ ἐρῶν, ὁ ἐραστής) and the recipient of eros, the beloved (ὁ ἐρώμενος, ὁ ἐραστός). Kataphygiotes makes use of this distinction in his syllogisms, but also discusses how this love and eros becomes mutual.

your heart and with all your mind (Deut. 6:5), and, *The Lord your God, the Lord is One* (Deut. 6:4). Here then the beloved is One, that is, the Triune God, and He of course must exist prior to the intellect's eros for Him. Therefore, the intellect must desire to ascend to the transcendent One, so that by attaining It and contemplating It a person's eros for it may shine forth, and so that he may become a fulfiller of both the natural law and the above commandment by *loving the Lord his God.*

24. When the intellect has ascended to the One beyond mind, it is impossible for it not to fall passionately in love with It. For it encounters an ineffable and inconceivable beauty springing from It, as from the root of all power. Then the intellect falls under the light of divine illuminations and marvels to behold the Beauty beyond intellect, like a net about to burst after landing a great catch of fish (cf. Lk. 5:7); it is intoxicated as if by wine and becomes, as it were, mad with ecstasy; it is seized with wonder beyond thought, and cannot bear the weight of the glorious sight[214] of such extraordinary Beauty. And so it is bound in the bonds of love, as if consumed with burning thirst. For the One beyond mind is One, and yet It is proclaimed by all things, for It is the Preoriginate Cause of all things: as beginning, as end, and as the power holding all things together. Again, It produced the beauty and goodness of all things beautiful and good in the superabundance of the power that makes all beautiful and good, while It Itself stands at an infinitely infinite height above all beauty and goodness as the unsurpassable and transcendent One. It alone is by nature the object of love (ἐραστός), above all loves, because It alone is properly Beautiful and Good, transcending all that is beautiful and good, and according to the law of nature and order It alone is truly lovely (ἀγαπητός) as the Cause of all things; It is so great that it surpasses all other loves and desires (ἀγαπητά, ἐραστά) in its excess of beauty and goodness; and It is indeed the transcendent One, as the only truly existent Being and Provider of being to all things. Let us return then, by the help of the Spirit and with a "good outcome" from God,[215] as people say, to the pursuit and knowledge of the One and Only, in whom originate the principles of all things and in whom are found their destinies; then the gate of divine love will surely open to us of itself by the grace of Christ (cf. Acts 12:10), and we will enter into the rest of our Lord (Heb. 4:3) with great joy and gladness, and will know the enjoyment of the One and receive a taste of divine bliss, having become *one* ourselves – no longer separated or divided into many – according to the Savior's prayer to the Father: *That they may be one, as We*

[214] Literally "unable to fit the sight inside of it" (μὴ χωρῶν καθορᾶν), continuing the fishing metaphor above.

[215] This popular phrase (ἀγαθῇ τύχῃ) originated in pre-Christian Greece as an invocation of the Goddess of Fortune. It was widely used to attest oaths, prayers, treaties, contracts, decrees, building projects and other endeavors of uncertain outcome.

are One (Jn. 17:22). Then we will also be exact keepers of the commandment that says, *You shall love the Lord your God with all your soul* (Deut. 6:5) *and your neighbor as yourself* (Lev. 19:18), and we shall even attain human perfection, as far as this is possible: *For the perfection of the law is love* (cf. Rom. 13:10), upon which not only do *all the Law and the Prophets hang* (Mt. 22:40), but also all who are perfected by God in Christ.

25. For everything that is by nature unified in the Spirit, division is degradation. Hence, if the intellect is ever divided in energy, it falls from the state of grace (κατὰ χάριν) proper to it. It suffers this when it gazes at various things, since it is impossible to remain undivided when it is dispersed in different directions. Indeed, if one supposes this to be possible, he will not find it easy to explain how the intellect engaged in stillness is different from the confused intellect, and will regard the intellect of the God-bearers as no different from the intellect disturbed by the commotion of the passions – which is absurd. For the intellect is such that it becomes like in energy to that which it sees, and thus when it looks on composites, it must of necessity become varied itself; again, when it falls short of simplicity, there is no way for it to remain undivided. And this state of subjection to division is more prone to sin than any other, and that is why this division of itself is condemned by those who are discerning in these matters. Thus, considering that it is natural for the noetic power of the intellect to taste the Beauty beyond nature with its noetic sense (νοερὰ αἰσθήσει) wholly unified, by contemplating the supreme and transcendent One, then this division is contrary to the state of grace.

Therefore we must hold fast to the transcendent One (Ἕν) and gaze only upon the One and Only with all our soul if we are to avoid division and differentiation (ἑτερότης). And not only that, but even if the intellect does look on a *single* thing (ἕν) that happens to be created (κτιστόν), even then it cannot remain undivided. For a single created thing (κτιστὸν ἕν) cannot be said to be simple in the proper sense, since it is limited and composite and circumscribable, and therefore nothing has the right to be called "simply and absolutely One", nor is the energy of the intellect simple and unified while gazing upon any "one" thing. For its contemplation will be limited and circumscribed with complexity, given the fact that it becomes like to that which it contemplates, and thus it will fall from the divine grace that renders it simple, beginningless, limitless, and uncircumscribable, and will remain apart from the hidden One that surpasses understanding. It will thus be deprived of its own glory, which is the single-minded enjoyment of the indivisible uniqueness, beginninglessness, limitlessness, simplicity, and formlessness of the One, and it will have no opportunity to 'suffer' the vision of the supernatural and utterly ineffable Beauty.

Hence, the intellect must gaze and lift itself up to the beginningless, simple, unlimited, and true One, and press on from there to be enlightened and united to the original Unity that gathers all, and so also be united with itself. This way, it will not only be loved by the Superior One (κρείττων), after being made like unto Him in limitlessness, simplicity, formlessness, and shapelessness, insofar as this is possible, but it too will come to love (ἀγαπᾶν) the Divine Beauty beyond beauty and One beyond nature by ascending to the aforementioned *likeness* to It (cf. Gen. 1:26). Indeed, since by nature things are usually disposed to love (ἀγαπητικὴ διάθεσις) other things like them, it should be quite clear that the intellect will be loved by God and love Him in return. For what is 'like' is of course like to what is like; and since the likeness always works both ways, it follows that the one will always have, in addition to its own loving, a reciprocal love from the other. There is nothing greater than this affection between God and the soul.

26. The intellect then goes beyond its nature when it fully arrives at the One beyond intellect, after becoming formless, shapeless, and wholly beyond form in God – beginningless and infinite, and, one might even say, after transcending its own union. As long as it still has its thinking power, even if it is engaging in divine and intelligible things, it is said to be moving and acting naturally and standing within the bounds of its own nature. But, naturally, the supernatural surpasses the natural and far excels it. Thus it should desire (φιλεῖν) and strive to attain the supernatural, which is far greater, in accordance with the command that tells us to *strive for the greater gifts* (1 Cor. 12:31). But again it is clear that when the intellect has attained the supernatural, it has attained God. For God of course is outside of all nature, since He is indeed the principal and absolute One. The intellect should thus ascend and strive to gaze and lift itself up to the principal and absolute One, so that by having ascended to the One beyond nature and surpassing its own natural energy, it may find fulfillment (βέλτιον) and transcend its own nature.

27. Each thing naturally rejoices and finds rest in its own principles (τὰ ἑαυτοῦ ἰδικά), all of which pre-exist in the primary Cause (ἀρχαιάτατον αἰτίον) in the sense that It is the single Principle of their causation (κατ' αἰτίαν ἑνοειδῆ).[216] Then the intellect will enter nature into true delights in fulfillment of its nature, and will have no fleeting pleasure, and will find profound rest, when it has surpassed and renounced all things and devoted[217] itself to that unique, original, and foremost Cause, and thus through noetic return attains to the One from whom all things and their reasons come to be (that is, their principles, means, and ends): to the One in

[216] This doctrine is likely related to St. Maximos the Confessor's teaching about the *logoi* (principles, reasons) of created things in God the *Logos*. See the reference to the *logos* of causality at the end of this chapter. Cf. *Ambiguum* 7, *On the Cosmic Mystery of Christ* (trans. Blowers), 45-74.

[217] The word "devote" (ἀνατίθημι) refers specifically to an offering in a sacred place.

whom all things subsist and are sustained; to the One by whom all things being perfected fulfill their ends; to the One in whom they receive joy and gladness; to the One who created the very intellect to be as it is. For the intellect has a certain way of returning to itself when it returns to that principal Cause of all, which is its true archetype. And because everything naturally loves itself, and this is especially the case for the intellect because it is an exceedingly beautiful image of the inconceivable beauty of the One beyond understanding, it has a great love to look back to its own Cause through return, for as I have said, it sees itself in It and loves beyond love (ὑπεραγαπάω). Besides, all things have a natural loving affection (στοργή ἀγαπητική) for that from which they come, as is also true *vice versa*, that parents fiercely love their children. For this reason there is an abundant and ineffable pleasure that arises for anything that returns to the One, the Cause of all things, because by returning to That from which it came, it also returns to itself, as we have explained. Indeed, That is the Cause in which all things pre-exist through the *logos* of causality, and so the intellect too, being one of them, exists in the One beyond understanding, since It is its archetypal Cause.[218]

28. Every essence comes from the Being beyond being and essence, and every nature comes from the One beyond nature, and all temporal and composite beings come from the timeless and the incomposite, and indeed all creatures came to be from the uncreated. Likewise every form has come to be from the formless, and the many phenomena come from the One beyond the universe. Thus he who neither devotes himself nor directs his gaze to the formless One as the One on which he depends, but instead looks to one of the formed and created things, such a person has placed what is incomparably lower above the Transcendent, and perhaps stands near to the idolaters. For that to which someone devotes himself and directs his gaze is the object of his desire; what he desires is what conquers him; and what conquers him is what enslaves (δεδούλωται) him (2 Pet. 2:19). Indeed, such a person truly worships the creation instead of the Creator (Rom. 1:25), because, following this reasoning, each person's intellect worships, becomes a servant to (δεδούλωται), and loves that on which it sets its gaze and devotes itself. Hence, if setting one's devotion and gaze on anything but the simple and formless One is a cause for such stumbling, let us apply all our diligence and knowledge to the formless and simple One through noetic return and ascent, whence come all the treasures of knowledge (Col. 2:3); all who arrive there find repose and relief (ἀνάπαυσις καὶ ἀπόπαυσις) from all acts of contemplation, quiet

---

[218] Here St. Kallistos is not saying that the essence or material of all created things exist from all eternity, but that, while they are created *in time* and *out of nothing*, their principles pre-exist in God inasmuch as He is their Cause. Again, see St. Maximos' doctrine of the *logoi* in *Ambiguum* 7, cf. n. in ch. 27.

rest from intellection, silence beyond intellect, and inexpressible exultation in great wonder.

29. If all beings desire being, and the cause of the being of all things is contained in the One beyond being, then all beings, especially rational ones – as long as they move rightly and properly – actually desire the One beyond being in their desire for being. Therefore the intellect that does not rise towards the One beyond being, and does not desire It, is engaged in a perverse and misguided (ἡμαρτημένος)[219]motion and falls short of its proper dignity: the knowledge of the One beyond being, the supremely divine unifying unity, and the love of It surpassing intellect.

30. Causes (τὰ αἴτια) have greater beauty than their effects (τὰ αἰτιατά), and moreover, the universal Cause of all things is the One beyond essence. So if the intellect turns its attention to something subsequent to the One beyond essence, regarding it as beautiful or somehow worthy of noetic attraction, it has obviously missed its mark (ἡμάρτηται ὁ σκοπὸς αὐτοῦ), because it is essentially *philokalic*.[220] But owing to its ignorance or indolence, instead of moving toward the first and principal One beyond essence (by which all beautiful things become beautiful through participation), it moves toward the things that have derived their beauty from It. However, the intellect that directs itself successfully extends the gaze of the mind to the One above essence, for it is sure that it will find even more than it yearns for, because through this noetic vision it reaches the Cause; and it is quite sure that nothing can communicate to it its own goodness or beauty but the One above essence. But even if it thinks that there are certain things that have the power to communicate their own properties, still, these by nature do not remain forever in the loving intellect (ἐραστὴς νοῦς). For it has faith that only the Holy Spirit can do this, who is active however and wherever He wills – for He is Lord, shares in the Sovereign Nature, and is a Person of the Trihypostatic Unity. Hence the intellect must return to the One above essence, whence comes not only the source of all good things, but also the bestowal of inalienable gifts.

31. All things naturally desire good, and again, the One is truly Good, although many are called "good". For among the many you will find nothing absolutely good and altogether perfect, as it were, but every good is only called "good" by having a certain share in the Good, that is, by participating in the Good and One above essence, and not by possessing goodness of itself. For only that One beyond

---

[219] Or "sinful".

[220] "Loving the beautiful" or "loving the good". Here we have translated the term φιλόκαλος as "philokalic" because of its pertinence to the title of the *Philokalia*.

essence is absolutely good and beyond good and the source of all goodness, being communicative of Its own good; It alone naturally restores to Itself every essence, existence, condition, power, motion, energy, property, and every form of beauty and goodness. Indeed, absolutely all things, and the realities we contemplate about them, have received their manifestation through being created by the One beyond essence. Therefore, the intellect that is directed to anything else but the simple One beyond essence has misdirected motion; it may even be moving towards some good, but not towards the proper and absolute Good, which in the superabundance of its benevolence improves and fulfills with goodness all that requires improvement and fulfillment (βελτίωσις) in goodness.

32. The intellects of "the many" (οἱ πολλοί)[221], which are subject to division because of their folly and distracted by the many (τὰ πολλά), do not know the good that is absolutely One, nor do they even seek It or take interest in It. Concerning such people the Spirit says through David, *Many say, 'Who will show us the goods?'* (Ps. 4:7) They do not say "the Good", as is to be expected, because they are *anxious and troubled about many things, when One is necessary*; sharing in this One is called the *good portion* in the holy word of God (Lk. 10:41-42); however, they either run past it in their ignorance or miss out on it in their negligence, and do not even think to seek what is most worthy to be sought. But those who have been led and taught by David and have seen fit to follow in his footsteps, say, *The light of Your face, Lord, has been signed upon us* (Ps. 4:7), which is to say, "The knowledge of your unique glory has been displayed to us as in a mirror." Thus, the vulgar and 'many' masses rejoice in 'many goods', but in contrast, those who live in the Spirit are enlightened and transcendently illumined in the knowledge of the single and absolute Good.

33. Just as the force of a stream of water is greater when it flows in a single cascade than when it is divided and split into many channels, so the gaze of the intellect and its natural motion and desire will grow stronger if it applies itself without being variegated and distracted, in a unification without division. This is naturally done by raising the intellect, beholding, and contemplating the transcendent and absolute One, for the transcendent and utterly simple One is what truly has the power to gather and unite; and once the intellect is made worthy to gaze upon It, it is then impossible for it not to be conformed to It, like an image,[222] and to become uniform in an order of unity – simple, colorless, formless, without attribute, impalpable, limitless, infinite, shapeless – and even to become itself an 'absolute transcendent one' by being gloriously arrayed with the rays of divine and

---

[221] That is, "most people", "the common people", the "hoi polloi".
[222] Or "icon" (εἰκών).

transcendent eros in the revelation of mystical knowledge, crowned with speechlessness and unknowing beyond reason, speech, and intellect, and enthralled with spiritual exultation and heavenly delight. It is further *transformed* into what is more divine and takes on a divine form (cf. Ps. 76:11), being formed in the Spirit by what is simple, shapeless, formless, and One, in addition to the other properties mentioned. However, if this has not occurred to the intellect and it has not suffered this divine transformation, then it has not yet attained the transcendent One through Its contact and manifestation (ἐν ἐπαφῇ καὶ φαντασίᾳ). For God is indeed the Unity that unifies and Intellect beyond intellection; and then the intellect is transcendently formed in the vision of Him, that is, when, in addition to what we have said, it becomes one beyond intellection and experiences this through divine manifestation.

34. The Triune Divinity beyond essence is joined in transcendent concord, for God is a Trihypostatic Unity. Hence it is not possible for the soul to image forth a likeness of God, as long as it is still tripartite and has not yet become one with itself in a manner beyond nature. I call the soul tripartite not in respect to its rational (λογιστικόν), irascible (θυμικόν), and appetitive (ἐπιθυμητικόν) parts, for properly speaking, the soul is not "tripartite" in this respect at all, since the rational soul bears hardly any relation to appetite and anger. In fact, we have derived these from the irrational part and they have arisen as a consequence [of the Fall] for our present animal life, and are inherently irrational and darkened, while the soul is rational and its nature is full of noetic light. We should say that the things that properly belong to the soul are those attributes without which it cannot perform its own natural energy and activity. But it can certainly act apart from anger and desire; and that is precisely when it is truly active: when it acts without them. Hence, these are not truly parts of the soul, but as has been said, they are powers of the lower animal state and subsist alongside it. For the rational soul that noetically examines the higher things and beholds intelligible realities and rises beyond itself and, I might say, soars aloft to such a height rejects desire and anger as idle chatter, having no use for them where it has simplicity, the formless, the shapeless, the colorless, the unformed, and all the other qualities that presuppose a free and wholly simple intellect. Nevertheless, the soul is in fact tripartite in its own natural simplicity, because it is intellect equipped with reason (λόγος) and spirit (πνεῦμα), its most distinctive attributes which by no means spoil its simplicity. For consider how the threeness of the henarchic Divinity, which the soul resembles as an *image* (εἰκών), is not an impediment to His unity and simplicity, but the Divinity is in fact a simple One beyond essence, and yet is nonetheless an undivided Trinity. Therefore, when the soul – that is, the intellect (for soul is intellect, or the soul is the intellect taken in its entirety) – reason, and spirit become one in a manner beyond nature, we are afforded our proper *likeness* to the One Trihypostatic Divinity. Now, the only way this can happen is through

the vision and contemplation of the supernatural Triadic Unity. For the Trinity is the One who has made the soul thus and restores the fallen soul to this state. But without directing its gaze to It in contemplation, it is impossible for this to happen to the soul, and unless this occurs and the soul recovers this likeness, we will remain incomplete. I am speaking here about the contemplative part [of the soul] and about the truth, which are the things most worthy of attention, without which it is impossible for us to attain a state of dispassion.

For just as we must reach the good by means of action (πρακτικῶς) in order to be counted among the dispassionate, so we must also turn to the truth by means of contemplation (θεωρητικῶς) in order to be godlike (θεοειδής), by worshiping the God of all and desiring to become and live as gods by divine adoption according to the archetypal resemblance decreed by God. If then it is necessary for us to become one in order to be like the prototype of the transcendent One, this will naturally be brought about by our vision of the transcendent One – our contemplation, ascent, and noetic return through ever looking fixedly to the One. We must attempt in every way, then, to look to the transcendent One beyond mind, and to make ourselves wholly dependent on It, in all earnestness and with all our heart and soul; to nourish within us the love of the transcendent – the One and Only beyond simplicity – that this eros may bear us aloft like holy wings in our noetic flight up to Him. And thus, *up in the air* – in a formless, unified condition – *we shall always be together with the Lord* (1 Thess. 4:17), the true One, praising the Trinity in a trinitarian manner, that is, noetically, rationally, and spiritually, with mouths agape in due wonder,[223] at one with ourselves and at one with the One, in oneness beyond oneness

35. The sensible number one (μονὰς αἰσθητή) is the principal unit (ἀρχή) of every numerical quantity (πλῆθος), and the transcendent One (μονὰς ὑπερκόσμιος) is the principle (ἀρχή) of every perceptible and intelligible quantity (πλῆθος), and of everything that exists. So then, just as the principal unit (ἀρχή) of every number is one, so does everything that exists pour forth from the transcendent One in a mode of causation, either by being caused naturally or by being created. Now, the place value (θέσις) of the number one, because it is sensible, is dictated by its nature: since it is the principal unit (ἀρχή) of the whole number system, it must come first when counting sensible things (ἡ αἴσθησις ἀριθμοῦσα). But in the case of the transcendent One, which is beyond intellect, the opposite is true. For while It naturally stands *before* all things as the One, the intellect places It *after* all things. For no intellect has ever been able to start with the One as a beginning (ἀρχή) and

---

[223] τριαδικῶς τὴν Τριάδα νοερῶς, λογικῶς τε καὶ πνευματικῶς ἐξυμνοῦντες [...] ἐκκεχηνότες καὶ ἐκπληττόμενοι.

proceed from It to the many [as in a sequence], but on the contrary, it begins its ascent from the many and is gathered to the One.[224] In the former case, the sensible number one needs to be countable to make sense of advancing to the many, otherwise we cannot count or progress as we desire. But in the latter case, the intellect must start with the many in order to ascend and be recollected (εἰς σύμπτυξιν) to the transcendent One, for there is no other means by which it may ascend to the vision of the One as it desires.

Hence the intellect, by making use of the order and method natural (οἰκεία) to it, takes its beginning from the many and makes the transcendent and most-supreme One its end. For since the sensible, countable number one (τὸ κατ' αἴσθησιν ἀριθμητὸν ἕν) is easily grasped and well defined, we naturally count it first, as its nature dictates. But the transcendent One for which the intellect seeks, since It is supernatural and defies intellection, is so far from being placed (θέσις) in a natural sequence that the intellect can by no means begin with It. So then, because It is supernatural, instead of the intellect beginning with It, it finds It not as the beginning, but rather as the supernatural end of its journey (διάβασις) through the many – after it has, I might add, "enumerated the many."

Now, since the intellect by nature knows (νοεῖν),[225] but the transcendent One is in itself incomprehensible and unapproachable, the intellect tends to be occupied with the many, even inadvertently, because it cannot cease from the activity of knowing, and yet neither does it have the power to grasp (περιδράξασθαι) the supreme and transcendent One. Nevertheless, by turning its gaze to the many, it perceives in each one of these many things something intelligible that is not just each thing's being, but something belonging to the One.[226] When it gathers from each thing that appears to it (φαινόμενον) a particular intelligible quality that shines forth from it (προφαινόμενον), and perceives how all these things harmonize with each other instead of colliding, and how all things are like flowers naturally springing forth from a single root and shoot, it then accordingly proceeds from the many to the most-supreme One, from whom the all and the many come, and it is naturally gathered from natural realities to a supernatural order, by perceiving the One beyond nature and essence as in a mirror (that is, to the degree that it is possible for That which is beyond nature to be seen in Its simplicity from natural things). Then, when the intellect has ineffably looked upon the generous ebullience that brings forth all goodness and beauty and has taken delight in the One beyond essence, it no longer willingly returns to the many, even though they are indeed beautiful and participate in the good. For since the intellect is by nature *philokalic*

[224] May also be understood as "inferring" the One from the many.

[225] νοῦς φύσιν ἔχει νοεῖν. "The intellect by nature engages in intellection."

[226] ἐνορᾷ νοητόν, οὐχ ὅπερ ἐστί εἶναι, ἀλλ' ὅπερ τινὸς ἑνός.

to the greatest degree,[227] it does not willingly depart from That which is above all unless circumstances require it to. However, since the mode of each reality is different, and the intellect can have different kinds of noetic visions and can ascend through these realities to the transcendent and supernatural One in various ways, I deem it necessary to lay out a brief method and way of ascent through the 'many' to the transcendent One beyond essence, so that, as the intellect ascends, step by step, as it were, it may have full confidence that it is moving in the right direction and may recognize when it goes astray and whether it is where it should be; what the measure of its delight in the One is; what causes it to err and removes it from that beauty, rapture, and divine banquet; and how it might return to the state from which it has fallen. The intellect will come to know thereby the difference between the mist[228]of the passions and the clarity of the pure heart, will recognize the truth, become a partaker of heavenly visions as if by peering in a mirror, and know divine perception; it will not fail to notice its own spiritual progress (or perhaps its backsliding), will engage in the study of many wonderful realities, and will understand the purpose of stillness and seclusion. This is as follows:

All reality (πάντα τὰ ὄντα) is divided into sensible created realities, intelligible created realities, intelligible uncreated realities, and the uncreated One beyond intellect and reality (ὑπερούσιον). As the eye of the soul, that is, the intellect, turns and sets its gaze on them and takes up (αἱρούμενος) the ascetical practice of stillness, it is itself taken up (αἵρεται) from the right practice of seclusion as if climbing up the rungs of a ladder to the act of contemplation, that it may attain to true Reality (τὸ ὄντως Ὄν) and delight in heavenly things, circle around the rays of truth, exult and become infinitely rich in eternal things, and experience a wondrous pleasure and sweetness. It may perhaps even be taken up in rapture from the earth through the synergy of grace, and in time, through the manifest attainment of the noetic light, it will become impervious to present things by the inspiration of the One beyond intellect and by the manifestation (φαντασία) of the One incomparably beyond all good.

Now, this sacred ladder is divided into five segments and thus its rungs lead us up to the ultimate goal; there is no spatial distance between these rungs, but their difference and distance from each other is an order of quality or kind, not degree. For instance, both sensible created things and intelligible created things are

---

[227] See note in Ch. 30.

[228] The "mist" (ἀχλύς) is a pervasive feature of Greek mythology. It usually refers to an ethereal shroud separating the realm of mortals from that of the gods. It clouds the eyes of dying warriors (Il. 5.696) and fills the House of Hades (Od. 20.357). When the gods envelop mortals in the mist, they turn invisible (Il. 20.321), and when it lifts, men can see the spirit world with their waking eyes (Il. 5.127).

realities, but the latter are as far superior to the former as the peculiar beauty of the intellect is superior to sensation. Again, uncreated intelligible realities far outrank created intelligible ones, while both sets belong to the category "realities" (ὄντα). However, uncreated intelligible realities are dependent (ὑποβεβήκασι) on the uncreated One above intellect. And hence it is clear that for the intellect to be established in the One that is superior to all realities, after having passed through action (πρᾶξις), and for it to come to that most-supreme Hiddenness (ἀποκρυφιότης), which dwells exceedingly far above all sensible and intelligible things: this is its superior vision (ἀπόβλεψις) and contemplation, while its humbler vision is found in the contemplation of sensible created realities, or even more so, in the practical stage.

Moreover, because the intellect is *philokalic* by nature, it should desire what is superior in every way, not only to enjoy it, but also to 'suffer' (πάσχειν) the superior *change* beyond intellect (cf. Ps. 76:11), because, as we have said, the mind also undergoes *change* in accordance with what it sees and delights in. However, the variability intertwined with the nature of the intellect will never leave it as long as today is still called *today* (cf. Heb. 3:13), and as it is said, *until the shadows depart* (Song 2:17), that is, until we depart from the present life, which shows us the truth *as in a mirror, darkly* and as in a shadow (1 Cor. 13:12). Therefore, when we fall short of the contemplation and vision of the uncreated One beyond intellect, we must try to stand as close as we can to the uncreated intelligible realities, so that our re-ascent to the uncreated One beyond intellect may be all the swifter. But when there falls a thicker mist (ἀχλύς) that obscures noetic activity and engulfs the intellect in despondency (ἀκηδία) regarding contemplation, then we should turn to the practitioner's prayers with a humble heart. After the darkness has subsided by the power of prayer and weeping, let us again consider the sensible created things as a kind of support and base (ὑποβάθρα), while the noetic light already acquired will continue to dwell in the heart by enhypostatic spiritual energy,[229] and the intellect will already possess through much experience the power of practice, by which it naturally climbs up, as it were, to a peak or summit and contemplates things that are not only invisible to most, but even unsought and inconceivable; without the power of practice no one will even be able to see himself, and still less will he see God (cf. Heb. 12:14). So then, it surely would not be outside the scope of the present discourse to give a cursory explanation of this ascetical practice.

---

[229] προενοικοῦντος τῇ καρδίᾳ ἐν ἐνεργείᾳ πνευματικῇ ἐνυποστάτῳ. A good reminder that the contemplative life and method described here presupposes the indwelling of the Holy Spirit ("enhypostatic spiritual energy") in the heart, the basis of hesychasm, as described in the other writings of this volume, e.g. Kallistos and Ignatios Xanthopoulos' *Exact Rule and Canon* 38, 41, 55, 60, 68, 76 and Kallistos Angelikoudes' *Chapters* 43, 52.

36. Three things within the soul require ascetical practice (πρᾶξις): the rational, appetitive, and irascible parts. Likewise, three things outside of it: the desire for glory, pleasure, and gain (τὸ πλεῖον). When the soul wisely considers these two triads [in the light of] Christ's life in the flesh, the intellect is healed by the grace of the Lord Jesus through the corresponding four cardinal virtues, namely, prudence, justice, temperance, and courage,[230] and thus the soul enables the intellect to be lifted up unhindered so as to perceive divine things and contemplate God.

When the Lord Jesus was led *by the Spirit into the desert* to defeat[231] the devil (Mt. 4:1-11), He healed the appetitive part by fasting, the rational part with vigilance and silent prayer, and the irascible part by rebuking the devil. Regarding the love of pleasure, he went hungry and did not seek for the stones to be turned to bread, as the devil suggested; regarding the love of glory, He refused to cast himself down from the pinnacle of the Temple to be glorified by the crowds for suffering nothing from the fall; regarding the love of money, He could not be persuaded to worship the devil with the promise of receiving the wealth of all the kingdoms, but with spirited (θυμοειδής) contradiction he rebuked Satan; this He did by means of prudence, justice, temperance, and courage, and thereby taught us how to thwart all of the devil's attacks. This is moreover what one may also perceive and understand from the Cross of the Savior. For at the time of the passion does the Savior not pray after removing Himself from the disciples (Mt. 26:36)? This is the healing of the rational part of the soul. Is He not wakeful and vigilant, suffering from thirst on the cross (Jn. 9:28)? This is medicine for the appetitive part of the soul. Does He not refuse to contradict, *contend, or cry out* despite being slandered (Mt. 12:19), and does He not even pray for His persecutors (Lk. 23:34)? This is for the proper ordering of the irascible part of the soul; that is, to reject the devil by contradicting him, but to treat the human beings who abuse Him with silence and long-suffering, since they themselves are abused by the devil, and to recompense them with prayer for their sake. Again, is He not spat upon, receiving blows and enduring mockery and ridicule (Mk. 14:65)? This is the cure for the love of glory. Is He not given vinegar to drink and bile to eat, crucified on a cross, and pierced with a lance (Mt. 27:34, 48; Jn. 19:29-30, 34)? This is the cure for the love of pleasure. Is he not hung naked, publicly exposed, alienated on the cross, despised

---

[230] The four cardinal virtues were first proposed by Plato and later became a mainstay of ethical teaching in antiquity, both Greek and Roman. Plato applied each virtue to a distinct domain of the tripartite soul, each as its goal to strive towards: temperance for the appetitive, courage for the irascible, prudence for the rational, and justice to govern the relationships among the various parts (Rep.427e; 435b).

[231] Literally "to wrestle into submission" (καταπαλαίω).

by all, like a *poor man and a pauper* (Ps. 69:6)? This is the abolition of a greedy disposition.

Hence the Savior has twice shown the healing of both internal and external passions. At one time, when He began to manifest Himself bodily to the world, and at another time, when He was about to depart from the world. Therefore, he who looks to Him, His teaching, and His cross, imitating His example as far as possible, with prudence, justice, temperance, and courage like His, will abolish the energy of these passions for evil, and will thus learn to make proper use of these and everything stemming from them, and will be a man who is a true practitioner, well-suited to ascend to God and to devote himself to inner noetic perception. And thus, after the intellect has taken its beginning from the many – that is, by starting with sensible created things – and seen the good fruit of their cultivation, and after perceiving created intelligible things and proceeding to intelligible uncreated realities, it will have already climbed up four rungs of the ladder. Then follow divine ineffability and silence and astonishment beyond intellect, and to sum up, the vision and contemplation of the transcendent One and union beyond intellection; it is the crown of stillness, the ultimate and perfect object of desire (ἐφετός), as far as this can be attained in the present life; the conclusion of the truth, the fruition of faith, the radiant illumination of the glory we hope for, the foundation of love, the measure of the intellect, the rest (στάσις) of its perpetual motion (ἀεικινησία), its inconceivable repose and unified state, the activity (ἐργασία) of the life to come as a foretaste, the cause of unimaginable joy, the treasury of peace, the quenching of carnal thoughts (Rom. 8:6), detachment from the present age and devotion to the age to come, separation from the impassioned life, affinity with dispassion, the glad rejoicing of the soul and the concentration, repose, and securement of its movements and powers, and, to summarize, divine knowledge and dispassion.

Therefore, whenever the intellect is restrained by its own laziness or by an external distraction, it must resolve to restore itself to its rightful (οἰκεῖος) contemplative beauty by removing the passion that impedes and prevents it from its purpose, to examine how far removed it is from the ultimate desire and why, and whether its contemplating activity is turned to sensible created realities, or to intelligible created ones, or to intelligible uncreated ones, or whether it has been distracted by vain thoughts or any other matter from the aim of its pursuit – the only true and transcendent One beyond all unity; and [the intellect must] accordingly remove the barriers between them, to return in a unified manner, as the proper order (τάξις) requires, to the contemplation and vision of the transcendent One. For when the intellect is found anywhere else but in the transcendent uncreated One beyond intellect, then it is subject to division and is not directed to the truly Beautiful (τὸ καλόν), even if its motion is good and fair (καλῶς), for the super-essential, uncreated, simple One beyond intellect is the supreme Beauty, and This is the true ultimate objective goal of the intellect, and hence as long as the intellect moves in a healthy way, it ascends through the stages we have mentioned and ultimately 'suffers' union beyond intellect. Let us therefore pursue the Infinite with all our strength, search for the One beyond intellect, contemplate the formless One, and take the Incomprehensible by storm,[232] that we may acquire the unique inheritance of the One and supreme God, by the grace of our Lord Jesus Christ and the Life-Giving Spirit, by whose illumination we are made worthy of the grace of contemplation and become gods adopted and deified by the gift of God.

37. When the intellect has ascended to the realm of divine Hiddenness (ἀποκρυφιότης) it naturally keeps silence,[233] unified in simplicity, and hence singularly illumined by the One beyond intellect by participation in the Spirit. For what might it have to say, after having reached beyond its own intelligence (νοερότης), and being brought outside all thought (νόημα), and stripped bare so as to be beyond intellection? For indeed if it still has any speech (λόγος)[234] to express, it is clear that it also thinks (νοεῖν), since all speech (λόγος) follows thought (νόημα). And if it thinks of something, how is it that it stands in the realm of Hiddenness? For that is not properly "hidden" which, although seen by no one else, can still be seen by the intellect itself; for otherwise many things could be called hidden, since so many, or I might even say, all of the things that the intellect sees, it sees in a way unknown to others (μὴ γινώσκοντος ἑτέρου). Hence, the amount of hidden things would approach infinity, which is absurd. For only One is hidden in the proper sense of the word, and it is to This that the intellect ascends after all things, as to the One from whom everything comes, whether visible or intelligible. And indeed the intellect, having ascended to the One above all things that can be manifested, spoken, and known, is established beyond knowledge, vision, and speech, but as long as it can still speak it has yet to ascend to so great a height, nor has it attained the divine Hiddenness. For this would imply that it knows and understands (νοεῖν), but the Hidden is in fact inconceivable, and thus also beyond

---

232 καταληπτέον ἐξ ἐφόδου τὸ ἀκατάληπτον. "comprehend the Incomprehensible", "breach the Impenetrable"; a play on the ambiguity of ἀκατάληπτος in the cognitive sense "unable to be grasped by the mind, incomprehensible" and in the military sense "unable to be captured; impregnable". Cf. Jn. 1:5, where generations of scholars have debated whether to read, "And the light shines in the darkness, and the darkness did not comprehend (κατέλαβεν) it" or "...and the darkness did not overcome (κατέλαβεν) it."

233 σιωπὴν ἀσκεῖ. We use the strange collocation "keep silence" to avoid connotations of "practice", since this is the stage of "contemplation", and to emphasize the special quality of this spiritual "silence".

234 λόγος is here consistently rendered "speech" in the sense of "rational speech" and "discourse", as the opposite of silence (σιωπή). *Logos*, like *nous*, is among the highest activities of human beings, but both must be transcended for the sake of union with God, who infinitely transcends them.

speech. Hence when the intellect has ascended to the realm of divine Hiddenness and become unified, it then keeps silence, not deliberately, but indeed quite naturally, since it is singularly illumined by the One beyond conception.

38. If words and reasons (λόγοι)[235] naturally cause the intellect to proceed and progress, then they must eventually raise it to a point that speech cannot reach, that is, to a reality that is fulfilled in silence. If words were a permanent feature of the intellect, and the soul were always meant to rely on them, then I, for one, do not see what progress the intellect could possibly have beyond reasoning. Indeed, reasoning is not only beneficial for practice, but also equally useful for contemplation. However, when the intellect ascends from words in the form of realities (λόγοι ἐν σχήματι τῶν ὄντων), up to That which is wholly formless beyond speech (ὑπὲρ λόγον) and absolutely and properly One, at that point all words appear superfluous, or even become obstacles, to put it more accurately. Words and reasons generally consist of transitions (μετάβασις) from one thought (νόημα) to another.[236] But how could the simple and absolute and unlimited and shapeless, which is entirely and properly One and lies beyond speech, possibly require words? What would it need to transition between? Or how could It be defined? For speech is wont to define things in a specific manner, yet the One is indefinable, being unlimited and formless. But if speech is not suited to the hidden One beyond intellect, since It is indefinable and formless, then what is suited to It is silence. Therefore those who have made progress in the *word* must conclude in *silence*, by advancing to a simple, unformed, and formless mode of contemplation.

39. If words and reasons (λόγοι) refer to things that are known, and the Hidden is unknown, then the Hidden is beyond word and reason. For if the unknowing of the Hidden is superior to all knowledge, and that which is superior to knowledge has no need for knowledge, much less speech. Thus the intellect that has ascended to the hidden absolute One naturally keeps silence (σιωπὴν ἀσκεῖ). If, however, it does not fall silent naturally and effortlessly, then it has not yet reached the hidden and supremely simple One in its ascent.

40. Just as hesychasts (ἡσυχίαν ἀσκοῦντες ἄνθρωποι) sometimes depart from their cell, and know by experience the great difference between sitting still and being out and about, so likewise those who have experienced (πάσχειν) silence and later resumed speaking, that is, those who devote themselves in contemplation[237] to the glory of God, recognize what state they are in when silence comes upon them by

---

[235] Again, λόγος can also be translated and understood as "discourse", "rational speech", and even "rational principle" and "definition".
[236] Cf. Ch. 44. Cognitive transition and discursion are treated as similar processes.
[237] Literally "sit by or near" (προσιζάνω).

nature but not by their own volition (φύσει, οὐ προαιρέσει), and what state they are in when they are disposed to speak; in fact, when silence comes upon them, they wish that they had never opened their mouths and pray that they may abide continually in that state. For then, like other angels set upon the earth, they are joined to the truth in a unified, formless, sightless, shapeless, and simple manner by motionless gazes of the intellect, possessing in themselves only amazement and wonder, without knowing anything by intellection, but simply casting its sightless gaze upon the beginningless and divine illuminations. But when the intellect has descended from that state through its inherent mutability, they return to speaking and intelligible discourse by means of many and varied discursions; and in order to bring back the state of silence, since it is vastly superior to speech, they embrace stillness and guard the senses from sensible things and employ any means to avoid speaking and even intellection, so that they too may say with David, *I became mute and was humbled and kept silent even about good things* (Ps. 38:3). For indeed, even speaking about good things is inferior to truly reasonable silence (μετὰ λόγου).[238]

41. The Divine is neither entirely manifest (ἐκπεφασμένος) nor again is It entirely hidden; for the fact that It exists is made clear and even quite obvious, but as to what It is, this is hidden. There is a vast difference between knowing *what* God is and knowing *that* He is; for the latter is shown by the energy of God, while the former refers to His essence, which even the angels before God could never hope to know, for God is infinitely infinite times beyond all existence, every intellect, and intellection. Therefore when the intellect apprehends the things that demonstrate God's existence it has many excellent things about which to speak (λέγω) and philosophize, and then it can be said to be both a philosopher and a theologian (θεολόγος). But when the intellect rises and ascends beyond the fact of God's existence, is enveloped in the divine Hiddenness, and receives the energy of the manifestation (φαντασία) of what God is,[239] and thus becomes altogether formless and intangible and visionless, then every word that would speak of God is futile, and the intellect comes to rest in unity, immersed in the inconceivable. And then the entire intellect is united with That which transcends all things, where there is neither speech, nor thought, nor any manner of conception that can introduce variation, but only simplicity and incomprehensibility, ineffability and amazement, the shapeless and infinite and limitless; and it paradoxically beholds the vision of the invisible and the form of the formless, having itself become completely free and formless; and in accordance with all the realities it invisibly

---

[238] Wordplay that can be read as "silence with speech" or "genuine silence".
[239] The use of the word φαντασία has nothing to do with "imagination", but here its use (and etymological meaning) relate to ἔκφασις, the word used to describe God's manifestness.

beholds and sightlessly perceives, it is re-adorned with all the colors of divine and supernatural beauty (ἀναχρωννύμενος), giving glory to God who created it thus.

42. God is called One not only because He is simple and exalted above all composition, but also because He alone is properly *the One who Is* (Ex. 3:14), among all things that are said to "be" (precisely because they have their being from Him). For whatever does not "exist" in the proper and absolute sense cannot be "one" in the proper and absolute sense either. Furthermore, since He is everywhere without being encompassed by space, and is alone dissimilar to all things, and unadulterated by any other thing (καθαρῶς πάντων ἐκτός); and because He is eternal, having neither beginning nor end; and because He shines the divine radiance of His providence on all things equally without being tainted by them (ἀχράντως) (although not all beings receive it in the same manner); and furthermore, because He makes Himself known to all without being conditioned by them (ἀσχέτως), He requires that the intellect be unvaried, formless, shapeless, colorless, untouched by all realities and wholly free in unbounded limitlessness, and that it ascend beyond time, space, nature, and everything pertaining to nature in order to behold Him somehow, in unity beyond noetic union.

43. Since the spiritual connection (συναφή) between God and the intellect transcends intellection, that is why it is said that the intellect is beyond its own nature at this time, as it freely receives the manifestation (φανταζόμενος) of the supernatural hidden One through noetic perception (αἰσθήσει νοερᾷ). Nevertheless, what the intellect experiences (πάσχειν) is in accordance with its nature, which has been purified by grace. For intellection is to the intellect what seeing is to the eye. Thus, he who opens his eyes into the darkness sees nothing, but nevertheless sees that darkness as one (ἕν), and can see that he does not see. Whereas if he had his eyes covered, he might assume he was surrounded by light and other objects. But with his eyes open wide he sees clearly that he does not see. Now, the ability of the visual faculty to penetrate into the darkness and to see things hidden is beyond the nature of the eye, but not its ability to see that it does not see. So then, as regards the intellect, when it has ascended to the divine Hiddenness and reached beyond intellection, it perceives (θεωρεῖν) nothing (for how could it see anything?), but nevertheless perceives that it does not perceive, and that That which it does not perceive is One, hidden away as in a kind of *cloud of darkness* (Ex. 20:21), and that from It pours forth (προχεῖται) every kind of reality, visible and intelligible, whether it be counted among created things or as an eternal uncreated reality. Again, if it did not perceive at all, it would not perceive itself being extended beyond itself.

But now with its noetic eyes wide open, it clearly perceives that it does not perceive, since it has transcended noetic contemplation (θεωρία), and that the One it fails to perceive cannot possibly be perceived. To penetrate and peer into the divine and unique Hiddenness beyond intellect is of course beyond the nature of the intellect; but to gaze upon the divine darkness of that Hiddenness and receive the manifestation (φαντάζεσθαι) of the ineffable Unity, which transcends all things in an unspeakable mystery, and to perceive that it can perceive nothing within the divine darkness, this is indeed the proper function of a pure intellect that contemplates in the Spirit. For the noetic eye of the intellect does not shut or blink, nor is it idle when it perceives that it perceives nothing but the divine and absolute One in Hiddenness, for that would be a sign of ignorance. But when it perceives with utter clarity, it soars up beyond intellect, at which point it perceives its inability to perceive while gazing into the Hiddenness of the utterly simple One. While it does perceive quite clearly that That from which all things come is One and that It is hidden, it does not perceive What It is. Hence the intellect is said to be raised to realities beyond its own nature as long as it continues to gaze on the utterly simple Hiddenness of God; and yet this *is* in accordance with the intellect's nature once it has become pure. And we can even go so far as to say that it is in the nature of the intellect to go beyond nature by casting its sightless gaze – that is to say, beyond noetic conceptions – on the divine and unique Hiddenness beyond intellect and simplicity. For then it has no kind of cognitive perception except that which is directed toward the underived (ἀνεκφοίτητος) One. And when it reaches It through the motion natural to it, it eventually comes to stability (στάσις) and rest. Of course, I do not mean that it ceases to know (for this would be the passion of madness), but rather stability and rest from the discursive motion from one thought or contemplation to another. For when the intellect has sprung up there, after it has plunged into the depths of the Infinite and Unlimited, immersed in noetic light, and encountered the incomprehensibility of that divine Hiddenness concealed from sight, it ceases and comes to a standstill, as it were, experiencing (πάσχειν) nothing but ecstasy in noetic radiance. And even though it does not move, it is nevertheless energized by noetic illumination and fixes its gaze on the Hiddenness beyond essence in single-minded unity, and is filled with wonder and beauty by the unapproachable inwardness of the underived Effulgence. Otherwise if it had left off contemplating, how could it undergo (πάσχειν) such ecstasy and radiance? But it is in this sense that the intellect is said to "stand still" (ἵσταμαι) once it has reached this point, in that it clings to the One immovably, contemplating Its splendor, yearning, rejoicing, shining, and standing (ἵσταμαι) without motion. This of course does not imply that it shuts off the [natural] enjoyment of its contemplation. In fact, this passion must be avoided, not praised, and is full of the darkness of ignorance, namely, to contemplate nothing at all.[240] The stillness (στάσις) of the intellect that we have mentioned is brought about by an unapproachable illumination of light, and it is contemplation that does not require discursion, but rather rest and stability (στάσις). For that supernatural and hidden and mysterious One above essence is infinite and inaccessible (ἀνέκβατον) to any intellect. And It does not allow the contemplating intellect to turn its contemplation anywhere else, to the extent that it has participated in the purification and divine aid proper to it. Henceforth the intellect does not fall away from this divine contemplation and exceedingly beautiful splendor and infinitude unless it is drawn away by the influence of some passion or preoccupation, or else by the natural mutability to which it is susceptible.

44. Intellection is the nature of the intellect, and intellection consists of motion and discursion. But when the intellect has come to God, it has transcended intellection and motion, and it might reasonably be said that the intellect goes beyond its nature when it receives the absolute manifestation (φανταζόμενος) of God. For it is clear that all knowledge naturally arises from a particular thing or reality (ἐκ πράγματος). But where no reality can be contemplated, neither can any knowledge come to be or exist. So then, since God can in no way whatsoever be seen as He really Is (πραγματικῶς), He naturally manifests Himself to the intellect from the realities surrounding Him, that is to say, the [energies] by which He acts, which possess a sphere of power that logically proceeds from a source of power (δυνατόν). So then, because, in respect to everything else, the intellect is accustomed to perceiving (θεωρεῖν) powers simultaneously with [their corresponding] sources of power, it also seeks to experience (πάσχειν) the same with respect to God. Yet being completely incapable of this inasmuch as it transcends the nature of every created intellect, it contemplates the realities around God and receives His manifestation beyond sight, as we have said, in simple and immediate perception (ἁπλῆ καὶ ἀθρόα ἐπιβολή). Then, after it has been taken up into the air of [noetic] stillness,[241] and attained divine favor, and received in itself the energy of the divine and worshipful Spirit, it is seized away from its habitual cognitive activity into a formless condition, simple and without quality, and swiftly enters the heart by the supernatural power of the Spirit. Moreover, by abiding (ἵσταμαι) in the manifestation of God and knowing (νοεῖν) nothing, but going beyond the activity of knowing, so just as it came to this point by beginning from the knowledge of realities around God, it likewise arises to the manifestation of the Divine, as we have said, after being restored to its simplicity, and then the

[240] A kind of contemplative *nihilism* (μηδαμῇ μηδαμῶς θεωρεῖν). The Buddhist teachings of *anātman, śūnyatā,* and *nirvāṇa* arguably fit this description.
[241] The image of rapture, or being "taken up in the air", is taken from 1 Thess. 4:17 and is part of the greater theme of the hesychastic life as anticipating the life to come.

intellect is said to exist (τελεῖν) beyond its nature because it is beyond intellection (τὸ νοεῖν).

45. Everything that is called "hidden" must possess something manifest by which one might get a sense of what is hidden; otherwise it would be nearly identical to non-being. For that which gives absolutely no recognizable indication of its existence whatsoever could be considered equivalent to that which is completely non-existent. Hence, along with God's hiddenness there must also exist certain manifest [signs], and as the intellect follows these tracks, as it were, it acquires a sense (δέχεται αἴσθησιν) of the Divine Hiddenness and follows God's knowability up to His incomprehensibility. When it reaches this state, it knows with certainty that there is Something that escapes its natural comprehension and that, being Supernatural, it lies beyond any kind of noetic comprehension, even angelic. And while It is the cause and principle and end of every nature and essence and every reality, It Itself is beyond nature and essence, dwelling infinitely higher than every existence, being ingenerate, beginningless, unlimited, and absolutely uncircumscribable in terms of nature, space, and time. This is the hidden One above intellect. And the divine apprehension (κατάληψις) that naturally proceeds from It is utterly abundant, and draws (ἐπανατείνουσα) us back up to Itself, restoring us and leading us as if guiding us by hand (χειραγωγίαις), back up to the original, hidden, supernatural One. It unites us with the One to the extent that we perceive that the One Is and that It is One, and yet also that it is inconceivable to know what This hidden One is in essence. Now, how could That which surpasses the intellect and eludes the mind possibly be explained by speech? Nevertheless, the Intelligible Reality[242] (νοητόν) which speech cannot explain can be contemplated by the intellect in a unified manner beyond conception, unutterably, ineffably, and silently, for It is Hidden; the intellect rejoices in It, for It is the Cause and Providence [of all]; it is astonished by It, for It is exceedingly radiant and good, supremely wise and powerful; and the intellect exults in divine gladness, for all the realities by which the hidden One beyond essence can be seen are infinite and unbounded; and this speechlessness is in fact the logical response of rational speech-endowed nature.[243] What would be illogical is for the intellect that dwells in such [realities] to attempt to make use of words and to give an account with discursive reasoning. Therefore he who does not practice silence but employs speech is deprived of the ultimate state of the intellect. For this is the intellect's ultimate state (as would even be admitted by those who think nothing of the truth): the attainment of the ultimate [fulfillment] of its activity (ἐνέργεια). And the

---

[242] referent? Divine energies, but in singular?

[243] Here there is a connection between λογική φύσις and λόγος in the sense of "speech", meaning something like, "Here it is rational for the speech-endowed nature to remain quiet."

ultimate fulfillment is its vision (ἀπόβλεψις) of the Ultimate, which is said to occur without sight, and thus all the more without speech.

46. As the intellect casts its sightless gaze (ἐπιβάλλειν) on the exceedingly divine, unique, transcendently principal (ὑπεραρχικός) and most-supreme Hiddenness, a reception (παραδοχή) comes to the intellect from It – also without sight. It is unified and unique, full of exceedingly beautiful, effulgent, and ineffable splendor, and it overwhelms the intellect with wonder and amazement in silence, after having prepossessed the heart with spiritual energy and sweet joy. This reception becomes for the intellect noetic illumination, enlightenment, and subsequently, divine eros and radiant joy, for it owes its cause to God, from whom comes *every good gift* (Jam. 1:17), provided the intellect is pure; it derives its material, one might say, from the various divine manifestations of the Scriptures and realities (ὄντα), provided they are contemplated with prudence and uprightness, in stillness and in prayer. For the hidden innermost One of divinity cannot be contemplated in just any manner, but only by means of the splendor that proceeds from It, filling the intellect abundantly with noetic vision and contemplation. Whoever has never experienced (πάσχειν) this may ascend externally – that is, rationally and cognitively – to the supernatural, hidden, simple One, but he does not yet have spiritual energy active in his heart, nor is he noetically enlightened.

47. The intellect's most resplendent unified and unique contemplation of God, which discerns both the unifying divine Hiddenness and the splendor flashing forth from It, and has become receptive to (παραδεδεγμένη) the divine effulgence of unoriginate and infinite radiance, requires not only silence of the mouth, but also silence of the intellect. For it is possible while one keeps the mouth silent for the intellect to deliberate (διατίθεσθαι) within, to progress in cogitations and intellections, and to be altered by them, this being a function of internal discourse.[244] But far from this state is the intellect that has soared aloft to the supremely simple unformed (ἀτύπωτος) Hiddenness of the divine Unity. For the contemplative power (θεωρεῖν) of the intellect is one thing, while its power to reason and think (διανοεῖσθαι) discursively, which belongs to internal discourse, is another. Hence, when the intellect approaches things that are created and composite, or otherwise varied, it first perceives, and then thinks and becomes varied itself, even to the point that it often finds many thoughts for one and the same thing. But in that unique and uniform and innermost divine Hiddenness it lifts and opens its contemplative eye and catches the rays of the simplicity of the divine radiance, although it is in no way capable of processing these discursively

[244] λόγος [...] τοῦ ἐνδιαθέτου. There is a classical philosophical distinction between λόγος ἐνδιάθετος (internal discourse/reason) and λόγος προφορικός (expressed discourse/reason). The silence of the latter corresponds to "silence of the mouth", silence of the former to "silence of the intellect".

and with thoughtful deliberation. For the single Simplicity eludes every kind of intellectual process (νοερὰν μετάβασιν) or varied deliberation, while the Hiddenness eludes the ability to express anything that is thought, whether by means of the mind's discourse or that of the mouth. Therefore the one who has ascended to the unique, most-glorious, divine Hiddenness naturally keeps silence in both his mouth and intellect.

48. When the intellect's direction is wholly turned to God, and its contemplative power yearns for the dazzling rays of divine beauty, and it rises formlessly to the simplicity and boundlessness of the hidden and formless One, even becoming one with itself through its ascent and gaze towards the One by the inspiration of the Spirit, it then surely attains that truly childlike spirit, receiving a taste of the ineffable and supernatural reality of the Kingdom of God according to the word of the Lord: *Unless you turn and become like children, you will never enter the Kingdom of Heaven* (Mt. 18:3). For then the intellect becomes free and altogether unconditioned (ἄσχετος) by anything, having soared beyond the limits implicit in all knowledge, in every manner of intellection, and in all composition and variation, and ascends to the Ineffable and Unknowable beyond intellect. Hence it naturally keeps silence in this state, which is not only beyond speech, but also beyond noetic energy, whereby it attains, in addition to the hidden and formless, also that which is supernatural, lovely, and pleasant for noetic enjoyment.

49. Contemplatives contemplate God as the unified One in His formless form, His immaterial, incomposite beauty far surpassing nature, and His supremely simple countenance: garlanded about with infinite goods, resplendent with innumerable beauties, brilliantly flashing forth luminous rays of beauty to every intellect; an ineffable and indescribable wealth, a generous and infinitely ever-flowing abundance of things good and beautiful, a treasury of glory – inexhaustible, unfathomable, unfailing – filling intellects deprived of sight with the most abundant delight, joy, and jubilation of heart, with gladness that is pure like an ever-streaming river mystically springing forth from that divine and supernatural Unity transcending all, concealed in Hiddenness. Moreover, just how vast, inscrutable, and uncircumscribable a sea of ineffable kindness, inexplicable love, and inconceivable providence It pours forth in boundless power and inexpressible wisdom is something incomprehensible to the angels, and even to the Seraphim, for it is established beyond all intellect. And in fact, even such things as we can grasp (συλλαμβάνω) at present by speechless reason (ἀρρήτῳ λόγῳ), and which in the age to come shall be restored (ἀποκαθίστημι) and as it were delivered (ἀπογεννάω) and brought to perfection, these realities astound the intellects of the Cherubim, and only somewhat dimly are they able to set their minds to even conceive of such [mysteries]. O the goodness and counsel of God, what love and

kindness, what power and wisdom and divine providence! Truly *blessed are those whose iniquities have been forgiven and whose sins have been covered* (Ps. 31:1), and, *Blessed is the man whom the Lord will instruct and teach by His law* and His Spirit (Ps. 93:12).

50. *In Spirit and truth* are revealed those realities that are invisible to those who dwell in *the world*, inasmuch as they *cannot receive the Holy Spirit*, as the Lord declared (Jn. 14:17). But to those who value spiritual retreat and a quiet life far from the world and worldly things, for whom the noetic light has shone on the eyes of their hearts through divine grace – *the Dayspring* of the intelligible Sun *from on high* (Lk. 1:78; Mal. 4:2) –, who have *received help from God* so that they *deliberate ascents in their hearts* (Ps. 83:6), and are made radiant by the illuminations of divine vision (θεοπτικαῖς), as is natural: to them these realities become visible and are seen quite clearly, along with so many other divine and intelligible realities and things worthy of spiritual vision, even the future eternal and unshakeable restoration of those who have lived piously, as it shall be not only above sense, but even beyond intellect. For the [righteous] will be completely changed, having wholly attained the state beyond intellect as well as the life and delight that transcend every conception, and just as gods adopted and set before Him who is God by nature, they will delight and rejoice in blessings beyond nature, which stream forth from the Ultimate and Only God by nature. They will stand encircled about Him celebrating the divine feast beyond intellect in utmost holiness and solemnity, participating in the one exceedingly joyful festival and celebration of that jubilation which is most longed for, together with all the noetic orders of angels. Indeed, that stream of pure exaltation, full of surpassing beauty, is abundant and inconceivable. Now, if a sensual beauty that reaches the intellect through the senses, being limited and fluid and neither simple nor uncreated, is still wont to bring no small delight to the soul, it is not difficult for those possessed of intellect to see and understand by analogy[245] what will occur when we not only attain to intelligible realities, but even to those boundless ones beyond intellect, which are not subject to flux and proceed from God from whom all things good and beautiful flow; for they are neither created, nor do they have a beginning in time, and they are meant for the delight, exaltation, and divine life worthy of that age and state [to come].

51. After the intellect has bid farewell to the intervals and extensions of time and space, as well as the properties that define the natures of things, and passed beyond them, then it is truly stripped down to unified simplicity and to a simple life without artifice. And without any screen or cover, it supernaturally ascends to an

[245] τὸ ἀνάλογον ἀναλογιζομένοις, "by reasoning analogically".

inconceivable and unspeakable state, beginningless and boundless, through a divine power and illumination of the heart brought about by the Spirit, and this illumination appears to co-extend to infinity together with the contemplation of the intellect. It is then that the peace of God dawns on the soul *from on high*, and the ineffable joy and inexpressible gladness of the Holy Spirit pours into it, and ecstasy beyond knowledge overwhelms the soul as it humbly chants, "Not only *will the God of the gods be seen,* but indeed already is He seen, *in Zion*" (Ps. 83:8), that is to say, within the intellect that has journeyed heavenward and looked on high; "*O Lord, God of hosts, blessed is the man who hopes in you*" (Ps. 83:13).

52. When the intellect stands illuminated in ecstasies inconceivable and inexpressible, and sees itself amidst the presence of God and the things of God, it then eats, if I may say so, the true fruits of spiritual knowledge, and is divinized and rejoices and increases in divine eros. It says nothing whatsoever, neither does it express any inner or outer disposition, nor again does it think, but rather sees noetically and simply in the light of the *Spirit and truth*, and safeguards the things it sees so as to delight in them constantly.

53. When the countenance of the intellect is turned within the heart and sees the illumination of the Spirit springing endlessly therefrom, then it is truly *a time to be silent* (Eccl. 3:7).

54. When the whole noetic countenance of the intellect sees God, or rather, when the whole intellect is found within God, or, to put it another way, when God is found within the whole intellect: this is of course, even more so, the *time to be silent* (Eccl. 3:7).

55. When, by participation in the Spirit, the intellect actually (κατὰ τὰ γινόμενα) stands before God in contemplation and rightly enjoys glory and splendor from the presence of God, it must, quite naturally, be silent so as to gaze in stillness and without distraction (ἀπερικτυπήτως). But if some misty (ἀχλυώδης) darkness ever creeps in between the intellect and God, the intellect [must] immediately cast a luminous and incandescent fire, as it were, at the exact cause (λόγον) of this darkness by means of a proper word (πεφυκότι λόγῳ) – a word briefly spoken (βραχύλεκτον) but infused with divine light. In this way, after swiftly extinguishing the darkness and the mist by means of light and warmth, and so brightening and warming the intellect by the same means, it can return to God's presence as before, contemplate His beauty, take natural delight in Him, and be beautified by Him. In short, it can 'suffer' the experiences of noetic perception through the reception (πάσχειν [...] τὰ κατὰ νοερὰν ἐπιβολὴν διὰ παραδοχῆς) of the Life-Giving Spirit from God, and may further be simplified and liberated from

all things by God *in Spirit and truth*, and even go beyond the realities around God. The contemplative attains this naturally and as a matter of course, but he who engages only in practice is far from this state because he has not yet been united with himself and, through himself, with God. It is no wonder, then, that he chants and speaks as much and as often as he can of the things of God, so that by these constant shafts of light (ταῖς συνεχέσι [...] βολαῖς)[246] he may terrify and put to flight the wicked enemy that fiercely wars against us. However, a time will come for the practitioner who patiently persists when, by the breath of the Holy Spirit, the shimmering sparks of so many divine chants, songs, and words will be gathered into one great torch. Then will he easily manage to strike a fatal blow against him, that is, by burning and dispersing, or rather, dissolving the enemy's darkness and illuminating and warming himself with this torch, zealously kindling the flame into divine and ardent eros, lifting up (ἀναφέρειν) a hymn to God in silence and ecstasy of the heart, and discovering for himself the most exceptional and wondrous mysteries. For it is not without reason that *those who patiently wait on the Lord* are said to be blessed, or that in time, being *meek, they shall inherit* the noetic Promised Land in Christ our Lord (Ps. 36:9,11; Mt. 5:5).[247]

56. When the intellect, enlightened by each ray issuing from the Spirit, is amazed and bedazzled and perceives itself being extended and altered into the infinite and unlimited, then is *a time to be silent* (Eccl. 3:7).

57. When, however, it feels somewhat weary from these dazzling insights and wishes to depart from this state to relax from the intensity and to take some respite,[248] then is naturally *a time to speak* (Eccl. 3:7), but only in moderation (βραχύλεκτα) and in accordance with divine illumination.

58. When the intellect has passed through the midst of the sea and escaped the noetic Pharaoh, spending its nights in the light of the fire and its days under the shade of cloud (Ex. 13:21), then there has surely come the time for silence and stillness and the true beginning of the soul's purification. But when the terrible noetic Amalek and the nations that follow him withstand it, barring its passage into

---

[246] St. Kallistos' presentation of spiritual warfare is striking for its imagery of light and fire repulsing darkness. See the phrase βάλλειν πῦρ "to cast fire" (cf. Lk. 12:49), with this fire being closely related to the proper use of λόγος, "word" and "reason", as we see in this chapter. βολή, cognate with βάλλειν, "to throw, to cast", can mean both a "cast weapon" but also "rays cast" from a bright object. Moreover, ἐπιβάλλω, the verbal form of ἐπιβολή, has been translated as "to gaze, look" throughout this work.

[247] The beatitude of Christ, *The meek shall inherit the land* (Mt. 5:5), is likely based on the promises of Psalm 36:9,11.

[248] διεξοδεύω, "depart" is elsewhere used to mean "explain discursively", that is, the activity of the intellect that engages in motion and logical discursion, rather than stillness and silence.

the Promised Land, then is a proper *time to speak* (Eccl. 3:7), but to God [in prayer], supported on the one hand by noetic practice and on the other by true contemplation, just like Moses of old, whose arms were upheld by Aaron and Hur (Ex. 17:12).

59. When, from the fathomless depths of the fountain of divine and noetic contemplation, spiritual power springs forth bursting from the heart, then naturally there has come the *time to be silent*. For then the intellect wordlessly conducts the worship and adoration of God *in Spirit and in truth* (Jn. 4:24), and this it does through true noetic perception.

60. When, by looking noetically to God, the rational part of the soul is completely filled with divine ecstasy, the noetic part with vision, and the whole soul with rejoicing, then is undoubtedly *a time to be silent*. For then, by the Spirit and in subtlety of perception, the intellect can gaze in concentration (συνεπτυγμένος) upon the truth and glorify in adoration the God who shines within it.

61. Those who properly *worship God in Spirit and truth* (Jn. 4:24) and rightly adore Him do not only worship and adore Him outside of space (οὐκ ἐν τόπῳ), but also to no less a degree outside of spoken discourse.[249] For just as the noetic sense that is raised in reverent uprightness has no desire to worship the uncircumscribable One in space since *He has no place of rest* (Isa. 66:1), so likewise, when it remains united with the truth, as it must, the infinite, limitless, unoriginate, formless, and perfectly simple, and in short, Him who is beyond intellect, the noetic sense is hardly wont to tolerate worship and adoration that consists merely of an assortment of words and set expressions. For when the time comes, by the empowerment and inspiration of the Spirit, for the intellect to be enlightened in a unified manner with the knowledge of divine truth (cf. 1 Tim. 2:4), at this time the intellect, having become completely free of all things and even gone beyond itself, finds good reason not only to refrain from speech, but even from intellection (ἀνοησίαν εὐλόγως ασκεῖν), since it then engages in contemplation of realities superior to word, reason, and intellect (τὰ κρείττω καὶ λόγου καὶ νοῦ) with exultation and ecstasy in noetic light, since it has become – somehow, by no contrivance of its own – immovable and unwavering in sightless perception through a union transcending its own nature.

---

[249] τῷ λόγῳ τῷ κατὰ προφοράν, could be rendered "expressed discourse", since it is very close to the term λόγος προφορικός.

62. The intellect must attend to itself[250] with diligence and direct its noetic disposition with understanding, wisdom, and judgment, and when it finds itself contemplating the simple and non-symbolic (ἀτύπωτα) mysteries of theology,[251] it must stand in stillness and silence, neither failing to marvel nor ignoring the energy and illumination of the Spirit in its heart. For then it is not only a time for keeping the senses completely still from all sensible things, but is also no less a time of silence from every kind of discursive speech (διεξοδεύων λόγος). And even more so for those devoted to knowledge (γνωστικοί), if I may say so, this is a time to practice noetic stillness and the art of unseeing. That is, one must train to acquire immobility in the senses, in speech and reasoning, in thoughts and perceptions, so that the intellect may directly – and, if necessary, in complete solitude – and freely and truly behold the infinite, unoriginate, and uncircumscribable in the unified and unique vision of the One and Only Triune God, as well as all the other divine and immutable and absolute [properties] and be united with them, having become transfigured (συνηλλοιωμένος) by contemplation, simple, and wholly deiform by divine grace with all delight and wonder. And since the intellect would desire, if possible, to abide in this state forever, but cannot because it is mutable and lives amidst mutable things and is joined to the body and to the circumstances surrounding it, it must take thought not to stray far from the unified vision whenever it falls away, nor should it say too much, but only a little; and even then, let its words be reflections of divine illumination, not only that it may swiftly return to union with God beyond intellect, but also that it may acquire a clearer and more lasting perception of this union. For the more the intellect preserves its concentration and avoids dispersion, the quicker it turns to divine union and the brighter – and indeed more fecund – are the flashes of light with which it is united in its ever-increasing familiarity with divine realities.

63. When the intellect, by experiencing (προσπάσχειν) the divine unified revelation through noetic vision, is transfigured (ἀλλοιοῦσθαι) and illumined by the Unknown beyond all knowledge, and becomes indivisible, simple, and limitless as if singularly dazzled by divine *darkness*, and contemplates Beauty indescribable in Its exceeding simplicity, Formless in Its superiority to all form, Unoriginate (ἄναρχον) in Its transcendence of any originating principle whatsoever (ἀρχή), Itself Incomprehensible while encompassing in Itself the limits and comprehension of all things, filling all things as the Super-Abundant One, all the while being Infinite in Itself; and in short, when the intellect sees beyond (ὑπεροψία) all realities through the sacred vision (ἐποψία) of the One, and sees

---

[250] A play on the common phrase τὸν νοῦν προσέχειν τινί "to pay attention to something", that is, by applying the *intellect* to it.

[251] We are following a reading based on St. Dionysios the Areopagite here, that is, mysteries contemplated directly without "types" or "symbols".

(ὄψηται) everything with an ineffable power of intelligence beyond intellection, then is *a time to be silent* (Eccl. 3:7), both mystically and transcendently, or, I might say, delighting without either sight or speech in the unique enjoyment of the truth in a yet more divine way of initiation. However, when these realities are absent from the intellect and division appears all around it, then is *a time to speak* (Eccl. 3:7); but let one say things worthy of leading (ἀναγωγή) the intellect back up to silence. For far superior to every rational word (λόγος) is that silence beyond reason (ὑπὲρ λόγον) which could quite reasonably be called "timely silence" (ἔγκαιρος σιγή), since Solomon, who preferred it above all else, says first, *There is a time to be silent*, and then, *a time to speak* (Eccl. 3:7). Timely silence is best and is given priority and first place. But if this has not yet come to the intellect, and it has yet to discern realities beyond speech (ὑπὲρ λόγον) in unified vision, then in any case let timely speech have second place. Furthermore, in order that this speech (λέγειν) may be close in affinity (συγγενές) and proximity (σύνεγγυς) to silence, let it be exercised in a timely manner as if in a hurry to return to silence, by speaking and thinking continually of divine things and by contemplating creation and how it reflects its Creator with such immense power, and even *speaks about* Him (διηγουμένης περὶ αὐτοῦ) (cf. Ps. 18:2). This is what we call "timely speech". At any rate, I should make a further note about these things, treating them as follows.

64. When the intellect, having passed through the things here below and ascended beyond them, gladly embraces silence in a natural manner, then is a time to delight in transcendent and unspeakable things; it is a time of illumination and noetic light, of union of intellect and contemplation, of simplicity, of limitlessness and infinitude and exceedingly radiant (ὑπερφαής) knowledge, and to put it briefly, a time for taking (ἀντίληψις) and partaking (μετάληψις) of spiritual wisdom, by which the intellect is perfected in stillness (σχολή) and silence, once it has received inexpressible exultation in ecstasy.

65. When the soul perceives through its perception of the truth that it has become *drunk from the cup* of grace, as from the *finest wine* (Ps. 22:5), and even gone out of its mind (ἔκνουν), then is surely *a time to be silent*.

66. When the disposition of the inner man desires to cry aloud, *Lord, why have they multiplied who afflict me? Many rise up against me* (Ps. 3:2), then is *a time to speak*; not, of course, to speak idle words, but to speak against one's enemies moderately and fittingly, as the occasion requires.

67. When *the light of the Lord's face has been signed* upon the soul (Ps. 4:7) so that it is made beautiful and radiant thereby and immersed in divine gladness, then is indeed *a time to be silent*.

68. When the soul sees *unjust witnesses rise up against it, accusing it of things it does not know* (Ps. 34:11) and putting it in turmoil, then is truly *a time to speak* and even to talk back in opposition.

69. God is the Supreme and, one might say, the Ultimate, or otherwise the Highest Beauty and Good over all existing things (ὄντα) and intelligible realities (νοούμενα). And among all visible things the human being *by nature* has the best nature by far and is without a doubt incomparably greater than all of them; however, *by grace* man is even superior to the angels. As the contemplative intellect approaches the One beyond conception in the midst of the vast multitude of realities between God and men, it simply stands in awe until it fully experiences the grace of illumination; but once it has tasted this through active (ἐνεργής) spiritual power in the heart, I venture to say that he then ascends to God, the Ultimate Beauty and Good, and enters Him through a gift yet more divine (κατὰ δωρεὰν θειοτέραν), seeing in unity and ecstasy, dwelling (αὐλιζόμενος) silently in the depth beyond intellect. This is truly the guarantee, as one might call it, of the first Sabbath rest,[252] the type of which is God's Sabbath rest after His creation of all things (Gen. 2:2-3). Another Sabbath rest, which Scripture inerrantly proclaims as *a Sabbath rest that remains for the people of God* (Heb. 4:9) – a greater rest of another kind – is that which man enjoys when he has turned from God to himself and known himself as an image of the Prototype, and indeed all qualities existing between God and men.[253] Then, not only does he pass over to realities beyond mind and intellect in wondrous amazement, but is also filled with such joy and spiritual jubilation as is impossible to express, and becomes truly jubilant (γαννύμενος γιγνομένως) in silence by the illuminations of divine vision and divinization (θεοπτικαῖς ἐλλάμψεσι καὶ θεουργίαις) that come upon him, although they are beyond him. And in this way he is united with the Unity of the divine and supernatural Divinity, in Christ Jesus.

[252] πρῶτος σαββατισμός. The "first" likely refers to the fact that it is man's first spiritual Sabbath rest, not only God's as Gen. 2:2-3 describes it, and that it is followed by a second "greater rest of another kind".

[253] ἑαυτὸν γνοὺς ὡς εἰκόνα μετὰ πρωτότυπον, καὶ τὸ ὅλον, τὰ μεταξὺ Θεοῦ καὶ ἀνθρώπων ὁποῖα. It is unclear whether this means to "know all qualities existing between God and man" "as an image of the Prototype", or simply knowing them.

70. When the intellect performs negation[254] of all created things as if they did not exist (ὡς μὴ ὄντα), it then, receives, by contemplating *in truth and in Spirit*, the unutterable manifestation of That which Truly Is (τὸ ὄντως ὄν) beyond noetic energy and union, infinitely superior to every kind of divine contemplation about existing realities (περὶ τὰ ὄντα). And then the intellect becomes unified, or even, so to speak "one", and is ineffably overcome with speechlessness; it becomes full of love and joy, and not at all of a common sort, but the love and joy that comes from the energy of the Spirit, a delight fit for angels.

71. Just as You cannot be grasped (ληπτός) according to Your essence by anyone in any way whatsoever, O Lord, whether by any kind of rational or intelligent nature (νοερά), or by means of any created knowledge, not even that of the cherubim, but You stand infinite times infinitely higher than all knowledge, so too, Your attributes (καὶ τὰ περὶ σέ), O Sovereign, are altogether infinite and limitless. Yet in Your unsurpassable care for us, you ordered the legislator of the Old Testament Moses to proclaim the fact that *You Are* (ὤν) and that You call Yourself *the One Who Is* (Ex. 3:14).[255] But even so, this did You say concerning Your attributes,[256] O You who are most-infallible and are alone the ultimate Truth, because You appear by means of them; Your name, however, You did not reveal (Gen. 32:29). For Your name is incomparably high *above every name* (Phil. 2:9), not only the names of all things on earth, but also of those in heaven. Furthermore, those who have been filled with Your light describe You as "Essence",[257] but this they do without predicating an underlying substance (ἐνυποκειμένου χωρίς), so that they might accordingly show You to be beyond being and essence; they also describe You as "Intellect" (νόησις), but entirely without any underlying substance (τι ὑποκείμενον),[258] so that You can be clearly known to be above intellect as well as infinitely unknowable and superior to all that can possibly be known. You are seen to be perfectly beyond time, unoriginate, being Life-Itself (αὐτοζωὴ ὤν), and boundless; You completely defy all spatial conception, You are everywhere present all at once (ἀθρόως), and are beyond everything, as the one and only Maker of all, and although you contain all noetic natures, You are a Region wholly

---

[254]ἀφαίρεσις, "negation, abstraction"; lit. "removal". Negation in the sense of ignoring or "removing" things "hypothetically" (ὑποθετικῶς) from the intellect with the goal of transcending them.

[255] ὄντα καὶ λέγοντα σεαυτόν. The LXX translates the Hebrew Name of God *Yahweh* ("he is"), from the formula *'ehyeh 'ăšer 'ehyeh* ("I am that I am"), as ὁ ὤν, "the One Who Is", or "He Who Is", the masculine participle "to be".

[256] περί τινων τῶν σῶν, ὅτι ὀφθεὶς αὐτοῖς. However, the MGk translation interprets this as "for certain of Your [people] for You appeared to them."

[257] οὐσία. "essence, being". Can also be rendered "substance", but οὐσίαand "essence" are both etymologically related to the verb "to be", in Greek and Latin respectively. On the other hand, "substance" stands closer to the corresponding Greek term ὑποκείμενον.

[258] cf. for this use of ὑποκείμενον, cf. Angelikoudes, *Chapters* 52.

uncharted, far exceeding the swiftness of the intellect and surpassing its intelligence (ἐπίνοια), since You are beyond everything; You are found to be the almighty hand indescribably holding all things, and are in no way subject to the bounds of nature, for You are unlimited not only in Your nature, being supernaturally incomprehensible, but also in Your natural properties, since you are Wisdom beyond wisdom and Power beyond power and Love and Goodness beyond every thought (διάνοια) of love and goodness. What might one call You? When You are called Light, are you not unapproachable? Hence You are beyond light. Or what else? When You are called Judge, do You not know everything before it even comes into existence? How could a judge possess such knowledge? Hence you are exalted far above a judge. What kind of Creator[259] might we call You, when You create all at once by the mere motion of your will, even these vast and diverse materials which we use to create? Then, as for immaterial things, O what depths of sublimity! I might say that with a single motion of Your Spirit immaterial things all partake of one nature, for they are spiritual; but they are also many and even infinitely many (πολλὰ δὲ καὶ πάμπολλα) in how they differ in disposition and, one might say, in personality (προσώπων διαφοραί); this is altogether wonderful, and far exceeds the conception of anyone possessed of intellect (νοῶν). Are these the abilities of a simple creator? Certainly not. Hence You are more than a creator. Are you called a Maker[260] and heralded as Craftsman (τεχνίτης)? Yet what maker is able to build without a foundation and on the basis of nothingness, or in short, in the manner You do, O Sovereign, who lay so great an expanse of earth, laden with mountains and stones and other matter, and found it *upon nothing* (Job 26:7) with such security? Or what craftsman is able to produce from completely non-existent material, and in but a moment, such works of art as You do? Would it be right for one to say Your works are those of a builder or a craftsman? By no means. Indeed, surely you are infinitely above the builder and the craftsman, being God.

What kind of love could one ever know, or hear report of, or even imagine in the slightest, is like the love which Your exceedingly marvellous kindness has shown us with such overwhelming evidence, by assuming our humanity in a love for us (φιλανθρώπως) exceeding anything we could hope for? Those who contemplate this, that is, such as have been made worthy by grace of this contemplation, enter into a vast and open sea of love and paradoxical providence and truly go outside

---

259 "Creator" (δημιουργός) has strong, concrete connotations of a craftsman who shapes, molds, and fashions raw materials into finished products. These everyday implications are part of the reason the author goes on to marvel at God the "Creator", who brings all things into being by His Word alone.
260 "Maker" (κτίστης) comes from the verb κτίζω, which properly means "to found, establish", as in a building, city, or institution. In the LXX, this word group was co-opted to describe God's creative activity and non-reliance on pre-existing material.

themselves in the sharpest pangs of divine eros, and they know not how properly to describe this economy.[261] For everything pertaining to Your Incarnation (ἐνανθρώπησις) exceedingly surpasses understanding (νοῦς) and speech (λόγος) and all manner of hearing and thought, O God who are supremely good. Are you, and are you rightly so-called, the Father of all? But you inexpressibly excel every kind of paternity, both as Cause and in terms of authority, care, admonition, long-suffering, and forbearance. Are you called King? But certainly not in such a way that You [could be considered to] reign in the present, and perhaps not in the future or not at all in the past. So how then? You reign marvellously, absolutely, and simply. *For Your kingdom is a kingdom for all the ages* (αἰῶνες) taken altogether, reigning over both the present, past, and future, *and Your sovereignty endures through all generations* (Ps. 144:13).

Therefore, in absolutely everything and in every way You surpass all intelligence in infinite measure, simply and absolutely, and to speak with brevity, You are exceedingly and infinitely transcendent, both You, O incomprehensible Lord, and the realities around You (τὰ περὶ σέ). When receiving their manifestation (ἃ φαντασιούμενος) in whatever way, the intellect is enthralled by the vision of You as far as possible, and when it is wholly inspired by the Spirit, it enters into a mystical darkness; it cannot see You perfectly there on account of Your infinite and unapproachable glory, and in this way You ineffably provide rest in transcendent repose to those who contemplate and truly love you with wonder; the intellect is not lacking in the least vision of You. So again do You satisfy them with divine and supernatural rest, O You who are in ineffable, inconceivable, uncircumscribable, incomprehensible, and wholly infinite in both essence and energy. Amen.

72. When the intellect ceases to entertain many thoughts (πολύνοια) by desisting (ἀποπείθεσθαι) from differentiations and fragmented concepts, it goes beyond mental dispersion by the inspiration and participation of the Holy Spirit, who unites it and constantly refreshes the heart with an ever-flowing breeze (ἀείβλυτα πνέοντος); and when the intellect loves to dwell continually in divine places, and has imbibed, as it were, manifestations concerning God, so that by simple noetic introspection it may see the reflection of all the realities around God in unity (τὰ ἡλίκα, ὅσα περὶ Θεὸν ἑνοειδῶς) with ineffable divine eros, then it has clearly attained divine rest and arrived at the enjoyment of a deep divine peace and an exceedingly holy and tranquil repose of the heart, in Christ Jesus our Lord.

---

[261] I.e. The Incarnation of the Son of God.

73. When the intellect converses with God in prayer, like a son to a father that is wholly affectionate in disposition, and takes inexpressible delight in seeing the light of Jesus, and becomes utterly ecstatic as it manifestly feels divine eros and the supernatural energy of the Holy Spirit in the heart, and desires to soar even beyond divine revelations and perfections in a mystical flight beyond the world, at that point it truly *rests from all its works* (cf. Gen. 2:3), that is, by going beyond intellection after engaging in intellection (ὑπὲρ τὸ νοεῖν μετὰ τὸ νοεῖν), and experiences wondrous pleasure (ἡδυπαθεῖν), and truly reposes in the peace of the Life-Giving Spirit of Christ.

74. *God rested from all the works He had begun to do* (Gen. 2:3), that is, after He had completed creation in Word and Spirit. In a similar way, the god-like (θεοείκελος) intellect rests from all the works it had begun to do from the beginning to complete the intelligible world of virtue. But it does this after having first examined and, as it were, continually worked the whole world anew along with the intelligible realities within it (ἐπεξεργάζεσθαι) through the Word of God and the Life-Giving Spirit, and having ascended from these – again in the Word and Spirit – to what some have called "metaphysical" realities,[262] and to peer into the simple and absolute mystical visions of theology. For then, in this rest from works, the intellect enjoys the utmost repose and peace in noetic truth, and is even deified in the light of knowledge and participation in the Life-Giving Spirit, in Christ Jesus, our Lord.

75. When God *rested from all His works*, He did not rest from absolutely all of them, but only from those *works He had begun to create* (Gen. 2:3); for He did not cease from the works that are beginningless, uncreated, and in a certain mode natural to Him.[263] Likewise, the intellect that imitates God, having passed through and gone beyond the visible creation by the grace of the Divine Word and the Life-Giving Spirit, cannot possibly rest from all the works natural to it, which have neither beginning nor end,[264] but ceases from visible works, which have both beginning and end. Hence, while bodily rest follows motionlessness in the case of one who has come to rest, the opposite occurs in the case of the intellect. For unless the intellect attains perpetual motion (ἀεικίνητος) through the constant Life-Giving inspiration of the Spirit as it turns its knowing gaze beyond visible things, it will

---

[262] μετὰ τὰ φυσικά. Lit."after the natural things". The title *Metaphysics* originally referred to the work that literally came "after the *Physics*" in the corpus of Aristotle's works, but in the course of time it also came to refer aptly to the study of realities "beyond nature."

[263] It may be noted that in Greek the word for "work" (ἔργον) is the basis for the word "energy, activity" (ἐνέργεια), hence it is quite natural for Kataphygiotes to refer to the uncreated energies, or at least their effects, as "works".

[264] This may refer to the intellect's participation in realities that have neither beginning nor end, which would be a work "natural" to the intellect inasmuch as it is created for union with God.

never realize that there exists a noetic rest which moves perpetually around God alone in unity and deifies the one who partakes of it with inexpressible and ineffable repose in Christ.

76. *Do not hasten to utter a word before the face of the Lord,* says Solomon. *For God is in heaven above and you are on earth below* (Eccl. 5:1). With such great clarity and precision he indicates to us what *the time to be silent* is (Eccl. 3:7). For he says outright that when you who are on earth below come before the face of the Lord who is in heaven above and are made worthy of such grace that you, being below, are able to *set your mind on* and discern *the things above* (Col. 3:2), and through noetic perception to stand before the face of the Lord, do not hasten to utter any word. For then is *a time to be silent*. That is, do not desire [to speak] when your intellect receives the energy of the truth in a unified and deiform manner (for this is what 'being before the face of the Lord' signifies, when the intellect contemplates the many realities around God in an undifferentiated manner (μονοειδῶς), in a simple and unitary perception of God; and do not hasten to utter a word when you experience (πάσχειν) this and stand before the face of the Lord. Otherwise, in your ignorance and willfulness, you rush to degrade and demean yourself. Or perhaps we should explain the meaning of this saying as follows.

There was a time when human nature was without care or sorrow and rightly stood afar from all manner of evil, being near to God; it contemplated God and enjoyed the glory of the beauty of His face with joy and wonder in the person of our forefather Adam, in immaterial, noetic, heavenly, and incorruptible delight. Moreover, abundant grace washed over the soul of the first man, and his deiform intellect was immersed in contemplations of spiritual knowledge and ascents (γνωστικαῖς θεωρίαις καὶ ἀνατάσεσι) to God, and within the sensible Paradise he also enjoyed the noetic Paradise and what I might call the happy and blessed life (μακαρία ζωή), being truly united with himself and with God, abiding in himself and even in God as is right, and cleaving to this unifying and truly deiform state, and quite naturally so, since he had been made *according to the image of God* (Gen. 1:26). Now these are precisely the good things that God intended for us to enjoy. However, for the enemy of our good inheritance and glory, that vengeful demon,[265] this was unbearable. For, stricken with envy, how could he not be? And hence this all-destructive one did much to deceive us and to dispel[266] our hope with seemingly fair-sounding advice, fanning our desire so that we would seek a deification higher than the one we already had, and the first worker of evil

---

[265] ἀλάστωρ δαίμων ἀλάστορες δαίμονες were fearsome spirits in Greek mythology sent to hound mortals for their sins and offences against the gods, and would not relent until they had exacted full retribution.

[266] Lit. "to hoist our hope out of reach" (ἀπαιωρέω).

slandered (διαβάλλειν) the sincerity (τὸ εὐθές) of God's commandment (Gen. 3:4-5).[267] From this deception we suffered piteous destruction and were banished from God and divine delight (Gen. 3:23-24). We wretchedly fell from the unified and spiritual life of the intellect and from our ability to contemplate the face of God and be glorified through being transformed by the radiance of divine beauty, and ended up – to our own hurt – divided and shattered into many and even perversely pleased with our divided lives and fragmentations. In fact, instead of honoring the one Triune Deity, we countenanced many different gods, who were not real gods, but deceitful and corrupting and hostile demons. We lost the true One and the life and order of unity, and were torn asunder into many and various parts, and were consequently stripped of our noetic strength and intensity (τόνος), or rather, upward tendency (ἀνάτασις), and we plunged into the bottomless depths of evil, and despite being ourselves images of God and worthy of the heavenly life above, we mindlessly set our minds on things below (cf. Col. 3:2).[268]

Nevertheless, because our nature is neither immutable nor immovable, it is still possible in any case, and the wisest course of action at that, for us to reverse this process, so that despite having slipped down from such abundant glory into the deepest disgrace, we may lift our gaze back up to look upon the most-illustrious face of God. We cannot, of course, see Him as closely as before, but can still from afar 'see and suffer (πάσχειν) the splendor' of His beauty.[269] For both the divine Moses and indeed all the prophets and even those before them, namely Abraham and those like him, beheld this beauty as far as it was possible, with great clarity, and they enjoyed the splendor of His beauty such as they could, and were astonished by His unapproachable glory. Some of them called themselves wretched (Is. 6:5), while others considered and called themselves "*dust and ashes*" (Gen. 18:27); some could not even speak on account of the exceeding glory of what they beheld, and deplored themselves for their *weakness in speech* and *slowness of tongue* (Ex. 4:10); and others experienced (πάσχειν) even greater and blessed things in glory. Presumably for this reason the marvellous David, yearning for the splendor of the beauty of the Lord's face, cries aloud to God, *When shall I come and appear before the face of my God?* (Ps. 41:3). And elsewhere, wishing to indicate the state of the soul that has seen the face of the Lord, he says, *The upright shall dwell before Your face* (Ps. 139:14). Again, wisely indicating how

---

[267] In Greek, the word διαβάλλω "to slander, oppose" is related to the word διάβολος, "Satan, the Devil", which is where we get our English words "devil", "diabolical", etc. The Greek διάβολος is a calque of the Hebrew *sâtân*, meaning "adversary, opponent", or in a courtroom setting, "accuser, prosecutor"

[268] Wordplay: ἀφρόνως φρονεῖν εἱλόμεθα.

[269] Gregory Nazianzen, *Oration* 45.7, On Holy Pascha.

great is the strength that is provided to the soul by the contemplation of God's face, he says, *You turned away Your face, and I was dismayed* (Ps. 29:8).

If when God turns His face away there is dismay (τάραχος), then by contrast, when He is present and appears spiritual peace comes to the soul, which is so magnificent a gift that it comes after divine love and joy in the list of the gifts, or fruits, of the Holy Spirit (Gal. 5:22). Moreover, David shows how those who live in holiness and devotion walk in the light of the face of the Lord, saying, *In the light of Your face shall they walk, and in Your name shall they exult all the day* (Ps. 88:16-17); here he refers to that spiritual day when the noetic and ineffable Sun sends forth its pure and life-giving rays to the inner man, and when the perception of supracosmic realities (τῶν ὑπερκοσμίων ἡ αἴσθησις) dawns on the intellect when all the remembrance (μνημόσυνον)[270] of the soul is taken up from the earth and transferred to heaven. Then man leaps with joy and rightly chants hymns and rejoices with such exultation, delight, and cheer, who could describe it? He glows with gladness and radiance from the splendor of the Lord's face. For this reason David elsewhere beseeches God, *Turn not Your face away from me lest I become like those who descend into a pit* (Ps. 142:7); for the absence (ἀποστροφή) of the face of the Lord is the cause of darkness, while its presence (ἐπιστροφή) is the cause of all noetic light, and is therefore also rightly the cause of spiritual joy. Thus he says about himself, *The light of Your face has been signed upon me,* and adds, *You have given gladness to my heart* (Ps. 4:8); again, he testifies that the spiritual gift of divine grace came to him from the illumination of the face of the Lord. And explaining who they are that stand near the face of the Lord and *seek His face*, he says that they are the noetically *rich among the people of God* (Ps. 44:13). For there are indeed many saints and people of God, but it is not possible for everyone to behold the face of God and to live an angelic life while still living on earth – certainly not! – but only those that acknowledge that the Divine ought to be adored with divine wisdom and knowledge and worshiped *in Spirit and truth* (Jn. 4:24). Indeed, these would rightly be called '*the rich among the people of God*', as they have been enlightened by mysteries of abundant contemplations with great wisdom and knowledge of a kind that not everyone possesses, according to Paul (1 Cor. 8:7), but only belongs to those who have a depth and wealth of wisdom and knowledge that are divine and spiritual. It is for this reason, as we have said, that the wonderful David says to God, *The rich among the people shall seek Your face* (Ps. 44:13).

---

[270] The language here is quite reminiscent of Orthodox memorial rites, but does not specifically refer to the departure of the soul at death.

Therefore, Solomon, knowing this better than anyone else, since he had been filled with divine wisdom more than anyone else (cf. 3 Kings 3:12), is the one who instructs us most adeptly, saying, *Do not hasten to utter a word before the face of the Lord, for God is in heaven above and you are on earth below* (Eccl. 5:1). When, by the gift of divine grace, you come before the face of the Lord, that is, when the intellect's contemplative gaze ascends there through divine and unifying manifestation, then is *a time to be silent*; do not then rush to utter anything, do not say even a single word as you would naturally be wont to, for it is no *time to speak* (Eccl. 3:7). For then you are becoming a god (*theos*) yourself while still upon the earth, since you contemplate (*theoron*) the face of God in heaven in imitation of the angels (ἀγγελομιμήτως),[271] just as the Savior has said: *They always see the face of our Father in heaven* (Mt. 18:10). Thus when you hear Solomon say in another place, *The righteous have light forever* (Prov. 13:9), you would be right to think that they experience (πάσχειν) this from the light streaming from the Lord's face, so that, by divine grace, just like angels (ἀγγελοειδῶς), *they always see the face of the Lord*, from which abundant light streams forth. For man becomes and truly is another angel, not to mention god, upon the earth. Of course, he is also restored to the gift of *the image* (εἰκονικὴ δωρεά) bestowed by the grace of the Lord, and you yourself become on the earth below, that which God is on high, that is, a god. You cannot explain this wonderful reality by discursive reason, nor by transitioning from one notion to another and the cogitations of your own reasoning,[272] so that you become divided in your intellect, but by perceiving in unity and contemplating like God (δίκην Θεοῦ θεωρῶν) without sight and without motion, through simple and unified vision, and by reveling in the utterly luminous and unapproachable splendor shining from the face of the Lord.

This, then, is the supreme state of the intellect before God that is most desired by the prudent-minded. It is the blossom of noetic purity, as it were, and *the unity of faith* we earnestly pray for (Eph. 4:13), which is perfected in the communion of the Spirit. It is the glorious fruit of divine and deifying wisdom, the foundation of spiritual peace, the refuge of unimaginable joy, the gateway to the love of God; the

---

[271] In this paragraph Kallistos revisits the etymological basis for contemplative deification (*theosis*), which is also mentioned in Ch. 2 and 19, according to which the contemplative becomes a "god" inasmuch as he participates in the Holy Spirit and the contemplation of God. While the connection between contemplation and divinity may seem unfamiliar, this association dates at least to Aristotle (*Nicomachean Ethics* 10). But whereas the intellect (νοῦς) in Aristotle is arguably inherently divine and God is described as Pure Intellect, in Orthodox theology the intellect is "god-like" by grace from God who is "beyond intellect", as the author emphatically repeats in this work. And furthermore, the human person participates in divinity through Christ, who "became man that we might become god" (αὐτὸς γὰρ ἐνηνθρώπησεν, ἵνα ἡμεῖς θεοποιηθῶμεν), in the phrase of St. Athanasios the Great, *On the Incarnation* 54.3.

[272] διεξοδεύων λόγῳ … μεταβαίνων … κινῶν τὸ ἴδιον λογιζόμενον. All these description of rational activity use words implying "motion" and "speech" (λόγος) rather than stillness and silence.

burgeoning of illumination, the cause of the overflow of inexhaustible waters of the Spirit from the heart; the true food and delight of the soul (of which manna was the type), as well as its growth and transformation;[273] the beginning of divine and unspeakable mysteries and revelations, the conclusion of the one and primary truth, the eradication of all sorts of thoughts (λογισμοί), rest from all intellections (νοήσεις), the understanding that surpasses the power to know (ὑπὲρ τὸ νοεῖν), the inducement of divine ecstasy; it is the conversion and transformation of the intellect beyond intellect so as to become simple, wholly limitless, infinite, unbounded, formless, and shapeless, free from variation, quality and quantity, intangible and transcendent, and the overall restoration to its likeness with God (πρὸς τὸ θεοειδὲς ἀποκατάστασις). Therefore, when you reach this state and are, in a manner, divinized (θεουργούμενος) through God's gracious love for man, *do not hasten to utter* a single word *before the face of the Lord* (Eccl. 5:1). For to Him be the one and simple glory, which ever shall be His unto all ages.

77. The intellect that desires to contemplate the intelligible realities beyond itself can see only obscurely, dimly, and with confusion unless it also has its heart cooperating to this end through divine grace. For this would deprive the intellect of its most fundamental pleasure, even if it counts itself happy in its ignorance, not knowing the taste, so to speak, of this delight, just as he who has eaten only barley bread somehow thinks he enjoys it, while remaining wholly deprived of the true pleasure of bread because he has never known the fresh taste of semolina bread.

78. After the noetic union of the heart through grace, the intellect sees unwaveringly by a spiritual light and reaches out for its desire, which is God; it goes beyond all sensation, that is, it is restored to a condition without shade or quality, and unaffected by the impressions of the senses.

79. The mind that is led by grace to contemplation truly partakes of spiritual manna at all times. For the sensible manna that Israel ate possessed a remarkable power to satisfy and nourish the body, but what it was in essence no one knew. For this reason it was given the name "manna", and this word signifies the "unknown", for [in Hebrew] this word means "What is this?" And thus, when they saw it and ate it and did not know its essence, they wondered, "*What is this?*" (Ex. 16:15). So too the contemplative is in a constant state of intellectual ecstasy and wonders to himself, "What is this?" For while it brings him cheer in his contemplation of it and satisfies his intellect as he spiritually partakes of it, in its own nature it utterly transcends intellection (ὑπερεκβαίνει δὲ τὸ νοεῖσθαι καθ' ἑαυτό), because it is divine and supernatural; and while it provides miraculous food and drink to the

---

[273] τροφή … τρυφήτε καὶ τρυφή/αὔξησις … ἀλλοίωσις. Wordplay in Greek.

intellect, it supasses the condition (κατάστασις) of the intellect, not only because it is incomprehensible in its essence, but also infinite and unlimited.

80. There are three witnesses to the truth, as I might say with good reason: creation (ἡ κτίσις), Scripture (ἡ γραφή), and the grace of the Spirit (ἐν τῷ πνεύματι). For from Scripture and creation, as long as they are perceived spiritually, one can contemplate the unique and simple truth, as well as the composite truth that comes from it. And when, having passed through the former three[274] one attains the latter two[275] and remains in them, he finds the unerring path by the grace of Christ. For when from the simple truth he reaches noetic heights and depths and a boundless expanse (cf. Eph. 3:18), he is filled with amazement on account of these, and sings in reverent fear. From the composite truth, in addition to what we have said, he also finds in his heart peace, love, and joy, and thus chants aloud full of love. However, man needs a great deal of time and effort and patience, until, by casting off the senses and sundering the intellect from sensible things, he may abide in intelligible things, after which the contemplation of the truth shines upon the soul. Of course, I am not saying that the truth itself needs such things for its discovery,[276] that is, the time or patience and effort required for it to be grasped, but I do say that man needs these. For the truth is of course One (ἕν) and Simple,[277] even if it is contemplated in a twofold manner in order to manifest itself; in fact it all but declares this everywhere, bearing witness of itself to those who wish to see it. But for man, being composite and interwoven with the senses and still subject to changes and alteration, there are times when, in a manner, he loses touch with himself, becomes his own opponent without realizing it, in his conceit does evil (πονηρευόμενος), and falls sick with disbelief. Moreover, through these three passions, that is, conceit, evil (πονηρία), and disbelief, man miserably falls away from the truth to which those first three witnesses testify, namely, Scripture, creation, and the Spirit. Hence, in order to cast off dreadful conceit and the other passions I have mentioned, the intellect must be humbled and believe with simplicity; and thence, directly through Scripture and creation by the grace of the Spirit, it will come to recognize clearly not only the simplest truth, but also the composite truth that comes from it; it will also understand what was preventing it from the contemplation of truth and, I might add, barring it from the enjoyment thereof.

---

274 That is: creation, Scripture, and the grace of the Spirit.

275 That is: the unique and simple truth and the composite truth that comes from it.

276 God, the One and the Truth, altogether transcends any notion of "need" or "necessity".

277 Here the feminine subject ἡ ἀλήθεια is given the predicate "one" in the neuter gender ἕν, that is the proper name attributed to God throughout the treatise, rather than in the feminine gender μία. So this "Truth" is another epithet of God.

Therefore the primary truth is alone One and Simple by nature. After it proceeds the truth that is composite for us, who are composite. And this is the ultimate and best pursuit (ἀντικείμενον) of our intellect, towards which every discipline and practice of those who pursue the spiritual purpose is eagerly directed, so that the intellect that is stripped as far as possible may see and enjoy the splendor radiating from both the first and only truth and the truth composed from it in a wondrous manner. This can be done in no other way but by humility and simplicity in faith,[278] through the witness of Scripture and creation by the grace of the Spirit. And when the intellect beholds the truth reflected in [these] three powers within it through the testimony of the three aforementioned witnesses, then as it returns to itself thereby, it becomes all the more humble and simple and, of course, faithful. It ascends from there with spring in its step (εὐθύμῳ ποδί), as they say, to the contemplation of the truth that is resplendent with glorious rays, by which it returns to itself on account of the magnificence of the glory it has beheld, descends into even greater humility and simplicity, and is filled with faith in amazement. And in this manner it revolves, as it were, in a kind of divine circle (τινα θεῖον κύκλον ἐπανακυκλῶν) as it cycles through humility, simplicity, and faith, rises in the vision of the truth, and is led by the radiance of the truth into ever deeper humility, entering into ever greater simplicity in faith. Moreover, it does not cease traversing this course for as long as the day *is called today* (Heb. 3:13), contemplating the truth in humility, simplicity, and faith through the testimony of Scripture and creation by the grace of the Spirit, and returning back to whence it first began its motion. And thus, as it is deified through grace day by day and illuminated by realities beyond intellect, living a life replete with abundant joy in Christ our Lord, it receives the enjoyment of future eternal goods as a foretaste and pledge (cf. 2 Cor. 1:22; 5:5; Eph. 1:14).

81. These three things naturally keep the contemplative life pure and inviolate, namely, faith, manifest participation in the Spirit, and the knowledge of wisdom. For contemplation is, to give a definition, the knowledge of intelligible realities within sensible ones; and sometimes it is even the knowledge of subtle intelligible realities apart from sense perception (αἴσθησις), which comes to the more advanced. Here, of course, faith is needed, for Scripture says, *Unless you believe, you will not understand* (Isa. 7:9), as well as the Spirit, since *the Spirit searches all things, even the depths of God* (1 Cor. 2:10). For this reason, too, the divine Job said, *It is the breath of the Almighty that teaches me* (Job 33:4). Then, in natural course, the divine energy that, as it were, stirs up within the heart and lives and so

---

[278] Humility (ταπείνωσις), simplicity (ἁπλότης), and faith (πίστις) are the opposites of the passions of conceit (οἴησις), evil/deviousness (πονηρία), and disbelief (ἀπιστία). Here πονηρός (cf. usually translated "evil" in the Lord's Prayer, cf. Mt. 6:13) also seems to have the later connotation of devious as opposed to "simple".

transcendently enlivens the intellect,[279] ineffably embraces (συμπτύσσειν) and gathers (συνάγειν) it to itself. It further prevents the intellect from floating away and enables it to see divine realities effortlessly, with tranquility, great cheer, comfort (παράκλησις), and divine love, to revolve around them, and to receive the manifestation of God in a new and wondrous manner. It accordingly rejoices in Him with ever-increasing and unbearable divine desires (ἀφορήτων ἐρώτων) and with fitting exultation. Next, as we have mentioned, wisdom is also needed, for, as Scripture says, *Wisdom will illuminate the face of man* (Eccl. 8:1). That is, it will illuminate it so that it may easily proceed from the realities of sense perception to intellection, and ascend from sensible things to intelligible and divine spectacles, and to look upon unutterable mysteries in noetic revelation; it will illuminate it to behold in contemplation the super-essential God and to receive His manifestation in unity. Hence, truly *blessed is the man whom you will instruct, O Lord, and You will teach him by Your law* (Ps. 93:12). For truly wise is the one who comes to faith through instruction and is taught the unspoken things of God by the teaching of the Spirit. It is a truly great thing to be a wise person who *walks by faith* (2 Cor. 5:7) in the supernatural union and communion of the Spirit. And as someone has said, "There are three things that are truly indomitable (ἀκράτητα): God, an angel, and a man who loves wisdom (φιλόσοφος)." He becomes, paradoxically, another angel upon the earth, a true sacred viewer[280] (ἐπόπτης) of the visible creation, and a genuine initiate (μύστης) in the uncreated divine processions (θεῖαι πρόοδοι) of God, or what one might call His gifts (δωρεῶν), laying hold of the Unseen in any way possible by directly discerning the knowledge of God in imitation of the angels.[281]

Such is, in sum, the man who is wise in faith by the grace of the Holy Spirit, and so is he blessed. Even though what Luke relates about the Lord in the Gospels, narrating how He was free of worldly things so as to excel in the power and praises of wisdom and grace, would by itself be enough for me to say and quell any doubts. For this is how he puts it in one place, writing, *Jesus progressed in wisdom and stature and grace* (Lk. 2:52), and elsewhere, *He grew and became strong in Spirit, being filled with wisdom* (Lk. 2:40). At any rate, since I am moved to say something even clearer in regard to these matters, I will further quote what the holy Solomon says to God: *The things in the heavens, who has searched these out? And who has known Your counsel, except He to whom You have given wisdom and sent the Holy*

---

[279] In Greek, the sequence "stirs up, lives, enlivens" is a wordplay: ἀναζέουσα, ζῶσα, ζωοῦσα.

[280] The language here is a Christian adaptation of the pre-Christian terminology of mystery religions, an adaptation that began to take shape as early as St. Ignatios of Antioch in the first century AD. ἐπόπτης alludes to the full-fledged viewer of mysteries, μύστης to the initiate, and πρόοδοι to festal processions.

[281] In this clause three words begin with the prefix ἐπί-, ἐπιδραττόμενος, ἐπιβολή, ἐπίγνωσις, intensifying the immediacy of this angelic knowledge.

Spirit from the highest?[282] *And thus the ways of those upon the earth were restored, and human beings were taught the things that are pleasing to You and saved by Your wisdom* (Wis. 9:16-19). Do you see how much power wisdom gains through participation in the Spirit, and how far removed from salvation is he who has not acquired wisdom and the Spirit from God, nor is guided by a wise participant in the Spirit? And if such things were written about the Savior, in whom *dwelt all the fullness of divinity* (Col. 1:19), and so, by extension, about the entire human race, it is not difficult to understand how much we need wisdom along with the power of the Spirit, and how much power and progress God, the cherisher of our souls, mercifully grants to the spiritual wise-man who *searches out the things in the heavens* and goes on to learn the counsel of the Most High; what wonder! But we must move on.

Thus having given such a detailed account about the contemplative, we should now speak about contemplation so as to provide a partial exposition and nourish, as it were, the reasoning faculty of the well-disposed listener. So let us speak and by no means shrink from the task at hand. For this is what God commands to all rational beings, namely, to pass on divine illumination and intelligible things generously (ἀφθόνως) to those below, and to receive what we can with reverence[283] from those above, and moreover to gather together with our peers (ὁμοταγής) in community (κοινωνικῶς) and converse freely about intelligible realities and God without ostentation or contention. For in this way not only will integrity and verity shine forth clearly in the Church of the Living God, but also that holy and exceedingly lovely feature (πρόσωπον) of love – the sign by which Christ's disciples are recognized (Jn. 13:35) – will shed its light forever in our hearts, poured into us by the Holy Spirit to love God and men perfectly and simply. And thus we might live an angelic life upon the earth, one that is truly blessed and no less than supremely delightful, for upon this divine and deifying dual-natured (διφυής) love hang all the Law and the Prophets (Mt. 22:40), and there is simply nothing sweeter to the soul, and especially when it proceeds directly from the contemplation and knowledge of God and divine realities, which is to say, from the grace of illumination.

---

282 Kataphygiotes seems to understand this passage from the Wisdom of Solomon as a specifically Christological prophecy in the light of the Gospel of Luke. It might also be noted that these passages about Christ's increase in wisdom refer to Christ's human nature (for in His divine nature He is "Wisdom beyond wisdom", ch. 71, and consubstantial with the Spirit from all eternity, ch. 2). As we see in the rest of the chapter, that which is attributed to Christ's humanity has universal implications for all humanity.

283 Subtle word-play: "receive with reverence" μετ' εὐλαβείας μεταλαμβάνειν.

So then, he who has well and wisely made the ascent to God his purpose and task in order to be united with Him and thus to be truly deified, that is, to be saved (for unless the intellect is deified, no man can be saved, according to the theologians [τὴν τῶν θεηγόρων ἐκφαντορίαν]), and who also puts the Lord's commandments into practice as much as possible, proceeds to the contemplation of both existent and visible realities (ὄντων καὶ φαινομένων), so that he has neither blind practice, which is cut off from contemplation, nor soulless contemplation, which is void of practice. Hence, with wisdom of reason (λόγος) and intellect (νοῦς) and the sacred study of the Scriptures, he is, as we often say, off to a good start by taking careful aim and setting his gaze on the world of the senses, examining it with reason (σὺν λόγῳ) as a manifestation (ἐπίδειγμα) of the infinitely powerful and boundlessly wise Creator; and eventually he comes to an appreciation of the Creator's infinite power and absolute Otherness – as far as his gaze can reach – and finds great delight and has his intellect (νοῦς) nourished in secret by secret things (κατὰ τὸ κρυπτὸν διὰ τῶν κρυπτῶν).[284] And then, over time, by quietly living a life of stillness and philosophizing[285] only about divine things through Scripture and visible realities, he makes the greatest effort he can to contemplate the creation spiritually in accordance with Scripture, and the symbols in accordance with the truth through an overarching, integral vision (δι' ἑνωτικωτέρας ὁράσεως).[286] When this is done, the intellect, by the venerable Spirit's favor and the energy He imparts, rises to the vision and understanding (ἐπιστήμη) of the sacred truth, and as the great Dionysios says, to the second sacred stage of contemplation, as it is called generally, that is to say, the sacred spectacles (θεῖα θεάματα) and perceptions (νοήματα) without veils or symbols (προκαλυμμάτων καὶ τύπων χωρίς).

After this, when the intellect is in a certain manner stripped, it strives to fill itself with both intelligible realities, which are stripped [of symbols], as well as divine manifestations through its own purity and effort to ascend to God, like brilliant rays of sun reflected in the brightest mirror. And after making further progress and maturing in grace by such means as it can, it proceeds to a kind of third stage, in which it refines (ἀνάγω) those many and blessed visions and divine processions in a more unified and concentrated manner from the many differentiations and raises them up to the ineffable love (ἔρως) of the immutable and hidden Unity, transforming them with all its noetic perception into a fiery, heartfelt, endless, divinizing (θεουργός) eros for God, just as the contemplator (θεωρός) is transformed by the Spirit who illuminates in *truth* and *remembrance* (Jn. 4:23;

[284] Wordplay: καὶ τρυφᾷ καὶ τρέφεται ("finds delight and is nourished").

[285] The monastic and ascetical life was termed the "philosophical life" in Byzantium.

[286] Two pairs seem to be at work here: reason and intellect (λόγος - νοῦς), Scripture and vision (γραφή - ὅρασις). Note the author's positive attitude towards creation, visible things, and the various spiritual means of contemplating it which assist the intellect's ascent to God.

14:26). And this is, once again according to the great Dionysios, inspired participation in the unifying power of the One Itself, as far as this possible.

So then, in these threefold stages of unifying participation in the Trinity, the divinely-minded intellect is borne aloft by God in thrice blessed bliss and clearly and manifestly delights in the unbearable spurs of divine ecstasy and the madness of divine eros, being *wounded by love* (Song 2:5); it sees itself, as it were, burst into flame from the ardor of this condition, and becomes enthused and indeed goes outside itself, since it has entered into the apophatic mysteries of theology with a radiant countenance; it feasts on the unoriginate, infinite, incomprehensible, wholly inexpressible, and altogether inconceivable One through perceptions beyond sight. And it conceives of God as "a kind of infinite and boundless ocean of being (πέλαγος οὐσίας), transcending every conception of time and nature," according to the renowned Theologian.[287] And this is, as St. Dionysios also says, the banquet of sacred vision (ἡ τῆς ἐποψίας ἑστίασις) that nourishes the intellect and deifies everyone who ascends to it, beginning of course from the contemplation and knowledge of realities (τὰ ὄντα), as this guide to sacred rites[288] says, in the place where he clarifies the meaning of the sacred symbols of our ecclesiastical hierarchy. And as the Basil the Great also says: "When one has passed beyond the beauty of visible things in contemplation and stands before God Himself, whom naturally only the pure hearts can see, then, having ascended to the highest realms of theology, one can become a sacred visionary (ἐποπτικός)." Again, about the saying of David who speaks in the Spirit, *In the morning I will stand before You and will behold* (ἐπόψει με) (Ps. 5:4), Basil the Great says, "When I stand before You and approach the very vision (αὐτῇ τῇ περὶ σοῦ θεωρίᾳ) of You with my intellect, then I will receive the energy of divine vision (ἐποπτικὴ ἐνέργεια) through the illumination of knowledge." One can hear much the same when listening to St. Maximos, who directly illustrates how much progress comes from the contemplation and knowledge of God through Scripture and creation; and how by means of these the illumination of knowledge is wont to shine, and through this illumination, blessed deification by direct perception (κατ᾽ ἐπιβολήν), something which has never been so rare and difficult to find among those who live the hesychastic life as it is today; for they have no teacher from the age of grace who can teach from experience, as the ultimate guide to stillness, St. Isaac the Syrian, says in his discourse about the spiritual sense and the contemplative faculty. Moreover, St. Maximos says: "We call the teachings of the saints

[287] Gregory Nazianzen, *Oration* 38.7.

[288] The "hierophant" (ἱεροφάντωρ/ἱεροφάντης) was in charge of explaining sacred rituals to the faithful. This would look different depending on the context: in Rome, this was the pontifex maximus; in the Eleusinian mysteries, this was the senior "viewer", who passed on holy knowledge to the initiates; the word could even refer to the Jewish High Priest, or even Moses the Lawgiver.

'divinizing lights', because they impart the light of knowledge and deify those who obey them." In this he clearly agrees with the most-holy Dionysios, who says: "Into all the other divinizing lights, in accordance with the oracles (τὰ λόγια) [of Scripture], which have been revealed to us by the mystical tradition of our inspired guides (ἐκφαντορικῶς), we too have been initiated." And elsewhere he says, "Divine knowledge lifts up those who reverently (ὡς θεμιτόν) look up to it – in a manner appropriate to each – and unifies them in the simplicity of its union." And again: "Every procession of light sent and kindly bestowed on us by the Father uplifts and fulfills us as a uniting power (cf. Jas. 1:17), and brings us back to the unity and deifying simplicity of the gathering Father; *for from Him and to Him are all things* (Rom. 11:36)."[289] Do you understand concerning the one who returns to God by lifting himself up to Him, that is, by divine perception, and with great wisdom becomes simple in God, whether he comes to the contemplation of God by ascending through realities (τὰ ὄντα), or through Scripture – either through symbolic [theology] or perhaps divine [insight][290] – that such a person is united with God and deified, and not only that, but is even called a god? For Dionysius says again: "All noetic and rational beings that have turned with all their power toward union with the thearchic Hiddenness and that incomprehensibly lift themselves as far as they can to Its illuminations, in an imitation, if we may say so, of God Himself – inasmuch as this is possible – are even counted worth of the divine name." And as Gregory, whose tongue speaks so wisely about God (ἡ Γρηγορίου πάνυ θεολόγος γλῶττα), says clearly that man is "a living being that is supervised here (οἰκονούμενος) and then moved elsewhere, and this is the consummation of the mystery: he is deified in his motion toward God."[291] Again, St. Maximos says: "The intelligible form of Sacred Scripture transfigures by its wisdom those who have progressed in knowledge and leads them to deification through the transfiguration wrought by the Word within them, as they *behold the glory of the Lord with unveiled face* (2 Cor. 3:18)."[292] Hence, as we have said, the contemplative life requires these three things: faith, participation in the Spirit, and the knowledge of wisdom in Christ Jesus our Lord.

82. The contemplative life lived with the grace of the Life-Giving Spirit mystically fills the [sacred] visionary (θεωρός) with many breathtaking intelligible visions (θεάματα), not of course all at once, nor all together (οὔτ' αὐθωρὸν οὔτ' ἀθρόον), but over time and a lengthy life of philosophy, arranged in a certain order like the rungs of a ladder. And you might now hear a contemplative say, as he contemplates

---

[289] *On the Celestial Hierarchy* 1.1. Also quoted in Ch. 17.
[290] This "divine insight" may be referring to the mode of contemplation "stripped of symbols" mentioned above.
[291] Gregory Nazianzen 38.11.
[292] *Centuries on Theology* 1.97, *Philokalia* Vol. 2, Ch. 97.

in deep stillness, having fled from all things but God: *I will be alone until I depart* (Ps. 140:10). Again, at another time, when he considers created things (τὰ ὄντα), he proclaims, "*How magnificent are Your works, O Lord; in wisdom have you made them all*" (Ps. 103:24), and, "*The scent of Your garments is like the scent of an abundant field which You have blessed, O Lord!*" (Gen. 27:27). And at times when he is striving to lift himself and his gaze higher and engaged in ascent to noetic heights, he is urged to say to God, "*I will run after the scent of Your perfumes*" (Song 1:4), and, "*I will exalt You, O God, my King, and I will bless Your name for ever and to the ages of ages. The Lord is great and greatly to be praised, and of His majesty there is no end* (Ps. 144:1,3), and, "*Your knowledge is too wonderful for me; it is so great, I cannot endure it*" (Ps. 138:6). Again, in other cases, as the beholders ascend to the vision of the One beyond essence, they are moved to praise Him thus: "*You are the Most High for ever, Lord, and You are remembered from generation to generation; You have been greatly and exceedingly exalted above all gods*" (Ps. 101:13; 96:9). At times, the contemplative life leads them on to cry aloud with stark negation,[293] "*There is none like You among the gods, O Lord, and there are no works like Yours*" (Ps. 85:8). Again, to those who contemplate in the Spirit it reveals the *mountain* of knowledge and *holy place* of God, where *those of clean hands and a pure heart may ascend* and *stand* (Ps. 23:3-4), and further enables them to see such ascents as reach *up to the heavens* as well as descents *to the depths* (Ps. 106:26), that is, to the heights and the depths of the Spirit's mysteries

Again, at times the contemplative life may arrest the intellect with wonder as it beholds the personal manifestation of God as Trinity (τοῦ κατὰ τὴν Τριάδα προσωπικοῦ θεάματος), and at other times, it causes one to gaze with ecstasy in contemplation of Jesus, His Incarnate economy, and the supernatural mysteries that follow it. But even then, after so many blessed visions (θεάματα), it does not relax its grip on the contemplator, until it has brought him illumined to the very *bosom of God* (Jn. 1:18) – O what amazing grace! – in true rest (κατάπαυσις) and inexpressible repose, spiritual supernatural delight, not to say inebriation from the intoxicating beauties of God, and a more divine ecstasy. In that bosom[294] of surpassing blessings is the profound depth of divine secrets and it signifies well the perception of God's transcendence beyond essence. Abraham received this bosom as an inheritance (κληρονομία) from God when God Himself became his

---

[293] "Negative statement" ἀπόφασις. This word constitutes the basis of "apophatic" or "negative theology," a theological method that makes use of statements concerning what God is *not* in order to lead the intellect to contemplate God beyond thought, creation, and even intellection. It might be pointed out how "apophatic" theology begins as early as the Old Testament.

[294] The discussion of the "bosom of God" may seem odd, but an important aspect of hesychastic theology is the spiritual, or "anagogical", exegesis of difficult Scriptural passages with the purpose of raising (ἀνάγω) the reader to higher truths.

"possession" (κλῆρος), as He said, *I am the God of Abraham* (Gen. 26:24). Since God is, after all, *the God of Abraham* in an eminent sense, it follows that the very bosom of God is the bosom of Abraham (Lk. 16:22). Therefore, contemplative life in the Spirit raises the intellect to the bosom of God, or as one might say, to the bosom of Abraham, and leads it into perfect simplicity with exceedingly loving gladness, and truly deifies it and makes it blissful (μακάριος) with merriment and great and ineffable delight; that is, the intellect that has partaken of wisdom and engages in the vision [of things] above with the utmost diligence, in Christ Jesus our Lord.

83. After both creation and Scripture are unfolded by the Word of God and perceived spiritually, they secure the intellect and *all its powers* in the sacred vision and understanding (κατανόησις) of God, once the heart has first received the energy and motion of *the Spirit*, and this the holy David teaches us with the greatest wisdom (Ps. 32:6), saying, on the one hand, when intellects *are established by the Word of the Lord* (which he here calls '*heavens*') and *all their power by the Spirit proceeding from His mouth*, and, on the other hand, when the intelligible *earth*, that is, our heart, appears *full of the mercy of the Lord* (Ps. 32:5), that is, full of the active power and energy of the Spirit, and this he explains with keen perception and clarity. Indeed, before the intellect senses this energy and active power within the heart, not only will it not possess firmness (τὸ στερέμνιον) by contemplatively and spiritually studying creation and Sacred Scripture and gathering all the things contained in them into one *logos*,[295] but there is also much reason to fear that it might perish through false conceptions and imagination (παραφαντάζεσθαι). Therefore, if we are going to engage in the contemplation of God from Scripture and creation, by concentrating (συμπτύσσειν) in a unified and undifferentiated manner the many *logoi* and perceptions (θεωρήματα) of beings into one *logos* and one spirit, by seeing through unifying, simple, and formless contemplation in a limitless, infinite, and unoriginate state, let us first seek to find the treasure of our heart within us and implore the Holy God to fill our earth with His mercy. And then with all our power let us set our intellect free to ascend to the unified, undifferentiated, simple, formless, eternal, infinite, and limitless understanding (κατανόησις) of God, through the contemplation and help of the Logos and the Spirit.

84. When man, with sincere and simple disposition of soul, walks the path of virtue, practicing these virtues and keeping his thought humble in the patience and hope that faith gives him, then the life-giving and ever-streaming power and energy

---

[295] "studying" ἀναλέγεσθαι can also mean "to gather up, collect; read, recount". The root λέγω means "to speak" and also "to gather", and forms the basis for the word λόγος, transliterated here as *logos* because of its relevance to St. Maximos the Confessor's doctrine of the *logoi*. Cf. n. in ch. 27.

of the Holy Spirit comes to reside in the heart, truly illumining the powers of the soul. And as this energy moves manifestly (περιφανῶς) in accordance with the Comforter's nature (πεφυκότως), it 'comforts' and immediately calls to itself[296] the intellect activated in energy (τὸν ἐνεργείᾳ νοῦν) and ineffably unites itself with it, so that in that moment the intellect can truly and unequivocally become *one spirit* with divine grace (cf. 1 Cor. 6:17), and that is precisely when and then at long last the intellect comes to contemplation, both of its own accord and aided by the inspiration of grace, that is, after it is brought to an inexpressible rest from its rovings and ramblings (περιφορὰ καὶ περιπλάνησις) by the energy and light of the Life-Giving Holy Spirit, and enters into revelations of intelligible divine mysteries. And by utter silence and stillness, with a gaze proper to his nature, he attains initiation (ἐμβατεύω) into supernatural and unspoken hallows (ἄρρητα). And regarding the person who has received the energy of God in the Holy Spirit, [it may observed that] the more he contemplates and is seized with divine inspiration (θεωρεῖ καὶ θεοληπτεῖται) and lifts himself as far as he can to the vision of God by learning the things of God (ἐπιστήμη τῶν θείων) and gathering them from sacred readings, the more he seeks solitude in humility and prayer. So then, he is in no way deprived of theology, but is precisely then a true theologian, and can hardly ever refrain from theologizing. Yet without the heavenly gift that we have mentioned, and without the breath of the Spirit moving in his heart at all times, alas! all that the intellect sees are its own imaginations (φαντασίαι) and all its theology is but vain words scattered to the wind, and does not stir the senses of the soul as it should, for all they hear is words coming from outside. Here the most grievous delusion (πλάνη) concerning intelligible realities and theology itself has crept in uninvited, since it does not come from a heart in which the Illuminating Spirit operates, which is where the unified and unchanging truth of theology is generally found. For in a heart where the life-giving and illuminating power and ever-streaming energy of the Spirit is not manifestly present, either by 'breathing' upon it, as one might say, or by 'streaming' over it,[297] there is no noetic union but rather division; nor is there power and stability, but weakness and variability; nor, at any rate, is there light and the vision of truth, but rather darkness and the vain fabrications of the imagination, and the twisted path of all folly and delusion. For, according to the Fathers, the intellect can pass through three stations or paths,

---

[296] "it comforts" (παρακαλοῦσα. This verb, meaning "to comfort exhort, help, advocate" is the characteristic activity of the Holy Spirit as the *Paraclete (Παράκλητος)*. Note the alliteration with προσκαλεῖται "to call, summon". Various derivatives of καλέω are associated with the Holy Spirit in Orthodox theology, e.g. the *epiklesis* prayer in the Divine Liturgy when the Holy Spirit descends.

[297] Word-play on the rhyming participles "breathing" (πνέουσα) and "streaming" (ῥέουσα), which are both verbs used to describe the activity of the Holy Spirit in the Gospel of John (cf. Jn. 3:8, 7:38-9).

namely, the natural (φυσικῶς), the supernatural (ὑπερφυῶς), and that which is contrary to nature (παρὰ τὴν φύσιν).

When the intellect contemplates something intelligible in a substance, then it sees in accordance with nature (φυσικῶς), but with the supernatural (ὑπερφυής) energy of the Spirit. When it sees hypostatically and not in a particular substance (whether that substance be a demon or an angel),[298] then if the intellect is united in peace and the torch of the Spirit is kindled to a blaze,[299] he sees supernaturally (ὑπερφυῶς) and hence without error; but if by seeing visible things the intellect is divided and darkened and the life-giving power is quenched (1 Thess. 5:19), then it sees contrary to nature (παρὰ φύσιν) and what it sees is only a delusion. For this reason, if we wish to have a healthy and prudent intellect we must not hypostatically raise the intellect to spiritual vision, nor put any confidence in vision, unless the heart receives the energy as we have mentioned above, and is moved by the power of the Holy Spirit.

85. Some attempt, and indeed they do very well, to heal (ἐξιάομαι) the flame and fever of their passions with the heavenly dew of grace; about them it is written: *The dew You send brings healing to us* (cf. Is. 26:19). For others, this dew, joined with some additional divine help, is transformed into manna and, in a manner similar to how wheat becomes bread, it is ground to contrition by the humbling of the heart, moistened by the water of tears, and baked in the fire of spiritual knowledge. And when it undergoes (πάσχειν) this process as it should, it even becomes food fit for angels. About these it is most aptly written, *Man ate the bread of angels* (Ps. 77:25). Again, there are others whose nature has become and appears to be pure manna since they have advanced to an even greater height. About these the Gospels say, "That which is born of the Spirit is spirit" (Jn. 3:6). The first station is that of the wise hesychasts, the second that of those who practice silence with divine knowledge, and the third that of those who have attained complete simplicity and transformation[300] in Christ Jesus, our Lord.

---

[298] Ὅταν ἐν ὑποκειμένῳ τι νοητὸν ὁ νοῦς θεωρῇ, κατὰ φύσιν ὁρᾷ, μέντοιγε μετ' ἐνεργείας ὑπερφυοῦς τοῦ Πνεύματος. Ὅθεν δὲ ὑποστατικῶς ὁρᾷ καὶ οὐκ ἐν ὑποκειμένῳ, δαίμονα τυχὸν ἢ ἄγγελον. Cf. Angelikoudes, *Chapters* 52, which passage has almost identical terminology. This does not imply demons as worthy objects of contemplation, but seems to identify the two extremes of existence: the entire range of created things from the lowest to the highest, i.e. this supernatural "hypostatic" vision is wholly beyond nature.

[299] ἡ δᾳδουχία τοῦ Πνεύματος ἀναζωπυρεῖται σφοδρότερον. Vibrant words used to describe the illumination of the Spirit, suggesting liturgical language (cf. also 2 Tim. 1:6).

[300] Wordplay: "simplicity" (ἡπλωμένων) and "transformation" (ἠλλοιωμένων). Note that in spoken Greek, the distinction between the smooth and rough breathings (spiritus lenis, spiritus asper) had long since disappeared.

86. The intellect that has, through grace, noetically[301] escaped Pharaoh and Egypt with its plagues and toil, as well as the fleshly life, flooded with the bitter waves of passion and the filthy brine of evil, and arrived at the noetic desert, that is to say, to a state free of the noetic army of Pharaoh; and which, in brief, has suffered and overcome in a noetic manner all the woes that befell the Hebrews in a sensible manner at that time, such an intellect then goes on to eat noetic manna securely with the sense of the soul (αἴσθησις ψυχῆς), for the sensible manna that Israel ate in ancient times (Ex. 16:1-36) was a type foreshadowing this noetic manna.

And in the beginning, of course, there are times when the intellect desires the noetic meat of the Egyptian sacrifices, just as the Israelites desired the sensible meat (Ex. 12:8), something extremely dangerous and equally misguided. And there are also times when it undergoes temptation because God turns away (ἀποστροφή), until it has properly propitiated the Divine through supplication by turning back in repentance. And indeed, if it is gradually filled up with manna through stillness, the passing of time, and the addition of power and strength of grace to it, it can clearly and manifestly perceive its noetic flesh being, as it were, changed into the nature of manna. For the intellect that partakes of manna there are spiritual weights and balances (Lev. 19:36), and by measuring with these he eats the manna in moderation, and does not gather more than the daily portion, lest it be spoiled with worms by exceeding due measure and altogether perish (Ex. 16:20-21) and the self-indulgent intellect have nothing to eat and perish along with it. It is clear that the intellect that eats manna, even though it eats nothing else, lives a fairer life than all, no matter what it is or how it eats; I am of course referring here to noetic realities in the intellect. For indeed, the intellect itself is somehow changed and takes on the quality of manna by keeping this diet, and the sign of this is its complete lack of appetite for any of the foreign foods it formerly desired; then it is able to partake of manna anywhere and becomes childlike by cleaving to faith in God. And it is surely no wonder that someone should change[302] into the state (πρὸς ἕξιν) of the food that he constantly eats and stores up in his body over a long period of time, and likewise it is not unreasonable for the intellect to transform into the state (πρὸς ἕξιν) of manna, since, of course, a steady and exclusive diet of anything naturally tends to make its consumer more like itself. So then, not only does the intellect clearly hold the rank of an angel, but even becomes a partaker of divine adoption, and in accordance with this dignity it goes from spiritual *glory to glory*

---

[301] The references to various Scriptural images as "noetic" are characteristic of the patristic spiritual/allegorical exegesis of Scripture. There are, as it were, "intelligible" signs in each detail of Scripture which the intellect discerns in order to make progress with the help of the Spirit. This method is also frequently employed in Orthodox hymnography.

[302] μεταβάλλεσθαι. Although *metabolism* is an English neologism, it provides a fortuitously helpful way of understanding the logic of this passage.

(2 Cor. 3:18), and not only does it gaze at the One, but also becomes one with itself, and lives in this One and transcendently delights in It and enjoys, so to speak, unspeakable secrets in a God-like and God-loving manner in the Holy Spirit. Moreover, it actually changes (γιγνομένως γινόμενος) in accordance with that which it sees and praises, in such a way that it can see itself becoming like the state (πρὸς ἕξιν) of manna. Hence, this station is much higher and more honorable than the one in which the intellect is aware of itself partaking of manna, but not yet being changed into the state (πρὸς ἕξιν) of manna. For the intellect may experience (πάσχειν) the former at some point in the beginning while concentrating (συμπτύσσειν) in itself in noetic union, but the latter is a clear manifestation of a more perfect union, of the revelation of the mysteries of knowledge, and of the ultimate liberation of the intellect from all things in a state of supreme simplicity.

87. The intellect is by nature simple, for it is obvious that the Divine, whose image it is, is simple as well. Since it is simple, it loves to act simply (ἁπλῶς ἐνεργεῖν φιλεῖ), for everything loves what is natural to it; the intellect is diffused into variation (ποικίλλεσθαι) however, not of its own accord, but because of the senses and the sensible things which transmit to it the receptions (παραδοχαί) of intelligible realities. But when the intellect establishes its own reason (λόγος) to judge and adjudicate between itself and the senses – as well as sensible things – to the best of its knowledge, so as not to make the senses duller than they should be, then immediately the intellect becomes one with itself and simple, restored to its proper nature, and removed from the things dividing it; it neither rashly covers over the beautiful aspects of sensible things nor crudely panders to them in a way that deprives the intellect of its strength to remain detached from them; but rather, [reason] distributes to each what is fitting, and the intellect naturally begins to love the One and Simple again and to act (ἐνεργεῖν) in a unified and simple manner, and seeks to do so out of love (φιλῶν). And by seeking thus it takes its flight beyond all composition until it finds That which is truly and properly One and Simple, who is God. Thence, as the intellect is at one time sheltered and at another time raised to great heights by His wings alone, it rejoices, for it is right for the intellect that is embraced and borne up by God to rejoice.[303]

88. It is as if a thick mist (ἀχλυώδης) of the passions had fallen upon the clear sight of the soul, and then it made it see things other than true being (τὸ ὄν). But when the intellect engages in frequent prayer and fulfills the commandments and lifts itself to the contemplation of God through grace, it dispels this thick mist and can see clearly of its own accord that it is seeing God; it requires no interpreter

---

303 "the intellect that is embraced and borne up by God" in Greek there is a word-play: θεοφρουρούμενον καὶ θεοφορούμενον νοῦν.

(ἑρμηνεύς) to explain this to it, just as one who sees with his sense of sight has no need of a teacher, unless of course there is something disturbing and covering over the pupil of the eye. For just as healthy senses naturally perceive sensible things, so also the intellections that are cleansed of the cloud (νέφος) of the passions are designed (ᾠκείωται) to perceive intelligible realities. And just as understanding (κατάληψις) comes from the sensory perception of sensible things, so also insight (ἐποψία) into intelligible realities naturally comes from noetic vision; after these follows the simple contemplation of God by the power of grace, a contemplation without form, quality, or image that takes possession of the intellect, releases it from all things whatsoever, both sensible and intelligible, and encloses it within an unfathomable depth of infinitude, incomprehensibility, and boundlessness in amazement and wonder, such as no words (λόγῳ) can describe.

89. O Sovereign, You are the Principle (ἀρχή) ruling all things visible and intelligible, almighty One! Your rule (ἀρχή) is without beginning (ἄναρχον), uncreated One; Your definition is indefinable, infinite One; Your nature is supernatural, unencompassable One; Your essence is super-essential, unbegotten One; Your form is formless, invisible One; Your property is eternal,[304] incorruptible One; Your figure is shapeless, inscrutable One; Your place (τόπος) is uncircumscribable, boundless One; the comprehension of You is incomprehensible, unsearchable One; the knowledge and contemplation of You is unseen and unknown, for You are unapproachable and unknowable; Your word is unspoken, inexpressible One; the explanation of You is unexplainable, ineffable One; the understanding of You is inconceivable, unthinkable One; and absolutely everything posited of You is negated in Your transcendence of it, O You who are beyond divinity. You are all wonder and serenity and courage and love and sweetness and gladness and trust in everything, and true peace (ἀμεριμνία) and joy, and You alone are enhypostatic (ἐνυπόστατος) glory and dominion and wisdom and power.[305] Hence You naturally and ineffably become ecstasy[306] out of all visible things and our rest from all intelligible ones, and repose in You is wondrous for all those who contemplate You through participation in the Holy Spirit, O unspeakable God!

---

[304] Wordplay: ἴδιον τὸ ἀΐδιον ("Your property is eternal").

[305] Enhypostatic. That is, God's glory, dominion (βασιλεία), wisdom, power are not qualities external to Him, but are eternal energies innate to the Hypostases of the Trinity. It may be noted that in Orthodox liturgical doxologies these attributes are constantly ascribed to God. "For Thine is the dominion, the power, and the glory, now and ever and unto the ages of ages. Amen."

[306] "Ecstasy" (ἔκστασις) means "stepping out of sth", either literally ("taking leave of, disengaging with") or mystically ("spiritual rapture, transport"); here it has both meanings.

90. Gregory the Theologian proclaims, "As we wonder at the Divine, we desire Him; and as we desire Him, He purifies us; and as He purifies us, He makes us like God (θεοειδεῖς); and once we have become akin to Him, He communes with us as with His own (οἰκεῖοι)."[307] And this is not only from God's perspective, but also those who have been purified thus encounter divine things and God Himself as realities akin to them *in spirit and in truth*. For this reason the Theologian also adds, "God is united with gods and is known by them." Do you see how wondrous this union is? For "God," he says, "is united with gods." And if there is such a union between them, it is clear that their dispositions and joys in this union will also be the same. For this reason he says, "and is known by them." So then, just as those who are deiform (θεοειδεῖς) and gods by grace commune with God and divine realities and know them as realities akin to them, so God in an analogous manner contemplates, communes, and is united with those who are 'deiform gods' as we mentioned above. Thus, the greatTheologian is right to explain further: "And God is made known to them", that is, to the pure and those who have become such gods, "perhaps to the same degree that He now knows them,"[308] that is, in a manner analogous to how He who is God by nature (φύσει) makes them gods by adoption (θέσει).[309] So then, do you see how far your theology may reach when you reason aright?[310] Indeed, they are very blessed who properly lift themselves to visions and contemplations of God with all the strength of their soul and with spiritual understanding, when you see all those who abide in God being in a state of wonder beyond wonder and of such great amazement before God's incomprehensibility (ἄληπτος)[311], on account of the beginninglessness, boundlessness, uncircumscribability, and perfect eternality and infinitude around Him. For this reason their *soul clings to God* with divine eros (Ps. 62:9); and they 'suffer' (πάσχειν) unbearable desire as they contemplate His divine face and its surpassing beauty and pine away with bliss. And then, following this, they are purified

---

[307] Gregory Nazianzen *Oration* 38.7.

[308] It might be noted about this bold statement (which St. Gregory himself admits with the phrase τολμᾷ τι νεανικὸν ὁ λόγος, "this idea breaks new ground") that Gregory begins and ends this quotation with apophatic statements about God's incomprehensibility, but also suggests God's paradoxical knowability. As Kataphygiotes' commentary shows, this knowledge is not so much rational as it is relational ("their dispositions and joys in this union will be much the same". A similar use of the word "to know" (γινώσκειν) is seen in the Last Judgment, Mt. 7:23.

[309] Or "by status". We have chosen to translate it as "by adoption" because of its relevance to the Scriptural teaching of "adoption as sons" υἱοθεσία (Rom. 8:14-15; cf. Eph. 1:5), which is so essential to Kataphygiotes' doctrine of deification, cf. ch. 10.

[310] In Greek, this succinct phrase has a wordplay: Πόσον τοίνυν εἰκάσαις τὸ εἰκὸς λογιζόμενος. The verb εἰκάζω suggests theological conjecture or, rather, analogical reasoning.

[311] ἄληπτος is the word Gregory Nazianzen uses, referring to the "incomprehensibility" of God that inspires the wonder at the beginning of the quotation: τῷ δὲ ἀλήπτῳ θαυμάζεται ("he wonders at His incomprehensibility"). From the time of St. Maximos, Gregory the Theologian's works were regarded with such reverence that they were often even exegeted in ways similar to Scripture and bound in splendid illuminated manuscripts.

through and through divinization (θεουργία) even become 'deiform gods' and are united with God in knowledge (γινωσκομένως). And He, indeed, becomes Himself knowable through the enrichment of those who are deified (περιουσίᾳ τῶν θεωθέντων) and by means of the supernatural gift of their deification and divine union, He enraptures all their noetic sensation in wonder and all their desire with His supreme beauty; He draws them around Himself like other angels, chanting in unbroken harmony, *God stands in the assembly of gods, and in their midst He will judge gods* (Ps. 81:1), and, *The Lord, the God of the gods, spoke and called forth the earth*, that is, the sons of earth, *from the east to the west* (Ps. 49:1). And for this reason *the rulers of the peoples were gathered unto the God of Abraham* (Ps. 46:10) and then took their place around God as *the Seraphim stood around Him* (Isa. 6:2), receiving divine illuminations of transcendent mysteries and cleaving to God inseparably, who is infinite times infinitely removed from all things. If, then, according to the beatitude of the Lord, *The pure in heart are blessed, because they shall see God* (Mt. 5:8), how could contemplatives not be most clearly blessed, as they are purified in their wonderment at the knowledge of God and ascend to the dignity of god through spiritual progress? So then, if we desire this beatitude and the experience (πάσχειν) of deification and thus to stand motionless as Cherubim around God, we must engage in contemplative knowledge and practice with all our diligence, in Christ Jesus, our Lord.

91. I so greatly desire to see You, and so then to praise You, O Life-Giver, the life of those who see You by any means possible, O Lord, my God, but although I desire to, I am unable to say anything worthy of You and I am truly overwhelmed and at a loss. O, how intimately does the intellect relate to You (οἰκείως), O Sovereign and all-wise Creator, and it has but only to see You and it can enjoy peace and its long-desired rest! For indeed, being intellect, it naturally desires to know (νοεῖν) and truly to comprehend (διανοεῖσθαι) by its own natural alacrity the highest things and by virtue of its own immateriality to cling all the more to the finer realities (τὰ ἰσχνότερα), once it has been freed from its wandering amidst external and visible things and come to stillness (σχολάζειν) in itself (cf. Ps. 45:11). In fact, by reason of its very nature it ascends spontaneously, as it were, to that which is higher than all things and even beyond all immateriality. It is also clear that the intellect, receiving the aid of the power of the Holy Spirit through faith, as it must, and thereby lifting itself up; or rather, since it is intellect itself, being actively drawn up to You by the intelligible realities around You (as if by things akin to its nature), intensely longs to see You with all the ardor of its soul. Then what wondrous and blessed things does it experience (πάσχειν), in accordance with its nature! For since it is in the intellect's nature, just as I have mentioned, to engage in intellection (φύσις νοερά) and it can wing its flight further and swifter than all other created things, and thus desires intelligible realities (τὰ νοητά), it therefore needs to know (νοεῖν) in the same way sensible animals need

to eat. For just as eating is proper to living, sensing beings, so is knowing proper to the intellect. Hence the intellect's true life and growth and enjoyment and delight come to it through the act of knowing, just as these qualities come to sensing animals through consumption. It experiences (πάσχειν) these things of course through action (δρᾶν), that is to say, by excelling in knowledge, and even more so when it reaches and inexpressibly attains You by the graciousness of Your Spirit, and its desire is mingled with the enrapturement of Your ineffable glory. For what might a creature with such desire naturally experience (πάσχειν) when it encounters something so ravishing (ἑλκτικός), and indeed so ravishing as You, to be enraptured – and this is just as Your providence saw fit – by something so desirable as You? For You, all-wise King, all-powerful and supremely good Lord, having created the intellect as a living being endowed with intelligence, You have wrought it such that it is able by nature to rejoice exceedingly in Your properties and to become ineffably possessed with Your divinity (ἐν κατοχῇ τοῦ θείου σου) in the ecstasy of divine eros, and even to fall madly in love with You, as it were, out of divine intoxication and enthusiasm (βακχικὸς ἐνθουσιασμός). And the intellect, having been created as so great a lover of goodness and beauty (φιλόκαλος), also has the precise attribute of being *philokalic* by nature, so that it is consequently endowed by Providence with the desire to know the best things and always to desire the things that are higher and further beyond (πρόσω) as well as to rejoice in anticipation of ever greater things. How then do You appear to it and enthrall it with the utmost wisdom, ravishing it by the eros of Your vision (θεωρία) so that it becomes ecstatic with all its soul, going beyond absolutely everything but You alone?

O Delightful One, You do not reveal Yourself to be only varied or simple, comprehensible or incomprehensible, fearful or gracious, but at one time You are this, and at another time that, so that by all these means [of manifesting Yourself] the motion and even the mutability of the intellect has nothing to turn to that is outside of Yourself, whether it is supposedly for the sake of variety or for the sake of simplicity, for the desire of the incomprehensible or the comprehensible, for the sake of solemn fear or gentleness. And in summary, since You are the all-comprehending Good and Beautiful One and even beyond goodness and beyond beauty (ὑπεράγαθος καὶ ὑπέρκαλλος) as the Creative Principle of all good and beautiful things, it is altogether impossible for the intellect to contemplate and abide and take delight in anything – in all the many and varied ways [that it desires] – except in You. For You have all things in Yourself as their Cause (αἰτιολογικῶς) and are found above all things, as their Creator, and You are infinite times infinitely beyond all beauty. Thus, while You are one in essence, O God, You are contemplated in many ways (ποικίλως) in Your energies, for they are many (πλῆθος), and again, as the great One, (πολύς), for they are great (μέγεθος). And what is even more wonderful and astonishing is that however You become comprehensible (ληπτός) to anyone, You still remain the same in the precise manner that [You manifest Yourself].[312] For You who are altogether incomprehensible according to essence are still by no means comprehended according to Your energy and therefore also Your power. For who can find the measure of Your power? And who has known Your wisdom? And who has fathomed the ocean of Your goodness? And, in short, who has come to a complete understanding of any one of Your properties (cf. Wis. 9:17; Is. 40:13)?

Nevertheless, You are certainly comprehensible (καταληπτός) in another manner. For surely when the intellect begins to contemplate the intelligible realities in visible things, it then eagerly ascends to the unity and incomprehensibility around You, O Savior. And because That which is comprehensible in You is lovely and altogether delightful, and the intellect itself is a lover of goodness and beauty (φιλόκαλος), it hastens in all diligence and ardently strives (φιλονεικεῖ) to rise even further beyond, as far it can. But when it can go no further, rightly considering that the object of its desire (φέρετρον) assuredly eludes it in its transcendence, it then becomes possessed and captivated by an intense kind of divine eros and is thus intoxicated with mad love for You (μανικῶς ἐκβακχεύεται), and it kindles fervent desires in the soul, making what is comprehensible of the Incomprehensible into fuel for divine love and rendering the impasse a passageway to greater desires (τὴν ἀπορίαν πορισμὸν ἐρώτων τιθέμενος). It is not so much attracted by what it comprehends about You, all-wise One, as it is excited by what eludes it, and because of the unattainability of this knowledge it is filled with great wonder and extraordinary yearning. And I would add that it persuades the intellect to seek, not of course what You are according to essence (since this is more than impossible to anyone whatsoever, in any case, and in any way), but the incomprehensible [aspect] of the divine power and energy of Your essence (οὐσιώδης)[313] and, in short, of the intelligible realities contemplated and theologically discerned around You, which are, as I have mentioned, infinite in magnitude (μέγεθος) and inscrutable in multitude (πλῆθος).[314] That is to say, even though it is impossible for the intellect to reach their limit (εἰς πέρας), since they are infinite (ἄπειρα), it is nevertheless possible for the intellect to proceed, by approaching You through purification (κάθαρσις) and gazing upon Your beauty, to brighter and clearer visions of the realities around You and to become deified in due measure. And thus do you inflame with the wound of divine eros (cf. Song 2:5) the intellect that rightly

---

[312] This paradox seems to resolve the question of divine simplicity.

[313] The fact that this energy is called οὐσιώδης ("of the essence", "essential") is one of many indications of the inseparability of energy and essence, although they are distinct.

[314] This seems to be the clearest statement Kataphygiotes makes concerning the identity of the divine energies with the intelligible realities around God.

waits on you, illuminating it more and more and leading it into impenetrable mystical visions beyond the heavens.

O heaven-sung Unity and Trinity of matchless worth, O bottomless profundity of power and wisdom! How, from this starting point, or rather starting line as one might say, you lead the intellect into Your exceedingly divine darkness (γνόφος), after it has been purified according to the rules of the race,[315] and guiding it *from glory to glory* (2 Cor. 3:18), and often even letting it dwell in the dazzling darkness (ὑπέρφωτος γνόφος). I do not know, as You know, whether it is the same darkness that Moses entered in ancient times (Ex. 20:21), or if the darkness Moses entered is an image of this darkness, or if this darkness is an image of the one he entered. However, that this darkness is manifestly an intelligible darkness and that within it the mysteries of spiritual union and love are divinely and supernaturally and ineffably celebrated in the secret place of the soul, this is what is understood with perfect clarity by those who have entered it by the torch light (δαδουχία) of the Illuminating Spirit.

92. Who, O Lord, Holy Trinity, being in this state, does not rejoice in seeing You who are the King and everlasting ruler and distributor of every beautiful and good thing and their bountiful source? And who, before seeing the vision of Your almighty sovereignty, can rejoice with true joy? No one, certainly! For this reason truly *blessed are the pure in heart* (Mt. 5:8), for they behold You with the eyes of the soul, You who are surpassing spiritual joy itself. And indeed they rejoice with gladness and great jubilation and are filled with unbearable yearnings (ἔρωτες), even though they often struggle with bodily ailments and suffer from demonic assaults. For the spiritual light shining from the beauty of Your face, Lord, is infinite times infinitely above any kind of worldly sorrow that may befall the person who receives its radiance through grace.

For this reason You go before us, who are all *sweetness, all desire* and holy yearning and ineffable eros (Song 5:16).[316] Then Your love leaves those who see You through some conception (κατά τινὰ ἐπίνοιαν) *wounded* with unbearable and immaterial pangs of *love* (Song 2:5). Here the souls of those by whom You are seen pursue and run *after the scent of Your perfumes* with intense and unyielding desire, O ineffable God (Song 1:4), and they strive by any means to draw You to themselves, wholly conquered and undone with wondrous longing for You. Hence they keep You in their intellect without forgetting, since they are captivated by Your supernatural beauty. Or rather, You Yourself first take possession of their

---

[315] There is a subtle athletic metaphor here.

[316] Cf. *Exact Rule and Canon*, 58.

hearts by day and by night, at all times through Your Spirit, and sleep flies from their eyelids; and the delight [...][317] But again, even when they do sleep, their *heart is awake* (Song 5:2) since they exult on their beds, as the prophet says (Ps. 149:5). And thus do they [always] see and are preserved in this state and are unable to grasp what is occurring, and they wonder (ἀπορεῖν) and become ecstatic because of the unspeakable radiance of Your face, the majesty of the glory of Your holiness, the transcendent ascents and mystical revelations they experience in themselves, the myriads of unutterable and ineffable secrets, the supremely good and beautiful gifts around You, Father [...] and may You support those who *dwell before Your face* in uprightness (Ps. 139:14)!

[317] This is a lacuna in the MS; see also below.

Saint Symeon Archbishop of Thessaloniki

ON THE SACRED AND DEIFYING PRAYER

Chapter 296

This divine prayer, the invocation of our Savior, in which we say "Lord Jesus Christ, Son of God, have mercy on me", is a prayer (προσευχή) and vow (εὐχή) and confession of faith; it invites the Holy Spirit and is a provider of divine gifts; it is a purification of the heart and a scourge of demons, an indwelling of Jesus Christ, and a source of spiritual perceptions and divine thoughts; it is redemption from sins, a hospital for souls and bodies, a bestower of divine illumination, a wellspring of God's mercy; it rewards us with revelations and divine initiations for humility, and is the only thing that saves, inasmuch as it bears in itself the saving name of our God. Indeed, the only name we invoke is that of Jesus Christ the Son of God, and we can be saved *in no one else*, as the Apostle Peter says (Acts 4:12). So then, it is a prayer (προσευχή), for through it we seek divine mercy. It is a vow (εὐχή) because we commit ourselves to Christ through His invocation.[318] It is a confession, for in confessing it Peter was called blessed (Mt. 16:17), and it invites the Spirit, for *no one can call Jesus Lord except in the Holy Spirit* (1 Cor. 12:3), and is a provider of divine gifts for on account of this confession, *I shall give to you,* Christ says to Peter, *the keys of the kingdom of heaven* (Mt. 16:18-9). It is a purification of the heart, for through it one sees God, and it beckons and purifies the beholder (Mt. 5:8). It is a scourge of demons, for in the name of Jesus Christ all demons were, and continue to be, driven out. It is an indwelling of Christ, for by calling Him to remembrance Christ is in us, and through this remembrance He dwells in us and fills us with gladness. For as Scripture says, *I remembered God and was made glad* (Ps. 76:4). It is a source of spiritual perceptions and thoughts, for Christ is the treasury of all *wisdom and knowledge* (Col. 2:3), and He bestows these treasures to those in whom He dwells. It is redemption from sins, for because of it, *all that you loose,* Christ says, *shall be loosed in heaven* (Mt. 16:19, 18:18). It is a hospital for souls and bodies, for the Apostle Peter says, *In the name of Jesus Christ, rise up and walk* (Acts 3:6), and also, *Aeneas, Jesus Christ heals you* (Acts 9:34). It is the bestower of divine illumination, for Christ is the True Light (Jn. 1:9), and He transmits His brightness and grace to those who call upon Him. And Scripture further says, *Let the brightness of our God be upon us* (Ps. 89:17), and, *He who follows Me shall have the light of truth* (Jn. 8:12). It is a wellspring of divine mercy, for it is mercy that we seek, and the Lord is merciful and has

[318] εὐχή means both "prayer", "vow", and "wish" in Ancient Greek, all of which imply "a word" that is given wholeheartedly. In Modern Greek, the Jesus Prayer is often simply called η ευχή.

compassion on all who call upon Him, and quickly vindicates those who cry out to Him. It rewards revelations and divine initiations to those who are humble, for even Peter, a humble fisherman, is given this confession through a *revelation* from *the Father in Heaven* (Mt. 16:17). Paul was *caught up in Christ* and heard revelations (2 Cor 12:2-4); and the prayer works (ἐνεργεῖ) in this way at all times. It is the only thing that saves, for *there is no one else*, as the Apostle Peter says, *in whom we must be saved* (Acts 4:12), namely, the Christ, the Savior of the world (Jn. 4:42). And for this reason, on the last day, *every tongue shall confess*, willingly or unwillingly, *that Jesus Christ is Lord, to the glory of God the Father* (Phil 2:11). And this is the sign of our faith, since we are and are called *Christ*-ians. It is the testimony that *we are of God* (1 Jn. 4:6). For *every spirit that confesses that the Lord Jesus Christ has come in the flesh is of God*, as we have said before, and *any spirit that does not confess this is not of God*. And this is precisely the spirit of the Antichrist: that which does not confess Jesus Christ (1 Jn. 4:2-3). Therefore, all believers must unceasingly confess this name, both for the proclamation of the faith and for the love of our Lord Jesus Christ, and nothing should ever separate us from this love (Rom. 8:35); for the grace from His name and forgiveness, redemption, healing, sanctification and illumination, and above all salvation. For it is in this divine name that the Apostles even wrought wonders and taught. And the Divine Evangelist says, *But these things have been written that you may believe that Jesus is the Christ, the Son of God*. Behold, what faith! *So that by believing, you may have life in His name*. Behold, salvation and life! (Jn. 20:31)

Chapter 297

That all Christians, clergy, monastics, and laypeople, should pray in the name of Jesus Christ, at least at a specific time, according to their strength.

Let every pious Christian say this holy name in prayer constantly, both with the intellect and with the tongue: both while standing and while travelling, while seated and while reclining; while saying or doing anything; and let him always compel himself to say this prayer. And in so doing he shall find the greatest serenity and joy, as those who have been diligent in this prayer know by experience. But since this task is beyond those living in the world and beyond even those monks who live in the midst of distractions, it is necessary for each of them to have a specific time set aside for this prayer, and all people, including clergy, monastics, and laypeople, should set this as a rule of prayer and practice it according to their strength. Those who live the monastic life, since they are in monastic orders for this purpose and have it as their necessary duty – even if they are serving amidst distractions – should force themselves at all times to keep the prayer active and to *pray unceasingly* to the Lord (1 Thess. 5:17), even in the case that they are prone to mental wandering and confusion and that which is, and is rightly called, the "captivity of the intellect". They should not be neglectful lest they be snatched away by the enemy, but rather return to the prayer, and rejoice in returning. Moreover, let the clergy be given charge of this apostolic work, for it is carried out as both divine preaching and divine actions, and represents the love of Christ [to men]. And let those in the world practice it according to their strength, keeping this prayer as a seal upon themselves, as a sign of faith and safeguard and sanctification, and a repellant against every temptation. Hence, everyone, including clergy, laypeople, and monastics, as soon as they arise from sleep should have Christ in their thoughts first and call Him to remembrance first, and they should offer this as the first-fruits of every thought in sacrifice to Christ. And since Christ who has saved us and so greatly loved us is deserving of our remembrance before every thought,[319] since we are and are called Christians. Indeed, we were clothed in Christ at Holy Baptism (Gal. 3:27), and were sealed with Him by the Consecrated Myrrh, and have partaken and continue to partake of His Holy Flesh and Blood. We are *members of His body*, and His *temple* (1 Cor. 12:27; 2 Cor. 6:16). We have *put on Christ*, and He dwells in us. And for this reason we ought to love Him and call Him to remembrance at all times. Therefore, let everyone set apart for this prayer a specific amount of time or a certain number of repetitions, each according to strength, as this is everyone's duty. But let what has been said suffice for now, since there are a great many things that can be learned by those who seek instruction concerning this subject.

[319] ἔννοια (thought) can also be translated "intention, plan".

A MARVELLOUS ORATION

On the Words of the Divine Prayer: "Lord Jesus Christ, Son of God, Have Mercy on Me"

How abundant is the power of the prayer, "Lord Jesus Christ, Son of God, have mercy on me"? And what manner of gifts does it bestow on those who practice it? And to what great dignity does it bring them? It is impossible for us to say and express this, since it is indeed beyond our strength. We may only say about the prayer of the Lord Jesus Christ whence it began and who were the first people who said the words of the prayer. So then, this prayer received its origin even from the very beginning, from Holy Scripture, and the three chief Apostles of Christ our Master spoke the words of the prayer, namely, Paul, John, and Peter, and we received the words from them like an inheritance passed down from one's forefathers;[320] and these words are divine mysteries and revelations of the Holy Spirit and utterances of God. For indeed we believe that all the things that the divine and Spirit-bearing apostles said or wrote are the words of Christ, which He spoke through the mouths of the apostles, since our Lord granted such a promise to them in the Holy Gospel, namely that He the Son, and the Father, and the Holy Spirit would *come and make their dwelling in them* (Jn. 14:23), and not only in the Apostles, but also in each and every Christian that keeps His commandments. Hence, the most divine Paul, who was made worthy to ascend to the third heaven, says, "Lord Jesus", saying, *no one can say "Lord Jesus" except in the Holy Spirit* (1 Cor. 12:3). And in saying this, the Apostle Paul shows in a truly marvellous way how this name is far more exalted and superior to all other names, so that it is not even possible for anyone to say it in any other way but by the Holy Spirit. Then, John the Theologian, who thundered forth[321] spiritual and theological words, took the end of Paul's words and made it his beginning, saying, *Every spirit that confesses that "Jesus Christ" has come in the flesh is of God* (1 Jn. 4:2). And again, when the divine apostle states this, he makes it clear how the name and confession of Jesus Christ comes from divine grace of the Spirit and does not come simply by chance. Likewise, Peter, the chief of the apostles, took John's end – that is, *Christ* – and made it his beginning. And at the time when our Lord asked His disciples, "*But you, who do you say that I am?*" Peter says, "*You are the 'Christ, the Son of God'* ", which *God the Father revealed to him from heaven* (Mt. 16:17), as our Lord testifies in the Holy Gospel. Consider, then, how these most sacred apostles of Christ say these words, and in what manner they are bound together, as in a circle; for the one mystically transmits divine utterances to the other, so that what

[320] Cf. Kallistos and Ignatios Xanthopoulos, *Exact Rule and Canon* 50.
[321] A reference to John the Theologian as one of the "sons of thunder", or "Boanerges", mentioned in Mk. 3:17, along with John's brother James.

the first says that word the second then takes as his beginning, as does the third, and so together they complete this prayer. For Paul says "Lord Jesus," John says "Jesus Christ," and Peter says "Christ, Son of God." Indeed, a marvellous circle is set in motion, so that the end, "Son of God", meets back at the beginning, "Lord". And this is because there is no difference between saying "Lord" and "Son of God", for both these titles manifest the divinity of the Only-Begotten Son of God. Now in order for everyone to understand this, we draw the circle here:

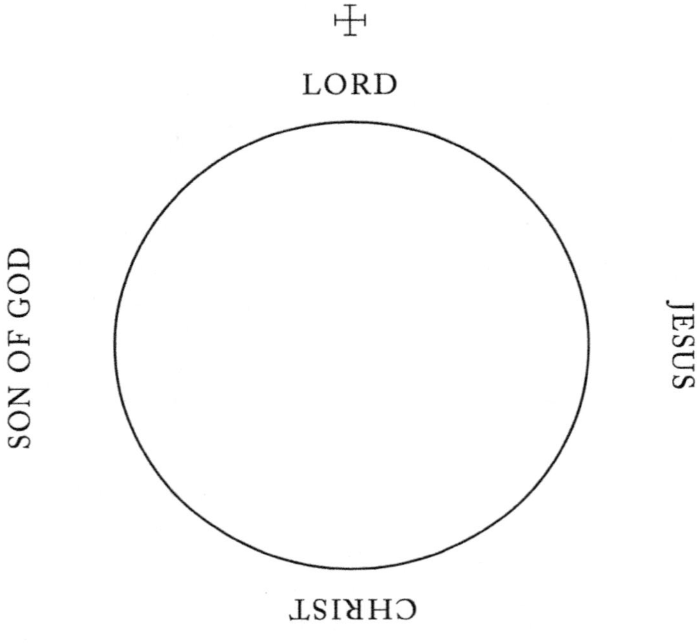

In this manner the blessed Apostles have passed down to us the tradition of both saying in the Holy Spirit and confessing: "Lord Jesus Christ, Son of God". And since there are also three of them, they are also trustworthy, for *every word is established* and confirmed by *three witnesses* (cf. Deut. 19:15; 2 Cor. 13:1). Even the order (τάξις) of Apostles who spoke these divine words was not without reason, but has its own explanation. For because the first who speaks is Paul, and the intermediary is John, and the last is Peter. The mystical tradition of the prayer of the Lord Jesus Christ began with Paul, who is a later disciple of Christ, coming after the others, and by means of John the prayer is passed on to Peter, who came first, and there it ends. And as far as I know, this signifies our orderly (τακτική) progress and union with God through practice, contemplation, and love. For Paul symbolizes practice, as he himself says, *I labored more abundantly than all* (1 Cor. 15:10), John symbolizes contemplation, as even his title "Theologian" indicates, and Peter symbolizes love, as our Lord shows when He says, *Peter, do you love Me? Tend My sheep* (Jn. 21:16). Therefore, whoever persists in this prayer makes progress in practical virtue as well, and from practice he ascends to contemplation, and thus acquires the love of God and is united with Him.

And these divine words do not only signify the things we have just mentioned, but they even reveal the correct doctrine of our faith and refute all the heresies of the heretics. For "Lord" reveals the divine nature of Christ and refutes the heresy of those who have claimed that He is only a man and not God.[322] Again, saying "Jesus" reveals the human nature of Christ and refutes the heresy of those who have claimed that He is only God and not man, but rather just appeared to be a man in an illusory manner.[323] Saying "Christ" reveals His two natures, the divine and the human, how both are united in one person and in one hypostasis, and it refutes the heresy of those who have claimed that Christ has two hypostases which are divided from one other.[324] And saying "Son of God" reveals how in Christ the divine nature remains without confusion even after its union with His human nature, and likewise His human nature is without confusion, and this refutes the heresy of those who have claimed that the divine and human natures in Christ were fused together and mixed up with each other.[325] Hence, these four words, as divine utterances and spiritual swords, overthrow and confute these two pairs of heresies, which, although they are diametrically opposed in the wickedness of their heresy, are also equal and alike in impiety. Again, here is an example for greater comprehension:

Lord
Overthrows the teachings of Paul of Samosata
Christ
Overthrows the teachings of Nestorius
Overthrows the teachings of Eutyches and Dioscoros, i.e. of the Monophysites
Over throws the teachings of the Armenians, i.e. of the Theopaschites
Son of God
Jesus

---

[322] e.g. Paul of Samosata.
[323] e.g. Theopaschites (cf. docetists and gnostics).
[324] e.g. Nestorians.
[325] e.g. Monophysites.

These have been passed down to us by the Holy Fathers who were wise in the things of God and perfect and Spirit-bearing men. In addition to handing down each of the divine words "Lord Jesus Christ, Son of God" as a tradition, they also received the impression of these words deep in their hearts and greatly loved them. Indeed the sweetest name of Jesus, which they alone kept as a perfect and complete prayer in for which they struggled unceasingly all their lives – how could they possibly be satiated with the sweetness of Jesus? They were always hungering and thirsting for Jesus. Indeed, they were filled with inexpressible spiritual joy and enjoyed divine gifts and were even brought outside of this world, and it is as if they were angels upon the earth or heavenly human beings, to such a height of virtue did they ascend by means of the sweetest name of Jesus. However, to us who are beginners and imperfect, they rightly passed down the tradition of saying "Have mercy on me" in addition; that is, "Lord Jesus Christ, Son of God, have mercy on me." Not for any other reason than for us to recognize our limitations and our condition, and how we need the rich and abundant mercy of our Holy God. We are like the blind person about which the Sacred Gospel speaks, who desired to receive the light of his eyes, and so cried out the moment our Lord was passing by and said, *Jesus, have mercy on me* (Mk. 1:47). So we too are like the blind man in our souls, calling out to God for him to show us His mercy and to open the eyes of our soul that we might see Him noetically. And hence, they also prescribed for us to say "Have mercy on me." Moreover, others who wish to observe the commandment to love one's neighbor in this manner say the prayer as follows: "Lord Jesus Christ, our God, have mercy on us." And they make supplication on behalf of all their brothers, for they have come to know how love is *the fulfillment of the law and the prophets* (Rom. 13:10; Mt. 22:40), and is a virtue which contains every commandment and spiritual work in its own principle. Thus, they unite their prayer with the love of neighbor too, and they supplicate God to have mercy on both themselves and their brothers, and in this way they move God more greatly to have mercy on them. For they address God jointly, namely, as the God of us all, because they seek His universal mercy for all the brethren. And certainly then the mercy of the All-Holy God is wont to come to us when He sees how we keep the right faith in our doctrines and the fulfillment of the commandments in our deeds, both of which are encompassed within the short line of the prayer, "Lord, Jesus Christ, our God, have mercy on us."

Furthermore, regarding the divine names "Lord Jesus Christ," if we also wish to examine the times when they were initially spoken, we will again find them in the order in which we say them. That is, we say "Lord," and then "Jesus," and lastly "Christ." For in the Old Testament we find in all places, both before and after the law, the Son and Word of God being called "Lord," as in the time of Lot when Scripture says, *The Lord rained fire from the Lord* (Gen. 19:24), and in his psalms

David says, *The Lord said to my Lord* (Ps. 109:1; Mt. 22:44). Then, when Gabriel announced the good news of the Incarnation of the Son of God to the Theotokos and tells her, *You shall call His name Jesus* (Lk. 1:31). For truly the Son and Word of God the Lord and Master and God of all, in His supreme goodness and compassion willed to become man in order to save man, and for this he is also called Jesus, which means 'savior' and 'redeemer' of man. Lastly, saying "Christ" reveals the deification of the human nature that our Lord assumed when He was incarnate and became man. Before His passion and death he prevented His disciples and did not yet allow them to proclaim Him as the Christ. But after His passion and resurrection, with great outspokenness before the Jews, the Apostle Peter calls Him Christ, saying, *Let all the house of Israel know that God has made Him both Lord and Christ* (Acts 2:36). For when the Son and Word of God assumed our human nature, it was immediately anointed[326] by His Divinity, but after He was crucified, rose from the dead, and ascended to heaven, took His seat at the right hand of the Father, it was then raised to equal honor with God. This is why only after the Ascension did the time come for the title of Christ to be revealed and for the Apostles to preach Him as Christ and Son of God and God. And so it is that we first say, "Lord," then "Jesus," and lastly "Christ" and "Son of God" as it appears in the prayer, "Lord Jesus Christ, Son of God, have mercy on me," which our Fathers wise in things divine received as an ancestral inheritance from the Holy Apostles, and which they passed down unto us. About these words of the prayer we have spoken only as much as is in our power, as if picking flowers from a great and beautiful tree. But let the fruits which are found to be so bountiful in these divine words be described by others, namely, by those who over a long period of time and experience have progressed in the labor of this prayer, and tasted the sweetness of its fruit, and reached perfection.

---

[326] Christ (Χριστός) means the "Anointed One".

An Interpretation of the Prayer "Lord Have Mercy" Beneficial for Every Christian[327]

The prayer "Lord Jesus Christ, have mercy on me", as well as the briefer form "Lord have mercy", was given to Christians from the time of the Apostles, and it was appointed for Christian to say it unceasingly, just as the Apostles themselves said it. Moreover, what the "Lord have mercy" expresses is known by very few people today and alas! every day they unprofitably and vainly cry out "Lord have mercy!", without receiving the mercy of the Lord since they do not know what they are seeking. Hence we must understand how the Son and Word of God was incarnate and became man, suffered such torments, was crucified, and how by the shedding of His All-Holy Blood He redeemed man from the grasp of the devil, and thereafter became the Lord and Master (ἐξουσιαστής) of human nature. Indeed, even before His Incarnation was He Lord of all created things, visible and invisible, as their Creator and Fashioner; however, humans and demons who did not want Him as their Lord and Master did not accept Him as their own Lord, even though He is the Lord of all the world. For since the All-Good God made angels and humans self-ruling (αὐτεξούσιοι) and granted them reason, so that they might have knowledge and discernment, in His truth and righteousness, He did not wish to remove their self-rule (αὐτεξούσιον) and to become their Lord by force or against their will. Rather He rules and becomes Lord over those who desire to be under His authority and care (κυβέρνησις). And again, He lets those who do not desire this to do their own will, since they are endowed with self-rule. Thus Adam, who was deceived by the apostate devil and so became apostate himself, chose not to obey God's commandment, and God left him to his own self-rule, not wishing to rule over him with force. However, the envious devil who had deceived man from the beginning, did not cease leading him further astray until he made him resemble the senseless beasts in his irrationality, and so man came to live as an irrational and senseless animal. Nevertheless, the All-Merciful God had compassion on him and looked from heaven and descended to earth and became man for the sake of man, and with His All-Immaculate Blood He redeemed man from the slavery of sin, through the Holy Gospel He taught him how to live a God-pleasing life. Moreover, according to John the Theologian, he granted us the *authority* (ἐξουσία) *to become children of God* (Jn. 1:12), and by Holy Baptism he gave us a second birth and refashioned us, and by His immaculate mysteries He nourishes every soul and gives it life. In short, in His perfect wisdom He has found the way to remain

[327] Anonymous author.

unseparated from us at all times and we unseparated from Him, so that the devil might no longer be given any room to interfere.

So then, those Christians who, after being made worthy of so many graces and receiving such benefits from Christ the Master, have again been led astray by the devil, separated themselves from God through the world and the flesh, and are dominated by sin and by the devil by doing his will, but are not so completely insensitive as not to sense the evil they have suffered, understanding their error and recognizing their enslavement; seeing that they cannot save themselves, these Christians run towards God and cry out, "Lord have mercy!" so that the All-Merciful Lord may show compassion and have mercy on them, accept them as the Prodigal Son, and grant them His divine grace again in order to be delivered from the slavery of sin, to separate themselves from the demons, and to receive back their freedom to live in a God-pleasing manner and keep the commandments of God. These, then, are the Christians who, as we have said, cry out "Lord have mercy," in a desire to attain by all means the mercy of the All-Good God, genuinely wishing to receive His grace to be freed from the slavery of sin and be saved. But if Christians have absolutely no knowledge of the things we have mentioned, then neither do they recognize their own misfortune of being enslaved to the will of the flesh and worldly things, nor do they have the opportunity to consider the slavery they are in, and without any sense of purpose only say "Lord, have mercy", more out of habit than anything else. But how is it possible for them to receive the mercy of God, and indeed such a wondrous and boundless mercy? In fact, it would be better for them not to receive God's mercy than to receive it just to lose it again, since this would only serve to bring double the blame. Likewise, if someone puts a precious gem into the hands of a little child or any boorish man that does not know its worth, and they lose it as soon as they're given it, it is clear that it wasn't they who lost it, but rather he who gave it to them.

And so that you might better understand what has been said, consider how in this world, he who is poor and in need and desires to receive alms of mercy (ἐλεημοσύνη) from a rich man will go up to him and say, "Have mercy on me." That is to say, "Take pity on me for my poverty and give me care (κυβέρνησις)." Or again, he who has a debt and desires to give what he owes to the lender goes to him and says, "Have mercy on me." That is to say, "Take pity on me for my want of means, and spare me the debt I owe." Similarly, the offender, who desires sympathy from the one he offended, goes to him and says, "Have mercy on me." That is to say, "Forgive me for how I offended you." But if the sinner cries out to God, "Lord, have mercy," yet does not understand what he is saying, or why he is saying it, or what the mercy of God is which is seeking, or how the mercy that he seeks benefits him, but says only out of habit, "Lord, have mercy," he finds nothing. And so, how can God give him His mercy, seeing that he does not understand it, neglects it, swiftly loses it again, and even sins more?

God's mercy is none other than the grace of the All-Holy Spirit, which we sinners must seek from God, and unceasingly cry out, "Lord, have mercy," meaning: "Take pity on me, my Lord, I who am a sinner in a pitiable condition, and receive me again into Your grace. Grant me a spirit of strength, to strengthen me to resist the temptations of the devil and the evil habit of sin. Grant me a spirit of moderation, that I may have self-control, and that I may come to my senses to be corrected. Grant me a spirit of fear, so that I may fear You and keep your commandments. Grant me a spirit of love, so that I may love You and no longer be separated from Your presence. Grant me a spirit of peace, to keep my soul peaceful and that I may gather all of my thoughts and remain still (ἥσυχος) and undisturbed. Grant me a spirit of purity that I may keep myself clean from every defilement. Grant me a spirit of meekness, that I may be gentle towards my fellow Christians and refrain from anger. Grant me a spirit of humility, that I may not think highly of myself with arrogance."

So then, he who recognizes what he needs judging from all of the above, and seeks such things from the All-Merciful God by crying out, "Lord, have mercy", will most certainly receive what he seeks and will attain the mercy of the Lord and His divine grace. But he who understands none of the things we have said, but only says "Lord, have mercy" out of habit, will never be able to receive God's grace. For even after having received many graces from God, he has not recognized them, nor has he thanked God for granting them. He received God's mercy already from the moment he was fashioned and made as a human being. He received God's mercy when he was refashioned through Holy Baptism and became an Orthodox Christian. He received God's mercy every time he was rescued from all the dangers of soul and body he has experienced in his life. He received God's mercy all the times he has been made worthy to partake of the Immaculate Mysteries. He received God's mercy as many times as he sinned against God and grieved Him with his sins, and yet was not destroyed or chastised as he deserved. He received God's mercy from all the ways he was shown goodness by God although he did not recognize it. Indeed, he has forgotten all of these things and has absolutely no concern for his salvation. So then, how can such a Christian receive God's mercy if he does not perceive and recognize that he is receiving such great grace from God, as we have said, or if he does not, is what he is saying, simply crying out, "Lord, have mercy," without any purpose or goal, but only out of habit?

Saint Symeon the New Theologian

DISCOURSE ON FAITH

and instruction addressed to those who claim that it is impossible for those who are in the world and have worldly cares to reach the perfection of virtue; and an explanation regarding this in the beginning, which is greatly beneficial.[328]

My beloved brothers and Fathers, it is very good, and brings great benefit to the soul, for us to proclaim commonly to all people the great and boundless mercy of our All-Good and Most-Merciful God, and to make known to all our Christian brethren the unsearchable sea of God's compassion and goodness towards us. And so I, as you can see, my brothers, and as you know very well, although I did not do many or strenuous fasts, or vigils, or spend many nights sleeping on the ground, or any other similar strenuous hardships of the body, but simply recognized by unworthiness, repented of my sins, condemned myself and was humbled, and in this way the Most-Compassionate and All-Good Lord saved me, just as the Divine David says, *I was humbled, and He saved me* (Ps. 114:6). And to put it in a few words, I only believed in the words of God, and my Lord and God received me by this faith. For one to acquire humility, he finds many obstacles that hinder him. But somehow, there is no obstacle that can keep him from finding faith and believing in the words of God. For if we were to wish to find faith with all of our soul, we would find it immediately without any effort. For faith is a gift from the All-Good God, who has bestowed it upon us so that we may naturally have it within our reach, and to have it when we so desire, with our own free will. For this reason we can see how the Tatars and barbarians and all of the nations naturally have faith, and each one believes in the words of the other, which shows how they have faith amongst themselves. And that I might demonstrate to you what I am saying with acts and not just words, hear the following story.

There was a man by the name of George, quite young in age, about twenty years old, who resided in Constantinople in our own times. He was charming in intellect but had an external bearing such that many held him in low regard, especially those people who are accustomed to looking at only the outer appearance of man without knowing what is hidden in each person, but condemn them and become indiscriminate critics of others. This young man became acquainted with a most holy monk who dwelt in a monastery in Constantinople, and he revealed to this monk all of the hidden things of his heart, and even told him how he yearned for

---

[328] This text is not translated from Ancient Greek, but from a Modern Greek translation in the original edition of the *Philokalia* for the purpose of accessibility.

the salvation of his soul and had a great desire to depart from the world and become a monk. And that honorable elder praised him for his goal, and he instructed him as needed and gave him the book of St. Mark the Ascetic to read the part *On the Spiritual Law*. The young man took the book with such eagerness and reverence as if it were sent to him by God, and he had such faith in it, as well as hope that he would receive the greatest profit from it. So on his way home, he immediately began reading with great attention and read through the whole thing with much reverence three or four times, and never again did it leave his hands. Just as he had hoped, he benefited greatly from that book. However, he picked out just three chapters to learn by heart, and decided to put them into practice and to keep them with all his attention.

One chapter said the following: "If you seek to find healing in your soul, make sure to have great diligence and care in guarding your conscience well so that it does not reprove you in any matter. And whatever good deeds your conscience tells you to do, do not grow tired or hesitant, but do them, and you shall find great benefit."

The next chapter said the following: "Whoever seeks to acquire the gifts of the Holy Spirit without having first kept God's commandments is like a slave who requests a certificate of freedom from his master the very moment he is handing over the silver to purchase the slave."

And the third chapter said: "He who prays with his mouth but has neither acquired spiritual knowledge, nor learned how to pray noetically, is like the blind man who cried out in his blindness, *Son of David, have mercy on me*! (Mk. 10:47). But he who has acquired spiritual knowledge and prays noetically and has opened the eyes of his soul, is like this same blind man after the Lord had healed him from his blindness, when he received the light of his eyes and saw the Lord and no longer called Him 'Son of David' but rather confessed Him to be the Son of God, and worshipped Him as he ought (Jn. 9:38)."

The young man liked these three chapters very much and he greatly marveled at them; he received assurance in his soul, and believed without a doubt that he would greatly benefit if he took good care of his conscience, as St. Mark says, so that he might enjoy the gifts of the Holy Spirit and His energy by keeping God's commandments, and how in the third chapter he said that by the grace of the Holy Spirit one could be made worthy to open the eyes of the soul and to see the Lord noetically. Thus, in hoping that he would see the unspeakable beauty of the Lord, he was wounded in his heart by this eros and love for God and had a great yearning for it. However, he did nothing else, as he assured me later with an oath, other than doing the prayers and prostrations the holy elder enjoined him to do every night before he went to bed to sleep.

So then, a short time passed as he was attending well to his conscience, when one night, while keeping that rule of prayer the elder gave him, his conscience told him to do yet more prayer and more prostrations, and even to say "Lord Jesus Christ, have mercy on me" as many times as he could. He then obeyed what his conscience told him with great zeal, and immediately began to do it without any hesitation, having faith that the things it told him were said to him by God Himself. And from then on he no longer fell into his bed to sleep before first doing what his conscience told him he could. In this way he was obedient to his conscience and it ever increased and told him to do more, and in a little while his prayer greatly increased, as we have said, each night. During the day he did not have the opportunity to pray because he managed the whole household of an important magistrate with several cares, responsibilities, and daily visits to the Imperial Palace; but being left without time to pray by day, every evening he would pray before going to bed, as we have said. Then his heart would begin to feel warmth, compunction would come to it, and abundant tears would stream from his eyes; and he would often do a great deal of kneeling and recite other prayers to the Theotokos with sighs and pain of heart. It would seem to him as if he were standing before the Lord bodily, and he would fall before His immaculate feet and beseech Him with tears that he might be shown compassion, just as the Lord showed it to the blind man as the Holy Gospel says, and to grant unto him the light of the eyes of his soul. And day after day, his nightly prayer so increased that he would stay up till midnight and while praying he would upright like a column and never even shifted his feet or any other part of his body; neither would he turn his gaze from one place to the other to look around, but rather stood with great fear and trembling without growing weary, nor did despondency or sloth ever come to him.

Thus, one night while he was praying and saying noetically with his intellect, "God, be merciful to me, a sinner" (Lk. 18:13), a divine brightness suddenly shone upon him, and both the entire place and the young man were filled with that light. Now the blessed George, as I call him, remained ecstatic and forgot his very own self and whether he was even inside a house, for he saw light everywhere as if he were outside. He neither understood at that time whether he was stepping upon the earth or standing in the air, nor had he a single bodily or worldly care in his intellect, and completely forgot the whole world and was united and became one with that divine light. For it seemed to him that he himself became light and was wholly filled with tears and an indescribable joy. And then his intellect ascended to Heaven and there he beheld an even more resplendent light and there he saw standing near to that light the holy elder who, as we mentioned, gave him the book by Abba Mark and his rule of prayer. And I, having heard these things from the young man, understood how the intercession of the holy elder also assisted (ἐσυνέργησε) greatly in this miracle, and God so arranged (οἰκονόμησεν) it in order to show the young man how great a height of virtue this holy elder had attained, and for this reason he saw him standing in the midst of this light. Then, when this vision had passed and this young man came to himself, he was full of joy and wonder, as he described it, and tears streamed from his heart. And along with those tears followed an intense sweetness. Finally, he fell into bed so as to sleep a little, when the rooster began to crow, and not long after the church bells rang for Matins, and the young man rose to read the Matins prayers as was his custom. And that night he did not sleep at all, nor did any thought of sleep even come to him.

The young man himself told me about how these things occurred to him. He assured me that he did nothing else, but only the things you have heard, and moreover, he had faith and hope without doubt and for this he was made worthy to behold such a vision. Now, let no one tell me that he just did these things to test God, since he, as he told me, never even entertained the thought of testing God, but simply had undoubting faith. Thus, by rejecting every fleshly and worldly thought (λογισμός) from his mind (λόγος), he was most diligent in guarding his conscience and carrying out the good things his conscience told him, so that he grew indifferent (ἀναίσθητος) to the affairs of this world and no longer even felt them (αἰσθάνετο). He also no longer had any appetite to eat or drink, so that he often continued fasting. Do you hear, my beloved brothers, the kinds of things faith accomplishes? And how much power it has when it is secured by good deeds? Do you recognize how neither does our youth harm or hinder us in anything, nor again does our old age benefit us if we are lacking the fear of God? Have you now learned how neither the world nor our governments can prevent us from doing the commandments of God as long as we are willing? And how neither does departure from the world or living in the solitude of the desert benefit us if we still remain slothful and negligent? Do we not all hear how King David, while having so many cares and royal duties, kept his intellect completely and wholly dedicated to God? And do we not wonder and say, "How did he become *David* and not just anybody?" And consider how God's commandments were followed more closely by this young man than by David. For David received direct testimony from God Himself, was anointed both Prophet and King, and received the grace of the Holy Spirit. And if at one time he erred before God and lost the grace of the Holy Spirit and the rank of prophecy and was estranged from communion with God, and then later came to his senses, remembered the good things he had lost, and sought to regain them, what is wonderful in that? What is wonderful and worthy of praise is how a young man of twenty years, who had his intellect fixed on worldly and ephemeral things, thought of nothing higher than them (nor did any such though even enter his mind), simply listened to a word from that holy elder, read those three chapters of Abba Mark, immediately believed without a doubt in what was written and put them into practice with unequivocal hope, and by that little labor he was made worthy to lift his intellect to heaven and move the Theotokos to have compassion on him, so that by her intercession to God the young man was so reconciled to Him, that He even sent him His divine illumination from heaven and the grace of the All-Holy Spirit, which enabled him to reach heaven and to enjoy that light which so many desire but so few attain.

This young man, the blessed George, who neither fasted for long periods of time, nor kept vigil, who neither engaged in other ascetic struggles, nor ever slept on the ground, who neither wore bristly clothes, nor became a monk or physically depart from the world, became an earthly angel and a heavenly man simply through the little vigil and prayer he did; a man in appearance and bodiless in contemplation[329]; contained and uncontained; seen by all and only found with only present with God alone, who knows all things. In this way he was deemed worthy to see that sweetest light of the noetic sun of righteousness. And rightly so, for the love and longing he had for God caused him to go beyond the world spiritually, to forget both the world and the flesh and all of the vanities thereof, and to attend to God completely, and thus he became wholly spiritual and wholly light and capable of seeing such a great vision and enjoying such delight. And indeed he still dwelt in a city, and in the city he spent time in the Imperial Palaces, and had authority over a great estate, with so many servants and other assistants, services and responsibilities both great and overwhelming.

But what we have said is quite enough both in praise of that young man and to give you reason to desire this yourselves and to imitate him, so that you may be made worthy to receive such grace from God. Or would you like me to tell you even greater things than this? "But what is greater than the fear of God?" as Gregory the Theologian says. For is not *the fear of God the beginning of wisdom*? (Prov. 9:10). "For where there is fear of God, there is the keeping of the commandments, and where there is the keeping of the commandments, there is the purification of the flesh, which is that thick cloud obscuring the soul and preventing it from seeing the divine radiance. And again, where there is purification of the flesh, there is divine illumination. And where there is divine illumination, there is the fulfillment of divine longing."[330] Moreover, divine illumination and the enlightenment of the Holy Spirit is the unending end (τέλος ἀτελείωτον) of every virtue. And whoever

---

[329] ἄγγελος ἐπίγειος καὶ ἄνθρωπος ἐπουράνιος, ἄνθρωπος εἰς τὸ φαινόμενον καὶ ἄσαρκος εἰς τὸ νοούμενον

[330] Gregory Nazianzen, *Oration* 39.8.

reaches this goal (τέλος) has finished (ἐτελείωσεν) with sensible things and begun to attain the knowledge of spiritual ones.

These, my brethren, are the wonders of the Holy God. For this reason the All-Wise God reveals His hidden saints, so that others might imitate them and take up their way of life themselves. Or else, if they do not imitate them, that they might remain without a defense and have no excuse. For even those who are found amidst distractions and disturbances, as long as they conduct themselves well, are saved and made worthy to receive the great blessings from God simply through the faith they have in Him alone. So then, take pity on your souls, brethren, and believe with your whole heart in our Lord and His words without any doubt, and despise the false things of the world, leaving them and treating them as the fleeting things they are, and *draw near to God* and *cleave* to Him (Ps. 33:6; 62:9). For without God there is nothing in the world. All things are as nothing when God is absent. This is why I cry and lament and grieve exceedingly when I consider how we have a Master so generous and loving of mankind, who grants such gifts as we have never seen or heard of simply through that faith in His words and promises which we show through our actions, and yet we inconsiderately, like the irrational beasts, prefer the earth and earthly things and perishable goods, which the All-Good God gives lavishly to us in His utmost compassion for the needs of the body, that it might be cared for in moderation, with as much as needs to live. This is so that the soul too might not have any hindrance, but be concerned for itself and behave as it ought, to be nourished itself by noetic food, and by the grace of the Holy Spirit.

For this is why man came into the world: to find reasons in all the things of the world for glorifying God who granted them to him, and to know his Benefactor and His benevolence, to yearn after Him and give thanks to him, both with words of thanksgiving and with God-pleasing deeds done in gratitude to Him. And thus is he made worthy to receive yet other benefactions from God, gifts even greater and eternal. But alas! We are completely unconcerned about the things of the future, but are wholly given to present ones, we take thought for these and act diligently to acquire them, to be filled with them, while giving no thought to Him who has given them to us. In fact, we show tremendous ingratitude towards Him and become like demons or even worse, to tell the truth. And this is why we should be punished even more than they, for we have also received greater benefactions having been born and baptized as Christians, received such mysteries and spiritual gifts; moreover, we believe in One God who became man for us and suffered such torments and and lastly death on the Cross so that he might free us from the deceit of the devil and from sin. And for all this, we believe Him with words alone, while by our deeds we completely deny him. Is not the name of Christ proclaimed everywhere today, in the cities, villages, monasteries, and desert? But, allow me to say, have you examined the matter precisely to learn just how many Christians keep His commandments? Even with difficulty will you find among them a single person who might truly be Christian in both words and deeds. Did our Lord not say in the Holy Gospel, *He who believes in Me, the works that I do he will do also; and greater works than these he will do* (Jn. 14:12)? Now who of us dares to say, "I do the works of Christ and I rightly believe in Him"? Do you see, brethren, how will be found to be faithless on that fearful day of judgement (cf. Lk. 18:8)? And we are more deserving of condemnation than those who do not know Christ at all, nor believe in Him? For it is necessary that either we be judged as unbelievers, or our Lord Jesus Christ, who is Truth Himself, shall be shown forth to be a liar, which is impossible.

Thus, I have written these things, my brothers, not with the intent to prevent Christians from departing from the world or from *hesychia*, preferring the way of life in the world. May this never be! Rather my intention is to inform those who read the present work that whoever wants and desires with all his heart and soul to do what is good and attain virtue has received power from the Almighty God to be capable of doing so in every place, and even to become worthy of divine gifts and divine contemplations just as that blessed youth George, whom I beseeched as my acquaintance and dear friend to narrate these things to me, just as I have written. For this reason, my brothers in Christ, I exhort us all to also have willingness and desire in our hearts to do good and to walk with undoubting faith and hope that we might fulfill the commandments of God. For our Lord is faithful and there is no falsehood in Him (Jn. 7:18; Thess. 3:3; Tit. 1:2). Let our faces not be ashamed (Ps. 33:6). Most assuredly we desire to be given the strength to accomplish every good thing wherever we may be: in cites, in villages, in monasteries, or in desert places. For the All-Good God, according to His promise, opens the doors of His Kingdom to everyone who ceaselessly knocks, and He grants the grace of the All-Holy Spirit to everyone who seeks it, and it is impossible for the person who seeks with all his soul not to find the wealth of the gifts of God (Mt. 7:8-9), to whom be the glory unto the ages of ages. Amen.

DISCOURSE ON THE THREE FORMS OF PRAYER[331]

There are three forms of attention (προσοχή) and prayer (προσευχή) through which the soul is lifted up and progresses, or else cast down and lost. For as long as the soul practices each aspect of these three forms at a suitable time, as it should, then it makes progress; but if it practices them foolishly and in an untimely manner, then it is cast down. And so, attention must be as bound to prayer and inseparable from it as the body is inseparable from the soul, and the one cannot stand without the other. Thus attention should go before to watch for enemies like a guard, and first battle against sin and resist evil thoughts that come to the soul. Then, attention must be followed by prayer, which extinguishes and destroys all those wicked thoughts. It is on this war waged jointly by attention and prayer that the life or death of the soul depends; for if we guard and maintain pure prayer with attention we progress. However, if we do not take heed to keep it pure, but leave it unguarded and defiled by evil thoughts, then we will become vile and stalled in our progress. So then, since we have said how there are three forms of attention and prayer, let us speak about the characteristics of each form so that the person who loves and seeks salvation may choose what is best and avoid what is unprofitable.

On the First Form of Attention and Prayer.

The characteristics of the first are as follows: When one stands in prayer, he raises his hands, eyes, and intellect to heaven, and with his intellect he ponders divine thoughts and imagines (φαντάζεται) the blessings of heaven, the hosts of the holy angels, and the tabernacles of the saints, and, in brief, he gathers with his intellect all that he has heard from the Holy Scriptures and then thinks about them at the hour of prayer; he looks up to heaven and stirs his soul with them to divine love and eros, and sometimes he cries and weeps; but little by little, his heart may become prideful without his realizing it, and it appears to him as if the things he does come from divine grace for his reward and consolation, and he asks God to always make him worthy to engage in this work of prayer. But these are signs of delusion (πλάνη). For what seems to be good is not good when it does not come about in a good and proper manner. For such a person, if he were to engage in extreme *hesychia* in solitude, it would be impossible for him not to go out of his mind and lose his wits. Or else, if by some chance he does not go mad, he will still

[331] Ascribed to Saint Symeon the New Theologian in the original *Philokalia*. This text is not translated directly from Ancient Greek, but from a Modern Greek translation from the original Greek edition of the *Philokalia*.

never be able to come to the knowledge and acquisition of the virtues or dispassion (ἀπάθεια).

While using this method of prayer there have also fallen into delusion those who have seen light and illumination with their bodily eyes, perceived sweet aromas with their sense of smell, and heard voices with their ears, and other similar things. Again, others have become possessed by demons and go roaming from place to place having lost their minds. There are yet others who accepted Satan when he appeared to them disguised as an angel of light (2 Cor. 11:14), deceived by him, and remained stubbornly irremediable to the end, without heeding advice from any of their brothers. There have even been some who were moved by the devil to kill themselves, by casting themselves down from cliffs or hanging themselves, and who can tell the different deceits of the Devil by which he leads them astray? Such things cannot be told. But from what we have said, any prudent person can understand what kind of harm may come from this first form of attention and prayer. Even if one happens to engage in this form of prayer and does not suffer any of the evils we have mentioned because he is a part of a community of brethren (since monastics who live reclusively are the most prone to such evils), he will still spend all of his life without progress.

On the Second Form.

The second form of attention and prayer is as follows: one concentrates his intellect within himself, removing it from all sensory things, guards his senses, and gathers all of his thoughts to keep them from musing about the vain things of this world. Sometimes he examines his thoughts, and at other times he attends to the words of the prayer he is saying. At one time he recovers his thoughts which had been taken captive by the devil and dragged into evil and vanity, and at another time with great effort and forcefulness he comes back to himself after having been dominated and overcome by a passion. And since he has this constant struggle and battle within himself, it is impossible for him ever to be at peace, or to find time to practice the virtues and receive *the crown of righteousness* (2 Tim. 4:8). For such a person is like someone that fights his enemies in the darkness of the night. He hears the voices of his attackers and receives their blows but cannot see clearly who they are and where they are coming from, or how and why they are assaulting him. For the darkness he finds himself to be in is in his intellect and the confusion is in his thoughts (λογισμοί), and they cause him great harm and it is impossible for him to flee from his enemies, the demons, to keep them from destroying him. And the unfortunate person endures the toil of this fight all in vain, for he loses the reward by being dominated by vainglory (κενοδοξία) without realizing it, and it appears to him as if he were actually attentive. Moreover, he often even despises others out of pride and judges them and commends himself, imagining in his own fantasy that he is worthy of becoming a shepherd and pastor of sheep and of leading them himself. He is like a blind man who claims he can lead other blind men (Mt. 15:14).

This is the second form, and everyone who desires salvation has the duty to learn about the harm it can bring to the soul and to take good care. However, this second form is still better than the first, just as a moonlit night is better than a gloomy, moonless midnight.

On the Third Form.

The third form is truly wonderful and difficult to explain. And to those who do not know it, it is not only difficult to understand, but it appears to them almost incredible and they do not understand how such a thing can be done, because in these days this form of prayer is not found among many, but only among few. And as I think, this good thing departed from us when we forsook obedience, for the obedience of each person toward his spiritual father is what makes him free from care and anxiety (ἀμέριμνος), for when he has cast his care upon his spiritual father (cf. 1 Pet. 5:7) he is then far from the anxiety and passion of this world and becomes a very willing and earnest practitioner of this third form. That is, as long as desires to find a true and unerring (ἀπλανής) teacher and spiritual father who has no delusion. For he who dedicates himself and all of his care to God and his spiritual father in true obedience no longer lives his own life, so as to do his own will, but becomes dead to every passionate attachment of the world and of his own body. What sort of temporal matter can defeat and enslave such a person? And what sort of care or concern could he have? So then, by this form of prayer together with obedience, all of the machinations of the demons and all the devices they employ to drag the intellect into many and diverse thoughts of distraction (λογισμοί), are ruined and destroyed. And then the intellect of that person remains free from everything and with great freedom and with proper timing it examines the distracting thoughts that the demons bring to it, successfully dispels them, and offers its prayers to God with a pure heart. This is the beginning of the true life, and those who do not begin in this way labor in vain without realizing it.

Furthermore, the beginning of this third form is not for one to look up to heaven and lift up his hands and to have his mind in the heavens and seek help there, for those things which we have said are the features of the first form and are characteristic of delusion. Again, neither is it guarding one's senses with the intellect and being attentive to this with one's whole self; and it is not the internal battles of the soul in which his enemies keep him from seeing or being able to attend to their attacks, for these are the features of the second form, and whoever engages in this form is struck by the demons, yet he does not strike them back. He is wounded, yet he does not know it. He is captured and enslaved and cannot take vengeance upon those who have enslaved him, but his enemies always, whether overtly or covertly, wage war against him and make him conceited and proud.

But you, O beloved, if you desire your salvation, must carry out this third form from now on. Together with accepting the complete obedience that you should keep toward your spiritual father, as we mentioned, it is also necessary for you to do everything with a pure conscience, as if you are standing before the face of God. For without obedience there is no way for the conscience to be pure. And your conscience must be kept pure in three ways: first, before God. Second, before your spiritual father. And third, before other people and the things of the world.

Before God you have the duty to keep your conscience pure. That is to say, that you do not do the things that you know grieve God, and that do not please Him. Again, before your spiritual father, do everything that he asks of you, neither more nor less, but rather do what is according to his intent and will, and thus shall you progress. Before other people, you must keep your conscience clean, and *do not do to them what you hate* (Tob. 4:15) or what you would not wish for them to do to you. Again, in regard to the things of the world you have a duty to guard yourself from abusing them. That is, make use of everything in a proper manner, both food and drink and clothing. And, in short, you must do all things as if you were standing before God, and let not your conscience reprove you in any of your deeds or prick you by doing something wrong. And thus, make good use of the true and unerring (ἀπλανής) path of the third form of attention and prayer, which is as follows.

The intellect should guard the heart at the time of prayer and ever dwell therein, and inside, from the depths of the heart, let it send up prayers to God; and when from within the heart the intellect *tastes that the Lord is good* (Ps. 33:9) and perceives this sweetness, then it will not depart from the place of the heart. And then the person will say the same words the Apostle Peter spoke, *It is good for us to be here* (Mt. 17:3). Thus the intellect will ever look within the heart and be active there, in a certain manner driving out and expelling all the thoughts (νοήματα) sown there by the devil. Now, to those who have no understanding of this salvific work (σωτήριον ἔργον) and do not know how to do it, it often seems quite laborious and distressing. But those who have tasted its sweetness and enjoyed this pleasure within the depths of their heart cry aloud together with St. Paul and say, "*Who shall separate us from the love of Christ?*" (Rom. 8:35), and the like.

For our Holy Fathers, when they heard the Lord saying in the Holy Gospel, *from out of the heart proceed evil thoughts, murders, adulteries, fornications, thefts, false witness, blasphemies* and how *these things defile a man* (Mt. 15:19–20), and again, the part of the Gospel in which He orders us to *clean the inside of the cup so the outside may be clean also* (Mt. 23:26), they left all other spiritual work and put all their labor into this one, that is, the guarding of the heart, since they were assured that with this work they would easily acquire every virtue. For without it, it is impossible for virtue to be acquired and for virtue to remain. This work was called "stillness of the heart" (ἡσυχία καρδιακή) by some of our Fathers. Others called it "attention" (προσοχή). Others "*nepsis*" and "*antirrhesis*",[332] and others "the examination of the thoughts and guarding of the intellect." For all were engaged in this work and by it they were made worthy of divine gifts. Regarding this the Preacher of Ecclesiastes says, *Be glad, O young man, in your youth and walk in the ways of your heart blameless* and pure and remove your heart from evil thoughts (Eccl. 11:9-10) And regarding the same thing, it says that if the assault of the devil rises against you, *do not let him enter your place* (Eccl. 10:4),[333] and by 'place' he means 'heart.' Our Lord also tells us in the Holy Gospel, *Do not have an anxious mind* (Lk. 12:29). That is, do not scatter your intellect here and there. And in another place, He also says, *Blessed are the poor in spirit* (Mt. 5:3). That is to say, happy are they who do not store up any thought or concern of this world in their heart, but are *poor* in regard to all worldly thoughts. In fact, all our Holy Fathers wrote much regarding this work and whoever wishes to read their writings will notice them: the things written by St. Mark the Ascetic, and said by St. John Climacus, St. Hesychios, St. Philotheos of Sinai, Abba Isaiah, Barsanuphios the Great, and many others.

In summary, whoever does not attend to guarding his intellect cannot become *pure in heart* so as to be made worthy to *see God*. Whoever does not have attention cannot become *poor in spirit*. Nor can he *mourn* and lament. Nor can he become *meek* and gentle. Nor can he *hunger and thirst after righteousness*. Nor can he become *merciful* or a *peacemaker*. Nor can he be *persecuted for righteousness' sake* (Mt. 5:3-11). And to put it generally, it is not possible for anyone to acquire the other virtues by any other means but this attentiveness (προσοχή). This is why you must be diligent in it more than anything else, so that you may understand the

---

[332] *Nepsis* (νῆψις) ("watchfulness", "sobriety"), hence the "Neptic Saints". The New Testament uses the verb form of this term, cf. 1 Thess. 5:6-8; 2 Tim. 4:5; 1 Pet. 1:13, 4:7; 5:8. Also, the use of the rarer term *antirrhesis* (ἀντίρρησις) "rebuke, contradiction", that is, the practice of rebuking the devil and evil thoughts also has a biblical basis in Ecclesiastes 8:11 LXX. Cf. *Antirrhetikos* by Evagrios of Pontus.

[333] "If the spirit of the ruler rise up against you, do not leave your place." This passage was understood to refer to the assault of the devil.

things I tell you by experience. And if you wish to learn the method by which you practice it, pay close attention and I will tell you about this too according to my ability.

It is necessary for you to guard three things above everything else. The first is your freedom from anxiety (ἀμεριμνία) about anything, whether it is a reasonable concern or unreasonable and vain, that is, by dying to the world. Second, a clean conscience in all things, as we have said, so that it does not find any reason to reprove you. And third, complete freedom from passions (ἀπροσπάθεια), without your thoughts inclining towards any worldly thing. And then, sit down in a remote and quiet place alone in a corner, close the door, and gather your intellect from every temporal and vain matter. Then rest your lower jaw, that is, your chin, on your chest, so that by this method you attend to yourself with your intellect and your bodily eyes.[334] Hold your breath a bit so that your intellect may find the place of your heart, and there shall your intellect be as well. Now, in the beginning you will find a darkness there and a great blindness and hardness. But later, when you are engaged in this work of attention unceasingly, day and night, you will find – O such wonder! – an unceasing joy. For when the intellect struggles in this labor it will find the place of the heart, and then, within there it will immediately perceive such things as it has never perceived before, nor ever known. For it perceives the space that is found there within the heart, and its whole self, bright and filled with all manner of wisdom and discernment. From then on, wherever any distracting thought (λογισμός) arises or appears, even before beginning to consider or form it, it drives it out and makes it disappear by the name of Jesus, through the prayer "Lord Jesus Christ, have mercy on me". At this point, the person's intellect begins to feel contempt and resentment towards the demons, and it wages unceasing war and raises its natural anger against them, pursues them, strikes them, and destroys them. And the other things that follow and come afterward, you shall learn these for yourself by experience, with God's help, through the attention of your intellect and by holding Jesus in your heart, that is, through the Jesus prayer. For as one Father says, "Sit in your cell, and it will teach you everything."

---

[334] This psychosomatic method is not essential to the third form of prayer commended by this author, but may possibly provide benefit so long as it is practiced with the guidance of a trustworthy spiritual guide, as he repeatedly mentions starting from the beginning of this section. In any case, the whole human person, body and soul, engages in prayer, as can be seen in the rich liturgical life of the Orthodox Church.

Question: Why is it that the first and second forms of which we have spoken cannot achieve these things?

Answer: Since we do not practice them properly. Thus St. John of the Ladder says these forms are like a ladder with four rungs, and he says, There are some who humble themselves and decrease the passions. There are others who chant, that is, pray with their mouths. Yet others engage in noetic prayer (νοερὰ προσευχή). And finally, there are those who come to contemplation (θεωρία). So then, those who wish to ascend these four rungs ought not begin from above and come downward, but climb from the bottom upward. So they rise to the first rung, and then onto the second, and next onto the third, and lastly onto the fourth. In this manner one can rise from the earth and ascend to heaven. First of all it is necessary for one to strive to decrease and put an end to the passions, and second, for one to be engaged in psalmody, that is, to pray with the mouth. For when the passions decrease, then prayer naturally brings pleasure and sweetness to the tongue, and the person becomes well pleasing to God. Third, one should pray noetically, and fourth is for one to ascend to contemplation. The first is for beginners, the second is for those who have increased in progress, the third is for those who have come to the end of progress, and the fourth is for the perfect.

Thus, the beginning is nothing other than the diminishment of the passions, which do not decrease from the soul in any way except by the guarding of the soul and attention of the heart. For *out of the heart proceeds evil thoughts which defile a man,* as our Master says, and that is where we require watchfulness and attention. And when the passions cease and decrease with the war and opposition that the heart wages against them, then the intellect begins to desire and seek to be reconciled with God, and thus it increases prayer and devotes itself to it. Again, from this longing and prayer, the intellect is strengthened and dispels all the distracting thoughts which wander about in attempts to enter the heart, striking them by prayer. Then a war takes place and the evil demons oppose it with great tumult, and by means of the passions they bring about confusion and dizziness in the heart. However, by the name of Jesus Christ, they all *vanish and melt as wax before the fire* (Ps. 67:3). Yet having been expelled from the heart, they do not rest, but disturb the intellect externally through the senses. For this reason, the intellect very quickly perceives the serenity and stillness that takes place within it, since they do not have the power to disturb the intellect at its depth, but only from outside at the surface of the intellect. But again, it is impossible completely to escape spiritual warfare and avoid being attacked by these evil spirits. For this is a state that belongs only to the perfect and to those who have completely withdrawn from everything and engage in attending to their heart at all times.

Hence, whoever practices these things in their proper order, each according to its proper time, can later – after his heart has been purified from passions – become wholly devoted to psalmody, and fight against distracting thoughts, and look up to heaven with his bodily eyes (if he sometimes has the need to) and with the noetic eyes of the soul contemplate heaven and pray with purity in truth, as he should. Nevertheless, he should only gaze up to heaven very rarely for fear of the evil spirits that dwell in the air and hence are called 'spirits of the air', which produce many and diverse delusions 'in the air', and concerning these we must be cautious (cf. Eph. 2:2). For all that God demands from us is for our hearts to be purified by guarding them with attention. And then if *the root is holy*, as the Apostle says, it is clear that *the branches are holy as well*, along with the fruit (Rom. 11:16). But without the form we have described, one lifts his eyes and his intellect to heaven and will imagine noetic realities, sees fantasies and things false and far from the truth, since his heart is impure. And as we have often said, the first and second forms bring no spiritual progress to man. For just as when we wish to build a house, we do not first place the roof and then the foundation, because that would be absurd, but rather first we lay the foundation, build the house, and afterward set up the roof, we must do likewise in spiritual things. First, we should place the foundation, that is, guard the heart and decrease the passions from it. Next, we must build the spiritual house, that is, dispel the disturbance of the evil spirits that war against us through the senses, and then escape from their assault as swiftly as possible. And then do we place the roof, that is, withdraw completely from everything and acquire peace as we should, and give ourselves completely unto God. Thus do we complete the spiritual house in Christ Jesus our Lord, to whom be all glory unto the ages of ages. Amen.

Note on the Omission of the Texts by St. Gregory of Sinai

We have omitted the texts by St. Gregory of Sinai because they are already published from the original Greek in Volume 4 of the *Philokalia*. Moreover, they appear to be the only texts in the *Philokalia* that are repeated twice, that is, first in Byzantine Greek and then in a Modern Greek paraphrase, and this repetition was meant for Modern Greek readers who had difficulty reading Ancient and Byzantine Greek.

FROM THE LIFE OF OUR HOLY AND GOD-BEARING FATHER MAXIMOS THE HUT-BURNER

When St. Gregory of Sinai met St. Maximos and conversed with him, amongst other things he asked him, "O my most honorable father, please do tell me: Do you keep the noetic prayer?" And he smiled a little and told him, "O honorable father, I do not want the miracle of the Theotokos that happened to me to be kept hidden from you. From my youth, I have had great faith in my Lady the Theotokos and I would supplicate her with tears that she might grant me the gift of noetic prayer. And one day while on my way to her church, as was my habit, I beseeched her again with all the immeasurable fervency of my heart. And then, the moment I was greeting her holy icon with yearning, I immediately felt within my breast and my heart a warmth and flame that came from the holy icon; it did not burn me, but refreshed me and brought sweetness and great compunction to my soul. From then on, O father, my heart began to say the prayer from within, and my intellect took delight in the remembrance of my Jesus and my Theotokos and in remembering them both constantly. And from then on the prayer has never left my heart. Forgive me."

And St. Gregory then said to him, "Tell me, holy one, while you have been saying the Jesus Prayer, has a divine change, or ecstasy, or any other fruit of the Holy Spirit ever come upon you?" And St. Maximos replied, "O father, this is the reason I went to a desert place and always yearned for *hesychia*, so that I might enjoy the fruit of the prayer even more, which is exceedingly great love for God and a rapture of the intellect to the Lord." And St. Gregory said, "Please, father, tell me: Do you have those things of which you speak?" And St. Maximos again smiled, and told him, "Give me something to eat and don't ask about a delusion of mine (πλάνη)." Then St. Gregory told him, "Oh, if only I myself had this 'delusion' of yours, holy one! But do tell me, at the time your intellect was seized up to God, what did you see with the eyes of the intellect? Was your intellect then perhaps able to lift up the prayer together with the heart?" And St. Maximos answered him, "No, it could not. For when the grace of the Holy Spirit comes to man by means of the prayer, then the prayer itself ceases, since the intellect is wholly overcome by the grace of the Holy Spirit and it can no longer exercise (ἐνεργήσῃ) its own faculties, but remains at rest and submits to the Holy Spirit alone and the Holy Spirit takes it where He wills (Jn. 3:8), either to the immaterial realm of divine light, or to other indescribable visions, and often even to conversation with God, and, in short, just as the Comforter – that is, the Holy Spirit – wills, so does He exhort and console his servants. He gives His grace to all in a way suitable to each. And anyone can clearly see what I am describing in the prophets and apostles, who were made worthy to behold such great visions, although people mocked them and took them for people who were deluded (πλανημένοι) and drunk (Acts 2:13). In this way the Prophet Isaiah saw the Lord lifted up on an exalted throne with the Seraphim surrounding Him (Is. 6:2). And the first martyr Stephen saw the heavens opened up, and Jesus at the right hand of the Father (Acts 7:56), and so on. And in such a manner, even to this day the servants of Christ are made worthy to see various visions, which some people do not believe or accept to be true in any way, but take them for delusion and consider those who see them to be deluded. And I marvel greatly at this and wonder what kind of people are they, who have become so insensible, as if blinded in soul, and do not believe that which God – who cannot lie – promised, by the mouth of Prophet Joel, regarding what He would give to the faithful, saying, *I shall pour out the grace of My Spirit* onto every believer, *on both my servants and my handmaids* (Joel 3:2).

"The Lord gave us this grace, and gives it even today, and until the consummation of all things He will continue to give it, according to His promise, to all his faithful servants. So then, when this grace of the Holy Spirit comes to anyone, it does not just show him ordinary things or the sensible things of this world, but reveals such things as he has never seen or imagined. And then that person's intellect is taught by the Holy Spirit mysteries sublime and hidden, and which, according to St. Paul, cannot be seen by the bodily eye of man, nor can the intellect of man ever contemplate them by reason alone (cf. 1 Cor. 2:9). And that you might understand how our intellect sees them, think about what I tell you now: When candle wax is far from the fire, it is solid and can be grasped, but when you put it into the fire it melts, and there it burns in the flame and catches fire and becomes all light and so finds a perfect end in the fire. There is no way for it not to melt in the fire and pour out like water. So too, while man's intellect is by itself, without encountering God, it thinks that everything is solidly in its power. But when it draws near, as it were, to the fire of Divinity and the Holy Spirit, it is completely dominated by that divine light and becomes all light, and there within the flame of the All-Holy Spirit it is set aflame and softened by divine perceptions. And in that fire of Divinity, there is no way for it to consider its own concerns and desires."

Then St. Gregory asked him, "But, my dear hut-burner, are there things that resemble these that arise from delusion?" And the Great Maximos answered him, "The signs of delusion are one thing and the signs of grace quite another. For when the evil spirit of delusion approaches man it confuses the intellect and makes it savage. It hardens and darkens the heart. It causes cowardice, fear, and pride. It makes his eyes wild, disturbs the mind, and causes the whole body to shudder. By means of the imagination, it reveals a light to the eyes that is not radiant and untainted, but reddish. It also makes his intellect mad and demonic, and prompts him to say with his tongue words indecent and blasphemous. And he who has received this spirit of delusion is usually angry and full of wrath and has not known real humility, or true sorrow and weeping, but always boasts about the good things he has done; he is vainglorious, without compunction or the fear of God, and is constantly entrenched in the passions. Last of all, he goes completely out of his mind and ends up in total perdition. May the Lord save us from such delusion, by your prayers! On the other hand, the signs of grace are these: when the grace of the All-Holy Spirit comes to man, it gathers his intellect and makes it attentive and humble. It brings it the remembrance of death and of its own sins, of the coming judgment and of eternal damnation, and makes the soul more willing to repent with weeping and mourning. It makes a man's eyes gentle and full of tears. And the more it draws near man, the more does it calm the soul and console it through the holy sufferings of our Lord Jesus Christ and His boundless love for man. It moreover brings sublime and true contemplations to the intellect. First, about how, by His incomprehensible power, God created everything and brought them from nothing into being by a single word. Second, about His infinite power, which holds all things together and rules over them with providence for everything. Third, about the incomprehensibility of the Holy Trinity and the inexhaustible ocean of God's being, and the like. And then, when man's intellect is seized, as it were, by that divine light and illumined with the illumination of divine knowledge, his heart becomes calm and utterly meek and it gushes forth the fruits of the Holy Spirit: joy, peace, long-suffering, goodness, kindness, love, humility, and the rest (Gal. 5:22), and his soul enjoys an inexpressible exultation." While listening to these things, St. Gregory of Sinai remained ecstatic and marvelled at all that St. Maximos told him, and he no longer called him a man, but an earthly angel.

HOW ALL CHRISTIANS SHOULD PRAY WITHOUT CEASING

My Christian brothers, let no one think that only the clergy and monastics have the duty to pray unceasingly and at all times, but not the people in the world. No, this is not so! All of us Christians have the universal duty to be engaged in prayer always. For as the most-holy Philotheos, Patriarch of Constantinople writes in the life of St. Gregory of Thessaloniki, St. Gregory had a dear friend by the name of Job, who was a very simple man and quite virtuous, and one day St. Gregory was conversing with him about prayer and how absolutely every Christian should struggle constantly in prayer and even pray unceasingly, just as the Apostle Paul universally enjoins all Christians to *pray without ceasing* (1 Thess. 5:17). And as the Prophet David also says, despite the fact that he was a king and had all the responsibility and care of his kingdom, *I have seen the Lord always before me* (Ps. 15:8). That is, 'I see the Lord always before me noetically, by means of prayer.' Moreover, Gregory the Theologian teaches all Christians, saying that we must remember the name of God in prayer more often than we breathe. And thus, while speaking about these and other things to his friend Job, St. Gregory also says how we too must be obedient to the precepts of the saints, and how not only should we pray at all times, but also teach everyone else, both monastics and laypeople, both the wise and the ignorant, both men, women, and children, and encourage them all to pray without ceasing. When he heard these things, the elder Job thought of it as something new and began to dispute it and tell the saint that praying unceasingly is only for ascetics and monastics who are outside of the world and away from its distractions, but not for the people in the world who have so many cares and obligations. Again, St. Gregory gave him yet other testimonies and proofs in opposition, but somehow the elder Job was not persuaded. So St. Gregory, wishing to avoid talkativeness and contention, grew silent, and each of them went to his own cell.

Then later, while Job was praying alone in his cell, an angel of the Lord appeared before him, sent from God who *desires for all men to be saved* (1 Tim. 2:4). And through the angel, He put him to great shame because he had quarrelled with St. Gregory and resisted illustrious things from which the salvation of Christians is effected, and he ordered him on behalf of the Holy God to take heed to the following: from then on he must take care not to say anything against any such work so beneficial to the soul (ψυχωφελέστατον ἔργον), for this is opposed to the will of God. Moreover, neither should he accept in his intellect any thought opposed to the teaching of St. Gregory or think differently from him. Then that most simple elder Job went immediately to the saint and fell down at his feet seeking forgiveness for all his opposition and contention, and he made known to Gregory all that the angel of the Lord had told him. Do you then see, my brethren, how all Christians, young and old, have the common duty to pray at all times with the noetic prayer, "Lord Jesus Christ, have mercy on me"? And how they should accustom their intellect and heart to say it always? And further consider how God is so well pleased by this endeavor and how it brings such benefit that in His utmost love for mankind He even sent an angel from heaven to reveal this to us so that we might no longer have any doubts about it.

But what might people in the world say? "We are caught up in so many affairs and worldly cares, and how is it even possible for us to pray unceasingly?"

And my reply to them is this: that God has not commanded us to do anything impossible, but rather to do all that is in our power. So then, it is possible for every one that diligently seeks the salvation of his soul to achieve this. For if it were impossible, it would be completely impossible for everyone in the world, and there would not be so very many people in the world who have achieved it. Among so many, let Constantine the Wonderful, the father of the above St. Gregory, serve as an example. He was immersed in royal matters, was called the father and teacher of the Emperor Andronikos, and was involved in all of the imperial affairs on a daily basis – let alone the affairs of his own household, for he was very wealthy, owned many properties, and had servants and children and a wife – and yet despite all these cares, he was so inseparable from God and so devoted to noetic and unceasing prayer, that he usually forgot the things that the emperor and the magistrates of the palace would say to him regarding imperial affairs, and he used to ask again about these same matters once or twice. Oftentimes the other magistrates who did not know the reason were confused at his behavior and reproached him for being so quick to forget and for bothering the emperor with his second set of questions. But the emperor, knowing the reason, defended him and said, "The illustrious Constantine has his own thoughts and they do not let him attend to our words concerning temporary and vain affairs; rather the intellect of the blessed man is fixed on true and heavenly things and because of this he forgets the earthly ones. For all of his attention is set on prayer and on God." Thus, Constantine was revered (as is described by the most-holy Patriarch Philotheos) and beloved both to the emperor and to all the highest ranking officials and magistrates of the empire. At the same time, he was loved by God, who even made this renowned man worthy to work miracles.

Once (as the most-holy Philotheos says in the *Life of Saint Gregory*, his son) he boarded a sailboat with his whole family to visit an anchorite practicing hesychasm in an area above Galata,[335] for the sake of his prayers and blessing, and on the way,

---

[335] A neighborhood in Constantinople located at the northern shore of the Golden Horn.

he asked his servants if anyone had brought any food for them to bring to that Abba as a gift. They told him they had forgotten due to the rush and that they had brought nothing with them. The blessed man grew a little sad but said nothing, and only went a little further up the sailboat, dipped his hand in the sea and with silent and noetic prayer he asked God, the Master of the sea, to grant him a catch of fish. And shortly after (O how marvellous are the works, Christ our King, with which You wondrously glorify Your servants!) he pulled his hand out of the sea holding a gigantic sea bass, which he then tossed into the boat before his servants, saying, "Look how our Lord has cared for us and for the Abba, His servant, that He has sent him something to eat!" Do you see, my brethren, with what kind of glory Jesus Christ glorifies His servants who are always present with Him and who call upon His all-holy and sweetest name at all times?

And was not the righteous St. Evdokimos also living in Constantinople, involved in the empire and imperial affairs? Did he not associate with the emperor and with the magistrates of the palace, with countless cares and distractions? For all that, he still always had the noetic prayer inseparable from his thought (λόγος) (as Symeon Metaphrastes narrates in his life), and thus the thrice-blessed one, while living amidst the world and worldly things, lived a truly angelic life beyond this world and was made worthy by God, who rewards His servants, to receive a blessed and divine end as well. And so many others, impossible to count, were in the world and yet completely devoted to this noetic and saving prayer, as we can find in the stories written about them. And so, my fellow Christians, I, together with St. John Chrysostom, beseech you for the sake of our souls' salvation, do not be neglectful of this work of prayer. Imitate those about whom we have spoken and follow their example as much as possible. And if this initially seems difficult to you, be certain and fully assured, as from the very face of God Almighty, that this same name of our Lord Jesus Christ which we call upon unceasingly each and every day will ease all of our difficulties; and after much time, as we grow accustomed to it and learn to sense the sweetness in it, then we will know by experience that it is neither impossible nor difficult, but both possible and easy. And for this reason, St. Paul, who knew better than us the great benefit that prayer brings, enjoined us to *pray without ceasing* (1 Thess. 5:17). And he would never advise us to do something so difficult or impossible that we could not do it, only for us to appear as disobedient transgressors of his injunction as a consequence, and so be condemned through it. But the intent of the Apostle when he said, *Pray without ceasing*, was for us to pray with our intellect, and it is possible for us to do this constantly. For while we are doing handicrafts, while we are walking, while we are sitting, while we are eating, and while we are drinking, we can always pray with our intellect and engage in noetic prayer that is true and well-pleasing to God.

Let us work with the body and pray with the soul. Let the outer man carry out every bodily service and the inner man be completely dedicated to the worship of God and never absent from this spiritual work of noetic prayer. As the God-Man Jesus Christ commanded us in the Holy Gospel, saying, *But you, when you pray, go into your chamber* (ταμεῖον), *and when you have shut your door, pray to your Father who is in secret* (Mt. 6:6). The chamber of the soul is the body. The doors of our body are the five senses. The soul enters its chamber when the intellect does not wander here and there anxious about matters of the world, but is found within our heart. Moreover, our senses are shut and remain sealed when we do not let them fixate upon sensible and visible things. And in this manner our intellect remains free from every earthly pursuit, and through hidden and noetic prayer you are united with God your Father. And then, the Lord says, *Your Father who sees in secret will reward you openly*. God, who knows the hidden things sees your noetic prayer and rewards it with manifest and magnificent gifts. For this is the prayer that is true and perfect, and it fills the soul with divine grace and spiritual gifts, just like myrrh: the further you close it into a vessel, the more fragrant it becomes. And so it is with prayer: the further you seal it within your heart, the more it is filled with divine grace.

Blessed and happy are they who have made a habit of this heavenly work, for by it they conquer every temptation of evil demons, just as David conquered the proud Goliath (1 Sam. 17:51). By it they quench the unruly desires of the flesh, just as the Three Youths quenched the flame of the fiery furnace (Dan. 3:16-28). By this work of noetic prayer they soothe the passions, just as Daniel calmed the wild lions (Dan. 6:18). By it the dew of the Holy Spirit descends upon their hearts, just as Elijah brought down rain upon Mount Carmel. This noetic prayer is what ascends up to the throne of God and is kept in golden bowls so that the Lord may be censed by it, as John the Theologian says in the Apocalypse, *And the twenty-four elders fell down before the Lamb, each having a harp, and golden bowls full of incense, which are the prayers of the saints* (Rev. 5:8). This noetic prayer is a light that ever illumines the soul of man and ignites his soul with the flames of the love of God. It is the chain that keeps and binds man to God.

O how incomparable is the grace of noetic prayer! It causes man to converse with God at all times. O how truly wonderful and extraordinary it is! For you to be together with men in the body and together with God with the intellect! The angels do not have material voices, but with their intellect they offer unto God unceasing doxology. This is their work. To this is their whole life dedicated. So you too, brother, when you go into your chamber and shut the door, that is, when your intellect is not dispersed here and there, but enters into your heart, and your senses are sealed and not fixed upon the things of this world, and when you pray in this manner with your intellect perpetually, then you become like the holy angels, and your Father, who sees your secret (μυστική) prayer, which you offer unto Him in the secret place of your heart, you shall be rewarded great spiritual gifts openly. But what greater and better thing could you desire than to be together with God at all times noetically, as we have said, and to converse with Him unceasingly? Without Him no man can be blessed either here or in the next life. And so, brother, whoever you may be, when you receive the present book in your hands, I fervently beseech you: remember to make supplication before God with one "Lord, have mercy", both for the sinful soul of him who has put his labor into this book and for him who has paid for its printing. They are in great need of your prayers. This is so that they may find divine mercy for their souls, and you for your own. May God grant this; may He grant it indeed.

GRACE BE UNTO HIM WHO DOETH GOOD THINGS FOR GOD

AND MAY HE DELIVER HIS FAITHFUL

FROM THE DREAD FIRE

GLOSSARY OF THEOLOGICAL TERMS

Nous (νοῦς): intellect. See Translators' Introduction.

Noein (νοεῖν): to know, to understand; intellection. The act or *energeia* of intellect (*nous*).

Noeros (νοερός): noetic; intelligent; pertaining to the intellect. Often used to describe prayer and contemplation with the intellect, e.g. *noetic prayer*.

Noetos (νοητός): intelligible; noetic; pertaining to the intellect. Roughly synonymous with *noeros,* but more often in the sense of "perceived by the intellect" (this applies to *nooumenos* (νοούμενος) as well. Often used to refer to spiritual realities discerned in created things and in Scripture.

Dianoia (διάνοια): mind, thought; discursive reason.

Noera aisthesis (νοερὰ αἴσθησις): noetic sense, noetic perception; noetic sensation.

Noera proseuche (νοερὰ προσευχή): noetic prayer. Prayer performed with the intellect (*nous*).

Aisthesis (αἴσθησις): sense, sense perception.

Aisthetos (αἰσθητός): sensible; physical; perceived by sense perception (*aisthesis*), often in contrast to *intelligible* reality, which is known through the intellect (*nous*).

Phainomenos (φαινόμενος): visible, apparent. Not always visible in the literal sense, but in the sense that the intellect can perceive it and conceive of it in the sensible world.

Anapausis (ἀνάπαυσις): repose; the "Sabbath rest" of the mind in contemplation of God; also the eternal repose of heaven. See *katapausis*.

Katapausis (κατάπαυσις): rest; similar to *anapausis*, *katapausis* emphasizes the cessation of earthly efforts and rest from labor.

Energeia (ἐνέργεια): energy, activity; working, operation. Not to be confused with energy in physics or Eastern philosophy. It refers to the innate activity natural to any created thing or to the uncreated energies and operations of God (often in the plural ἐνέργειαι).

Eros (ἔρως): eros, divine eros; intense love. *Eros* is nearly always used to refer to spiritual love between God and the soul.

Kardiake proseuche (καρδιακὴ προσευχή): prayer of the heart.

Logos (λόγος): *logos,* word, speech, discourse; reason; unifying principle; object of contemplation (in Angelikoudes and Kataphygiotes). The *Logos* of God is also the name of the second divine hypostasis of the Trinity, Jesus Christ (Jn. 1:1).

> *Logoi* (λόγοι): *logoi* (plural of *logos*), principles; the purposes and meanings of things; words, reasonings; truths contemplated by the intellect. Related to St. Maximos the Confessor's doctrine of the *logoi.*[336]
>
> *Logikos, logistikos* (λογικός, λογιστικός): reasonable, rational; reason-endowed; endowed with speech.
>
> *Alogos* (ἄλογος): irrational; dumb (without speech); foolish. e.g. "irrational animals."

Hesychia (ἡσυχία): stillness; silence.

Hesychasmos (ἡσυχασμός): Hesychasm, the monastic life of stillness and prayer, defended by St. Gregory Palamas and his followers in the 14th century AD.

Psyche (ψυχή): soul; life.

> *logistikon* (λογιστικόν): rational part of the soul. See *logikos*.
>
> *epithymetikon* (ἐπιθυμητικόν): appetitive part of the soul; desiring part.
>
> > *epithymia* (ἐπιθυμία): desire, appetite.
>
> *thymikon* (θυμικόν): irascible part of the soul; anger, spirited part.
>
> > *thymos* (θυμός): anger.

Katharsis (κάθαρσις): purification of the soul and intellect, especially at the beginning stage of spiritual life.

Photismos (φωτισμός): illumination. A similar term that is used is *ellampsis* (ἐλλαμψις), as in St. Maximos' phrase "enhypostatic illumination." Understood as the second stage of spiritual life.

Theosis (θέωσις): deification, *theosis*. When the human person is made deiform and "god by grace" (χάριτι) or by "adoption" (θέσει/θετός). This does not mean becoming God in His essence, but coming to know Him and being united to Him through the incarnation of the Son of God and through God's divine uncreated energies and love. Also called *theopoiesis* (θεοποίησις). Similar to *theourgia*

---

[336] *Ambiguum* 7, *On the Cosmic Mystery of Christ* (trans. Blowers), 45-74.

(θεουργία), translated as "divinization" here. Also known as "union with God", it is considered the third and final stage of spiritual life and salvation. Related to θεοπτία (vision of God) and ἕνωσις (union).

Theologia (θεολογία): theology. Mystical knowledge of God, and being able to "speak about God" (θεολογεῖν) or "theologize" on that basis. Sometimes meaning the study of God in Himself or of His providence, rather than in respect to His Incarnation (*oikonomia*).

Oikonomia (οἰκονομία): economy; God's plan and dispensation. Usually used to refer to the incarnation of God the Word as man.

Pathe (τὰ πάθη): passions; vices; the passivity (or in some cases "potential") of created things, sometimes ascribed to the "passible part of the soul".

> *Apatheia* (ἀπάθεια): dispassion. Freedom from the passions.
>
> *Paschein* (πάσχειν, παθεῖν): "to suffer", undergo, experience; receive. A common patristic term to describe the experience of God, based on a phrase "to see and to suffer God" from the writings of St. Gregory Nazianzen (*Or.* 45.7 On Holy Pascha). Also related to the "blessed passion" referred to by St. Maximos the Confessor. Cf. *On Union with God* 19-20.

Paideia (παιδεία): instruction, God's providential training of man.

Peirasmos (πειρασμός): temptation, testing, trial. This often refers to the devil's attempts to make us stumble.

Antirrhesis (ἀντίρρησις): rebuking demons and bad thoughts.

Praxis (πρᾶξις): practice, action; ascetical practice.

> *Praktikos* (πρακτικός): practitioner; engaged in ascetical practice and training.

Theoria (θεωρία): contemplation, vision of God and divine realities (i.e. the divine energies). Not to be confused with *theory*, which only has a very loose connection to *theoria* as understood in Orthodox theology.

> *Theoretikos* (θεωρητικός): contemplative. Kataphygiotes' *On Union with God and the Contemplative Life* provides an extensive account of the contemplative's activity.

Onta (τὰ ὄντα): realities, existing things; lit. "beings"; truths contemplated by the intellect. We have generally avoided the translation "beings" because of its association with "sentient beings" in English.[337] Moreover, St. Kataphygiotes even speaks about *uncreated realities around God* (see also *energeia*).

Ousia (οὐσία): essence, being. *Hyperousios* (ὑπερούσιος): God is beyond essence, beyond being. *Homoousios* (ὁμοούσιος): of one essence, "consubsantial.".

Hypostasis (ὑπόστασις): person, unique subsistence. The Holy Trinity is three uncreated *hypostases*, Father, Son, and Holy Spirit, who share one essence – *homoousios*.

Enhypostatos (ἐνυπόστατος): enhypostatic; the substantive form of a reality, established in *hypostasis*. Christian faith is substantive, *enhypostatic faith*, not based on blind faith or pure reason, but experience and *manifest* grace. Christ is *enhypostatic* Word (*Logos*) and Wisdom, i.e. Wisdom-Itself. Divine illumination is *enhypostatic* and from God, not sensible created light. The word is interpreted with great precision by St. Kallistos Angelikoudes.

Hypokeimenon (ὑποκείμενον): substance, underlying substance.

---

[337] We would like to thank Dr. Marcus Plested for his suggestions concerning this issue.

Bibliography

Aristotle, *De Anima.* ed. W. D. Ross (Oxford Classical Texts). Oxford: Oxford University Press, 1979.

Athanasius, *On the Incarnation.* trans. John Behr (Popular Patristic Series). Crestwood: St. Vladimir's Seminary Press, 2012

Basil the Great, *Letters*. trans. Roy J. Defferari. Harvard, 1926; repr. 1961.

Demetracopoulos, John, *Palamas Transformed: Palamite Interpretations of the Distinction between God's 'Essence' and 'Energies' in Late Byzantium* in *Greeks, Latins, and Intellectual History: 1204-1500*, ed. Martin Hinterberger, Chris Schabel (Recherches de theologie et philosophie medievales; Bibliotheca, 11). Leuven: Peeters, 2011; 263-372.

Dionysios the Areopagite, *Pseudo-Dionysius: The Complete Works*. trans. Colm Luibhéid, Paul Rorem. New York: Paulist Press, 1987.

Dostoevsky, Fyodor. *The Idiot*. trans. Constance Garnett. New York: Bantam, 1981.

Galen, *Method of Medicine, Vol. III: Books 10-14*. ed., trans. Ian Johnston, G. H. R. Horsley (Loeb Classical Library 518). Cambridge: Harvard University Press, 2011.

Golitzin, Alexander. *Mystagogy: A Monastic Reading of Dionysius Areopagita*. ed. Bogdan G. Bacur (Cistercian Studies). Cistercian Publications, 2014.

Gregory of Nazianzus, *Gregory of Nazianzus*. ed., trans. C.G. Browne, J.E. Swallow (The Nicene and Post-Nicene Fathers, 2nd series, vol. 7). Oxford/New York, 1894; repr. Edinburgh: T & T Clark, 1989.

John Climacus. *The Ladder of Divine Ascent*. trans. Lazarus Moore. New York: Harper & Brothers, 1959.

Joyce, James. *Ulysses*. London: Faber and Faber, 1975.

Maximus the Confessor. *On the Cosmic Mystery of Jesus Christ*. trans. Paul M. Blowers, Robrt Louis Wilken (Popular Patristics). Crestwood: St. Vladimir's Seminary Press, 2003.

———. *On Difficulties in Sacred Scripture: The Responses to Thalassios*. trans. Maximos Constas (Fathers of the Church Patristic Series). Washington, D.C.: The Catholic University of America Press, 2018.

Philokalia: the Complete Text, Compiled by St. Nikodimos of the Holy Mountain and St. Makarios of Corinth (vol. 1-4). ed., trans. G.E.H. Palmer, Philip Sherrard, and Kallistos Ware. London: Faber & Faber, 1979-2011.

Pieper, Josef. *Leisure: The Basis of Culture*. San Francisco: Ignatius Press, 2009.

Plested, Marcus. *Orthodox Readings of Aquinas*. Oxford: Oxford University Press, 2015.

Rodionov, Oleg, *The Chapters of Kallistos Angelikoudes: The Relationship of the Separate Series and their Main Theological Themes*, in: Byzantine Theology and its Philosophical Background, ed. Antonio Rigo (Studies in Byzantine History and Civilization, 4). Turnhout: Brepols, 2011, 141–159.

St. Gregory Palamas. Analogia (Pemptousia Journal for Theological Studies, Vol. 3, Issue 2). Athens: St Maxim the Greek Institute, 2017.

Staniloae, Dumitru. *The Experience of God: Orthodox Dogmatic Theology. Vol. 1.* ed., trans. Ioan Ionită, Robert Barringer. Brookline: Holy Cross Orthodox Press, 1994.

The Apostolic Fathers. ed., trans. Michael Holmes. Grand Rapids: Baker Academic, 2007.

———. *The Experience of God: Orthodox Dogmatic Theology. Vol. 2: The World: Creation and Deification*. ed., trans. Ioan Ionită, Robert Barringer. Brookline: Holy Cross Orthodox Press, 2000.

Φιλοκαλία τῶν ἱερῶν νηπτικῶν (Philokalia of the Holy Neptic Fathers), Vol. 4-5. Athens: Aster-Papademetriou, 1957.

Φιλοκαλία τῶν ἱερῶν νηπτικῶν (Philokalia of the Holy Neptic Fathers), Vol. 5. trans. Antonios G. Galitis. Thessaloniki: To Perivoli tis Theotokou, 1993.

Printed in Great Britain
by Amazon

27401381R00183